The Secret Diary of Kasturba

Neelima Dalmia Adhar was educated in a convent school and a reputed college in Delhi and has a Master's in Psychology with a specialisation in 'Personality'. Her first and only job was to teach Psychology to undergraduate students of Delhi University. A passionate 'people-watcher', she is drawn to oddities and thrives on writing about personalities and human behaviour, from the quirky to the mysterious to the bizarre, a subject she does chillingly close to the bone.

She lives in Delhi with her husband, children and two grandchildren.

Other books by the author

Merchants of Death
Father Dearest: The Life & Times of R.K. Dalmia
Radha: The Princess of Barsana

Neelima Dalmia Adhar

The Secret Diary of Kasturba

WESTLAND
NON-FICTION

First published by Tranquebar, an imprint of westland ltd, in 2016

Published by Westland Non-Fiction, an imprint of Westland Books, a division of Nasadiya Technologies Private Limited, in 2024

No. 269/2B, First Floor, 'Irai Arul', Vimalraj Street, Nethaji Nagar, Alapakkam Main Road, Maduravoyal, Chennai 600095

Westland, the Westland logo, Westland Non-Fiction and the Westland Non-Fiction logo are the trademarks of Nasadiya Technologies Private Limited, or its affiliates.

ISBN: 9788196011826

10 9 8 7 6 5 4 3 2 1

Typeset by PrePSol Enterprises Pvt. Ltd
Printed at Nutech Print Services, India

All the sparkling energies that unfailingly light up my being.

Mrinali, Nishant, Shyraa, Shauryaveer
and
Yameer, Sharnamli, Zaavian, Azarius

Acknowledgements

- Anubhav Nath who diligently assisted me in my research from the time of the inception of the book.
- Anish Maheshwari for initially transcribing my illegible scrawl onto Word.
- Sudha Sadhanand for her unending hours of patient and dedicated editing and re-editing the manuscript till it was perfect.
- The Westland team who believed in the merit and worthiness of Kasturba's Diary.

This is a story of the Yin and the Yang. A story of a relentless quest by these quintessential forces of nature, to unite and explode into a million particles that scatter in all directions and begin a renewed journey to find and fuse with each other again. The Yin is the moon, dark, feminine, passive, dormant and contracting, and the Yang, embodied by the sun is bright, masculine, dynamic, ever expanding and omnipotent. This story begins and ends with the union of these diametrically opposed energies of Shiva the godhead and Shakti his divine consort. This story is essentially the genesis of life on earth.

PROLOGUE

Aga Khan Palace
22 February 1944
6 pm

The coarse white handwoven sari, greyed with repeated washing, has chafed the skin of my shrivelled legs. Its narrow vermillion border rides up my ankles and lies carelessly wrapped around my exposed shins. I am curled up in a foetal position, my head cradled on the lap of a man who has been my husband for over six decades.

Inside this dank prison where I lie, there is an overpowering smell of death. It nauseates me. It hovers over me like a dark shadow and casts an ashen film over my wasting body. I feel a continuous trembling in my bones, my life ebbing out. My breathing is shallow and weak. A burning fever rages from my toes to my skull. It has set my eyeballs on fire. With each laboured breath, a knife turns inside my ribs and air rushes out in gasping sounds from my slackened mouth. Echoes and images come zooming in.

Two voices drone above me like floating spirits.
'No…No…No! No penicillin for her…it's evil…'
'But sir, the pneumonia? Her fever isn't coming down! Her heart cannot take it much longer. It can be fatal.'
'I'd rather she dies…let nature take its course.'
I hear this squabble between two men, a father and a son.
'Please Bapu, please, let them give her that penicillin injection. It's her only chance.' That pleading voice is my son.
'No! No Devdas, the penicillin will only prolong her agony. Don't make her suffer more. Let her go in peace.'
The older voice is edged with stern authority.

I hear more sounds; vivid images, loud beating of drums, crackling pyres, the chanting of Sanskrit verses—verses that spiral up to another "timescape". The sacred mangalacharan begins.

I am walking around a fire, bedecked with flowers and jewels, in a sari, the colour of blood. Six yards of luxurious silk, woven with threads of gold, swathed around me like bandages on a corpse. I'm holding the hand of a wiry, dark-skinned boy who leads me forward. We are two infants frolicking in merry pantomime. The bells on my silver anklets tinkle sweetly as I move. The priest's voice resonates loudly and then fades away. I can hear myself, an illiterate ignorant child-bride of thirteen years parroting the marriage vows mechanically.

'Take one step so that we may have strength of will,' says the priest.

'In every worthy wish of yours I shall be your helpmate.' I repeat.
The second step –
'So we may be filled with vigour,' he intones.
'In every worthy wish of yours I shall be your helpmate.' The third step–
'That we may have increasing prosperity.'
'Your joys and sorrows I shall share,' he says. I repeat.
Then the fourth...the fifth...sixth...and then the last step. Hark! What does he ask me to say now?
'It is the fruit of my past good deeds that I have you as my husband.
'You are my best friend, my highest guru. My sovereign lord, I shall serve you till my last breath. I am a fortunate woman. May death come to me before it takes away my lord and master.'
I hear my own voice echo as the priest drones on.

At thirteen years, a few months older than my husband, I am his third wife. The two before me have died in close succession when they were barely six months old, betrothed even before they began to crawl. I feel a burst of firecrackers inside my head and then a loud continuous pounding between my ears. Life is ticking away.

Now my feet are frozen and blue, I cannot move them. Now my ankles feel like lead. A new immobility surges up my groin forking into my bowels. My chest heaves and arches upwards. It wrenches into a violent spasm. A guttural rasp escapes from my mouth. My lungs are filling up with a pale red jelly. I feel suffocated as it closes in on me. I gasp and flail about to stay on the surface, but I'm immobile and the pull is too strong. I drift in and out of consciousness. Someone comes near me carrying an urn of holy water from the Ganga, forces open my slack mouth and dribbles a few drops on my parched tongue. My eyelids are glued together. I don't have the strength to open them. 'Let my death be an occasion to rejoice. I don't want any wailing and crying,' I mumble.

I don't know if anyone can hear my dying wish. I squeeze my eyes shut tighter.

'God, my refuge...Thy mercy I crave.'

Another image bubbles up into my head. My first sexual encounter; I am thirteen. I bleed. I am in pain. More images... Memories of an active sex life shared with a man who has a heightened libido, whipped by an overriding sense of guilt. Then a long, painful span of childbearing and what felt like single motherhood. And then a unilateral vow of celibacy—without my consent.

'How dare he?' I mouth my last irreverence to my lord and master, a man driven by surreal exhibitionism and megalomania.

And I can see that in my husband's relentless pursuit of truth and non-violence there is yet to come a lurid experiment with sex, another fervent attempt to put his vows of celibacy to test. In the devastating barrenness of the dual roles we have played all our lives, shame and scandal shall smear his frank disclosures. His attraction for the perverse and the bizarre will unleash an emotional holocaust that will shock the world, but I shall not live to see.

Now my thoughts freeze. My lungs are bursting. My breathing is rapid and shallow. I see all my dead ancestors dressed in black, filing silently around me. They shall lead me into that one-way street, away from this temporal pain into lightness—into bliss. A narrow tunnel of moving blue light appears before my eyes. I am being sucked into a chasm of serenity to become whole and pain-free once again. I feel myself floating upwards, a weightless balloon rising high above the clouds into the expanding ether. I let myself go; a total and complete surrender.

Miles below, amidst the swirling colours and scents of daffodils, cannas and marigolds in full bloom, I can barely see the wasted carcass that holds me captive no longer. I am consumed by a feeling of deliverance. I mingle into a quiet, immortal nothingness. He sits still on a metal charpoy under the shade of an old mango tree, slumped over my cold body, cradling my head in his lap, tears spilling over his gaunt face. A face wrinkled with grief; a gentle and enduring spirit that will not let go.

'Farewell Ba, my beloved!' he whispers as a long wail let out by grieving cellmates and the milling crowds outside rents the air.

He sits huddled in a corner all night, chanting verses from the Gita while my body is bathed, dressed and anointed with a freshly ground paste of sandalwood. The women mark a big red dot in the centre of my pale clammy forehead. He watches a set of six glass bangles of the same hue being eased onto each of my wrists. With all the symbols befitting a Hindu married woman in place, I'm lifted off the ground onto a bamboo bier bedecked with ropes of marigolds and roses. The bier is placed upon a pyre made of sandalwood logs. Melted butter is poured on it before it is set ablaze. The flames rise high above, crackling greedily, devouring the decaying muscle and flesh that lie beneath the shroud of a dead Kastur. The acrid odour of burning flesh snakes up his nostrils. He sits down near the flaming pyre, dejected and motionless. 'How can I leave her like this? She would never forgive me,' he cries. Uncontrollable sobs rack through his crumpled body.

Twenty-four hours later, scattered amidst the smouldering ashes of my charred remains, someone has found six red bangles covered in ashes and dust, intact.

'I can't imagine a life without her,' he laments as the loud chatter of the people gathered there gets drowned in frenzied cries of salutation.

'Long live Kasturba Gandhi! Kasturba Gandhi amar rahe!'

'Hail Ba! The ever faithful, loving wife, the symbol of purity, fidelity and devotion, a living tribute to womanhood; she has redeemed her debt to humanity. She shall be transported straight to heaven.'

❀ ❀ ❀

ONE

It was a calm April morning in the tiny "White City" of coastal Kathiawar that had acquired its name because of its high walls and homes built of white limestone. Inside a finely-furnished bungalow, set amongst a cluster of houses criss-crossed by narrow lanes, a young woman was writhing in labour for the fourth time. A toothless midwife with bad breath and rotting gums was poring over her, trying to facilitate a safe and easy passage for the unborn child. She was chanting mantras and kneading her bursting abdomen with practiced ease. Braving the agony of intense pre-birth contractions, my mother Vrajkunwer Kapadia lay there, praying fervently for a healthy child.

Hazardous labour notwithstanding, I was born to nobility and wealth, a fair and beautiful child with inherently weak lungs. My father Gokuldas Makanji Kapadia, the former Mayor of Porbandar, was a highly revered wealthy businessman with a well-established overseas business in textiles, grain and cotton. It was the year the British were preparing to announce the opening of the Suez Canal that purported to shorten the sea-route around the African continent by thousands of miles. It was to be the year of global jubilation for international traders. While the world waited to cheer the grandiose opening of the canal that would become the highway to India, a little house in the coastal "White City" decked like a bride, echoed with cheers of a different kind. Elaborate celebrations to mark the birth of a beautiful girl were underway while I kicked around in my cradle, oblivious of the exploding forces of nature that had predetermined my onward journey on earth. Suckling my mother vigorously, I was content in the touch of her body and secure in the feel of her warm, moist breath on my tiny forehead.

I was named Kastur after the seductive scent that the world knows as musk. This heady intoxicant is the rarest and most potent of aphrodisiacs that ooze from the follicles around the navel of a male musk deer. Down the ages, in his quest for this fragrant potion that symbolizes divine and sensuous love, men have slaughtered thousands of these hapless and beautiful creatures. The deer wanders around its habitat, maddened by this erotic odour that emanates from deep within its own stomach, till it is hunted down by human predators; a curse of its birth that drives it to certain destruction. Call it the curse of my birth, or the burden of my name, but there I was, Kastur, the youngest of three siblings enjoying a privileged position as my two elder sisters had died in childbirth. Considered to be a divine gift from heaven, my parents treated me with excessive indulgence and care.

Even as my mother Vrajkunwer Ba had been screaming with terminal contractions in her makeshift labour room, not too far away another woman, Putli Bai, the third and much younger wife of Karamchand Gandhi, had just completed her first trimester. She bore inside her a soul that was to wait patiently to connect to me, Kastur the newborn girl, just a few houses and three trimesters down the road. It would have to bide its time to fit into a highly complex matrix where these two souls were to intertwine and then stride out together in their lives ahead.

The glorious unborn seed of Karamchand and Putli Bai, churning in its mother's womb, was destined to be my betrothed. The one whom the world would eulogize as the harbinger of Indian political renaissance, the most powerful messiah of the downtrodden, a "mahatma" who would galvanize and deliver his people to freedom, and finally, fall to the bullet of a crazed assassin, his own countryman, with the name of the Lord on his lips.

The yet-to-be-born Gandhi, swam and kicked around in the amniotic fluid of his mother's womb, a tiny little embryo of barely twelve weeks. 'I'm waiting for you, my husband-to-be,' I cooed, my desires wafting into Putli Bai's womb. I could do this at will. It was my secret escapade, a frolic I loved and often indulged in.

'You will start moving downwards, head first when it's time. Don't be afraid, my beloved. It's a path I have travelled before. I'm waiting on the other side.'

For waiting was ordained to be my mission on earth.

On 2 October 1869, cheer rang through the neighbourhood. Temple bells tolled furiously and the deafening sounds of rolling drums rent the air to announce the birth of Mohandas, the fourth child of Putli Bai and Karamchand Gandhi.

I was six months old.

Two

We became playmates. It was a past life connect; he was my Mohandas and I his Kastur. I often ventured into the open courtyard of his home to mingle with all the Gandhi grandchildren. We spent hours playing ball, spinning wooden tops, aiming clumsily at clusters of marbles in demarcated circles on the ground, squabbling over little pieces of chalk, scribbling abstract frescoes on the tiled floor of the patio, acting out fictional dramas, tugging and pushing at our hair and clothes till we rolled over giggling hysterically. It was blissful revelry that continued all day.

But as soon as I turned five, my mother slapped an embargo on me. 'Nice girls don't!' 'You can't play with boys, Kastur. No, no! Not even Mohandas. You are a big girl now.' Her voice trailed off.

And thenceforth my trips to the neighbourhood were stopped forever. Mohandas, curious and restless as he was, was allowed a free run in the vicinity albeit under the hawk's eye of a maid, while I sat holed up in my home in anticipation of lessons on how to become a devoted wife and good mother. The discrimination was firmly in place. 'Nice girls didn't!'

Mohandas' antics and bratty behaviour soon took on a heroic spin that trickled into our home. He often gave his sister and the family maid the slip and sneaked off to a nearby temple, climbing trees, hanging upside down from the branches for hours on end, before wandering off outside the city limits to watch some passing parade. The poor maid, overcome with hysteria in trying to track him down eventually quit her job.

One otherwise uneventful day, Mohandas quietly removed the idol of the family deity from its sacred alcove in Putli Bai's prayer room and perched himself in its place. He sat there all day till someone spotted him just before the evening prayers and all hell broke loose.

'God have mercy on us!' Putli Bai cried out.

She dragged him off the pedestal, begging to be spared from the wrath of the Almighty and doomed to rot in hell. A family meeting was hurriedly summoned to discuss the grievous sacrilege and sterner ways to reign him in, but Mohandas didn't relent. Each day he would indulge in new pranks to exasperate Putli Bai who finally gave up. It was this restlessness, a proclivity for the unusual albeit a childhood pastime, that portended a peculiar kind of mind mapping in the boy. It was this internal wiring of a manic energy that would mould his conduct in the years to come. It left his mother wringing her hands in despair and soon, Mohandas was forcibly enrolled in a kindergarten school in the city.

For the truant boy, whose heart was anywhere but in the austere regimentation of a classroom, the atmosphere was oppressive. He found himself struggling to learn those fearsome alphabets and numbers that were being loaded on him. He had to find some escape, which he did in harmless entertainment by assigning comical names to his teachers and making fun of them. But escaping school was non-negotiable; he had to become literate.

Meanwhile, my schooling had begun on a less structured but more serious note. I was being indoctrinated with legends of glorious, heroic women from ancient Hindu mythology. Each day was a fable retold, a new ethic, a new lesson, and a new icon to emulate. I learned of Anusaya, the wife of a sage whose chastity was tested by none other than the Lord himself. And Savitri, who challenged and outwitted Yama, the mighty God of Death, to bring her husband back from his fearsome abode. There was Taramati, who underwent untold miseries and torture in order to protect her husband's vow of speaking the truth. And Sita, the persecuted queen of Lord Rama, who was subjected to a trial by fire after a washerman accused her of impropriety.

My heart bled for her and her miserable life. I wondered. Had the gods nothing better to do than to descend on earth with alarming regularity to test the chastity of women? And who had assigned women with the punishing duty to please these enraged gods, failing which they could incur the wrath of these entities and be banished into the netherworld forever? What kind of gods were these who excommunicated hapless women on a whim, sometimes turning them into gigantic blocks of granite? Who would be so cruel as to curse them with a gory death by burning on skewers in the blazing infernos of hell? Sadly, I could not speak out, but my mind, indoctrinated by an overload of folklore and mythology refused to be crammed with the fear of doom, should I choose not to comply with the wishes of all men.

My coaching was vigorously underway for the singular purpose of becoming a faithful wife and a devoted mother. I was gradually evolving from child to woman, shaping up for the specific purpose of procreation. It was my duty as a woman that I owed to all of mankind. Quite an absurd paradox, considering that I would soon be drawn into one man's resolute vow of celibacy.

THREE

The Dewan of Porbandar, Karamchand Gandhi, was a troubled man. The legacy of the title bequeathed to him by his father, who had before him also been Dewan to the local ruler, sat well upon his shoulders. But it was not the affairs of the state that had put him in a quandary; it was his son. His fourth and youngest child Mohandas had turned seven and was becoming dreadfully unmanageable each passing day. Adding to his woes was the boy's mother, Putli Bai, who was forever anxious that something terrible was sure to befall upon her devilish son. She wanted him married, hoping that it would make him responsible. Two earlier engagements had left her fearful because the infant girls had died in quick succession of each other, soon after being engaged to her son. But the greater urgency was because Karamchand had been appointed the Dewan of the princely state of Rajkot, which was the regional headquarters of British administrative officers. She desperately wanted Mohandas to be engaged, before his father got deeper into the affairs of state.

Stirred by different compulsions, my parents could think of no better alliance for me, their much adored and only daughter, Kastur. Mohandas was born of an illustrious pedigree. His family history and lineage was unquestionable. A local astrologer in Rajkot drew up birth charts for both Mohandas and me, and finding them to be compatible, identified an auspicious time for the engagement ceremony.

On the assigned day, Karamchand escorted a group of elders from his family into our home to present a formal proposal to my parents. Cheer rang through the Kapadia household. It tugged at the strings of my heart. I was delighted to be at the centre of so much attention. The local priest appeared with a large brass platter laden with fruit and flowers and ornaments made of gold. Fully attired in bridal finery, I held my mother's hand as she steered me out from the women's quarters into the drawing room. The heavy brass platter was balanced upon my head for a few moments while the priest chanted mantras to bless me. At that time, the enormity of the change that was being set into motion was lost on me, overshadowed as it was, by the gifts and attention being showered on me by my family and friends.

I was engaged to Mohandas Karamchand Gandhi in absentia. My fiancé, the boy whom the stars had ordained to be my husband, was nowhere to be seen. Nor was he informed of the nuptial contract till much later. The mention of his name, however, stirred some unfamiliar churnings within me. Somewhere from my not-so-distant past, the image of a lean, chocolate-complexioned boy with a sing-song voice and unusually large ears, flashed before my eyes. I felt a heady sense of elation. Finally I was going to acquire a full-time playmate who was no stranger to me, but more importantly was a boy.

The Dewan of Porbandar could breathe easy at last. A wide benevolent smile lit up his face as I dived to touch my forehead to his bare feet, stifling a giggle. We would have to wait six years before we were wed, but that was no cause for despair because for me, at the age of seven, time had no boundaries or relevance.

✂ ✂ ✂

The celestial constellations capered across the skies at their own pace, whilst I, Kastur, conforming to the endlessly mystifying mindset of a Hindu woman, embarked on a journey towards the most significant part of my life. Meanwhile my mother had begun teaching me the basics of Hindu rituals, for she believed that every girl should understand them thoroughly before she transitions into womanhood, in her husband's home.

Of all the Vedic ceremonies that a Hindu is duty-bound to execute from the womb to the tomb and beyond, marriage is the most defining one. These ceremonies are deemed imperative for the purification of an individual to attain divine deliverance from the mortal bond of this life and supreme veneration in the next.

For the advocates of the theory of reincarnation like I was taught to be, the fear of violation of this decree seemed paramount.

Unlike my prepubescent body that was totally unprepared for the act of sexual intercourse and the travails of impending motherhood, surprisingly my mind that had endured grilling tutorials in chastity, fidelity and obedience was in a state of supreme readiness. This would hold me in good stead till I left my home at the age of thirteen and then spillover beyond.

❊ ❊ ❊

In the summer of 1882 there were three Gandhi boys ripe and ready for marriage. Karamchand's two sons, Karsandas and Mohandas were sixteen and thirteen years old and his younger brother had a son Motilal, who had turned seventeen that year. It was only natural for the two senior Gandhis who were nearing the age of sixty to want to discharge their duties whilst they were still in good health. Given the urgency of the situation, the brothers in concurrence with each other decided on a triple wedding to be held in the autumn of that year. Predictably, none of these plans were voiced to the three prospective grooms who remained blissfully oblivious until after the engagements had been formalized.

Even though Mohandas was fully aware of his own seven-year-long engagement to one Kastur Kapadia, whom he faintly remembered as the sprightly little girl from his neighbourhood, he had never deliberated on the prospect of marriage, much less on the onus it bore. Unlike me, he had never received any tutoring in the very private but crucial subject for which I was being painstakingly groomed. As the significance of the impending event dawned on him, he could barely contain his excitement at the prospect of appropriating a new and permanent playmate. The Gandhi boys were withdrawn from school long before the family began preparing to travel to Porbandar, to partake in the weeklong festivities preceding the wedding.

Meanwhile, in the homes of the three brides of Porbandar, Ganga, Harkunwer and me, frantic activity was underway. In keeping with our social status and the incumbent demands of a triple wedding, a huge hall was hired and an elaborate menu drawn up to feed the *baraatis* accompanying the grooms. Opulent flower arrangements were set in place and a bevy of singers and flutists lined up to create the magic appropriate for the magnificent ceremony that would unite four adolescent and two prepubescent children in wedlock, a knot so permanent that only death could do them apart.

And somewhere in the thick of the hustle and bustle, I flitted bewildered and lost. As was the custom, my father and mother hand-wrote the first invitation card in red ink, which they placed ceremoniously at the feet of the deity in the village temple.

As the day of the wedding approached, I was made to undergo a special beauty regimen. A fragrant paste of almonds, turmeric, sandalwood, rose-petals and fresh dairy cream was whipped up by an old aunt. While the toothless wonder crooned a bawdy folk song in her hoarse off-key voice, I was made to sit on a low wooden stool in the centre of the tiled courtyard strewn with red and yellow flowers, amidst all my aunts and cousins. The concoction was smeared generously all over my face and head and then ladled onto my bare arms and legs by each of them in turn. The drone of the raspy chorus that everyone had joined in, made me laugh. Although I was in the grip of a heady exhilaration that I had never known before, I was aware that these were my last few days in the safe confines of my mother's home. I had to begin preparing for a long and final expedition to Rajkot, as a married woman, no longer protected by the cocoon of my parental nurturing, no longer the darling and only daughter of Gokuldas and Vrajkunwer. I was going to bid farewell to my siblings, my home, my family, my dreams, my innocence and my childhood; the wife of a strange boy from my past whom I had not seen in nine years. A mild anxiety crept up in me. I was leaving my parents home forever. Forever was an infinite word. It was never-ending. It had no comebacks.

As darkness fell, the chattering in the common room died down and the Kapadia household had retired. I sat up in my room before an ornately carved cedar-wood chest that was overflowing with new clothes. The bright outfits embellished with shining threads of silver and gold beckoned me.

'All these are yours, Kastur,' I said to myself, my eyes sparkling with delight. I prized open a red lacquer jewellery box made by skilled craftsmen from China that my father had specially imported for me. A dazzling array of gold bangles, carved bracelets, intricately designed necklaces, rings and earrings embedded with precious stones, nose pins and filigreed silver anklets caught my eye. I took each piece out of its socket, caressed it with my nimble fingers and slipped it on. I pulled out a purple and gold sari made of silk net and draped it over my head. Colour rushed to my cheeks as I peered into the mirror. My anxiety dissipated. It was time to rejoice.

The sound of approaching footsteps startled me. I dived under the cover sheet on my bed. It was my mother.

'Kastur! What are you doing? Are you still awake?' she chided. 'Go to sleep now, my child. Don't tire yourself. It's a long day tomorrow and if Mohandas sees dark shadows under your eyes, he may just go back without you.'

'Yes Ba, I know,' I mumbled from under the sheet. And she was gone. I heard the creaking door snap shut. I closed my eyes and drifted into a blissful slumber.

Descending from a dense cover of silver clouds, a dark boy riding a bejewelled chariot drawn by six magnificent white horses loomed before me. Hundreds of drums and temple bells came alive as he alighted and stepped forward, his arms outstretched. A veil of white jasmine buds covered his face. A heady aroma of raw musk was emanating from him. His bare body was anointed with a glowing yellow paste, similar to the one that I had been treated to a few hours earlier. The slender, half-clad figure moved closer. I felt his warm misty breath mingling with mine. The aroma of musk, sandalwood and roses consumed me. I felt myself melting like a lighted candle, my body merging with his. We were fused together in eternal divinity, the androgynous deity epitomizing the perfect synthesis of masculine and feminine energies, the "Ardhanarishwara". We rocked to the music of the rolling spheres, a glowing mass of cells, vibrating to a celestial melody, in complete harmony with the cosmos. We swirled around in unison till we became one miniscule speck in the ever expanding stretch of the universe and all that remained was the singular echoing chant of a never-ending Om.

Far away from the hubbub of wedding preparations in Porbandar, on the coast of the Arabian Sea in the bustling city of Karachi, the firstborn son of a prosperous merchant from Kathiawar was counting down to a special day. On the day of the yuletide spirit, when the Christians of the world commemorate the birth of Jesus Christ, this little boy, whose parents of Gujarati Hindu origin had embraced Islam just one generation ago, was waiting to celebrate his sixth birthday.

Completely oblivious of the forces of the universe that had positioned the soon-to-be wed Mohandas Gandhi and Kastur Kapadia in such freakish proximity with him, he trudged along, with no inkling that their paths were to collide in the not-too-distant future. They would come onto a common platform for a common goal to banish a common enemy, only to part as bitter antagonists in their individual fights for freedom. The boy who would grow up with little faith in his religious identity, would have no confidence in his opponent's doctrine of peace, secularism and brotherhood either. He would orchestrate and catalyze the bloodiest transmigration in history, of a people driven by terror and religious zeal. The two men would in time be sharply pitted against each other in a losing battle of ideologies. The little Muslim boy would go on to be lauded as Qaid-e-Azam Mohammed Ali Jinnah, the creator of Pakistan, in a brutally divided subcontinent.

FOUR

Bedecked like a bride, the city of Porbandar eagerly awaited the arrival of the special procession from Rajkot. Groups of men sporting orange and yellow turbans and women attired in claret reds, leafy greens and gaudy pinks floated around the venue. Some waited at the entrance with silver sprinklers filled with rose water to splash on the guests as they walked in.

The banquet hall, perhaps the largest in Porbandar, had been given a makeover. A fresh coat of paint, a medley of coloured lights and bunches of flowers in kaleidoscopic colours festooned every nook and cranny; they extended from the floor to the ceiling and outwards onto the fences and walls, snaking up the trees outside. An amber glow had illuminated the building giving it a surreal look.

Just as the sun descended over the western horizon, a radiant canvas of pink and gold came alive in the sky. Three palanquins decked with strands of marigolds, jasmines, roses and betel leaves, carrying three traditionally attired brides led by a retinue of singing and dancing relatives wound their way to the venue. The palanquins swayed gently from side to side as the bearers traipsed along. I sat inside mine, like the other two brides in theirs, adorning a red sari of Benares silk that weighed several times more than my body. Soaked in the oils of sandal and turmeric earlier that week, my skin had turned the colour of gold. My head was covered with a gauzy net *chunni*, woven with shiny metallic threads. A fine circular wire of gold pierced my nose. Beaded through it were two tiny pearls flanking a ruby droplet that caressed my lips. My palms were tattooed with a traditional pattern of henna that spread right up to my elbows. Ivory bangles with red paint on the rims covered the length of my forearms. My feet had been outlined with a special red dye, and on my ankles were a pair of silver anklets that had tiny bells fixed on them. I shook my feet vigorously to listen to the sound of the tinkling bells. They augured well.

The bridal palanquin was covered with a screen of flowers that blocked my view outside. The rope of flowers brushed against the side of my face. I felt a piercing pain shoot up from the large circular wire of gold that had impaled the right side of my nose. I cringed. I dared not touch it. My heart hammered inside my chest. I squeezed my eyes to shut out the pain.

'Help me, Ba! Take this cruel thing off,' I called out to my mother. My entreaty got drowned in the din of the rolling drums outside. My eyes brimmed with tears that rolled down my face and then onto my chest. I was alone, enveloped in an ethereal golden light that afforded no solace. And Ba was nowhere in sight.

The palanquin lurched gently as the bearers came to a halt. I was lowered onto the ground. The pain had somewhat dulled. My heartbeats became faster and louder till they merged with the deafening sounds of the *shehnais* and the beating drums. Someone held my hand and helped me climb up to a dais where a dark, slender figure holding a thick garland of red roses stood. All I could see through my lowered eyes was a face covered by a veil of flowers and a gigantic pink turban made of silk, on the small head of a thin boy with abnormally large ears.

If there were any signs of a deeply embedded repression in him that would incubate on the death of his father and then, after a long struggle with conflicting forces drive him onto the global firmament as a Mahatma, they were lost on me. And if someone had told me then, that this preadolescent Gandhi who stood there patiently waiting to garland me, would in the years to come indulge in bizarre sexual experiments and mind-bending cult practices, I might have fled!

⚭ ⚭ ⚭

On a cool and sunny morning two separate railway carriages, ferrying three newly-wed brides with the men and women of the wedding party of Rajkot, chugged out of the railway station of Porbandar. After a heart-rending farewell, I parted from my weeping mother and the Kapadia household.

'Don't send me away, Ba,' I sobbed. 'Please Ba, I don't want to go.'

I clung to her knees weeping hysterically before someone peeled me away and guided me to the waiting carriage. The sight of the other two weeping brides saddened me further.

The train roared ahead, picking up speed and one of the Gandhi women burst into a cheery folk song that lulled me to sleep. When I woke up my anxiety was gone. The thought of the enticing new world of my husband that was waiting to welcome me lightened my spirit. I had never in all my thirteen years stepped out of Porbandar. It was beginning to feel like a picnic.

At the flower-bedecked entrance of my new home, Mohandas' sister, Raliatben stood in the doorway, obstructing the entry of her three brothers and their brides. She would have to be paid the customary amount before she allowed us in. Suddenly I felt I had morphed into a new creature. Just as a snake casts off its scaly skin to assume a shining new form, I had cast off my innocence and childhood of thirteen years to submerge into a new identity; a role that was fraught with innumerable expectations and responsibilities, within a large joint family. I had become a Gandhi.

FIVE

As twilight enveloped the city and shadows of darkness cast spooky patterns on the floor of the tiled courtyard, everyone dispersed and headed to their quarters. Believing it would be a magical night as my older sisters-in-law had insinuated, I shyly followed Mohandas to his small room on the first floor of the house with my heart beating wildly. Mohandas bolted the door behind me.

The room was strewn with rose petals and a sweet aroma had diffused in the air around. An oil lantern that stood on a stool near the window was burning brightly. A tiny earthen lamp laden with layers of black soot flickered faintly in one corner. The bed was covered with a vegetable-dye counterpane that had tribal motifs patched on it. Mohandas sat down on the bed. I stood beside him with my head bent, not knowing what I was expected to do. He leaned back on the pillow and turned around to face me. He looked bewildered and I could sense his nervousness. He fumbled, unsure of himself. I stood there in silence waiting for him to speak. After what seemed like an eternity, he smiled.

'Come here, Kastur,' he said as he pulled me gently, and locked his arms around me in a tight embrace. I closed my eyes and yielded coyly unto him.

As we lay on the bed holding each other, he took my fingers and continued to caress my hands, cheeks, neck and chin till he stopped on the gauzy fabric that covered my throat. He tugged at it and it fell away. I blushed and instinctively covered my face with one end of my sari. Then I pulled the bed cover over me, right up to my chin. He drew me closer, but I shrank away awkwardly.

Mohandas rose to snuff out the lantern. The room plunged into darkness. Only a faint glimmer of the earthen lamp in the corner and the silver rays of a full moon filtered through the stained glass window, bathing our bodies in an ethereal blue light. He rolled me over into the crook of his arm.

I quivered. My entire body was seized by lightness, a feeling that was both euphoric and new. This was my lord and master and my mother had told me that he had a right on me, to do as he pleased.

All kinds of stirrings surged through my mind and body. A warm glow diffused slowly within me and I could feel a rapid throbbing. I slackened every nerve and gave myself unto him as if it was an offering to the gods, a complete and open surrender.

My marriage was consummated, seventy-two hours after we were wed. I had finally joined the exalted ranks of my sisters-in-law Ganga and Harkunwer.

The sight of four crescent-shaped scratch marks of my nails on his back aroused me. The feeling that Mohandas and I had embarked on a novel journey of passion, into a world of self-discovery and erotica was thrilling.

❈   ❈   ❈

It was the morning after that the sight of blood on the bedsheet made me recoil in horror. I stared at the despicable stain in panic, not knowing what to do. I felt betrayed. No one had told me there would be blood. Nor had anyone said that sex was painful. Surely Ba would find out what we had been up to and punish us. I held on to Mohandas and wept. He took me gently in his arms stroking the back of my head.

'It's ok, Kastur. We haven't done anything wrong. Ba won't be angry. Nothing will happen. It's ok. Don't cry, my beloved. I'm here with you. Don't be afraid.'

His tender, soothing words comforted me and I tiptoed down the stairs into the courtyard where Putli Ba's day had long begun. I prayed to god that the guilt on my face would not give me away. The heady feeling of intimacy, the secret trysts I shared with Mohandas, the excitement of being touched, disrobed, loved, and caressed by him lingered on. The fear of being punished for those vile bloodstains on my bed faded away.

❈   ❈   ❈

My unripe breasts and premature body were unprepared to face the brunt of sex and its natural outcome, childbirth. But my mind had been tuned differently. As the days rolled by, I sensed Mohandas' increasing passion and I daresay I began to crave for his touch on my naked skin. He was the one I adored, my singular playmate on whom I had a primary lien. The mere touch of his fingers could send ripples of pleasure deep inside me. I loved him dearly and he was mine to possess. I would stop at nothing to please him. Much like the raw odorous musk that oozes from the entrails of a wild deer, my pheromones too were beginning to peak.

Our sexual union, the mortal embodiment of Shiva and his divine consort, the final amalgamation of yin and yang was indeed a cosmic explosion. I would soon get accustomed to the appearance of normalcy, the feigned amnesia of couples who behind closed doors, naked in each others' arms, regularly engaged in passionate sexual exchanges and appreciate the quintessential but accepted duplicity of the flawed human race. As for Mohandas, he had acquired a toy; a living organism that could talk back, laugh, play, copulate and then return to being his bonded slave. For him I was a mere plaything that was not permitted to either think or protest.

Life changed for me as it did for Mohandas. He was sent back to school and I got entangled in the household affairs as a fledgling appendage in the long chain of serving Gandhi women, whom it had became my duty to serve.

✂ ✂ ✂

The Dewan of Rajkot had an endless stream of visitors everyday, who had to be entertained and fed. Unlike my parental home where there was a retinue of servants to wait on us, here we had to do everything ourselves. My routine kept me busy all day. The household tasks, which I performed willingly for all the older women, were no longer tedious. Putli Ba was wise and kind. Unlike most dictatorial women of her ilk, she played no favourites. She instructed by example and not by authority and I grew to love her like my own mother. It made the chores easy and the hours fly fast.

But all day long, I hungered for the private moments in my bedroom. That was my impetus, my addiction, my personal sanctuary and my life.

I could not exhibit any physical proximity or overt contact with my husband in the presence of family elders. That would be a dreadful breach of conduct, but behind the closed doors of our own little room, we turned into a pair of wild deer, frolicking in the wilderness, driven by sheer animal passion, to indulge in a compelling, carnal, steamy erotic union, as much as to redeem our duty towards procreation.

And the tiny terracotta lamp, laden with thick layers of black soot, flickering in the corner of our room never burned out.

Sometime later, subtle changes began taking place in my body. The weave of my bodice felt constricting on my chest. It grazed painfully against my sore breasts that were fast swelling up. I could feel a peculiar and novel stirring inside me. Yes, the inevitable had happened. I was carrying Mohandas' child. The thought was at once thrilling and terrifying.

At home I had acquired a special status. I was being treated like a fragile entity and the attention I was getting from my hitherto intimidating elders delighted me. I did not want to think about the morbid ordeals of childbirth or the travails that had resulted in the tragic loss of my elder sisters. I knew that my rapidly changing body was a holy shrine. It was the abode of a new life that was growing within, a perfect entity that fed off my innards, bearing the blueprint of the extraordinarily pedigreed Gandhi-Kapadia gene pool.

In the meantime, Mohandas was undergoing a metamorphosis of his own. Deeply in love, he lusted for his new toy, Kastur all day long, and the thrill of fathering his own child temporarily dispelled his fear of losing the oldest link of the Gandhi chain; Karamchand's life was ebbing out. He had become terminally ill.

Six

With the passage of time, Mohandas assumed the role of a typical, authoritative Indian husband. His mind was crammed with things he had learned from street pamphlets. He had discovered a strange dimension to his "conjugal rights" that was a far cry from the simplistic and practical advice contained therein. This new identity came with an insufferable demand for fidelity and he took it upon himself to devise ways and means to extract it from me. Even if it was motivated by his innate passion for the tenet of truth, his manner of exhibiting it was downright abusive. Trapped in the throes of love and lust he dwelt on just one thing all day long…Kastur! His consuming passion had blocked out all else.

Much as I thirsted for our nocturnal sojourns and adored my Mohandas, the notion of becoming a bonded slave appalled me. He closely monitored my every move and I had to ask for his permission before I left the house even if it was to accompany his mother. I was disturbed at this arbitrary curtailing of my freedom. Captive of these stifling restrictions at fifteen and carrying Mohandas' child in my womb, I felt outraged and humiliated. Even more so because I hardly ever saw my older counterparts, Ganga and Harkunwer dart off in search of their husbands to seek permission before leaving the house. What made matters worse was the long and cruel lessons that were being forced on me each night by Mohandas in a futile bid to make me a literate, urban sophisticate worthy of the Gandhi surname. Fortunately for me, his lust always got the better of him which came as a great relief to me because I had never wanted to be singled out as different from Ganga and Harkunwer, both of whom were not only of less wealthy stock, but like me were also illiterate.

I was essentially conservative, but I could not allow myself to succumb to authority or be dictated to. Given that my outings were restricted to accompanying Putli Ba to a neighbour's house or sometimes just to the nearby temple, I felt constrained and humiliated. Even though I never consciously desired to flout tradition, one part of me scorned Mohandas' unreasonable and tyrannical embargo.

I revolted. The knocking down of my individuality had to be stopped and the need to assert myself became crucial for me. I would not allow my free spirit to be shackled. A grim resentment was simmering within. A quarrel was brewing and an open confrontation with my lord and master was inevitable. It would be our first in many.

One morning I accompanied Putli Ba on her usual trip to the temple. There was a buoyant spirit of defiance within me; I had not sought Mohandas' permission to leave. I had stopped doing this for a while now. His high-handedness no longer held any power over me. Expectedly he exploded. He made another attempt at clamping even greater restrictions on me, which I flouted again with impunity. He finally gave up when he realized that Kastur would not succumb to his oppression. He soon retracted and normalcy between us was restored. He had accepted his first defeat in our relationship somewhat calmly, but Mohandas was always distracted and restless, hardly at peace with himself.

Just then word came from Porbandar. It was time for me to go back to my parental home as was the custom that required young married couples to be separated for a considerable length of time during the wife's confinement. I was happy to go and easily settled into the comfort of my mother's domain with my overindulgent parents who pampered me even more, as I was with child.

Cocooned in the cozy confines of my childhood haven, my maid entertained me with endless tales each night while massaging me with soothing herbal concoctions. The stories were about the iconic and gallant Warrior Queen of Jhansi, Rani Laxmi Bai, who had led a troop of Indian soldiers to fight the Imperial tyrants to protect her kingdom. She was my all-time favourite heroine who had sacrificed her life in battle, defending her motherland just a few years before I was born. Her epic tales never ceased to infuse a burning fervour in me as my maid crooned folk lullabies extolling her honour and valiance. I fantasized being the proud and patriotic queen, charging on a white horse armed with a sword and armour. With my infant boy strapped to my breast, unmindful of the fatal wounds on my body, I would ride into the sunset with loud war cries resounding in the horizon, until I fell asleep.

Soon thoughts of Mohandas began to trouble me. I yearned to be back with him. My life in Rajkot beckoned me. Even though he had become irritable and mean, I missed him deeply. My problems had begun only because I had rebelled against his authority. If I had not revealed my desires for an independent life, everything would have been fine. I did want to be a good wife like many of those extraordinary women I had been regaled about right through my childhood. However, I had a duty to myself that I was not willing to forgo.

For now, the yearning to be with my Mohandas clouded all else. The next morning I asked my mother to send me back to Rajkot.

✳ ✳ ✳

Meanwhile in Rajkot, Mohandas had befriended an erstwhile friend of his older cousin Karsandas, Mehtab Sheikh. The son of a jail warden who had been employed by the British, Mehtab Sheikh was a tall and strapping athlete. A lazy and boastful waster, Sheikh's rakish manner, his powerful air of sexuality and his supreme confidence all but stoked the sleeping beast in Mohandas. A strong bond began to form between the two polar opposites.

Sheikh was not particularly liked by the Gandhis. Their explicit antipathy had less to do with his religious beliefs and more with his waywardness. As for Mohandas, he had found a mature and experienced confidante with whom he could share his inner fears and his irrational insecurities, something he had never been able to do with anyone in the family. Driven by his perverse attraction to the forbidden, a desperately lonely Mohandas had become addicted to Sheikh's wise words. He found it easy to express his embarrassing fear of the dark and his revulsion to snakes and wild animals, the terror he felt of ghosts and ghouls, thieves and dacoits and other phobias without the fear of being derided by him. For once he was able to speak out that he felt ashamed that his wife was not scared of any of these bogeys that so terrified him and the shameful pressure he felt at his own inadequacies.

'While I lie awake in terror, keeping an oil-lamp burning all night in my bedroom, fearing every shadow that falls on my window, Kastur sleeps soundly, unaffected by anything. She steps out alone into the dark. I feel small and humiliated because I can't,' he blurted out in one breath.

Mehtab Sheikh, his new-found mentor, would have ready answers and Mohandas was confident that under the influence of this god-sent master, he would turn into the man he yearned to be.

'I can fix anything for you, my friend,' boasted Mehtab Sheikh. 'Look at me! I can hold poisonous snakes in my hand like a piece of twine. I can battle a band of dacoits alone with my bare hands. They do not terrify me. And ghosts...? What are ghosts...? I don't believe in them. I'm a Muslim. I eat meat. My prowess is unchallenged. No one can outrun me. No one can outsmart me. And do you know why? Because I eat meat. You cannot get a powerful body or mind on a fare of just vegetables!' There was a devilish gleam in his eyes as he bragged on.

'Why do you think the British could conquer us so easily? Because they are white skinned, my friend and the white man doesn't eat *ghaas-phus* like you do, he eats meat.'

Mohandas sat for hours beside him goggle-eyed, hanging on to these precious pearls of wisdom. He felt cheated by the accident of his birth. Being a Vaishnav, his caste and lineage forbade him from eating meat. He had been taught that it was a sin worse than manslaughter. It would surely relegate him to the raging fires of hell. But the overwhelming lure of Sheikh's quick-fix cure deadened his conscience. If meat eating were the simple cure to all his phobias, then meat it would have to be.

Bracing for the ultimate tribulation, he dispelled his anxiety by consoling himself that some of his Hindu teachers at school were also meat eaters; so it could not have been that grave a transgression. As a consequence of this newly-acquired bravado, he rationalized that eating meat was a perfectly acceptable way of life and therefore he was making no violations of any moral ethic, other than the secrecy he would have to maintain from his parents.

Mohandas had always been somewhat of a rebel. The attitude of the upper castes was unbearable for him; any rules imposed by his community had to be broken. The cruelty meted out to the night soil cleaners, appalled him. "Untouchability" to him was a vile sin, much more damnable than eating the flesh of a dead animal. A deep-rooted churning had begun within him which would finally culminate into a massive upheaval. But for now, he had devised his own secret method to defy the upholders of this loathsome ethic.

His prepubescent rebellion had found one more avenue for expression. Fascinated by people who smoked, he mustered the courage to pick up a stubbed cigarette butt and took a long, deep drag. No smoke blew out of it or his mouth and he found the nicotine-ridden butt to be acrid and distasteful. To give it one more shot, he stole a few coppers from the servants of his house and bought himself a new pack, which he smoked with renewed enthusiasm. His secret tryst however, was short lived as the bitter taste of the tar and the smoke-induced bout of coughing banished the joys of that forbidden fruit forever.

By now Mohandas had completely stopped going to temples. The ostentatious show of wealth on bejewelled deities placed on gilded thrones outraged him. Skepticism gripped him and he found solace in proclaiming that he was an atheist. If there was any shred of guilt on his conscience for these transgressions, it soon dissipated, for he was destined to adopt a larger, more altruistic and noble cause. He was embarking on an experiment that was well worth the risk of eternal damnation to hell. Mohandas had begun a momentous albeit sinful journey, his mind dulled into apathy with the popular limerick foremost in his head,

Behold the mighty Englishman,
He rules the Indian small
Because being a meat eater,
He stands five cubits tall!

Mohandas was on a road to self-realization and freedom from the Imperial rulers. Both would elude him for a long time.

❋ ❋ ❋

By the secluded bank of a river on the outskirts of Rajkot, was a little clearing hedged by a thick shrubbery of overgrown ferns and wild grass, hidden from prying eyes. There lay a grand feast of roasted goat's meat and freshly rolled out rotis, which Mehtab Sheikh had spread out on a straw mat. Mohandas held his breath. He had never touched or smelled this kind of food before. With trembling hands, he gulped down the vile chewy stuff. He had adopted an air of bravado, not wanting to show his hesitation for fear of ridicule by his benevolent mentor. He ate a big portion of it quietly, holding his breath, fighting the urge to throw up.

'Well done, my friend!' Mehtab thumped his back, grinning widely. 'You are a man now! Just watch how your life changes from here on!'

But, back in the privacy of his room that night Mohandas felt violently ill. Revulsion, guilt and nausea gripped his throat. Deep inside, he felt painful stirrings that kept him awake through the night. Of the few hours that he did manage to sleep, graphic images of a live goat trapped inside his stomach, bleating piteously, jerked him to his feet. He found himself on his bed trembling in fear, drenched in perspiration. He had committed his first cardinal sin.

Mohandas was overcome with remorse, but he did not allow himself to weaken. His commitment to his country was of far greater importance than this squeamishness he felt for the flesh of a slaughtered animal. He would conquer it. The sacrifice of a few goats was indeed a tiny price to pay for the deliverance of his motherland. As an inchoate teenager, the first seeds of "freedom from white masters" had already germinated inside him, the absurdity of its formula, notwithstanding.

❋ ❋ ❋

Seven

Rajkot
16 November 1885

Karamchand lay in bed seriously ill. His anal fistula had turned septic and the pain emanating from that pus-filled laceration was unbearable. Each waking moment was an excruciating battle of nerves, for he had become too weak to even lift his head. Ayurvedic ointments and concoctions had stopped working. The *hakim*'s medicated plasters were ineffective and quick-fix magical nostrums from local quacks had failed. As a last ditch effort to ease his agony, he was taken to an English surgeon in Bombay who recommended immediate surgery as the only option.

Earlier, the family physician had vetoed the idea, fearing dangerous complications with his advancing age, so a crest-fallen Karamchand had returned to Rajkot to await the inevitable. Confined to his bed, he revolted at the idea of someone else tending to him; but his flesh was rotting and spirit weak, so he resigned himself to being bathed, cleansed, bandaged and sponged in turns by Putli Ba, Mohandas and an old family retainer.

Mohandas attended to the nursing duties assigned to him in earnest. He religiously cleaned and dressed his father's pestilent wound, compounding and administering medicines with great care. Each night he would stay up for hours, massaging the aching legs of a dying man, watching the laboured heaving of his chest, dreading to face the grim truth that Karamchand's life was ebbing out.

His own life had come to a virtual standstill. Between school and his ailing father, he had no time for anything, not even his mentor, Mehtab Sheikh. I was relieved to see that his dependence on that evil man had vanished.

A deep depression had overcome Mohandas. Gently kneading and massaging his father's legs every night, his mind compelled him to dream of the carnal pleasures that awaited him in the far corner of the house. His eyelids heavy with sleep that night, he drifted back to another incident that was fresh in his memory.

His father was lying in bed, temporarily dulled by the analgesic effect of the Ayurvedic plaster on the inflamed and festering lesion that was spilling toxins into his blood.

Mohandas tiptoed into his father's room, with a neatly folded sheet of paper in his hand. He came close to his bed and stood silently beside him not wanting to wake him up. Karamchand moaned and opened his eyes.

'What is it, my son? What troubles you?' he spoke in barely audible rasps.

Blinded by tears that streamed down his cheeks, Mohandas handed the note to his father and crumbled onto the floor in a heap near his feet.

Karamchand struggled to prop himself up. He unfolded the sheet of paper and glanced over it slowly. Mohandas' heart pounded in fear. He did not expect his father to show any mercy after reading what he held in his hands. He would surely lash out in anger and thrash him black and blue if he could, something that he had never done before. After a long torturous silence, Mohandas dared to look up at Karamchand's face. Tears were streaming down his gaunt cheeks. He had squeezed his eyes shut, folded the note and torn it to bits. The damp shreds fell to the floor as Karamchand dropped his head back on his pillow, racked with sobs.

Mohandas had wept inconsolably. The confessions of his sins, his thieving, eating meat, smoking cigarettes, they were all there in his handwriting. He had bared his soul to his father to purge his mind and rid himself of the guilt that had somewhat lessened. He lay there clutching onto Karamchand's feet, sobbing loudly. A huge weight had lifted off his chest. He had been vindicated, forgiven for his sins and freed from the fear of damnation.

A gentle nudge broke his reverie, bringing him back to the room where his father slept.

'*Beta*, I'm here, you can go now. Go and sleep. It's late.' It was his uncle, Karamchand's younger brother who had come to relieve him. It was also the night that would wound the innards of his soul and leave him scarred for life.

✂ ✂ ✂

There was an uneasy calm as a cold night descended like a shroud upon Rajkot. An eerie blue light enveloped the surroundings as far as the eye could see. Sleep eluded me as I lay on my crumpled bed, waiting. A slight draft stirred the faded orange drapes on my bedroom window. I felt an icy breeze tousling my hair, brushing against my flushed face. A chill crept upon my ankles and shin. I pinioned the edge of my sari under my heels and dug them into the soft mattress on which I lay. I tightened the loose end of the *pallu* around my neck like a scarf and pulled the patchwork quilt right up to my chin.

A low and continuous moaning of someone in pain echoed from the room where Karamchand lay. I had long sensed that piteous cry of a life ebbing out. A faint anxiety crept into my head. My heart began to beat faster. I heard two muffled voices across the landing followed by shuffling of feet and some urgent whispers. It was Mohandas and his uncle.

Just then, a violent stirring in my womb jolted me out of my bed. I felt a sharp kick within that sent ripples right down my back. As if that tiny life breeding inside was reminding me that it was there. I clenched my teeth, squeezing my eyes tightly to fight a wave of nausea. The voices had died down. I felt that uneasy stillness around me and those terrifying moans across the landing boomed right in my ears again. I heard the footsteps come closer. The door creaked open and then snapped shut.

Mohandas had entered the bedroom stealthily, his face out of focus in the dim light. I lay still, pretending to be asleep. I could feel his penetrating gaze on me. The little foetus inside me delivered another sharp kick to my abdomen. I clenched my fists holding back a desire to massage my throbbing stomach. Then all was quiet. A death-like calm had overcome us. He stood beside me, tearing off his clothes.

'Wake up, Kastur,' he whispered. 'Shhh! Don't make a sound. Bapu is not asleep yet.'

There was a savage passion streaming from his eyes. I felt his warm and moist body against mine. Just then, there was an urgent knock on our bedroom door. Breathing heavily, Mohandas rolled over on the bed. I heard another louder rap on the door and then a sharp voice, 'Hurry up, Mohandas. Your father is dying.'

Those words hung like frozen icicles in the midnight air. He lay still for a brief moment, his breath slowed down. Then he turned his glazed eyes towards me.

What the hell? What happened? Would death wait for him?

I lay there in shock shivering, rubbing my eyes trying to adjust to the darkness. I wanted to push him off, to scream at him, tell him to rush to his dying father's side, but there was a renewed urgency in his movements. I shuddered. The wriggling foetus inside me made one last violent convulsion before it lay still. A terrifying, dark, silence enveloped me. The painful moans from outside had stopped.

While Mohandas' body, fizzing with erotic need, had sought its release in the arms of his Kastur, death had sneaked in to snatch Karamchand away from the lap of his helpless brother. In a few moments the loud wail of a distraught widow, Putli Ba, rent the air. Mohandas jumped up from the bed, grabbed his clothes from the floor, hurriedly put them on and darted out. I lay under the quilt for a long, long time, cold, mortified and trembling.

On seeing the lifeless body of his father that had been lowered from the bed to the floor, Mohandas was gripped by an overwhelming sense of remorse. This fearsome image was going to haunt him all his life. He would have to bear the torment of having been seized by a fit of violent lust, to copulate with his pregnant wife while his father lay writhing in excruciating agony next door. What he did not know was that he had inadvertently ushered the shadow of "the grim reaper" into my febrile womb.

A few months later, I gave birth to a premature child. Mohandas could not bear to look at 'the poor mite, who scarcely breathed for a few days, and died.'

'That was expected,' he murmured caustically, 'it should be a lesson for all those in the evil grip of desire.'

❈ ❈ ❈

Eight

After the death of his father, Mohandas was a changed man. I found him unusually aloof and quiet. He showed none of his earlier tenderness and his fervour to teach me to read and write had vanished. This strange coldness was unnerving. Even the oil lamp that had burned all night in the corner of our room was gone. There was definitely something eating at his vitals. I knew instinctively that some strange experiment to attain selfhood had assumed a disturbing dimension.

Mohandas and I hardly spoke, not even in the privacy of our bedroom. He would return home late, go straight to bed in the dark and leave for school before sunrise each day. He would rarely eat dinner at home complaining of indigestion on being questioned by his mother. I knew he was hiding something dreadful from me and that he was lying to his mother. It did not take me long to figure out that Mohandas had begun to eat meat and for me, a devout Vaishnav, that was tantamount to consuming human flesh. That evil Mehtab Sheikh had turned him into a pagan, a demonic violator of everything that was sacred to us.

Soon I noticed some other vices that had probably lain dormant inside him so far, raise their heads. He always smelled of stale cigarettes, meat had become his cherished daily fare and he was involved in petty thieving. In the erroneous belief that he was marching towards national, spiritual and personal liberation, he had turned into an evil man.

After twelve long months into this puerile journey, a thoroughly corrupted Mohandas, not even half a centimeter taller or any more robust as per the claims of his vile mentor, had stumbled upon yet another unfulfilled fantasy. Even though the guilt of having deceived his parents never stopped gnawing at his heart,

Mehtab Sheikh's continuous reminders that it was not prudent at this stage to lose sight of his higher goal, somewhat deadened his soul. In fact he got lured into another den of vice, where he was promised infinite satisfaction and ultimate absolution.

Uncertain of how women should react to sexual advances, another battle was raging within him. For a while my responses had been troubling him. He had begun to view them suspiciously and needed to know how and where I could have learnt my daring ways. Given his own lack of experience, he turned to his only saviour, "The Oracle" Mehtab Sheikh who knew it all.

'She rises on her toes and kisses my eyes and forehead, Mehtabbhai. I am at my wits' end. Is she a child or a woman? That wild passion in her is unnerving. And in that moment, I am scared. I fear for myself and for her too. In whose bed has she lain? Tell me please? My head is bursting. Has she betrayed me?'

Sheikh's answer must have indeed been alarming for Mohandas.

'Perhaps there is someone she likes better than you, Mohandas,' he said with a flourish, a fiendish grin etched on his face. 'This will need further investigation,' he said mockingly. The seed of suspicion having taken root, he easily seduced my jealous husband into visiting a nearby brothel to get a clearer picture on my perceived amorous behaviour.

❅ ❅ ❅

'You have been unfaithful to me, Kastur,' Mohandas lashed out in the cover of a cold dark night soon after, as he struck hard at my arm. The red bangles on my wrist shattered into tiny bits. A small fragment of glass pierced the skin of my palm and drops of blood trickled on the bed. I cringed back with fear. What was this?

'I'm going to send you back to your mother,' he ranted, his chest heaving violently. 'You have violated the holy vows of wedlock. Which man is more worthy of your body than me? You are not a "pativrata" woman! You do not deserve to be wedded to a Gandhi.' Possessed by a wicked demon as it were, he continued to mouth a string of lewd obscenities that I had never heard him utter before.

'I shall throw you out on the streets! Leave you to rot in hell… in hell…in hell!' His scathing words resounded in my head till I

clamped my palms on my ears to block them out. Some blood from
my bleeding wrist had stained the sides of my cheek.

I lay on my bed with my face turned up to the ceiling, my heart beating wildly. The room was dark and I was alone. I looked at my arms. There were no traces of blood. I was sweating profusely. Had it been a bad dream? I steadied myself and reached out for a glass of water, gulping it down in one breath. It was well past midnight. Mohandas was not back. I felt that deep restlessness again. I had tried desperately to dispel it, but how could a devoted Hindu *pativrata* wife, wrestle the demons that threatened her life and marriage and be at peace?

Pacing up and down alone in my bedroom, I was oblivious to the fact, that my truant husband had just stepped into a den of Satan in the seedy confines of the city's most infamous brothel, to verify the fidelity of his poor, unsuspecting wife. If anyone was in dire need of tenderness at that moment, it was I. A chill ran down my spine. I felt I had just received an icy hug from the Lord of Death!

✼ ✼ ✼

The master manipulator Mehtab Sheikh, the omnipotent sorcerer, the one who held answers to all that was ailing the universe, had tempted my husband Mohandas Karamchand Gandhi with the promise of a miraculous nostrum of carnal gratification. He had promised him pleasures of the flesh, the kind my blubbering, sexual, greenhorn Mohandas could never have dreamt of. He would then be able to tell with certainty, whether Kastur had been polluted by another man or not. Mohandas felt heady with the anticipation of this promised carnal release. After all, he was on the verge of an indisputable verification of his own misgivings and my fidelity.

✼ ✼ ✼

On the suburban outskirts of the city, at the bottom of a narrow winding road, bordered with dense overgrown shrubbery, a vile Venus flytrap lies nestled inside a seedy ghetto hidden from the public eye. It is a place where men dare to tread only under the cover of darkness. There inside a doorway, protruding with rows of rusted iron knobs, in the fading light of a moonless sky, the silhouette of a garishly made-up woman, barely in her Twenties, wearing a bilious yellow sari and blood-red lipstick beckons him.

He enters a tiny room with green cracked walls that is bare, except for a rickety wooden bed covered with a tattered mattress, two pillows and a faded counterpane. On one wall of the dimly-lit room hangs an oversized calendar with a dancing Shiva, printed in gaudy colours. A garland of orange and pink plastic flowers laden with dust hangs untidily on it. A thin trail of a sweet-smelling smoke curls up to the ceiling from an ash-laden incense stick that stands on the makeshift altar underneath the calendar. A lone, naked bulb suspended from a frayed wire from the ceiling lights up the dingy room.

The woman glides in behind him. She squirts a red trajectory of tobacco and her saliva into a tarnished brass spittoon, wiping her betel-stained mouth with the loose end of her sari.

'Paise laye ho na, Babu?' she coos coming close to him, curling her bare arms around his shoulders to check if he has any money.

Mohandas removes his jacket and sits nervously at the edge of the bed that creaks annoyingly with his weight. This harlot is no gazelle-eyed damsel in pastel robes of soft silk as he had imagined. She's a far cry from the velvet and gold-attired nautch girls of yore, or the famed *Devadasis* from Hindu temples that he has secretly lusted over in picture books.

Mohandas trembles. The coarse woman with betel-stained teeth and red lips looms above him. He fumbles, avoiding her thickly-kohled, penetrating eyes. Suddenly, she lunges forward. Fighting down a wave of revulsion, he stretches his arms and yanks her roughly on the bed by her pinned up hair that tumbles loosely around her breasts. The harlot lets out a shrill cackle and rolls over.

Mohandas has never felt so ill. He sits rooted to the spot in embarrassment, his libido snuffed out. He feels reviled by the foul, semi-naked creature that lies provocatively beside him. He turns his face away. A strong cocktail of mouldy odours, stale tobacco and a cheap jasmine perfume nauseates him. Fired by violent remorse, he jumps up from the swaying mattress, grabs his jacket from the floor that is littered with half-smoked *beedis* and burnt matchsticks and darts out leaving a clutch of soiled currency notes on the bed.

The bawdy creature breaks into a string of obscenities. Her lewd curses stream out of the crack in the door as he breaks into a run, blinded by his tears. How could he have besmirched the character of his beloved Kastur? He would beg her for forgiveness and fall at the feet of his ever-trusting mother begging for pardon.

Whether Mohandas had been saved from damnation that ominous night by his sudden loss of libido, or was it a lack of nerves that had rendered him impotent, I do not know, but his compelling carnality shall draw him back into Satan's Den again and again, till he can learn to crystallize the need for abstinence from sex, by taking a lifetime vow of *brahmacharya*. Either way, I was to be the casualty!

�֍   ✖   ✖

Nothing fixes a thought so irrevocably into the matrix of the human mind as the desire to forget it.

A deep guilt had consumed Mohandas. During all his waking hours, he obsessed about his sins. They preyed on his vitals plunging him to abysmal depths of remorse. He desperately needed to appease his conscience for he could no longer bear the burden of his transgressions alone. A broken and desolate Mohandas finally brought himself to redemption at my feet. Amidst copious tears, he poured out his heart to me begging for forgiveness.

The mother in me took his head onto my lap, running my fingers through his hair silently while his tears flowed out in torrents amidst racking sobs. He wept for long like a child. That night my beloved husband, a crumpled and dejected boy, sat before me with his head bowed in shame, unable to look me in the eye. I could feel a sharp constriction in my throat. My eyes filled up. My future loomed before me. Mohandas was repentant. He was vulnerable and damaged. He needed me for support and I knew somewhere deep down that this was the role destiny had ordained for me. Mine would be a life of waiting and sacrifice. Wiping his face with the loose end of my sari, in what was deemed to be the first test of our conjugal vows, I embraced him tightly and we wept. I had tided over the first crisis of my life with patience and maturity far beyond my fifteen years.

I was also pregnant for the second time, with Mohandas' child.

✖   ✖   ✖

NINE

With the passing away of Karamchand, bad times fell upon the Gandhis. The pension that he had been getting from the ruler of Rajkot stopped. He had left them no savings. Some minor investments in property were of little consequence. His two older brothers, who held low-level legal positions in the state, were unable to sustain the expenses of the growing family. And neither of them had a command over the English language that was essential for higher placements in the government; so the future looked dismal.

The responsibility of the family naturally fell upon Mohandas. It was imperative for him to complete his higher education in order to get a job that would bring in enough to cover the family expenses. Given his track record as an average student, this would pose a challenge, but providence favoured him when he passed the matriculation examination at Samaldas College; one of just four who qualified with him at nineteen years.

Ninety miles away from home, the college in Bhavnagar where Mohandas was sent to live alone for the first time in his life away from Putli Ba, the family and me, made him terribly homesick. The teaching was of a high standard; English lessons were cumbersome and his marks poor. He had lost precious time during the months preceding his wedding preparations and later tending to an ailing Karamchand. He lagged behind in class. He was disheartened and pined endlessly for his beloved wife. Also the prospect of impending fatherhood greatly distracted him.

On returning home at the end of the first term, Mohandas poured his heart out to me. He voiced his anguish at the futility of this higher education. A mere graduation would not suffice to get him a job of high office and hardly reward him with his deceased father's mantle of Prime Minister, which he so longed for. Putli Ba turned to her husband's friend Mavji Dave, whose views and counsel the family relied upon after Karamchand had gone. A learned Brahmin scholar, well versed in the ways of the world, he proposed that it would be in everyone's interest to send Mohandas to study for a barrister's degree at the renowned Inns of Court in London. That three-year course he felt was his best and only recourse.

Mavji's words rang sincere and deep. Words that were indeed well meaning and wise, but how would the family cough up the requisite three-four thousand rupees to cover the costs of his studies? They had barely scraped together the fees for his college at Bhavnagar which was only ninety miles away. Moreover, an orthodox Vaishnav was not supposed to violate the religious decree by crossing the seven seas, to dwell amongst alcohol-consuming and meat-eating, white skinned people. The prospect of ritual pollution and a total corruption of her beloved son terrified Putli Ba, but fate ordained otherwise. All apprehensions were soon brushed aside by Mavji Dave and frenetic preparations to send Mohandas away in the spring of 1888 had begun.

Mohandas was overjoyed. The prospect of going off to England to pursue a higher education thrilled him.

'If I go to England,' he mused, 'not only shall I become a barrister, but I'll be able to visit the land of philosophers and poets and live at the epicentre of one of the greatest civilizations of the world.'

Mohandas however had no say in the matter. The decision to send him away was not his. His family decided his course of study. His natural aptitude for medicine was shot down as it entailed the dissection of dead animals; something that was totally against his religion. He was expected to follow in his father's footsteps to take over as Prime Minister of Rajkot for which law and not medicine would be of use to him. The fact that law was not conducive to Mohandas' nature was completely disregarded by everyone and no one imagined that it would be a long haul before he could become a lawyer, even of mediocrity.

Now all they needed was the right recommendation and the funds.

❇   ❇   ❇

TEN

4 September 1888

On a muggy September morning, Mohandas Karamchand Gandhi set sail aboard S.S. Clyde from Bombay harbour across the perilous "seven seas" westwards to London. Sailing across the Arabian Sea and the Red Sea via the Suez Canal, the Mediterranean Sea, the Straits of Gibraltar and then northwards across the Atlantic Ocean to the English Channel, it purported to be a treacherous voyage that would take more than seven weeks.

It had been a long, grievous struggle for Putli Ba to raise funds for the trip and tuitions, but much worse was braving the threats of excommunication from the Modh-Bania community. Putli Ba, the defiant widow, had taken a stand. Mohandas would go to study law at the Inns of Court at London, no matter what. She had complete faith in her son. She had reinforced her confidence by extracting a vow from him in the presence of her god and a Jain monk who was also a trusted family friend. Mohandas pledged never to give in to temptations of the flesh, alcohol or meat of any kind in what she deemed was the white man's den of vice. After that Putli Ba feared no transgressions on her son's part and whole-heartedly supported the decision to send him far away, the inevitable and ignominious threat of excommunication notwithstanding.

Earlier that year during the long periods of separation from Mohandas and pregnant for the second time, I had been going through my own travails. Plagued by a consuming anxiety that spilled over from my first pregnancy and a premature child who did not survive four days, it was impossible to keep my fears in check. Every morning I accompanied Putli Ba to the village temple to pray for protection and a safe passage of the unborn child growing in my womb. I prayed fervently for a healthy child, a boy.

Around that time, my older sister-in-law Nandkunwer was also pregnant and that brought us much closer to each other. In the spring of 1888 she gave birth to the first Gandhi grandchild, a lovely healthy girl. Jubilant celebrations ensued, but I sensed a distinct underlying restraint. No one voiced it, but the disappointment was palpable. Now all eyes were fixed on me to accomplish the heroic feat of delivering the much-awaited son and heir to the Gandhi clan.

Even as hectic plans to send Mohandas to England were underway, in the winter of 1888 I went into labour. The family waited anxiously for good tidings while I lay writhing in agony, braving the torture of pre-partum contractions. A loud wave of euphoria ran through the Gandhi household when the news broke. I had delivered a normal, healthy, bonny baby boy. All apprehensions dispelled, the mood was one of gaiety and joy and the overhang of Mohandas' uncertain future was temporarily forgotten. Putli Ba was ecstatic. Relatives were notified with the speed of lightning and plans of a grand celebratory feast were set into motion. Boxes of sweets and meticulously packed gifts were distributed to all those who mattered. The celebrations were no different in scale and design to those of a wedding.

After six days of the birth of my son, I was brought out of the birthing room for the elaborate Hindu ritual of purification of the mother and child. This was followed by a solemn ceremony where the Lord Almighty was invoked to come down to earth and script the destiny of the newborn baby with his own hands. It was believed that the child had to be given a name on that day to enable the Almighty to identify him. Quite appropriately, the boy was named Harilal, the Son of God, thereby eliminating any scope for error in god's judgement and a life of fortitude and prosperity was a foregone conclusion.

Alas! Fate had chalked out other plans!

Harilal's arrival, momentous as it was, only provided a temporary diversion from the troubles that plagued the family. Between a deep emotional struggle on Putli Ba's part to fight religious misgivings about sending her son away to the land of sin and feverish attempts by the brothers to raise funds, the atmosphere at home was anything but peaceful. The shadow of gloom fell upon Mohandas as well.

Mohandas had immense faith in his own persuasive powers. Putli Ba was going to be easy, but the real challenge lay in obtaining a fully paid scholarship from Frederick Lely, the British Political Agent and advisor to the Rana of Porbandar. In those days, political agents were the resident officials, "superimposed" upon the 600-odd Indian rulers by the Crown. They were in effect the de-facto rulers of the respective states to whom in exchange they guaranteed protection and retention of wealth.

In what turned out to be his first personal encounter with British officialdom, Mohandas' hopes came crashing down. Lely's tone was curt and the reasons stated unclear. To be eligible for a scholarship, a college degree was mandatory and poor Mohandas' application was summarily and sternly dismissed. Had Lely known at that time that he was facing a man who would spell the ruin of the British Empire, perhaps his stance would have been different; but for now, Mohandas had been shooed away.

After a motley mix of divine forces at work, letters of recommendation, friendly cousins pitching in and the selling off of my jewellery finally bore fruit. On 10 August, amidst a large gathering of relatives and friends, Mohandas bade a final farewell to Rajkot, his family and to me. He hugged Putli Ba who had covered her face with her palms, unable to stifle her sobs. And then he went from person to person, bending to touch their feet to ask for their blessings and bid them goodbye.

Mohandas came to bid me farewell in the privacy of our room. He could see I had been crying all night. I stood before him broken in spirit, paralyzed and mute. He took me in his arms and kissed me gently. My body racked with violent sobs, I melted into his arms, wetting his chest with a pool of tears. My voice was heavy with pain and all that escaped my lips as he left the room was, 'Don't go!'

But Mohandas was gone. Putli Ba and the family experienced a weird sense of both relief and pain. Expectedly, the Gandhis were excommunicated from the Modh-Bania community for violating its religious decree and I at nineteen, the mother of a ten-month-old boy had begun a lone, solitary vigil that would last for three long years.

ELEVEN

Mohandas' excommunication from the community had such far-reaching consequences that they triggered off disturbing changes in my life. Being his next of kin, Harilal and I were inherently a part of the religious expulsion. My visits to Porbandar had to be stopped as they amounted to violation of the caste decree. My parents, who were also Modh-Banias, were no longer allowed to associate with us outcastes. Most nights for me were sleepless hours of misery and I bore the brunt of separation from my loved ones all alone, seeking momentary solace in the adorable antics of my growing child.

Putli Ba was no ordinary matriarch. She commanded the same love and respect from her family that she had enjoyed when her husband was alive and her status in the household remained unchanged. For me, Putli Ba was everything. Ever empathetic she stood by me, filling up the place of my parents and now absent husband. She was sensitive to my pangs of separation from Mohandas and showered me with extra love and care. From Harilal she sought consolation for her missing son, for whom she pined as much as I did for my husband.

The infant's frolics often brought tears to her eyes.

'Look at him, Kastur, he's just like his father,' she would say, her eyes shining with pride and voice laced with love.

Indeed little Harilal had filled up an aching void in our lives; for me, it was a state of constant learning, just to watch Putli Ba nurture her grandchild whom she had taken under her wing; a task that I could scarcely have accomplished on my own.

As the days rolled by slowly, the Gandhi household underwent distinct changes. The visitors who thronged the house when

Karamchand was Prime Minister were no longer to be seen. Money was scarce and it was becoming increasingly difficult to maintain our standard of living. Moreover there had been two additions to the family. Nandkunwer had given birth to her second daughter and Ganga and Karsandas had been blessed with their first child, also a girl. With two more mouths to feed and the astronomical cost of Mohandas' education in London which had turned out to be far greater than the original estimate, the family had been pushed deeper into debt.

I too had become acutely conscious of the cash crunch. Realizing that I was dependent for my maintenance on Mohandas' brothers who had their own wives and children to feed, I began squirrelling away small savings to keep me going. Gone were all the extravagant ways of my pampered childhood. Now new clothes were a rarity for me, and I had to make do with saris borrowed from my sisters-in-law on special occasions if I was bored with my own. I missed all the jewels and finery that I had been given at my wedding and was no longer able to dress like I did before. Following Putli Ba's example of eating my meals after everyone else had been fed, I began to cut down on my food; so long as Harilal was being properly fed, I could manage with very little.

Yet amidst all this chaos, uppermost in my thoughts was my beloved Mohandas. I missed him deeply. I yearned for his warm touch and love. I missed indulging his sweet tooth with his favourite *mithai* made of wheat flour, molasses and ghee; and any chance I could get, I would make the *golpapdi* he loved and send it to London, which to me was a distant land of fantasy. For hours I would sit by the window awaiting the arrival of the postman. My mind would take me on frequent flights to England, trying to imagine what Mohandas would be doing, who were the people he mingled with and where he lived. If there had been a lack of privacy between us before Mohandas' departure, it totally vanished after he left, because all letters from him came to Putli Ba and they were read out in the presence of the family since I was unable to read. They were always addressed to his brother Laxmidas and sometimes all I could get were snippets of information gathered by his wife Nandkunwer.

After an eighteen-month-long wait, the postman brought an envelope with a photograph of Mohandas in the morning post. My sister-in-law came running up to me excitedly. 'Look look, Kastur! Just look at our Mohandas! He's become a *bada sahib*! Look at his *Angrezi* suit and fashionable hairstyle!' She blurted out in one breath. 'How fine he looks! I'm sure he's found a *gori-mem* there, Kastur. You'd better watch out, *haan*!' She winked as she spoke, leaning forward to hand me the envelope.

I grabbed it with my trembling hands, my heart beating wildly. The image stunned me. An urbane sophisticate in a dark European-style suit with no turban on his head, hair parted to one side and sleeked down, a white-collared stiff-winged shirt and a sharp bow tie stared back at me. Could the man in the picture with his meticulously combed down hair and deep-set eyes really be the father of my infant Harilal? This was not my Mohandas who had left me broken-hearted and weeping in Rajkot not too long ago. He looked so different from that rustic, old-fashioned man I knew. I stared at the photograph in disbelief for a long time and held it close to my chest. The sight of his familiar protruding ears somewhat comforted me.

It was indeed my own Mohandas, my beloved husband whom I had not seen for eighteen long months. I was stirred by feelings of anxiety. Thousands of fearful thoughts darted through my head. With the total transformation that he had undergone, would things ever be the same between us when we met again? And what if he had really found a *gori-mem* in that hateful land of vice and sin?

I scooped my baby Harilal from the floor and ran up the stairs; he was the only solace in my dark desolate world. I tightened my arms around him and wept, while the half-torn envelope with that black and white photograph of Mohandas in his new avatar lay on the couch of the sitting-room downstairs.

⌘ ⌘ ⌘

TWELVE

At the end of the three years, Mohandas had undergone a complete transformation in England. From the shy and blundering nineteen year old who had disembarked at Southampton in a slick white flannel suit that could scarcely keep him protected from the bitter chill, he had become a stylish, highly accomplished, barrister who had mastered two new languages, Latin and French. He had completed his law degree and had been invited to "the bar" to be enrolled in the High Court. To his list of accomplishments was playing bridge, taking classes in social dancing, playing the violin and public speaking. Of all these carefully acquired skills, it was the last one that would hold him in good stead in his later years. He had travelled extensively around Europe. Baffled by the Eiffel Tower in Paris, he was at his wits' end, trying to figure what purpose a monument of that nature could serve!

Although he appeared totally anglicized and all efforts to become the perfect English gentleman had come to fruition, the futility of this outward transformation quickly dawned on him and he began to concentrate on his studies. To cut back on expenses, he discontinued his bridge and violin tuitions and stopped his dance classes. He moved into a cheaper accommodation and no longer used public transport, choosing to walk to school and elsewhere. It's here that he acquired the habit of speed-walking that stayed with him till the end of his life. He began keeping a detailed record of his personal expenses, thus training himself in accounts and bookkeeping, another habit that would last all his life. English and law became his principal focus. He took to reading the newspapers everyday in an effort to improve his English and studied law books at the Inner Temple all day.

In June 1890, after consistent efforts at a private tuition class where he had learned French and Latin, he made his second attempt at Matriculation and passed the examination. A proud matriculate from London, fluent in English, Latin and French, Mohandas could compete with any Englishman his age. The scathing insult that the stiff upper-lipped administrator, Frederick Lely had flung upon him some years ago, by refusing him a scholarship for an overseas education for lack of a proper matriculation degree, had finally been avenged. God had been kind to Mohandas.

❈ ❈ ❈

The city of London was overflowing with temptations. Mohandas struggled hard to preserve the vows he had made to his family back in India. But food had really become a problem. He was fed-up of his bland home-cooked porridge and hot cocoa milk that was now his daily fare. After a while he stumbled upon a vegetarian restaurant, Central, not far from the Inner Temple, where he savoured his first vegetarian meal since he had left India. He came in contact with a few members of "The Vegetarian Society" who were a group of free thinkers, attempting to change the attitude of Victorian society towards vegetarianism. According to them, the only "humane and morally defensible diet for humankind" was a vegetarian one and Mohandas finally became a true convert.

While I struggled within my cocoon, beset by insecurities, suspicions and forced austerity, my husband was rapidly moving towards incorporating vegetarianism into his own spiritual mind map. It portended a sweeping change in the man who had at one time considered vegetarianism a moral necessity, but meat eating scientifically superior. This was one of the many vicissitudes that were beginning to mould Mohandas into a whole new individual. And contrary to my mortifying thoughts, it was no *gori-mem!*

Although he began to work as an active member of "The Vegetarian Society", he was soon elected to its executive committee and started regularly contributing articles for its publications. Drawn into the Theosophical Society that was closely linked to the society of vegetarianism, Mohandas read an English translation of the Bhagavad Gita, as also the Bible and a detailed narration on the life of Prophet Mohammed. In his pursuit of law in an alien land deemed to be Satan's Den by the heads of his Modh-Bania community, Mohandas had embarked on a journey of spiritual realization to rediscover his roots and his motherland.

The expectations that his family had cast onto his shoulders, burdened him, unsure as he was of being able to realize their grandiose dreams. But if he had known that thousands of miles away in his native Indian peninsula, his beloved mother Putli Ba was breathing her last, he may have given up everything and rushed back to be by her side.

THIRTEEN

On the tenth of June after duly enrolling in the High Court, Mohandas, a fully accomplished and qualified barrister, set sail from Tilbury aboard the S.S. Assam with sadness in his heart. The joy of returning to his homeland was clouded by the gloom of leaving England that had become his haven for three years. But a far greater misery was to hit him on his return to Rajkot.

Earlier that year, death had struck the Gandhi household. After a brief illness, Putli Ba had died suddenly without being afforded that one last glimpse of her favourite son, Mohandas. She left behind a shocked, grieving family and her unexpected death pushed me into a deeper melancholy. It was hard for them to decide whether Mohandas should be informed about the passing away of his mother in the midst of preparations for his final examination or wait till his return. After long deliberations, they decided to wait.

I was somewhat relieved by their decision. Even though I ached to be with my husband, the lengthy separation had frayed my nerves and I dreaded to think of how I would handle a heartbroken, grief-stricken Mohandas? Memories of his breakdown on the death of his father came flooding back. And now Putli Ba's sudden passing away would deal another excruciating blow to him; more so because he had not seen her for three long years.

With Putli Ba abruptly snatched away, the family had plunged into gloom. I too was overcome with a deep insecurity. With the protective umbrella of her love gone, and with my husband thousands of miles away, I felt miserable and alone. All kinds of fears crept into my mind. What if he returned with an alien white woman? What if he found me too inferior and shunned me? What would become of my child and me?

The family expected too much from Mohandas. Would he be able to deal with their expectations and the responsibility of a wife and child? While the crumbling household waited impatiently for his return to a gloomy home, all I could do was hope and pray. I looked into the eyes of my son and began an agonizing countdown to his father's return.

✄ ✄ ✄

In the second week of August, S.S. Assam ferrying Mohandas sailed into Bombay harbour. A jubilant Laxmidas, who was waiting patiently for his brother on the Ballard Pier, had travelled alone from Rajkot to welcome and escort him home. He scanned the passengers who hurriedly filed past him. There was no sign of his brother. And then he spotted him. His chest swelled with pride at the sight of Mohandas. He couldn't imagine how he had failed to recognize his transformed younger sibling, a full-fledged barrister! Tears filled his eyes. For a moment, his joy clouded over with an uneasiness as he embraced him.

'Will Mohandas ever be able to fit into the conservative Gandhi household in this new avatar?' He mused. The thought was unsettling.

The two brothers stayed on for a few days in Bombay at the house of a family friend, Dr. Pranjivan Mehta. It was here that the news of Putli Ba's death was broken to Mohandas. Mohandas felt numbed. He felt his chest would explode. The pain of never being able to see his mother again was unbearable. But he had matured into a man with great self-restraint, so no outpouring of grief was evident. He lamented in the privacy of his room.

'You could have waited for me, Ba. Forty-one is no age to die.'

Try as he did, he couldn't stop his tears.

In accordance with Putli Ba's last wish, the excommunication of her family from the community had to be withdrawn before Mohandas returned to Rajkot. She had wanted her son to do whatever it took to get readmitted into the Modh-Bania community. Hence, an elaborately planned purification ritual was underway.

✄ ✄ ✄

FOURTEEN

The bigotry of the sanction imposed on us by the Modh-Banias could not have been more evident than at the time of Putli Ba's death. The glorious Gandhi matriarch, who had lived the magnificent life of a chaste Hindu woman of impeccable character, deserved a royal send-off in keeping with her lineage and status; but the upholders of the faith showed her no mercy. They shunned her even in her last mortal hours. The premonition that she had had before her death, her apprehensions about having become an outcaste who would be rejected even at the time of her funeral, were not unfounded. The deeds of her rebellious son had cast a dark cloud on her family and her death delivered no redemption. Much to the dismay of her grieving relatives, several rituals at the funeral had to be curtailed and some totally omitted.

Along with the funereal gloom, a sense of foreboding gripped the Gandhi household. It had become imperative for Mohandas to seek penance and regain his position in the community or else it was feared that his career as a lawyer would also get impacted. To Mohandas it was of no consequence, either way. He had matured enough in his mind and spirit to understand that religious sanctions were meaningless, but in compliance with his brothers' wishes and the advice of the community elders, Mohandas stayed back in Bombay to go through the elaborate rituals of penance and plead forgiveness for violating the sacred decree, of having dared to sail across the seven seas to the forbidden land of sin.

Shortly after, Laxmidas and Mohandas left from Bombay to the city of Nasik for their final pilgrimage of purification. In the presence of several witnesses and loud ritualistic chants, Mohandas immersed himself in the holy waters of the river Godavari to cleanse his polluted mind and body.

In Rajkot, the other two brothers, Laxmidas and Karsandas hosted a grand feast where all the caste elders were invited to partake in the holy ceremony. Adorning just a cotton dhoti, with his upper body bare, Mohandas was made to serve food to each of his guest seated inside a large banquet hall. By doing so, he had enacted the ultimate act of penance as ordained by the religious decree; and by accepting food touched by the repentant infidel, the upholders of the faith had finally forgiven him. The ban was lifted and he was allowed into the haloed confines of the Modh-Bania community, with his honour restored.

To Mohandas this was a senseless exercise that mocked at his rationale, but following the diktat of his deceased mother, he accepted his redemption and re-entered into the fold, a position he neither recognized nor valued.

All formalities out of the way, it was time to return to Rajkot where everything had been transformed to receive the distinguished "foreign-returned" Gandhi. The house had been given a total makeover in keeping with European tastes. Dinner plates had replaced old *thalis* and serving dishes and cutlery sets replete with knives and forks, hitherto alien to the Gandhi household, had been put in use months before his return. A dining table was placed in the centre of the room, where the family once sat on the floor at meal times. A new order was in place.

❈ ❈ ❈

Back home in Rajkot, I was bursting with excitement to get the first glimpse of my husband whom I had not seen for thirty-six months, except in that single photograph. My heart raced. My hands trembled. I could barely contain my nervousness. I had no way of knowing if Mohandas had changed in these three years and what he would expect out of me, now that he had tasted life in the land of the "white man". How would I reacquaint myself to the stranger whom I had pined for all these long and sleepless nights?

That morning before sunrise, I bathed with rose water and put on a pretty sari of pastel pink that I had borrowed from my sister-in-law Ganga. I glanced in the mirror on my bedroom wall and drew a big red *bindi* in the centre of my forehead. I smeared a thin line of red *sindoor* in my parted hair that sparkled in the diffused light of dawn. I carefully combed my long black tresses that tumbled down right below my hips in rolling masses of unruly curls. I patted them down and pinned the end of my sari that was looped over my head. A bright glow lit up my face and my large eyes smouldered beneath their kohled outlines. The thought of being with my beloved made my heart thump uncontrollably. It was a long while before Harilal's cries broke my reverie.

❄ ❄ ❄

Our initial union was a bit awkward, but it was evident that Mohandas was struck by my blossoming beauty and innocence. At twenty-two, I had become a full-bodied, beautiful woman. Overcome by a strong sexual urge that was compounded by the prolonged spell of celibacy, he took me into his arms and pressed me into his chest in a crushing embrace.

'My lovely Kastur,' he whispered into my ear running his fingers through my hair. 'How could I have forgotten how beautiful you are?' He caressed my face, brushing over my long curling lashes with his moist lips. He lay me down on the bed, gently pulling away my clothes. Every pore of my sensuous, petite body, supple under the soft folds of the sari that now lay in a heap on the floor, responded thirstily to his touch. 'You are so beautiful, my sweet Kastur…! God, how I missed you,' he whispered. An urgent, erotic, spasm had consumed me.

After the rush of our long awaited union died down, we lay there in each other's arms, satiated and spent. A quiet blissful contentment engulfed us. The lonely vigil of three long years had come to an end at last. It was comforting to know that England had neither changed Mohandas nor had it weakened the lust he'd felt for me when he left home. The natural love for his three-year-old child, whom he had effortlessly won over on his return, was also intact. I heard the silver bells on my anklets tinkle sweetly as I moved my legs from under him. Who knew that they were heralding the new soul that was taking root in the deep innards of my womb?

❄ ❄ ❄

FIFTEEN

In the weeks that followed Mohandas' return to Rajkot, the Gandhi household changed drastically. The old celebratory spirit was back. The expiation of the decree that had deemed us outcastes made the family buoyant. Besides, the return of a qualified barrister from England was a matter of great pride and jubilation for us. Things were finally returning to normal.

Even though the influence of western culture had trickled into our home long before Mohandas returned, his homecoming ushered in even greater changes. To begin with, he wanted Harilal and all the other siblings to be raised like English children. He wanted them to be tough and hardy like "white men". So much so, that a breakfast of porridge made of English oatmeal and cocoa was incorporated into everyone's meal plan. No longer were the children allowed to walk around bare feet. He bought each one of them new shoes and socks, took them on long walks in the countryside and drew up a strict regimen of exercise that he supervised each day. I offered no resistance to these sweeping changes. It made me happy to see him take charge of the children and groom them in the ways of the western world. Nandkunwer and Ganga were equally pleased and cooperative.

Shortly after, a restlessness resurfaced in Mohandas. In his zeal to modernize the Gandhi household, he now trained his sights back on me. Once again I was going to be subjected to his punishing nocturnal, literacy plan. I dreaded the prospects of these lessons, and his indefatigable fervour made it worse. Much to my dismay, a rigorous timetable to educate me was put into place. Days passed in the tug-of-war of persistence and resistance and woefully other disturbing patterns began to appear. I soon discovered a dominating, suspicious, controlling, jealous husband still lurking beneath the sophisticated veneer of Mohandas' highly coveted English barrister's degree. Once in a while, the old fears and accusations of being made a cuckold by a slanderous cheating wife also crept up. Nothing had changed. It was a frightening repeat of the same tortuous exercise. He was the same, persistent, bullying, Mohandas; the same boy who could think of nothing else but teach me to read and write and much the same aborted classroom sessions that ended in lustful nights of sex.

Much as I felt flattered that after all these years he still found me intensely desirable and the need to have me by his side all the time, warmed the cockles of my heart, but his behaviour had begun to border on cruelty. This constant hounding was getting to me. I was feeling suffocated. Surely a "London-returned" barrister should have found something more meaningful to do, than to chase his wife all day and then make false allegations and hurl preposterous charges of infidelity at her. I was being emotionally abused. This was cruelty. I had had enough.

That night, after my usual half-finished lessons that were followed by routine sex, I mustered up the courage to speak.

'You are so obsessed with English education and inculcating your western ways in the children that you have lost all regard for your brothers and family. Do you need to be reminded that you have duties towards your two uncles? Have you forgotten that they ran up huge debts to help you through your education in London? And now that they are without jobs, isn't it your duty to help them? You were sent away to England to study, not to turn into a beast, bullying your hapless wife, hounding her all day. Are you so blinded by lust? You have become very selfish, Mohandas! What will it take for you to understand? I don't want to be literate. Let me be.'

Mohandas' piercing glare did not unnerve me. I had made my point. The night ended in another round of intense sex, but for the first time in all my married years, I slept peacefully while Mohandas tossed and turned beside me all night...

The next day I woke up in a sombre mood. The air was heavy with a spillover of the previous night's outburst. Mohandas avoided looking me in the eye. Not a word was exchanged between us and a few hours later I was bundled off on a train to Porbandar, along with my four-year-old Harilal. It was to be my first visit to my parents' home after the Modh-Banias had revoked their sanction and if this sending away was meant to have been some sort of punishment, Mohandas was grievously mistaken. I suffered no remorse for I had done no wrong; and I was looking forward to being with my parents who had been pining to see us, without fear of violating the religious ban. I felt a sense of exhilaration at leaving Rajkot and Mohandas.

The train raced across the countryside on the new broad gauge railway line. I sat by the window with Harilal in my lap, engrossed in the changing landscape flying past me. My thoughts drifted back to Mohandas. His paranoia and allegations of infidelity had pushed me to the end of my tether. I was not prepared to live in an abusive relationship with a pathologically obsessive man. It was best to let Mohandas fight his own demons alone. This separation should jolt him into sorting out his mind. I breathed easy. The sadistic thrill at being in control was a novel feeling.

The train picked up speed as it raced onwards to Kathiawar, the nearest railway junction to my parental home, and I dozed off with Harilal clinging to my bosom. Secure in the knowledge that this crucial separation from my beloved would soon end, I could dream of a happier tomorrow.

Sixteen

I had barely been a month in Porbandar, when I was summoned back to Rajkot by Mohandas. Believing that these thirty days of separation should have made me thoroughly miserable, he had condescended to end the punishment and allowed me to return home.

Back in Rajkot, I found Mohandas a changed man. He had become unusually quiet. There were no more accusations being hurled at me; and none of those beastly tutorials forced down my gullet. At first I was a bit unsettled, but soon this new Mohandas stirred maternal feelings within me. I yearned to draw him into my bosom like a mother would her child. A compelling tenderness in me wanted to pay heed to his fears and insecurities, to dispel them.

Late one night, Mohandas spoke. His voice choking with remorse, all his pent-up emotions came pouring out. It was almost as if he was talking to himself.

'What have I done! I have been so cruel to you, Kastur! I have neglected my duties towards you. My brothers and my family have also been neglected by me. How could I have been so blind and so insensitive? My adoring brothers have broken their backs to fund my education. All their hopes are riding on me, and I have done nothing for them.' His voice trailed off in heart-rending sobs.

I drew him into my arms. I did not speak a word. He lay quiet for a long time.

'People will laugh at me, Kastur. I cannot start practicing law in Rajkot. Alas! The three years of study in London are not good enough for me to practice in India. No one will employ me. I don't even have the knowledge of a junior clerk.'

I could tell that Mohandas was terribly distraught. He was well versed in Common Law and even Roman law, but Hindu and Muslim law he knew nothing about and that would pose a problem. 'Why, even a home-trained *vakil* such as my brother knows more about Indian law than me. Tell me Kastur, who would pay me my due as a barrister from England? Who would cough up ten times the fee of an Indian *vakil*? Can I be so arrogant as to believe that I can make it big here, under these circumstances? No, Kastur, no! It is stupid. To believe that I am ten times more capable than my brothers is defrauding myself.' Mohandas' body racked with uncontrollable sobs.

I did not move his head from my chest that felt wet with his tears. I let him speak, stroking his head continuously with my fingers. 'Don't despair, my beloved,' I said. 'Speak out your mind to your brothers. Ask them for guidance. They will surely help you find a way.'

'No, Kastur! No! I am a sinner. I shall burn in hell. I have wronged my parents. How can I ever forgive myself? I was not there when they needed me. Forgive me, Ba! Forgive me for not being there for your last rites. Forgive me, for not being by your side in your dying moments, Bapu. Will the Almighty ever forgive me?' He was mumbling in broken sentences.

The long hours of the dark night ticked by slowly. Cradling him in my arms, I rocked him to sleep. 'Don't despair,' I whispered. 'It was not your fault. Ba and Bapu are showering you with their blessings from heaven. All will be well. I am here for you... shall always be.' I spoke quietly into his ear. It felt good.

Locked in each others' arms we dozed off, two souls merged into one, content and secure. But the agonizing guilt that had burrowed deep into Mohandas had already wrecked his peace.

⁂

A new plan was put in place. It was decided by the elders that the best way forward was to send Mohandas to Bombay where, unlike Rajkot, opportunities abounded. Porbandar and Rajkot did not offer enough work for the existing lawyers, with soon more added to the list, that too of Mohandas' calibre, would be of no use to anyone in these small provincial towns. Bombay promised better chances. It would help him familiarize himself with Indian law and earn some money. A deep sense of despair overcame me. The thought of another long separation from Mohandas was agonizing, but it was time for him to shoulder familial responsibilities and repay his debt to his brothers. It was time for him to go away. It broke my heart.

'Don't fret, Kastur.' He pulled me into his arms that night. 'You and Harilal will have to stay away from me for a short while, but I promise that as soon as I can afford it, I shall take you with me to Bombay and never leave you alone again. I'll set up a home there for the three of us, Kastur. I'll never let you go, I promise.' He kissed my eyes that had welled up with tears.

The next day, we bade him a tearful farewell. Both Harilal and I, stood at the door for a long time after he left, staring at the vacant landscape outside. I was lost in mixed feelings of both sadness and hope. A sharp churning in my stomach sent a wave of nausea up my throat. Harilal tugged at my elbow.

'Ma, I'm hungry,' he lisped.

I scurried into the kitchen to give him lunch and filled up my plate to sit beside him and eat. The new being growing inside me also needed to be fed. I hadn't told Mohandas that I was pregnant.

It was not the right time. I looked at the greasy food on my plate and retched.

❈ ❈ ❈

On the train to Bombay, Mohandas was feeling listless. A deep remorse descended on him. Directionless, uprooted and unsure of himself, the grief of losing his mother, weighed him down and the guilt surrounding his father's death never abated. It mocked at his obsessive carnality that had prevented him from being with his father while he lay on his deathbed. It festered inside like a pestilent wound. It would create havoc in his mind and unnatural complexes would dominate his conduct in the years to come. Not only would it drive him to bizarre methods of penance, he would resort to unholy practices of testing the limits of a self-imposed celibacy that would shock the world.

But for now, his lack of experience and low self-worth made him apprehensive. Deep down inside he harboured a secret—the reality that he was a lawyer of a very low calibre loomed large.

✂ ✂ ✂

Bombay was a bigger dampener. Mohandas rented a room and hired someone to cook for him but the food was so inedible that he ended up cooking most times. He had to walk miles to and from the High Court where he spent most of his time mingling with and observing the lawyers at work, to imbibe the ways of the Indian system. He bought some law books and began educating himself in the Civil Procedure Code and Evidence Act.

Meanwhile all his expenses, meagre as they were, were being borne by his brothers and their debts continued to mount. As the weeks passed, a crushing sense of failure came over Mohandas. He could find no work that could bring him money or merit. In his desperation, he applied to a local boys' high school for a job as an English teacher at a salary of seventy-five rupees per month.

But poor Mohandas! His application was turned down. This time the rejection came because the school only wanted teachers with graduate degrees from Indian universities. His fancy London Matriculation degree with Latin as a second language did not merit the qualifications for the job. Life couldn't have been more ironical!

After many unsuccessful attempts at seeking law-suits, a petty court case came his way. For the first time in his homeland, Mohandas appeared proudly before the judge in the Small Claim's Court, donning his grand-looking English wig and gown. But just as he rose to cross-examine the witness, he was gripped by panic. His fear of public speaking had got the better of him. He could not utter a single word. He sank into his chair wishing the earth would swallow him at that moment when a loud ruckus of mocking laughter drowned out all else. Mohandas left the court room that day, a forlorn, dejected man. He swore never to appear at a hearing, until he had overcome his fear of speaking in public. He refunded the thirty rupees he had taken from his client as an advance payment and trudged home.

Some days later, a letter arrived with good tidings. It was from his brother Laxmidas, asking him to return to Rajkot. It also mentioned the coming of our second child. The news of my pregnancy did little to lighten Mohandas' spirit. Burdened by a crushing sense of responsibility and the prospect of one more mouth to feed, he boarded the train to Rajkot with a heavy heart. His Bombay experience had so far been disappointing; his expenses were proving to be unaffordable as he had failed to establish even a semblance of a legal practice in the city.

'Come back...try your luck in Kathiawar, Mohandas,' his brother's words pounding in his ears got drowned in the din, as the train roared out of the station.

❈ ❈ ❈

On 28 October 1892, I gave birth to a boy who was named Manilal. It was time to rejoice. The arrival of a baby boy who was healthy and beautiful portended good times ahead. Sweets and gifts were distributed to friends, relatives and visitors who came in droves laden with presents for the newborn baby and me. All my earlier angst melted away when I set eyes on my baby. My little Manilal would surely herald happy changes in the fortune of his parents and life would become comfortable for us once again.

On the fortieth day after Manilal's birth I took both my sons to a nearby temple to thank the Lord for his benevolence. I felt an acute sense of pain for not having Putli Ba by my side.

❈ ❈ ❈

Seventeen

While Mohandas was desperately struggling to set up his legal practice in Rajkot, a ray of hope suddenly came his way. A merchant firm in Porbandar offered to hire him to fight a compensation suit in South Africa. Dada Abdulla, of Dada Abdulla and Company, was an illiterate gold trader with vast business establishments in Natal. His operations spanned across India and South Africa where he had struck rich during the gold rush of 1888, after which his fortunes had multiplied several-fold.

Abdulla was looking for an intermediary who could be a conduit between him and his battery of lawyers in South Africa, since his own knowledge of English was poor and they spoke no Gujarati. Fluent in both languages, it was a job custom-made for Mohandas. Armed as he was with his impressive British barrister's degree, Mohandas was recruited for the job with a fixed remuneration of a hundred and five pounds sterling per month. They offered to undertake all the expenses of his boarding and lodging and a fully-paid return ticket to Durban. He would have to be based in Natal till the matter was resolved.

Although the endowment did not really excite Mohandas, but given the desperate circumstances, he accepted the offer. The family heaved a sigh of relief. God had answered their prayers. As for me, I was happy that Mohandas had finally found an opening; but the thought of being alone with my two sons, for an indefinite period of time racked my nerves.

I could see that he was also torn between the looming prospect of another prolonged period of separation from us and the only chance of making a living. The disomfort of working in an unfamiliar terrain without me by his side rattled him as much. I reckoned that this parting was going to be far more difficult. That night when I came face to face with him, I steeled myself and held back my tears.

In the privacy of our bedroom, he held me close and put his lips to my ears.

'We shall meet again after twelve months, Kastur. I'll be back before you know. You will wait for me, my beloved…won't you?' His low voice laden with emotion, quivered as he spoke.

'Yes I will, my beloved. I will wait for you. These twelve months will pass quickly,' I said but I couldn't conceal the pain in my voice. 'And I shall be able to use those pounds that you earn for all the household expenses. I shall hold my head high, for I shall live off the earnings of my husband.' My voice trailed; I steadied it, stifling a sob.

My pride had been severely stung several times in the past. Living off my brothers-in-law who themselves were deep in debt made me feel small. They did not have to provide for my sons and me, but all that was about to change.

I lay in his arms savouring each precious moment, not wanting to let go. I saw his eyes brim over. I stroked his cheeks gently. Each drop of his tears that touched my palms, were like the elixir of love. It was a beautiful dream that I never wanted to be broken.

'Go, Mohandas…go! My heart tells me that success awaits you across the seven seas. Go, my beloved! Your Kastur shall be counting the hours till you return.' A torrent of emotions burst like a broken dam. We hugged each other and wept.

In the second week of April, Mohandas boarded a train to Bombay, from where he was to sail across the forbidden "black waters" of the Indian Ocean once again. My four-year-old Harilal, who stood three feet tall on the railway platform and my six-month-old Manilal pressed close to my breast, waved a teary goodbye to him. All three of us watched the train leaving a trail of grey smoke as it chugged out.

The shrill whistle of the guard, punctuated with the chopping sound of the racing wheels, would haunt me.

❀ ❀ ❀

Eighteen

While Mohandas set sail to an unknown and faraway land to seek his fortune, Harilal, Manilal and I, three souls whose lives were irrevocably woven with his, had begun another twelve-month-long vigil for the return of the prime arbiter of our destinies.

Mohandas stood on the rails of the deck, inhaling the crisp winter air as his ship cruised into Durban harbour. Bright sunlight illumined the beautifully manicured boulevards and serpentine coastline. A sea of unknown people could be seen charging noisily up the gangway to greet the arriving passengers. Totally unprepared for what lay ahead, Mohandas climbed down amidst the unruly crowd. Glaring signs of racial discrimination were evident as the natives and whites jostled for space, climbing up the ramp. The whites expected the gangway cleared of the native, lesser mortals. They pushed and swore at them loudly. Mohandas was appalled. Nothing he had ever witnessed in England or at home, could have matched this blatant display of discrimination. His first impression of Durban made him edgy. He cringed.

He scanned the crowd. A tall, distinguished man stepped forward to greet him with his hands outstretched. This had to be Dada Abdulla. Mohandas was overwhelmed. He had not expected the most influential partner of the firm to be there in person to receive him. He noticed that even Dada Abdulla, a well-positioned and respected Muslim, the owner of a highly reputed trading firm, was not spared the white man's scorn. Contemptuous affronts from white-skinned strangers milling around the harbour flew thick and fast. He saw Dada Abdulla being roughed up and pushed aside by some unknown white men. Dada Abdulla seemed unmoved. Why wasn't he reacting? Why did he not lash out against this brazen misbehaviour? Mohandas was furious, more at Dada Abdulla's apathy than the insults heaped on him. Simmering with indignation, Mohandas climbed into the waiting car and drove off in silence with his self-effacing new employer. He stared wistfully at the beautiful terrain of this foreign land.

'How beautiful it is on the outside,' he thought, 'but what a hideous underbelly!'

A seed of rebellion was taking root within.

Meanwhile, miles away on the west coast of the Indian peninsula, as the sun dawned on my horizon, my restlessness grew. As the mother of two sons, one of six years and the other under twelve months, I was consumed by severe anxiety. I watched every miniscule change in their faces and bodies, wondering where and how their father must be. How unfortunate he was to be deprived of the pleasure of marking the milestones of his lovely children's growth. I had watched Harilal take his first doddering steps. I had savoured the sweetness of his first uttered word, his first tooth, the pain of his first fall, all by myself and now with Manilal, it was going to be the same. He would not have his father to share these little joys of growing up.

Holding the wailing infant in my arms, I put his tiny mouth that knew nothing other than the taste of mother's milk to my breasts. I did not want to think of their father in absentia, my missing husband, and the tortuous wait before we could be united again. Try as I did, I could not hold back my tears.

Not that life was looking up for the debutant lawyer in a hostile, foreign land.

❇ ❇ ❇

As soon as Mohandas landed in Durban, work commenced at a feverish pace. Donning a sharp European suit that distinguished him from others of his ilk, his turban remained the only symbol of his Indian lineage. It sat stubbornly on his head, lending him a quaint and conspicuous uniqueness. At work, the long pending lawsuit for which Mohandas had been hired needed urgent intervention, so Dada Abdulla packed him off to Pretoria almost as soon as he arrived. This entailed an overnight train journey to the Transvaal border, a dangerously hostile territory, from where he was to take a stagecoach to his destination.

While I lay sleepless on my bed faraway in Rajkot, with both my sons lying on either side in deep slumber, my gaze travelled to the peeling paint on the ceiling. The damp patches on the bedroom walls made me uneasy. I closed my eyes and began to pray for the safety of my beloved; my husband of over six years, the father of these two innocent boys. I had no way of knowing that he had embarked on a momentous journey that would lead to a deep awakening within him, with far-reaching ramifications.

That night I had a hard time quelling the pain and loneliness that was beginning to fester like an open wound inside the depths of my soul.

✂ ✂ ✂

The first class compartment of the train from Durban had a warm, plush interior. The journey was long and the night bitterly cold. An icy blast from an open window stung Mohandas' face. He pulled the shutters down and settled into his seat with a book. The train gathered speed and soon lulled him to sleep.

Just fifty miles short of Pretoria, the train halted at Pietermaritzburg. A white man with an expensive looking suitcase entered the compartment. The sight of the dark Indian who sat by the window, engrossed in his book, enraged him. He grimaced as if he had seen a leper.

'You!' he hissed contemptuously waving a finger at Mohandas. 'What are you doing here?'

'Travelling to Pretoria, what else?' Mohandas replied. He was taken aback. He had done no wrong. 'This is my seat, sir. Look, I have a first class ticket,' his voice trailed off. He waved an orange piece of paper in the fuming foreigner's face. The man grimaced again and stormed out, swearing as he left.

Mohandas steadied himself and went back to the pages of his book. In a few minutes he saw the man enter the compartment again, this time with a uniformed officer. He was a stern looking, slightly stout white man, with a salt and pepper handlebar moustache and deep furrows on his freckled forehead. The officer peered down at him, a sneer etched on his lopsided mouth.

'What are you doing here, Mister? Come on. Get up and get out. Go to the third class compartment, will you?' he snarled.

Mohandas looked up at them, straight in the eye.

'I have a first class ticket, sir. I have paid for it. I have every right to sit here. I was allowed in here at Durban and shall only leave when I get to my destination. I shall not leave my seat before that. Throw me out if you must, sir, but I shall not move from my seat. I have paid for it.' The next thing Mohandas knew, two mean-looking constables appeared from nowhere looming menacingly at him. Along with the two white men, they yanked him by the collar, roughed him up and shoved him out of the train, on the freezing cold platform. They tossed his bags behind him, swearing loudly.

'Take that! And don't ever show us your wretched face again,' the official bellowed. 'First class ticket, have you? Huh! Get out of here, you filthy Indian dog!'

Mohandas sat down on the hard ground of the railway platform, smarting more with the insult than injury. The cold night chilled him right through to his bones. He saw the train race out of the station in a blast of smoke that followed the shrill sound of a whistle that rent the icy air.

Bewildered and humiliated, a raging fire consumed his insides. 'The ultimate sin is not oppression, but silence,' he muttered under his breath, 'silence is more lethal...it's unforgivable... unforgivable.' He felt the shooting pain of a bruised ligament on his twisted ankle as he steadied himself and hobbled towards the waiting room of the railway station.

� ✼ ✼ ✼

A peculiar restlessness had kept me tossing and turning in my bed that night. I felt a sudden chill run down the small of my back. I put my arms around the boys sleeping on either side of me, pulling them close to my body. Their shallow breaths and warm bodies felt comforting, but sleep eluded me for a long time.

Huddled inside the dark, freezing waiting room of the railway station, Mohandas had suffered a long, sleepless and agonizing night. He glanced at the clock on the wall. It was still three hours to midnight. He could do nothing but wait for the next train or for daybreak. Shivering and hungry, he sat on a hard metal bench in the stark waiting room lost in a whirl of thoughts. Kastur, Manilal, Harilal, his warm bed in Rajkot, the passionate embrace of the woman he loved, freshly cooked, piping hot food straight off the fire…a chill gripped his heart and razored its way into his skull.

What was he doing in this foreign land, surrounded by hostile strangers who were out to humiliate him? The soft and beautiful face of his Kastur, smiling, tender, inviting and that of his two playful sons, zoomed in and out of his head.

He felt a tug at his heart. He was tempted to take the fastest ship back to India; but he feared the failure that would plague him for the rest of his life, so he quickly dismissed the thought. He couldn't let his family down once again. And his poor Kastur! How could he put *me* through this?

Shivering and miserable in the cold, thousands of miles away from his motherland, the twenty-four-year-old was sowing the seeds of an order that would shatter the conventional method of protest and give birth to a new credo of non-violence. Call it a stroke of providence or a deeply ingrained Jain spirit of truth and ahimsa. Call it injured pride, or a fierce compulsion to fight against evil, but Mohandas would never be the same again. His intolerance to injustice and oppression had never been stoked so vehemently before.

✂ ✂ ✂

That night in Rajkot, a horrific feeling of anxiety continued to consume me. I was missing Mohandas. When would this long year of torture end? Harilal and Manilal would have to grow up without their father, and I….? My throat choked. I sat up and straightened Harilal, pulling him closer to me. He had moved to the edge of the bed. Manilal stirred. He began to cry. He was hungry. I picked him up and put his tiny mouth to my breast. My tender gaze lingered on his face. He shut his eyes and his fingers curled over mine in bliss as I stroked his cheek. The little infant, untouched by the raw brutalities of the world outside, looked snug and secure in my arms. Just then a loud thud startled me. Harilal had rolled off the bed and fallen on the floor. I rushed to him, scooped him up into my arms and patted him back to sleep on my lap.

Unbeknownst to me, some thousands of miles away, in the cold, distant, alien, southern hemisphere, a wiry twenty-four-year-old Indian lawyer had been shoved onto a hard railway platform on a dark freezing night for having had the audacity to retaliate against a white man.

Whilst there was no visible sign of bruising on Harilal's body after he fell off the bed, the blood flowing out of the invisible gash on his father's soul would never stop.

Nineteen

After the horrific incident at the railway platform, Mohandas continued onwards to Pretoria for three days in a gravely hostile terrain. Memories of that ghastly insult continued to plague him. Being Indian warranted being treated like a lowly animal. It was not going to be easy to erase this ugly truth from his mind.

Mohandas was no longer a stranger to the Indians of South Africa. His sharp European suit, accessorized by an Indian turban, made him an oddity in the courtroom where being Indian in any case was a matter of abject disdain. The magistrate peered down his spectacles that were perched on the bridge of his nose and commented, 'You will have to remove that comical contraption on your head, Mister…er…what did you say your name was? Speak up, Mister. Yes, Ghandy is it? You Indians have such long unpronounceable names, Mr. Ghandy. Take that ugly thing off your head before you present your case to this court. And do hurry up, Mr. Ghandy, I have other matters of pressing importance to look into, as you would appreciate.'

Mohandas winced at the mockery and the mispronunciation of his name. He pursed his mouth in a stubborn sneer, swept up his papers and said, 'No, Your Lordship, I shall not!' Holding his head high in defiance, he stomped out of the courtroom.

The face of the magistrate turned a flaming red, even as a hushed silence descended upon the people in the room. The local press picked up the episode and Mohandas found himself pitchforked to the front pages of the newspapers the next morning. They had made him a celebrity overnight.

Emboldened by the response of the locals and even more resolute in his mission to liberate his fellow Indians, he decided that he would continue wearing his turban in South Africa as a mark of solidarity to all those of his ilk. So the vibrant turban, native to his homeland, the symbol of his defiant and proud Indian identity, stayed fixed on his head till he was ready to return home.

❈ ❈ ❈

After twelve long fruitful months of hard work, it was time for Mohandas to return to India. Dada Abdulla hosted a grand lunch for his favourite employee. He was extremely sad to see him go. Almost every distinguished Indian had been invited to partake in the celebratory farewell feast, for a man who was now recognized not only as a lawyer of great repute, but as someone who fought for the cause of his countrymen in South Africa.

As the celebrations began, Mohandas sat browsing the morning newspapers. A tiny news-item placed innocuously at the bottom of the page caught his attention. It reported the introduction of a Bill in the Natal Legislative Assembly that purported to disallow Indians their voting rights. This was preposterous, thought Mohandas! His fighter instinct aroused, he sat up and pondered over the repercussions of what he had just read. The draconian Act that was hitherto confined to the Boer Republic was soon to be applicable in Natal. 'Look! Have you seen this, my friends?' he exclaimed. 'You are about to lose your right to vote. Do you realize how serious that is?' The anger in his voice apparent, he read out the snippet to the guests sitting around him.

A hushed silence fell upon the people. Then Dada Abdulla spoke. 'We are illiterate businessmen, Mohandas,' he said. 'To us newspapers are merely instruments to study market trends. Politics does not interest us. For that we have our European attorneys to act as our eyes and ears. This snippet means nothing to us. What can we do? Our lives are controlled by the whims of these Englishmen.' Mohandas was silent. A deep conflict began lashing inside him. He was to sail back to India the next day, away from the unbearable oppression that his fellowmen were being subjected to, away from the land where the whites inflicted atrocities and insults upon them. He had not been spared either. The humiliation that had been heaped upon him time and again, only because his skin was of a different colour flooded his thoughts. How could he turn his back on his hapless fraternity?

'No no! We cannot let this happen. We will lose all our respect, and our rightful place in this country shall be in serious jeopardy. And then, don't you understand my friends, it won't stop here. Some other rights shall be curtailed. We have to put an end to this right now.' His emphatic words had caught the attention of all the people present in the room.

Dada Abdulla had really grown to love Mohandas. He looked at him beseechingly. 'But we are powerless. You had infused us with enthusiasm, but now that you shall be gone, we can't fight them. Without you we can't fight them.' He said.

Mohandas was torn apart by his words. There was no way he could leave South Africa at this crucial moment of calling. He asked Dada Abdulla to cancel his departure for India.

'God has sent me on a mission,' he said. 'I shall not leave it unfinished. Cancel my ticket. I cannot leave you. Not at this juncture.'

Cheer rang out amongst the people gathered there. The jubilant community promised to pay for his stay and provide him all the money and manpower they had at their disposal, in his fight for justice for them. Mohandas' ticket was cancelled. The farewell lunch had turned into a celebration of a different kind. It heralded new beginnings and radical changes in the lives of Indians living in South Africa. They were confident that they would emerge victorious under Mohandas, who they began to believe was the messenger of god.

❈　❈　❈

I sat in the wide verandah that jutted out of the first floor of our house, staring at the starry night sky. My long wait had finally come to an end. Through the lonely countdown of over twelve months, I had somehow managed to keep myself together, tending to my two sons and to my never-ending domestic duties. Mohandas was soon to set sail from that distant land to be united with us. My heart bursting with anticipation of the happy reunion ahead, I found it hard to keep my spirits in control. Sleep eluded me again that night.

The next morning a letter from Mohandas arrived in the mail. I ran out excitedly hoping to hear more news about the day and time of his arrival, my boys in tow. My brother-in-law had torn open the envelope and was waiting to read it out to me.

The Indian community here needs me to fight for their rights. I have to stay back for a while to help them battle the discriminating laws that are impinging on their dignity.

I fell back on a chair in a heap. Harilal began to cry. I bundled him into my arms and slithered away. All the earlier jubilance I felt had vanished. I did not know how many long and lonely nights were ahead for me and how much longer my sons would have to wait before they could be united with their father? A father they had hardly known!

A little later, I fought back my misgivings. I rationalized—Mohandas was needed by the people there. If they had ignited in him a mission of manic zeal that would drive him beyond himself, who was I to stymie that? But what about his sons and me? Surely he owed as much of a duty to us.

My sons were growing up without a father. Unlike me, who in her formative years, was the centre of the universe for my family, Harilal and Manilal were deprived of their father's attention. I felt a tight constriction in my chest. Now six years old, what memories would Harilal have of his father? Perhaps only as a visiting relative. And Manilal was a little child—over two years old. He would remember nothing of him.

Mohandas look! Your son walks. You will not recognize him, nor he you… This time is never going to come back. While you rejoice in raising slogans in a foreign land and defy rules to restore the rights and dignity of your ilk, shouldn't you spare a moment for the welfare of your wife and sons?

No one heard my silent cries. That night as I lay on my bed, haunting phantoms of unfulfilled desires and suppressed passion threatened to consume me. Even my distant dream of a happy reunion with my beloved, living faraway in a house of my own with only him and the children, seemed to have slipped away. I mustered up the strength to pray for my husband's well-being in that vile faraway land and murmured to myself...

Have a safe journey on the treacherous seas, my love; when you return!

Twenty

Impassioned by the staunch faith the Indians of South Africa had bestowed upon him, Mohandas plunged headlong into their cause, refusing to accept any remuneration for his work. The community however, promised to keep him flushed with enough legal work so as to cover the cost of his stay in Durban. Soon after, around twenty merchants appointed him their standing counsel and in keeping with his imposing barrister status, he rented a pretty, two-storied house overlooking the beach, which Dada Abdulla undertook to furnish.

It wasn't as if his life was ever strewn with roses, but now it was throwing up even greater challenges at him. On his arrival, the Law Society of Natal fiercely opposed his application for a license to practice as a barrister in the Supreme Court. After a long-drawn-out battle with the authorities that entailed a surfeit of correspondence back and forth, he finally obtained a favourable order from them, on the condition that there wouldn't be any distinction between the whites and non-whites in his practice. They also decreed that he would have to do away with his turban during court appearances. This was the one time that Mohandas rescinded to a compromise of his faith. In the larger perspective, he reasoned, this was a minor concession.

Mohandas had perforce, turned into a suit-attired, white-collared, tie-sporting European gentleman, who was fairly successful as an imposing barrister in the Supreme Court of South Africa; but for me, trapped in the distant confines of my primitive home in Rajkot, it portended another long wait, another lonely separation from my beloved. The only consolation was that Mohandas would be earning enough to take care of us and pay back the debts his family had incurred. I continued to bide my time with little communication from him. The occasional letters to his brothers that brought short impersonal messages for me were most often conveyed to me by my sister-in-law Harkunwer. She would come bounding down the stairs, shouting at the top of her voice, '*Arrey*, come out Kastur. Where are you? I have some news from *pardes*. But you'll have to give me something very nice in exchange. What will you give me? Tell me! Tell me, or else I won't give you his message.'

She would break into peals of laughter, tweaking my flushed cheeks between her fingers.

'Your Mohandas is not coming back. I told you he's found a very stylish *gori-mem* there, Kastur.' She had cupped one hand around my ear, her voice dropping to a whisper, 'Now you are doomed. He doesn't want you there! You silly woman. Stop pining for him. He's a *pardesi*…he's flown away…left you alone and gone!'

The feigned mockery in her words was not always amusing. More so on the day I was told that he had opened his own law office in Durban and had no intentions of returning to India in the near future. Nor had there been any mention of sending for the boys and me to be with him in his new habitat.

I exploded with suspicion and fear. I hated Harkunwer for the stupid pranks she played, but what if he really had found a wicked *gori-mem* in Africa? How lucky my two sisters-in-law were. They had their adoring spouses with them all the time. They would never have to suffer those awful pangs of insecurity and separation like I did.

As the days passed in this humdrum, my daily chores became even more burdensome. I tended to the boys as best as I could, but there was never a moment when the pain of being away from Mohandas abated. The thought of him in his independent and stylish house, where he had hired a cook and moved some of his office clerks, made me even more jealous.

Would I ever be a part of his life again? I wondered. What if Mohandas had transformed into a strange being and was living sinfully with a loathsome white woman all these days? Was that the reason he had stayed back? The prospect of being permanently isolated from his life terrified me.

Indeed Durban had changed Mohandas. The journey that he had set upon for the discovery of truth was helping him to formulate new strategies, set new patterns and inspire future generations to become a part of his passionate crusade for equality and justice. That one-time, under-confident husband of mine was racing ahead, transforming into a messianic leader of humankind —a far cry from the sexually-driven, blubbering boy who would collapse into my arms at the slightest setback; his carnal release in bed being his only solace!

Twenty One

Mohandas' law practice in Durban had become a roaring success and the Gandhi name a household word, synonymous with social reform. As the standing counsel for several Indian businessmen, he earned enough to manage his household expenses, send money to support the family in Rajkot and also have a tidy sum leftover to spend on public service.

Fired by the zeal of his calling and the response from local Indians, he founded an association called the Indian National Congress of Natal. Although his movement was centred around social and political causes, he never lost sight of his innate search for god and began studying the Hindu scriptures, Zoroastrianism and the life of Prophet Mohammed. As a true philosopher's mission to amalgamate diverse religious idioms, he had begun dreaming about the infinite possibilities of universal love and brotherhood.

By the end of June, two years later, Mohandas decided to go back to India for a period of six months. He wanted to acquaint his fellow-Indians with the plight of their counterparts in South Africa. And then there was also his family that he had not seen for over three years and planned to bring back with him to Durban.

For me the summer of 1896 had brought sweet tidings. Mohandas was home in Rajkot. I was jubilant and the family in bliss, but if living away from him had been a period of prolonged misery, living with a man who had transformed so drastically was infinitely more challenging.

My feelings lay bottled up inside. I could neither weep nor laugh. As a wife, I was not allowed any public display of emotions towards my husband, not even in front of my children. The tiny consolation of cooking Mohandas' favourite dishes, and to feed him myself was not going to be granted to me. I could not come out of the kitchen to serve him when he was surrounded by family elders; that privilege was now with the natural successor of Putli Ba, my eldest sister-in-law Nandkunwer. Oh! How I envied her. To sit by my husband's side and partake of a meal had become a distant dream for me.

All these days I had been bursting with hundreds of questions that I needed to ask my husband. There was so much that I needed to share. I needed to ask him if those shameless *gori-mems* were in any way better than me, his Kastur; if he had really been in the arms of those enticing sirens; if he still found me beautiful and loved me no less than before.

During those three painful years tending to his sons and the family, I had suppressed every trifling occurrence of my life. I had waited patiently to share my joys and the pain of those long lonely nights with him. But that was not to be. Even my late-night bedroom sojourns had become a rarity.

'I have come to take you back with me, Kastur, and the children will come with us,' he said to me one night. I looked up at him shyly and just melted into his arms.

Beach Grove Villa sounded like the house of my dreams, my own private haven, with just my two boys and the man I adored. 'At last we would have him all to ourselves,' I mused. A sense of euphoria that I had not felt in a long time overcame me.

That night Mohandas lay in my arms for a long, long time. I ran my fingers through his matted hair and gently kissed his dopey eyes caressing the dark circles under them. We lay there locked in an embrace, my gaze trailing over his tanned face. I tried to peel back the invisible layers that covered the body and mind of the stranger who lay beside me, totally oblivious of the raging inferno that burned inside. His entire life reeled like a film before me. The once cowardly schoolboy controlled by that evil Mehtab Sheikh, that cruel possessive child-groom, that distraught son who struggled endlessly with the trauma of losing his parents and the overriding guilt of that night of sin, that carnal tryst with his wife while his father lay dying in an adjacent room; that dejected young man who failed to make a living to support his family. All those faces had fused into that of a proud Indian who had made a mark of distinction in a hostile foreign land. This new Gandhi, totally consumed by his mission, one that I could neither comprehend nor ignore, felt alien to the old-fashioned and illiterate me. The thought of a new life in a strange land without the security umbrella of my family was a bit unsettling, yet I could not hold back the exuberance of living with my beloved in a house that I could call my own.

Every night I heard Mohandas speak about the plight of his countrymen in South Africa. 'Our basic tenet is to conquer hatred by love, Kastur,' he would say. Those unforgettable words stayed deep in my subconscious mind till the time I was lost to the world around me.

Our Rajkot house soon became the bustling headquarters for Mohandas' mission in India. He began distributing a hand-written pamphlet on bright green paper titled, "The grievances of British Indians in South Africa", free of cost to everyone in the city. All this while, I kept devising ways and means of getting Mohandas to connect with his sons.

'Listen!' I said. 'Harilal can help you with making copies of the pamphlets. His handwriting is really neat, and Manilal can paste stamps on them for mailing.' My efforts bore fruit, not only for my sons, but also hordes of other children from the neighbourhood school who were roped in to assist Mohandas, and the task finished in record time.

A few days later, a dreadful plague broke out in Bombay. Scores of people died and the threat of it spreading to nearby areas drove Mohandas to join the local sanitation committee that was working to prevent it. He toured the city extensively, inspecting homes and latrines, while educating the citizens about cleanliness and disease-breeding conditions. Unlike other members of the team, Mohandas freely entered the homes of "untouchables", oblivious of the fact that it was considered most disdainful an act by society.

As he set about his endeavour in earnest, the need for establishing equality amongst all humans had taken deep root inside him. In his future reformist missions, he would urge his volunteers to do away with the contempt they felt for "lowly tasks", by getting them to carry and dispose off buckets full of night soil.

Soon the Indian press took notice of the hand-written green pamphlet and it found mention in several national newspapers. A Reuters correspondent reported the stir it had caused in India, to his office in London. The London office cabled a distorted three-line summary of the report to Durban wherein Mohandas was mischievously misquoted as saying, 'The Indians in Natal are robbed, assaulted and treated as lowly beasts without any redress.' Published in *Natal Mercury*, a local journal of Durban, it was followed by a huge public uproar that would cause serious problems for us in the near future.

TWENTY TWO

Two ships, Courland and Nadir, had set sail simultaneously from Bombay harbour ferrying a group of impassioned Indian passengers to Durban. As I boarded the Courland with my husband and my sons, I felt an uneasiness come over me. I had never ventured outside Rajkot, except a hundred miles to the city of Porbandar. The dangers of crossing the "seven seas" terrified me. Even if I did survive the forbidding journey, I did not know what my life would be in a strange land, far away from my loved ones. The thought of having my own home with my sons and Mohandas, or even the thought of being accompanied by Raliatben's ten-year-old son Gokuldas, who had just lost his father, did little to ease my discomfiture.

My heart went out to Raliatben who would have to suffer endless pangs of separation at sending her child away. I feared that she, a lonely widow, would never see a united family again. I knew that pain of separation and loneliness so well. And then, leaving Rajkot was making me nervous. I had begun to fret about everything – the travel plan, the journey, choosing appropriate clothes that would retain my native culture, but suit western sensibilities, all of which was irksome.

Mohandas believed that in South Africa, as the Parsis were regarded as a highly cultured group, the attire of its women, a sari with a long sleeved blouse worn with shoes and socks seemed just the right combination that would accord us the respectability he sought. I had never worn closed shoes and socks in my life. They shackled my feet. They deprived me of my freedom. Was this imposition symbolic of what lay ahead for me? I did not want to forfeit my identity to this alien dress.

On board the ship, instructions were being heaped upon the boys and me constantly. We were ordered to put on our shoes and socks from daybreak to nightfall and never be bare-footed any waking moment. The boys were traumatized. The shoes and socks regimentation was cumbersome. Their feet hurt and their socks soaked in perspiration emitted a foul odour, but there was to be no respite. Mohandas had forced us into a gruelling routine. Every day we were made to march up and down the deck of the ship with those torturous shoes and socks that bound our feet and literally gagged our tongues. During the drill, he walked alongside, all the while studying my posture and scrutinizing the faces of the boys.

'Stand erect... Hold your head high... Walk small steps...'

The regimentation was tiresome and endless. Some days I had to muster up all my grit to avoid collapsing during the punishing drill. Sometimes I felt a violent need to retch. But he never let up. Wasn't there someone who could tell Mohandas that we had had enough?

My reprieve only came at bedtime, when I could throw off my hellish shoes to let my feet breathe freely and go to sleep. There were plentiful and repeated chidings 'Don't slouch. Your shoelaces are undone.' Mealtimes were even more torturous; to sit at a table, eating out of small china plates, with unwieldy knives and forks. I'd rather have remained hungry.

'The knife in your right, the fork in your left...Eat with your mouth closed...Don't talk with food in your mouth...' The nagging never stopped. It was much worse than those wretched tuitions in Rajkot. At least they ended in intimate frolics and love-making that took the edge off that arduous learning schedule.

But here I had no respite. How on earth could I possibly shovel food into my mouth with metal contraptions? The taste of food would be destroyed if I didn't use my fingers. And who could chew with their mouths closed? Food was supposed to be relished with slurping noises and gigantic chewing movements. This food was anyway foul, boiled vegetables and bread. We had never set eyes on this kind of stuff in Rajkot. But I swallowed it down along with my injured pride, held back my tears of frustration and prayed fervently for the journey to end. How I ached to be back in Rajkot. The freedom, the happy memories of the years gone by where there was no decree on dress code, where I could stay bare-foot for as long as I liked, where I could eat on or off the floor with my fingers. Alas! That was a distant, fading dream.

Barely five days away from our destination, a violent storm seized the ships which were being tossed about on the ocean like paper boats. Gigantic waves beat around us and many terrified passengers had cleared the decks and retreated to the safety of the cabins below. The air was rent with the howling of gales lashing against the railings and a garbled chorus of prayers could be heard above the din of the waves and the furious windstorm.

The violent pitching and rolling of the ship made most passengers acutely ill and in a few moments, it became unbearable. Harilal, Manilal and Gokuldas had doubled over. Our churning stomachs felt as if our intestines were being yanked out through our mouths. I had never known such nausea before and the three boys, pale-faced and terror-stricken just looked at me helplessly, retching and throwing up. Surprisingly, Mohandas remained calm with no signs of any nausea. He settled me and the boys in the cabin, consoling us with tender words, patting the children on their heads, reassuring them that this would soon pass, and then went out of our cabin to help other passengers on board.

I was left alone with the boys. I was furious. How could he leave us and go off to assist strangers in this hour of crisis? I took the boys into my arms and lay on the cabin-bed holding the groaning and weeping children close to me and praying for an end to the frightful, stormy night on the seas. Each time the ship rolled sharply on its side, I prayed more fervently fearing that we were all going to sink to our death in the dark dreadful ocean. Where was Mohandas? He should have been here with us, holding on to the terrified children who had never needed him like they did that day! I screamed.

Help us God! We are going to die!

A cold apathy had gripped me. Where the hell was he?

Between cries for deliverance to the Almighty, I murmured,

Charity begins at home…I shall never again step on a ship in my life, if I survive this calamity.

My heart hammered against my chest that heaved up and down rapidly. I felt the dark swirling waves close in above me and the painful cries of the panic-stricken children pierced my ears. Mohandas never returned to the cabin, till the skies cleared up after twenty-four hours.

The gloom lifted and with sanity restored, most passengers celebrated the triumph of life over death and an air of gaiety returned on board. I too resumed the drudgery of my daily walks on the deck with the boys. Those biting, strangulating shoes no longer seemed so painful. Everything paled in front of the fear of death that had gripped us a short while ago.

Five days later, on 19 December, the ship sailed into Durban. A ripple of excitement broke out at the prospect of being on land after a long and death-defying journey, but this was not quite the journey's end! Because of an outbreak of the plague earlier that year in Bombay, health authority officers at Durban boarded the ships as we sailed in, declaring that we would be quarantined for a period of five days, before we could disembark. Five more days of forced incarceration aboard a ship that lay anchored just outside Durban harbour? My nerves, already at the end of their tether, snapped. However, Mohandas true to form, was unperturbed. He devised various ways to divert the attention of the weary passengers and organized entertaining games for them to pass time. For once, even the boys joined in.

On Christmas day, the mood aboard the ship became celebratory again. All the passengers and the crew were invited to join in a feast organized by the captain of the ship. Extolling the virtues of Christianity in fluent English, Mohandas had everyone riveted. He spoke eloquently about the greatness of the religion comparing it to all the other great religious orders of the world that had propagated peace, equality and non-violence. I sat there in ignorance, amongst a group of strange foreigners trying to grasp his extempore speech. A devout Hindu at heart, I began to question the righteousness and injustice of having to celebrate a Christian festival that meant little to me. I was more concerned about the welfare of my boys after the nauseating sea voyage that had traumatized all four of us; a voyage the likes of which I had vowed never to embark on, again.

Meanwhile, unbeknownst to us, a turbulent storm of another kind was brewing in Durban that was to have far-reaching consequences.

TWENTY THREE

In Durban, malicious press reports had caused massive resistance to the entry of Mohandas and his entourage. Believing in the mischievous canards spread against him, the people of South Africa were afraid to allow these rebellious Indians whose rabble-rousing ring-leader had condemned the European community for ill-treating his fellowmen.

Rumours were rife that Mohandas was arriving in Natal with two shiploads of Indians. South Africans dreaded the clearance of 800 passengers who would swamp their homeland and demand equal rights. The government was in a state of panic. Even some European friends of Mohandas were overcome with terror. Loud public protests were witnessed everywhere. Angry crowds carrying incendiary placards collected every night at the city centre, demanding immediate expulsion of the "brown rebel". Exaggerated reports of expelling Indians from Natal were floating around and the air was thick with warlike hostility.

Even as these rumours trickled down to us on board, all the passengers were overcome with fright. Those who had homes in South Africa were in a complete state of panic. Several others began mentally preparing to return home, lest some unforeseen disaster befell them. Mohandas spent a considerable amount of time trying to assuage their fears. If his words had any calming effect on my co-passengers, they did little to appease me. I was petrified. At the end of a long and torturous journey, my frayed nerves could no longer withstand another threat to our very survival.

'Don't be afraid, Kastur! I have done nothing wrong. I have nothing to fear. I have only stated the truth for which I shall fight till my last breath,' he said. 'Have faith in god. He shall see us through this crisis. I know He shall!'

Mohandas' words fell on my deaf ears and the crisis raged on.

For eighteen agonizing days of uncertainty, we waited outside Durban harbour, while the incensed crowds continued with their protests to scare us into returning home. Meanwhile on board, tension was mounting with each passing moment. Supplies of food and water ran out and there was no sign of replenishment. It had been forty-four days since we had departed from Bombay when the government lifted the quarantine and we sailed into Durban, exhausted and ill. This was indeed my first taste of victory by peaceful resistance.

All day the boys and I, dressed in our brand new clothes with our bags packed, waited eagerly to disembark. There was no sign of Mohandas till late afternoon. He had been summoned to the Captain's cabin hours ago. Our impatience and anxiety mounted as the hours dragged on painfully. I was sick of the mouldy smell emanating from the ship, and even more of these endless delays. Never before had I yearned to have my feet on firm ground as I did that moment. It was agonizing to watch all the passengers making their way out while we waited for Mohandas. Manilal was sleepy and restless. What could you expect from a five year old? Harilal and Gokuldas were worse. They groaned and moaned like captive animals in the suffocating cabin. Every few minutes, Harilal looked at me, 'How much longer, Ba?' his sleepy eyes staring at me. 'I don't know,' was all I could say. By now, I was completely exhausted and aching all over.

A little while later Mohandas returned, but not with the news we needed to hear.

'We can't leave the ship yet, Kastur! The captain has advised us to wait here. He says it's not safe for us to disembark. Not until it's dark,' he said.

'Oh God, no!' I cried out in desperation. 'What kind of beasts live in this wretched place? Why did I ever agree to come here?' I wrung my hands in despair.

'Listen to me! There are people all around; angry whites protesting against my entering Durban. But don't you fret, Kastur... all will be well. They have been dispersed. No harm shall come to us. My friend Harry Escombe who is a highly placed government official has cautioned that it is not safe for us to leave before it gets dark. Just be patient for a bit longer…. No harm shall come to us.'

I had turned pale as Mohandas' voice trailed off, but the cacophony bursting inside my head had risen to a deafening pitch. I sank in the bed of my cabin in a crumpled heap. The boys began to weep.

The hostility of the atmosphere outside had seeped into the crevices of my brain. I found it hard to control my tears. Mohandas had been equally perturbed at the idea of sneaking out like criminals in the dark to avoid confronting his adversaries, but we had no option. The long wait ended in silence. When the captain sensed that things had settled and it was safe, he sent word that we could leave the ship just before nightfall.

We disembarked stealthily, as the threat of being lynched by irate locals loomed large. An uneasy calm had descended on the city that night. A port carriage organized by the Durban authorities was waiting to take us to the house of a friend, Jiwanji Rustomji, who was a wealthy Parsi merchant and member of the Natal Indian Congress. 'You go in the coach with the children, Kastur,' Mohandas whispered to me as we shuffled out. 'I shall be walking behind you with Mr. Laughton.'

I clutched his hands tightly, with panic writ large on my face. 'We have nothing to fear…' He added. 'Just go.'

'I want to walk with you. I don't want you to go alone.' I protested meekly.

'No no, dear! It's a long walk, almost two miles. You are all tired. Just sit in the carriage and go. I'm right behind you. You will be drained by the time we reach and we cannot send the boys to Rustomji's house by themselves … go with them now. Please do as I say. Just go!'

Mohandas' firm words did little to allay my fears. I sensed there was an imminent danger to his life and I wanted to be by his side; not away from the public eye, driven by strangers in an alien hostile city to an unknown person's home. That was not where I wanted to be, but I had long learned that protesting was futile. I was bundled into the coach with the children. I took one last look out of the carriage window at Mohandas. He stood on the rail of the ship alongside a tall European man.

'That must be Laughton,' I mumbled as I sat up straight with the boys, pulling the Parsi-style sari over my head looking every bit the proud wife of a very, very controversial Indian! I did not know whether to smile or to cry.

Mohandas began his walk to Rustomji's house soon after our carriage left. On a route that normally witnessed lean traffic and hardly any pedestrians, he spotted a crowd of young men looming before them. His heart skipped a beat. The rowdy group lunged forward and closed in on them shouting, 'Gandhi! Go home! Go Home! Go back, Gandhi!'

The blood-curdling cries must have rattled him as much as they petrified us. They were being jostled and jeered at by over a dozen rabid protesters who were joined by many more.

Despite all his good intentions, Laughton had delivered Mohandas right into the lap of an irate mob. What followed was perhaps the worst nightmare that a lone man could have suffered in the midst of a violent crowd. Mohandas was pinned down by people on either side who were roughing him up. His turban, pulled off his head, lay in a trail on the ground and rotten eggs and stale fish were being hurled at him from all directions.

'Go back, infidel! Gandhi, go home! Down with Gandhi!' The maniacal mob pushed poor Laughton roughly onto one side and threw Mohandas to the ground, punching, slapping and kicking him.

A lone white woman, the wife of the superintendent of police of Durban, who was strolling on the Esplanade that day, heard the murderous cries of the angry mob that was raining blows and shouting abuses at someone who had been taken down. To her horror she saw Mohandas, the spirited young Indian barrister whom both she and her husband had known and held in great respect, being brutally pummelled. She jumped right into their midst with her open parasol and held it above Mohandas' head to shield him from the egg-missiles and blows. Seeing a white lady amongst them, the crowd fell silent and began slinking away.

Meanwhile alerted by another Indian passerby, a group of constables arrived on the scene. They dispersed the mob and Mohandas was rescued from a near death.

It had been over two hours since we arrived at Rustomji's house and I was getting restless. I paced up and down my room but there was no sign of Mohandas. I was gripped with panic. I knew something was terribly wrong. When he did arrive, bruised and bloodied, torn and dishevelled, the stains of blood and mud on his face, I rushed to him weeping uncontrollably.

'Oh my God! What have these beasts done to you?' I screamed.

Unmindful of the unconventional display of emotions in public, I took him in my arms and cradled his head on my lap.

'What have these brutes done? Let's go back home. I do not wish to live here amongst savages…' my face was streaming with tears.

My bewildered boys crowded around, clinging to my side.

'Get me a dish of warm water someone…' I had begun to swab his bleeding wounds with my *pallu*, 'someone call a doctor, please!' I screamed hysterically.

Mohandas however was unperturbed. He held my hand gently and said. 'It's nothing, Kastur! Don't worry, I'm okay!' I could feel the pain in his voice.

By the time the doctor arrived, I had cleaned up his face and bandaged his bleeding wounds. Luckily they were only surface abrasions and the doctor left after examining him.

At dusk, a small crowd had gathered outside Rustomji's house. Word had spread that we were holed up inside. The irate mob hadn't quite finished with Mohandas. The crowd got bigger and in a few hours it turned into a violent horde shouting abuses, threatening to break down the doors of poor Rustomji's home. Meanwhile, the police superintendent also arrived with a posse of constables, but he was aware that dispersing the bloodthirsty mob was going to be an impossible task.

'Down with Gandhi! Send Gandhi out! We want Gandhi out! We must have Gandhi!' Just then, from somewhere in the distance, loud garbled words of a song wafted in:

We'll hang old Gandhi...
on the sour apple tree…

Crouching behind the bolted doors of Rustomji's house, a chilling panic gripped us. Harilal and Manilal clung to my sides weeping loudly and poor Gokuldas, dumbstruck with fear stared vacantly outside. My heart went out to the little boy who had lost his father barely a few months ago, and had travelled with us on a perilous sea-voyage to this awful land. He didn't deserve this fate! How would poor Raliatben come to terms with losing her son? I was sure that we were going to be lynched to death any moment, in this dreadfully hostile, foreign land. I closed my eyes and prayed.

God have mercy on us!

Finally, the terrible night ended with Mohandas leaving the house disguised as a constable on the advice of the superintendent of police.

'I'll be back soon to take you home. Don't worry, you are safe with Rustomji, Kastur. I'll be back soon.' His words of reassurance notwithstanding, a sense of foreboding gripped me as I watched him race down the stairs accompanied by two detectives disguised as Indian merchants. While I paced restlessly all night, Mohandas stayed at the police station till daybreak by which time the crowd had dispersed.

The Durban press carried exaggerated reports of the incident on its front pages the next morning. News of the assault on Mohandas had reached India and England. In Bombay, the Viceroy expressed grave concern at the dastardly attack and the Queen's Office in London shot off a cable to Natal instructing them to initiate an immediate inquiry against the instigators.

Mohandas, however, refused to press charges against his assailants and the matter was closed; but not without the public extolling my husband's ever benevolent conduct, which catapulted him to instant stardom.

✳   ✳   ✳

Twenty Four

We left Rustomji's house after eight days with mixed emotions of relief and gratitude. While I was extremely indebted to them for their generosity and the shelter they had provided despite a life-threatening risk, staying in a Parsi household was not easy for me. In their world, so starkly different from our conservative home, men and women freely sat together, ate together and went out together with no reservations. In Rajkot I had never even stepped out of the women's quarters without covering my face. Nor could I ever mingle freely like this with older male members of the family. To make matters worse, the food, which they so graciously had cooked for us was unpalatable. For me, a staunch Vaishnav Hindu, that fare of meat, fish and fowl was an unbearable assault on my sensibilities and the relief that flooded me at leaving Rustomji's home was far greater than the gratitude, which I felt for their generous hospitality. I looked forward to being in my own home with my sacred vegetarian kitchen and the independent life I had always dreamt of.

For the first time, at the age of twenty-eight, I would be in my own domain, not under the authority of anyone. My name would change to the very august sounding Kasturba! The sound of the new affix tinkled sweetly in my ears. I repeated. Kastur-ba-aa! It felt enchanting! I twirled around and repeated it again. Kastur-ba-aa-aa! As Kasturba, the lady of the regal manor, mistress of the grand Beach Grove Villa, wife of the renowned Mohandas, proud mother of his two sons, I had come a long way.

And Mohandas had also evolved into a highly revered man, adulated by thousands of people in South Africa. I had begun to see how ardently people followed his public pronouncements; he ignited a phenomenal passion in them and the perils that blind faith of this kind could bring upon their leader had begun to dawn on me.

Life had never felt better. Beach Grove Villa was a beautiful, spacious five-bedroom house with a sprawling sea-facing verandah, imposing wrought-iron gates and a pretty front garden. It was unlike any other home I had lived in. The scenic view of the ocean and fresh scent of the sea breeze brought back happy memories of my childhood in Porbandar.

The interiors of my new home were equipped with plush European furnishings. The living room had a luxurious carpet, a fully upholstered sofa, two comfortable armchairs, a round library table and a wooden bookcase that was filled with books of famous authors that Mohandas had collected. I saw among them, copies of the Bible and Quran and some biographies of Indian leaders. The dining room had an eight-seater rectangular table with bentwood chairs and a carved sideboard of the same wood. The bedrooms on the first floor were stark in comparison. There were bare wooden platforms that served as beds and simple wooden cupboards in each room.

I wandered around the house that had been locked up while Mohandas was away. Dust had covered the furniture and scratched the polish. A musty smell emanated from within. I pushed the doors and windows open to let in the cool breeze from the ocean. The rooms needed to be aired, swept and dusted. Our bags had to be unpacked and I needed to stock up provisions in the kitchen. Even with the help of the boys and the servants it would take a while before we were comfortable in a clean and functioning home.

But first I would have to learn to cook in this unfamiliar, modern kitchen that looked forbidding. I heard the boys cry out, 'We are hungry, Ba!'

It was time to rustle up a meal but my nerves were at a breaking point. I had never worked in a kitchen with my shoes on, standing upright intimidated by modern gadgets. In Rajkot, I had always squatted on the floor of the kitchen, to cook on live coal stoves. This kitchen was fitted with large wood-burning stoves that I could barely reach up to. I hadn't a clue as to how they were to be lit. It took me several weeks before I was able to master the intricacies of the cooking range and the drudgery of housekeeping began to diminish. However, my feet never stopped aching in the tight confinement of those vile leather shoes. And Mohandas' cruel command, "shoes to be kept on at all times" never let up.

As I stood gazing out of the window at the rolling ocean below, my thoughts drifted back to the easy flow of our lives in Rajkot. I yearned to be back in the bustling comfort of my home. How I missed being amongst the women of the Gandhi household, sharing chores, exchanging gossip and tending to each other's children. Every time news about my sisters-in-law came through letters that Mohandas read aloud, my heartache intensified.

For the first time I realized how privileged I had been to have enjoyed the love of my family and what a sharp contrast it was to live alone. But Mohandas was busy with an unending stream of visitors who dropped in at any time of the day to seek legal advice. The niche he had carved for himself in this strange, social milieu made my heart swell with pride.

Twenty Five

Beach Grove Villa soon became an open house. Mohandas even invited a few of his young law clerks to live with us. The hustle and bustle of these spirited and youthful interns boosted my spirits and the gloom of being separated from my beloved family back home in Rajkot, slowly dissipated.

Despite his busy schedule, I noticed that Mohandas was making an effort to spend time with the boys. Having lived away from them for so long, he began to feel the need to groom them and instill in them his values, something they had been denied all those years. Education in "race-conscious" South Africa was not easy; schools were discriminating, with superior ones reserved strictly for white children. Given the fact that they were Mohandas' children, getting admission into the haloed precincts of an elitist school was a privilege that could have been easily granted to our boys, but he shot down the idea.

'This kind of favouritism shall alienate the boys from Indian society,' he said firmly.

He rejected anything that was not universally available to all Indians. So no school was found to be suitable for his sons. Even the Christian missionary-run schools had an inferior and unqualified lot of teachers, so the children stayed home whiling away their time, while others their age were being schooled in institutions of some sort in the city.

I was in grave turmoil. While Manilal was too young, the two older boys needed to go to school. I constantly worried about Harilal, who was bright, diligent and eager to study. Gokuldas was undemanding, but he also required to have a regular academic schedule.

'The boys need to go to school. We can't keep them home all day,' I mustered up courage and said to Mohandas one day. 'I don't want them to end up like me. Can't you see they are being wasted?'

The more I pleaded, the more Mohandas hardened his stance. Till one day, tired by my constant needling he hired a white woman as a governess for the boys. She was to teach them English-reading and writing and some basic arithmetic.

But the boys could make no headway with her. They could not understand a word of what she said, so it became an utterly useless exercise and their illiteracy and my frustration endured.

Soon, Mohandas sacked the fancy white governess and we were back to square one. He then decided to homeschool the young boys and began conducting all the lessons in Gujarati, an equally arduous task that seemed to be making little progress. To me it was a grim reminder of the irksome lessons I was subjected to every night in Rajkot—a miserable duplication of his obduracy and failure.

I was forever strung-up. Mohandas found less and less time to teach the boys—when he came home late in the evenings, the children would be too tired to concentrate on his gruelling Gujarati-to-English lessons, and trying to rouse them from their slumber at that hour, was an impossible task for me. So, at this point, all of Mohandas' experiments had become impractical and guaranteed to fail. I had had enough.

'This won't do,' I blurted out to him one tedious morning, trying desperately to drag the boys out of their beds. Mohandas was startled by the defiance in my voice.

'You have to stop this madness,' I ranted. 'We have to send them to some school. Any damn school will do! At least they will learn something there. They are just wasting their time at home all day. And you can't find the time to teach them. Can't you see we are ruining their lives?'

My sharp words must have cracked open the chinks in his icy armour.

Mohandas stood staring at me in disbelief till I turned away and left the room in a huff.

I sat sulking on a cane chair in the verandah, trying to hold back my frustration. Feeling a queasy rumbling in my stomach, I ran into the bathroom and vomited all I had eaten that morning.

I discovered I was pregnant with Mohandas' third child. It was the last quarter of 1897.

✄　✄　✄

Running Beach Grove Villa in my current condition had become a tough challenge. I felt constantly tired and irritable, yearning to be in the comfort of my home in India, with my adoring family beside me. Yet I could neither complain nor slacken the efficiency of managing my ever-growing household.

The year had begun with many a conflict that had taken root in my mind. I had begun to resent the foul directive that Mohandas had imposed on all the inhabitants of Beach Grove Villa. We had been ordered, not just to clean our own chamber pots every day, but also to extend this service to other residents whose pots had not been tended to or cleaned properly. Every morning I had to fight down a wave of revulsion at the loathsome chore he had forced upon us. I was nauseated as much with the thought of doing this reviling job with my own hands as I was in the first trimester of my third pregnancy. I felt humiliated. How dare he subject me to this vile torture?

All my life I had looked upon the cleaning of toilet pots as the lowliest of jobs; a task that condemned those who did it as sub-humans, unfit to even reside inside the city limits where decent folks lived. I knew that even their shadows were unclean and deemed you ritually impure if they were to fall upon you. These wretched cleaners were allowed into our homes only in the thick of the night, so that no one set sight on their ill-omened faces while they went about their jobs of removing night soil from the homes of the upper castes. And now Mohandas tells me to defile myself and clean my own toilet and if need be, other's toilets as well! How dare he?

I felt my unborn child kick hard at the walls of my womb. Another wave of nausea hit my throat and I ran out into the garden for a breath of fresh air. A rancid stench persisted in my breath and my heart raced uncontrollably. I sat on a low chair facing the sea, till the melody of the rising and falling waves lulled me to sleep.

A few days later, a new Christian house guest moved into Beach Grove Villa. The atmosphere of our open and always welcoming home must have lured him to stay, but I felt a sharp twinge of loathing. That lowly *malech!* I couldn't bear to be eating from the same plate as him. And what if he touched the faucets of my kitchen and polluted them? My mind was running wild; I was frustrated and helpless at not being able to stymie his invasion into my sacred space.

Sure enough, the first assault to my battered nerves happened within twenty-four hours of his arrival. Unaware or probably unmindful of the rules of Beach Villa Grove, he had left his un-emptied chamber pot under his bed and was gone for the day. I was furious. I knew Mohandas would pick up the dirty pot of the stranger, empty it out, clean it and place it back for him to soil again. To prevent him from the humiliation, suppressing my own outrage and spilling tears, I yanked out the filthy pot, holding my breath as I dragged it down the stairs and emptied it out into the main collection trough.

I wasn't aware that Mohandas had been watching me and had heard my loud rumblings as I lugged the pot downstairs with anger pouring out of my eyes.

'*Ek toh malech! Upar se uska pot mai uthaaon?* I, Kastur, the beloved wife of the great barrister Mohandas, have to lower myself to this level and pick up the pot of this lowly beast!' I kept grumbling loudly.

'Wait!' I was taken aback to see Mohandas. 'What did you just say, Kastur? Lowering yourself, are you? I will not stand this nonsense in my house!' Mohandas' sharp voice rang out, piercing me like an arrow. 'If you want to do this task of emptying chamber pots, do so with grace and I must see a smile on your face,' he said. 'Or else, get out!'

My patience snapped.

'Keep your damn house to yourself and let me go! I do not want to live with you and your wretched ideals. Let me go!' I shouted back. Mohandas grabbed my hand. His fingers tightened against my glass bangles that broke, digging into my wrist, forming red welts from which blood oozed out.

'What are you doing? Have you no shame?' I pulled my hands back and cried. 'Have all your senses deserted you? Is this what you have brought me to South Africa for? And now you want to throw me out? But where can I go? I have no one here to turn to. Who is there to protect me from your cruelty?' I screamed loudly.

By then, Mohandas had dragged me by my arm, and taken me right outside the gate of Beach Grove Villa.

'Behave yourself!' I hollered. 'I'm not here to take your beatings, Mohandas. You are a cruel beast! God, how I hate you! Shut the gates and let's go in before we become a spectacle for the entire neighbourhood.'

I edged into the gates and stumbled in a heap inside the boundary wall of the house. I picked myself up and ran in, weeping hysterically, 'Where can I go? I have no one in South Africa whom I can turn to. I know you want me dead!'

Waves of severe nausea and the pain of humiliation were pounding at my chest. I ran into the bathroom and crawled under the faucet directing a sharp stream of water onto my body and began to scrub vigorously. I felt a sharp stinging pain where the glass had cut open the skin. I let the water drizzle over my hands till the bleeding stopped. I then lay down on my bed. The little foetus in my belly lay still as I stretched supine trying desperately to expel that horrific stench of the chamber pot that had suffused my entire being.

The persistant putrid stink, the nasty gash on my wrist, where Mohandas had grabbed me and dragged me to the gate, the rap on my dignity and the sting of salty tears on my chapped face kept me awake all night.

Indeed I was no saint, but Mohandas had become an abusive and cruel husband who had lost all regard for the one person he claimed to have loved the most. I felt suffocated and trapped.

'Sadist! Sadist! Sadist! Why don't you kill me once and for all?' Those silent reverberating shrieks did not cease until long after.

❄ ❄ ❄

Twenty Six

1898

I had witnessed a violent streak in Mohandas for the first time in our marriage of sixteen years. His ferocious outburst at being disobeyed, when he had nearly raised his hand on me had shocked me, but I was keen to put that ugly quarrel behind us. After a tearful session of apologies, Mohandas vowed he would never lose his temper with me again. I succumbed to the moment, also pledging that I would comply with all his wishes cheerfully thereafter. I fell asleep in his arms that night, drifting quietly into rosy ambrosia that accompanies a tender sexual exchange.

With peace restored between us, Beach Grove Villa sprang back to life again and I began preparing for the birth of my third child, who unlike the older two was going to be born in a foreign country amongst strange men with even stranger customs. It made me nervous. Beach Grove Villa had no birthing room like the one we had in the Rajkot house where Harilal and Manilal were born. Mohandas wanted me to have the best medical care through my last trimester, by engaging the services of a good doctor. But when I heard his suggestion, I paled. A male doctor delivering my child was a serious affront to my modesty.

'No no! Never! How can a man attend to my delivery?' I was adamant and refused to relent. 'Even if he's Indian, I won't have it.'

The presence of a strange male during that curiously female ritual of childbirth, was to me, grave sacrilege. However after much resistance, I finally gave in. I also agreed to let him hire a nurse to look after the infant and me.

'Only if she is Indian,' I said reluctantly. 'With you away in office all day, how will I communicate with a European woman?'

A slight smile played on Mohandas' face.

'Oh, Kastur! You are so innocent,' he said. 'Where will we find an Indian nurse in South Africa? It will be easier to find an Indian doctor here, my love!' he jibed.

He ruffled my hair and placed his hands on my swollen stomach, gently stroking it.

'Don't worry, little one,' he whispered. 'I am here for the both of you. Your Bapu will look after you.' His voice trailed off dreamily while I snuggled close to him, overcome by a deep sense of calm.

'I can look after my baby myself.' I murmured. 'If I had been in India, wouldn't I have taken care of my child?'

A few days later, I noticed that Mohandas ordered a copy of a popular book on childcare from India, written in Gujarati. It detailed a comprehensive account of the actual process of childbirth along with complete instructions on handling and caring for a newborn.

On a morning in May, after a prolonged and difficult labour in a tiny makeshift birthing-room on the first floor of Beach Grove Villa, I gave birth to Ramdas, my third son. Mohandas stayed by the doctor's side all through the procedure to assist him, which mildly relieved my embarrassment. The book he had studiously devoured had come handy. My post-partum recovery was difficult and slow. For weeks I was weak and bedridden with anaemia and severe exhaustion. I did not even have the energy to breastfeed my baby.

All that while, Mohandas displayed exemplary paternal instincts taking over the duties of a nurse: bathing, feeding, changing the newborn even as he tended to me and the older boys.

✸ ✸ ✸

While I slowly regained my strength in the months following the birth of Ramdas, I began to sense that Mohandas was restless all over again. I failed to understand the inner turmoil that was making him edgy and my attempts to speak to him yielded nothing. It was disturbing to see him like that....While we were in India, his meagre income had been a cause for concern, but here in idyllic South Africa his legal practice was booming. With close to a dozen employees working under him and an annual income in excess of seventy-five thousand pounds, we were living a very comfortable life. What then was troubling him, I wondered.

I soon realized that the very comforts we enjoyed as the family of a successful, wealthy barrister were becoming irksome for Mohandas. Our easy lifestyle violated his moral principles. It did not take him too long to tell me how our household expenses were wasteful and needed to be curtailed immediately so that more of his earnings could be diverted towards social causes and public service. It would also discipline us into a life of austerity and self-reliance, he said.

As a result of his austerity drive, the domestic staff was first dismissed. Each one of us was ordered to do our own work and help in the daily chores. The greatest burden of this cruel measure fell on me. Along with cooking meals for that houseful of boarders, washing clothes, cleaning and dusting, I had to teach the boys how to perform their duties, which was almost impossible. Mohandas also took on a whole chunk of the work himself.

It took me quite a while to get accustomed to watching him do household chores. Back home in Rajkot, the men never cooked, cleaned or washed. Those jobs were only reserved for the women. But life in South Africa was beginning to unfold in startlingly different ways. I began to settle into the change gradually. I noticed the immense faith people reposed in my husband. I looked at him bemusedly as he sat engrossed in a book, *Laundry and Care of Textiles.*

'He must be doing something right,' I murmured. My mind was somewhat at peace.

Twenty Seven

1899

In the month of November, as the year and the millennium raced to its end, I discovered I was pregnant with Mohandas' fourth child. As our laborious life in Beach Grove Villa persisted, deep in the throes of my pregnancy, I was often overcome with severe exhaustion. By now, Mohandas had taken on a sizeable part of the household chores. He had learned the intricacies of laundering and ironing, and had even managed, after a few hilarious blunders, to master the technique of starching laundered clothes.

Although his reputation as a successful lawyer-cum-social activist had grown rapidly, he still battled racial discrimination at various levels. On a trip to Pretoria one day, he stopped at a haircutting saloon for a much-needed trim. The English barber who owned the place took one look at him, and snarled, 'You Indians are far too presumptive, aren't you? I'm not so badly off that I need to sully my hands by trimming your dirty black hair! Go find yourself an Indian barber for this job, Mister. Get out!' He said and turned his face away in disgust.

The rude outburst did not unnerve Mohandas. He smiled at him politely and said, 'Okay brother! That's your choice and your loss, not mine! At this rate you shall have fewer and fewer customers each day. Bad business decision, isn't it? Bad decision! But it's not your fault, my friend,' he continued calmly. 'I am being made to pay a price for the discrimination we impose on our own people, back home. We prohibit our barbers from serving the poor untouchables whom we also socially scorn, like you do to me today! Ah! The will of the Almighty! He chooses to punish me here in South Africa, to open my eyes to my follies. No fault of yours, brother. Have a good day,' he said, as he proudly strode out.

Unfazed by the insult, he then went into the market, bought himself a pair of scissors and began to cut his own hair. Of course he made a mess of it, but over time his haircutting skills became so perfect that he could give the boys a trim at home, whenever the need arose.

While I grappled with the changes in my body, preparing for the birth of my child, I found Mohandas driven by a manic energy. That year, a terrible famine had broken out in India and Mohandas decided to set up a relief fund for the tragedy, in order to awaken a sense of duty amongst his fellow expatriates towards their homeland. Not only did wealthy Indians make sizeable donations to the cause, every one he knew also contributed generously. Following that, Mohandas undertook massive sanitization campaigns in local Indian settlements to educate the people on hygiene and dispel the general perception that all Indians were dirty and led slovenly lives.

Gradually, Mohandas' interest in public health and medicine became an obsession. He read up dozens of books on naturopathy and often prescribed simple home remedies to his ailing clients, all the while continuing voluntary work in the neighbourhood hospital.

About a month before I had discovered I was pregnant, a war had broken out in South Africa. A conflict had been brewing for over ten years, ever since gold was discovered in Transvaal, between the native Boers and British settlers, both trying to establish control over the mines. As the hostility escalated between the two groups, the Boers began to deny citizenship to the British and imposed heavy taxes on them. In turn, the British retaliated by sending troops into South African colonies, which became the flashpoint and the Boers declared war.

Meanwhile, the South African Indians were reluctant to get drawn into the *white man's* war. Believing to be the common enemy of the warring factions, they were scared of the aftermath —whatever may be the outcome. Mohandas however was deeply stirred by the unrest. His conscience would not allow him to be an indifferent bystander. He felt that his loyalty to the Empire was being challenged and he was duty-bound to support them. He sallied forth.

In keeping with his staunch belief in non-violence, he engaged the Indian settlers to side with the Queen, but without the use of arms. He wrote to the government of Natal offering to organize a corps of Indians to serve as medical orderlies and stretcher-bearers for the wounded. However, the English officials summarily dismissed his proposal saying that Indians could not be trusted as all of them were cowards.

Mohandas was dejected but he persevered. He recruited some eleven hundred volunteers and appointed forty leaders from amongst them for serving in the ambulance corps. He later enlisted the help of a friend, a British Medical Missionary who was chief superintendant of a charitable hospital, to train the volunteers and help obtain the requisite certification for medical practice.

In the meantime, there had been alarming developments on the battlefront. The Boers who had first laid siege to the city of Ladysmith, gradually took over Natal. In the beginning of December, the government of Natal, pushed to the brink, had no option but to allow Indian volunteers to fight the Boers. They provided the Indian Corps with uniforms and the much-needed transport for their services, and the battle raged on. Mohandas' dream had been realized. The official Indian Ambulance Corps was firmly in place.

The volunteers of the Corps however had a daunting task. They often marched twenty-five miles under the harsh summer sun through arid plains, carrying wounded men on stretchers from the battlefront to base hospitals, putting their own lives at risk. The senseless carnage and bloodshed seared through Mohandas' mind. His latent hatred for war crystallized deep within his soul and he once again resolved to shun violence of any kind thereafter.

But what was most remarkable in the terrible war-torn situation was the resilience shown by the Corps' volunteers who had come together to work during a challenging crisis, by putting aside their religious, caste and linguistic differences. Their self-sacrifice, courage and endurance earned them high praise from British officers and the ingratiated infantry. Even though many of his valiant men had lost their lives, Mohandas' heart swelled with pride as his ultimate goal was somewhat accomplished.

Mohandas sat early one morning by a roadside kerb, nibbling an army biscuit, with a gleam in his eye. His bearing was stoic and resolute, he was at peace. Indian pride and prestige had never before been so exalted. The crowning moment dawned when he along with thirty-six other members of the Corps were awarded the prestigious War Medal that provided further validation for his principle of fighting a war through non-violent means. He hoped that this would make the British modify their discriminative policies against his fellowmen and the new millennium would augur well for them.

Twenty Eight

After an unexpectedly severe onset of labour, I gave birth to Devdas, my fourth child, on 23 May 1900. The abruptness of the contractions had given us no time to summon a doctor. As I had lain writhing in the agony of a complicated and difficult labour that had me leeched on to the sides of my bed, drenched in perspiration and screaming for release, Mohandas had gone about the procedure with the precision of a trained midwife. The delivery left me too exhausted to even hold the baby and I kept fragile health for a long while thereafter, so it was Mohandas who took complete charge of caring for the newborn baby, the older boys and me.

Life rolled on comfortably for all of us soon after the new arrival. In spite of the house reverberating with the loud wails of a newborn, the animated chatter of the older boys and the noisy activities of the live-in guests, Mohandas' daily routine went on undisturbed even as he carefully nursed me back to health. Hobbling along, gradually regaining my strength each day, I was looking forward to my return to Rajkot, when our seven-year-old Manilal came down with a virulent attack of smallpox. All plans for an early return to India were indefinitely deferred thereafter.

Despite the uncertainty of our return and the well being of my children, there was something about Mohandas that stoked my anxiety, something that seemed to be preying on his mind all the time. He had started bringing files home and often worked late into the nights, totally exhausted by the time he came to bed. Worse, he always appeared cold and aloof.

Late one night, after the boys had gone to sleep and Devdas was lying in my lap after his night feed, he came into the room and sat on a chair by the window. He gazed quietly at the dark sky, wriggling his toes. Then in a low monotone he spoke. 'You will have to sleep in a separate bedroom, Kastur. We shall no longer be man and wife!'

His words tumbled out like a practiced monologue even as the indifferent tone slapped me hard in the face. I eased Manilal onto his crib and crumpled on the floor. A sweeping proclamation as this, delivered so matter-of-factly! What a cruel unilateral decree. No arguments, no defense, no explanation, nothing! Was this also a manifestation of his belief to shun violence in its most ferocious or feeblest form? Before I could look up at him, he had left the room.

A cold darkness enveloped me. I lay for hours on the dank floor of the room near Devdas' cradle, my heart and head pounding like a drum threatening to explode. Crazed thoughts criss-crossed through my head like strokes of lightening.

'What did I do wrong? Why was he punishing me thus? Was he in love with another woman, more beautiful, more polished and more educated than me? Was he being held captive by the lure of an *Angrezi* siren, or had he become a *param yogi* who could suppress his libido and internalize the trajectory of his semen towards the supreme *chakra* of his brain to attain *moksha*?'

Tears ran down my face. They drenched the front of my blouse. My nasal passages choked with the salty liquid that flowed out, obstructing my breath. Nothing could have prepared me for this terrible humiliation, this final severance of my worldly link to his body. How could this be happening to me? How would I face a loving husband each day, who was willing to perform every single duty towards his wife except the most vital one? I felt I had been strangulated by the morbid hug of death.

The loud wails of Devdas roused me from my death-like stupor. The cheery chatter of the boys in the front yard wafted in through the door. I stumbled as I jumped up from the floor and lifted him out of his crib. I put his hungry mouth to my breast. His vigorous suckling sounds sent deep waves of gratification down to my entrails. I folded my thoughts into a ball of quiet reticence. There were to be no more discussions about this hereafter. And even though his final vow of celibacy was to come later, I was not going to delude myself about what lay ahead. I felt something curl up inside me and die while Mohandas was gone for the day.

✄   ✄   ✄

Even after my earlier pregnancies had marred my feminine appeal and the birth of Devdas had contorted my body, making it uglier, I could never have believed that Mohandas would ever cease to desire me. I hated those unsightly stretch marks that were emblazoned deep on my slack belly, those hideous rolls of flesh hanging like saddle-bags on either side of my waist, my sagging breasts stretched to their limits after suckling four boys, yet I could never have imagined that my Mohandas would ever find me any less appealing. I was his beloved Kastur and he my wedded husband. He had pledged to be faithful to me till I died. It was his *dharma.*

Was the fear of becoming a slave to his sexual desires eating into his vitals? Was that raging conflict between his libido and his *dharma* consuming him? Was he trying to tell me that a legitimate conjugal relationship was a grave sin? Where had he learned that these energies were deflecting his spiritual growth? Why was he embarking on a journey of penance and celibacy oblivious of the people he would inadvertently victimize, wound and mutilate on the way? I thought my head was going to burst. I needed to scream.

Who has given you the authority to enforce a ruling on me that affects me with such a cruel, brutal force without my consent? Who?

But I did not dare to voice my cries of protest. Not now, not ever. For between us the discussion of sex was taboo. No one spoke about it. From mother to daughter, father to son, it was a silent flow of the unspoken word. You just learned the act by obeying your husband, not for pleasure but for procreation. Pain, ecstasy, orgasm or climax, you could not choose; it was his privilege and your lot. I tried several times in vain to draw him out, to speak, to evoke words and thoughts from him that could allay my fears, but he remained aloof and silent. Yet, I was not willing to give up so easily.

One night, after the evening shadows enveloped the city, I bathed in scented water and anointed myself with a rose fragrance that a young boarder had presented me. I parted my hair right down the middle and combed it till my thick, dark tresses shone in the diffused light of the moon like the starlit sky. I put on a light silk sari and covered my arms with its loose ends.

Mohandas had retired to the adjoining room. The light from his room spread out in geometric patterns from underneath the closed door. I stealthily pushed the door open and glided in. The rustle of silk startled him. He looked up from the file he was engrossed in. I saw his eyes mist over as he glanced at me. I walked up to his desk and went around him, facing his back. He did not move or turn his head but I could sense an icy undercurrent emanating from him. I let my *pallu* drop from my shoulders, and put my arms around him feeling his rigid back. My warm, moist breath fell on his cheeks and my scented hair settled like the tail of a peacock, gently caressing his neck and back.

'Mohandas,' I cooed into his ears. Those breezy words fell upon his deaf ears. Those brief moments of ecstasy vapourized into the air, dragging me down with the weight of a violent oncoming climax. His sharp voice jolted me out of my trance. 'Stop it, Kastur! Stop this, will you? What has come over you? Go back to your room and let me never see a repeat of this again. Do you understand?'

Those cruel words ripped through me like a million tons of debris from an exploding meteor.

The brutal shattering of my sensuous entreaties hit me hard. I gathered myself into a bundle, and ran out to the terrace under the clear, moonlit sky. The sobs that racked every pore of my being, resonated with the twinkling stars above. I looked up at them through a veil of tears. They were all weeping like me, while the moon shied away behind a wispy cloud.

❊ ❊ ❊

While eight-month-old Devdas lay in his crib, oblivious to the tumultuous happenings that deluged his mother, and the older boys lay in their beds all in deep blissful slumber, Mohandas was racked by violent emotions of another kind. He spent a turbulent night tossing in his bed, troubled by the demons of his curtailed libido, even more hardened in his resolve. All night each of us burnt in the fiery infernos of hell charred by the leaping flames that were corroding our souls. Each one in a separate world of gloom feeling betrayed by the other. But no one would ever dare to question him and no one would ever bother to ask me, are you happy, Kastur?

And, within Mohandas, a gnawing suspicion of Kastur having lain in another man's bed had taken root, firm and deep. He would never be certain either way.

Twenty Nine

By the time Devdas was eleven months old, his father's internal conflicts had taken mammoth proportions. His loathing for societal oppression, his aspiration for justice and equality and his desire for alleviating universal human suffering were driving him to challenge a gamut of established social norms. For the first time he felt the need to work towards the upliftment of women in India; he believed his duty towards mankind would be somewhat redeemed by his giving up the lure of material pursuits and going back to address the needs of his people.

Meanwhile, phone calls from Indian friends urging him to return and take charge of our ravaged homeland began flooding Mohandas. Gripped by intense homesickness, I too longed to get back after the four long years of separation from the family which seemed even longer, considering my two sons were born in faraway South Africa. How I yearned to go back and show them off to our relatives and friends. Our own "made-in-Africa" boys would do us proud. I couldn't wait to see the envy on the faces of my two sisters-in-law when they would set eyes on these handsome young men. Even though I had constantly fretted about their education, which was seriously impacted, particularly of the older two who had entered their teens, they were a delightful lot. I tried not to lament about the erratic tuitions they had received from their father who was always hard pressed for time. Yes, they could sweep floors, launder clothes and do other household chores skillfully; but what good was that? I consoled myself,

All will be well. Let's just get back to Rajkot!

The much-awaited day was set for the first week of October 1901. A teary-eyed Mohandas, who had finally decided to go home, pledged before a large group of friends to return to South Africa.

What followed was a spate of farewell parties where the Indian community headed by Dada Abdulla, Jiwanji Rustomji, and Ritchie conferred him with dozens of written testimonials. They showered us with expensive parting gifts which included a thousand pounds worth of gold and diamond jewellery, watches, pens and also an exceptionally beautiful necklace of gold specially crafted for me. I grabbed the necklace and put it on, admiring the exquisite design in the mirror. I saw Harilal pick out a silver watch and slip it on his wrist, his eyes gleaming with excitement.

'They are all ours, my child, and you can keep that watch. I know you don't want to let anyone else have it, do you?'

I ruffled his hair and pirouetted before the mirror caressing the links of my new gold neckpiece.

Mohandas however was deeply disturbed. Viewing the gifts piled up on the table, he paced up and down the house, clearly annoyed by our behaviour. Accepting gifts was in clear violation of a moral decree that he strongly upheld. On the other hand, rejecting tokens of an abiding friendship could have been construed as offensive to his friends. After hours of deliberation, he decided to donate all the gifts that were in tribute to the Natal Indian Congress, to be used for the benefit of South African Indians. He drew up legal documents to set up a public trust that would hold the valuables in custody and made his close friends and a few associates joint trustees. With a serious load off his chest, he finally felt at peace with himself.

All he needed was to break the news to me. Taking the two older boys, Harilal and Manilal into confidence, he convinced them that it was against all moral principles to keep the gifts.

'If Ba ever needs jewels for your brides-to-be, my sons, we can buy them then? We don't need to keep these, do we?'

Little Harilal, ever eager to please his overbearing father, swiftly took the watch off and laid it back on the pile. He spoke first.

'You are right, Bapu! If Ba ever needs jewels for us, we can buy our own.' And Manilal nodded in agreement.

Emboldened by the reaction of the boys, the trio marched into my room, but none of them had anticipated the tantrum they were about to witness. Fed up of Mohandas' constant emotional abuse, for me this was truly the last straw.

'No no no!' I shrieked loudly. 'I shall not give them up for your stupid Trust! These gifts are ours. And this necklace, it's mine. It was specially ordered for me. What right do you have over it? I will not let you take it away.' I grabbed the box with both my hands and pressed it close to my chest.

'I shall take it back to India along with all the other gifts. And don't you dare stop me!' My lips had pursed into an angry sneer. My quivering voice, crackled loudly at the three dumbstruck Gandhi men who stood quietly before me.

No one had seen this side of me before and I rambled on. 'Don't you see? When someone gifts you something out of love, you should accept it in the same spirit. You can't start lecturing about the ethics of it. You must accept it. And these are precious jewels. They are my security for the future. I shall preserve them and pass them on to my daughters-in-law when my sons get married, or who knows, should bad times befall us, we can use them to tide over. No, Mohandas…No. I shall not let you take these away from me. Not in a hundred years. Now go! Just leave me alone and go!'

My voice trailed off. My throat choked up and tears streamed down my eyes.

Harilal held my hand gently and said, 'But Ba, we don't need these things, really. We shall never marry women who demand jewels from us. Please listen to Bapu and hand him back these gifts.' His impassioned plea wrenched my heart. But I was not going to give up. 'Keep quiet, Harilal!' I snapped. 'I wasn't talking to you. And you, Mohandas! Don't try to convert these innocent boys into saints even before they have become men.'

I was frazzled, stretched to a breaking point, but continued to lash out at him. It must have been the forceful resistance in my words that shook up Mohandas for he paused, steadied himself, and in a softer tone said to me.

'When the boys get married, Kastur, and that shall not be for a long time yet, I shall provide you with all that you would want for their brides. Here now, look at me and stop crying.' He had moved closer and was trying to wipe my tears. 'Don't be so unreasonable. Give me that box.'

I pushed his hands away, tightened my grip on the box and said, 'Mohandas, you will provide me with what I need? You? What have you ever given me but pain? And what do you have, to give me Mohandas? You have already given everything away.'

Tears were rolling down my face; sparks of anger flashed from my wet eyes.

'Be reasonable, Kastur...come here,' he said firmly. He wiped the tears off my cheeks and slowly extracted the box from me. I turned around and allowed him to unhook the necklace. I knew I had lost the battle.

Later that night when the demons of hate, anger and unrequited passion overtook my mind, I rued the happenings of the day. I had a hard time digesting the bitter truth that my identity as Kastur Kapadia was now eclipsed and Mohandas would always, always have his way. Once again he had wounded me with an unsolicited decree, without as much as a fleeting thought for my emotions. I was only human. And surely being human was not such a nasty aberration?

Before we sailed from Durban, all those gifts including my precious necklace went into a bank vault. I knew I would never see them again.

THIRTY

December 1901

The turn of the century augured happy tidings for me, especially my return to Rajkot. Accompanied by Mohandas and the boys, I had sailed from South Africa with an over-burdened heart. But I was delighted to be back in Rajkot and the painful memories of those last few days in Durban somewhat faded away. Friends and family celebrated our homecoming with great jubilance. But Mohandas was not at peace. Aloof and restless at all times, the goings-on in our Rajkot home were of little interest to him.

On 17 December, barely three days after we had settled into our routines, he left for Bombay to join a group of delegates to attend the 17th annual meeting of the Indian National Congress. He felt that after a gap of five long years, it would be a good opportunity to renew his ties with Indian leaders and highlight the atrocities faced by his countrymen in South Africa.

Mohandas lobbied hard. En route to Calcutta, without wasting a single moment, he voiced his concerns to other leaders of the Congress party. But his enthusiasm was cut short; most were of the opinion that the conditions in India needed addressing on priority before any help could be extended to the community overseas. And the Calcutta session ended without much headway on a rather conciliatory note. Unwilling to give up easily, Mohandas stayed back in the home of a senior Congress functionary, Gopal Krishna Gokhale, accompanying him to the elite India Club each day. He began meeting several influential people, including members of renowned Bengali families, and wealthy patrons.

It was Gokhale who advised him to begin working for the liberation of his fellow Indians all over the world. He advised Mohandas to commence his mission by first travelling within the country so that he could acquaint himself with the condition of the poor.

Mohandas acquiesced to his mentor's advise. He soon made a short trip to Burma where he found the free spirit of its women extremely charming, but was appalled by the general indolence of men and the terrible sight of rats crawling over the country's sacred pagodas! He returned to Calcutta a few weeks later and bought a third class ticket for a week long train journey to Rajkot. Donning a Gujarati peasant-style dhoti and jacket, he boarded the train at the bustling Howrah station to begin his journey. In a sense, it was to be his first railway pilgrimage through parts of India that he had never seen before.

Surprisingly, this wasn't welcomed by Mohandas' mentor, Gopal Krishna Gokhale, for he had envisioned bigger things for his young protégé. But for Mohandas, this was more in keeping with his spartan way of life. His transformation had begun on a seat by the window in a three-tier, third class compartment, along with what had symbolically become his tool for a life that came to be synonymous with simplicity—a cheap canvas bag packed with a coarse towel, a rough blanket tucked under his arm, and a water bottle slung on his shoulder.

Standing on the crowded platform was Gokhale, immaculately dressed in a luxurious silk turban and expensive jacket, in stark contrast to the humble soldier of peace who was waving him goodbye. Mohandas clutched on to the farewell gift from his mentor; a brass tiffin packed with deep-fried *puris* and homemade *laddoos* that would hold him in good stead through the journey. As the train chugged out of the station, he fixed his gaze on the receding figure of a man he had come to acknowledge as his guru. His eyes misted over. He wouldn't see him in a long time.

For Mohandas this was a first. He had never travelled in a third class compartment before and never on a train which halted at every little station! However when the train stopped at Benares, Mohandas disembarked and after taking a dip in the sacred Ganga, he went to pay obeisance at the oldest and most revered Kashi Vishwanath temple.

The village-bazaar like atmosphere surrounding the vicinity of the holy temple of Lord Shiva shocked him. It was filthy, swarming with stray dogs, flies hovering over rotten flowers, the streets lined with wily shopkeepers operating filthy kiosks selling sweets, condiments and cheap plastic toys. Periodically, Mohandas was accosted by hordes of greedy *pandas* who mouthed dirty invectives after failing to extract money from him. Mohandas searched for the almighty God Shiva all day, but found no signs of Him in those filthy bylanes that were oozing with lucre and grime. The place nauseated him.

As the train progressed westwards through Agra, Jaipur and Palampur, stopping at each station on its way to Rajkot, Mohandas became increasingly pensive. The hard metal surfaces of the third class compartment were uncomfortable. There were no cushioned seats and no sleeping arrangements unlike the trains of Europe and South Africa that he was accustomed to. The trains were never cleaned and there were no regulations against overcrowding. The callousness of the authorities was as bad as the lack of consideration the passengers had for each other. They pushed, shouted, yelled, screamed and jostled around, unmindful of the discomfort they caused others. Half-smoked and crushed butts of *beedis*, peanut shells and chewed betel and tobacco stains made it appear like an overflowing garbage bin.

'Third class passengers are a wretched lot,' he mused sadly. 'They are worse than sheep or cattle…There is such a lack of civic sense! The only way to improve the condition of third class compartments is to encourage the educated to travel in them. People who would lead by example and protest against authorities.'

❈ ❈ ❈

For me the return to India was proving to be hectic. I had acquired a peculiar celebrity status, as the first woman from Rajkot to have travelled to a foreign land, despite the initial strictures passed on us for venturing out on that blasphemous ocean voyage. I had begun to revel in my unique and new-found acclaim. The never-ending welcoming festivities carried on even after Mohandas had left for Calcutta. For days on end I was busy entertaining visitors, narrating my adventures on the high seas and those in the distant land of South Africa. My older boys were also treated like heroes, while the younger two, "South Africa born", were hugged, extolled and pampered as if they were extraordinarily special! Yet, through this cacophony of revelry and excitement, the pain of having lost both my parents dragged me into an abysmal gloom. After I had left Rajkot with Mohandas in 1896, my parents, Gokuldas and Vrajkunwer Kapadia had departed from the world and my life forever. That pretty much severed my links with the Kapadia household and all that remained was happy childhood memories of my home in Porbandar.

I never visited my parents' home after I returned to India for I was made to believe that a daughter's link with her natal home ceases after her parents' death. Neither did my boys ever go back to Porbandar after 1901. But the ache of longing for my Ba and Bapu persisted till life tossed up bigger and tougher challenges and that great healer, TIME somewhat dulled my sense of a loss. And the memory of Ba, Bapu and Porbandar gradually faded away.

I settled back into the routine surrounded by a houseful of elders and children. In the five years we had been away, there had been two additions to the family. Nandkunwerben had given birth to two boys, almost the same age as my Ramdas and Devdas, and Gangaben had been blessed with another baby girl. We spent endless days sharing tales of birthing, teething, child rearing, the first steps taken by our children and the first words uttered; and the children found as much to do, as I did with my sisters-in-law. The older boys, happy to be with their cousins and uncles, had rediscovered the joys of a joint family life. I had not forgotten the role my brothers-in-law had played in the early years of Harilal's growing up days. I was reassured when I saw that that bond had not weakened and fourteen-year-old Harilal was quite at ease discussing his problems, apprehensions and confiding his fears to his uncles. While Mohandas had been away attending a session of the Indian National Congress in Calcutta, Harilal grabbed the opportunity to tell one of his uncles, Laxmidas about his keenness to study and his Bapu's reluctance to send him to school. Laxmidas heard his nephew patiently; the discord between father and son somewhat unnerved him, but he promised to do whatever he could to resolve it.

❃   ❃   ❃

THIRTY ONE

With each passing day, while I had comfortably adjusted into the home with my sons, Mohandas returned to Rajkot no longer the firebrand crusader that he had been in South Africa. Even as he floundered with the vast ills that plagued his motherland, he was struggling with his new identity, uncertain of the role he was expected to play.

Meanwhile, Mavji Dave, the old and trusted friend of the Gandhis who had persuaded Mohandas to go to London for a barrister's degree, referred three legal cases to him which he won with utmost ease. I took that as a propitious sign from heaven, believing that my husband's place as a successful lawyer in Rajkot had been destined by the stars.

But soon, it became clear to me that his ever-restless mind was pulling him in quite another direction. His benevolent mentor Gopal Krishna Gokhale, who in a sense had ignited the "service to motherland" spirit in Mohandas, was now compelling him to establish his legal practice in Bombay where the ageing leader lived for most part of the year. Mohandas was tempted but the memory of his failure in that forbidding city still haunted him.

Fate however, had other plans.

Mavji Dave called on Mohandas one day and declared in his authoritative voice, 'You cannot vegetate here like this, Mohandas. What good is your fancy London degree in Rajkot? You will have to go to Bombay. I insist!'

It was the command of a man in charge. Mohandas was quiet. In a low voice laden with diffidence, he said, 'Bombay is an expensive city. How will I survive there with my large family? I shall need a house and an office.' His trembling words trailed off as he lowered his eyes to the floor.

'Oh, don't you worry, Mohandas. You were made for bigger things. We shall send you legal cases from here. Why? We can even call you back here for advice, if needed.'

'Do you want to get rid of me?' Mohandas smiled nervously, his wry humour not lost on Dave.

'No, Mohandas! *Tamey shoo kahi rahya chho*? What are you saying!' Dave spat out emphatically. 'You are being wasted in this small town. Your London degree is not being put to use. Bombay is a big city. It is exploding with opportunities, Mohandas. Your love for social service and inner calling for politics will bear fruit there. Bombay will fulfil all your dreams.'

Mohandas looked Dave in the eye and smiled. By the end of July, all the requisite arrangements had been made. An office was rented in the busy Fort area of central Bombay and a small bungalow in Girgaun. We were all set to move house again.

Mohandas, the ever-dutiful son and brother had never shied away from taking charge of Gokuldas, his widowed sister's son, and began thinking of his schooling in Bombay. Meanwhile, Harilal who had been pleading with his elders for admission into a school, was now also considered as a potential candidate by his father. Mohandas zeroed in on two boarding schools—one in his home state in Gondal and the other in Benares. Since there was only one vacancy in each, the boys were asked to pick coins from a bag, and whoever got the one of higher denomination got the better school!

To Harilal's utter dismay, he picked the coin of lower value and was packed off to the lesser school in Gondal, but not without a feeling of utter dejection. I knew Mohandas had not played favourites, but Harilal felt slighted.

'Bapu is being unfair, Ba,' Harilal snuggled into my bed and whispered in my ear that night.

I could feel the pain and humiliation in his cracking voice. 'He is sending Motabhai to the better school. Why Ba? First he decides, "no school for Harilal". Then when Motabhai needs to be sent to school, I get the bad one. Sometimes I feel I'm his stepchild. He really hates me!'

I cradled my son in my arms and gathered him in a tight embrace.

'Now now, Harilal, you mustn't think like that. Bapu loves you. You are our firstborn, darling son. He loves you as much as I do.'

'No, Ba. I don't believe you,' he clung tightly to my bosom and his body heaved with sobs.

I kissed his forehead and held him close till the weeping stopped. 'Now go and wash your face, Harilal. Bapu must not see you like this. And don't forget my darling child, you did draw the lower coin from the bag, didn't you? Bapu was being more than fair!'

Harilal darted off to his room, straightening his clothes and wiping his nose on his shirtsleeve.

A twinge of sadness stabbed at my heart.

Hey Bhagwan! Don't let this fester in Harilal's mind.

I murmured after he was gone.

In early August 1902, we moved to Bombay with the younger three boys. For me this meant being uprooted all over again and a complete readjustment to life in an unfamiliar city.

Bombay with its exploding boundaries, a splendid harbour, bustling railway stations, gigantic textile mills, broad tree-lined boulevards, imposing colonial marble mansions with manicured gardens that housed the Indian royals and wealthy European nobility, was anyone's dream city. I could feel its pulsating energy in my bones as soon as I set foot there. Opulent markets bustling with wealthy people, shops stacked with expensive silks and brocades, gold and silver, beautiful jewels and lux textiles lured me.

The thought that the largest textile mill that belonged to my father was situated in Bombay, as were the homes of my brothers and some friends from Rajkot and Porbandar, made me nostalgic. But I settled into the noisy humdrum of the effervescent city, and the grim memories of my lonely days in Durban began to fade away.

However, the pangs of separation I felt at being away from Harilal kept me anxious and I prayed to god to restore the confidence and peace of my troubled fourteen year old. I lamented,

Oh Mohandas! If only you knew!

❊ ❊ ❊

THIRTY TWO

Ever since an episode of smallpox in Durban two years ago, which had left our second son Manilal with weak eyesight, Mohandas and I were always anxious about him, for he was given to falling ill easily. Just as we were moving to our house in Girgaun, Manilal took ill again; this time he contracted typhoid, which later complicated into pneumonia.

Mohandas summoned a local Parsi doctor who was of the opinion that Manilal needed a comprehensive nutrition plan to withstand the life-threatening, double onslaught and prescribed a protein-rich diet of chicken soup and eggs to boost his strength and resistance. We were already at the end of our tether tackling our son's fever and weakened lungs, and the thought of feeding him "unholy food" made us doubly distraught. My heart was bursting with fear. I held onto Mohandas' arm. 'Oh what will become of this child?' I moaned.

Mohandas took me aside. 'God is testing our faith, Kastur. We have to be calm,' he said.

'Yes I know. But what will happen to Manilal? How do we save this poor boy? Just look at him. If we don't do something fast, he is sure to die.' I began to cry.

'Kastur! Do not despair...wait.' There was a rare tenderness in his words.

'I want to carry out an experiment if you will allow me. I have read about a magical water cure that entails frequent hip baths. I have great faith in these remedies. Let me try this on Manilal. Trust me, he shall be well.'

I agreed reluctantly as Mohandas apprised the bewildered doctor of his plan.

'This hydropathic treatment was invented by a German doctor, Ludwig Kuhne. I shall be giving him several medicated hip baths through the day. He shall have no food except for the occasional sip of water or a few sips of orange juice. I know I'll be able to cure my son. But we need you to come and see him every day, Doctor *Sahab!*'

To my surprise, the Parsi doctor relented and the treatment began.

For the next three days, nothing changed. The hip baths and near starvation diet had worsened Manilal's condition. The doctor arrived each day, examined him and left after pronouncing a grim verdict. The child's health was rapidly deteriorating.

I sat by Manilal's bed all day and stayed up with him all night, but his fever showed no signs of abating. The nights were always worse, as my child had now become delirious. Soon my patience snapped. Although Mohandas refused to admit it the first time, his faith in this self-devised treatment seemed to falter. The effectiveness of his hazardous home remedy was in doubt, but Mohandas was not one to give up.

'Have patience, Kastur,' he said hesitatingly, looking into my imploring eyes. 'Don't worry. I shall make Manilal well again. I promise!'

But how could I not worry? I went about the task mechanically, assisting Mohandas while pretending to be unruffled, but my heart and mind were exploding in panic.

I shall never forgive myself or you, Mohandas. If Manilal dies, you shall have the murder of your son on your hands.

On the fourth harrowing night, I called Mohandas to the room where the dying child lay. Manilal's nails had turned blue. His breath was shallow and rapid. His face was pale and lips dry. He was babbling deliriously. His condition had worsened. I touched his burning forehead and checked his fever. It was 104 degrees Fahrenheit. I closed my eyes and began to pray,

Don't do this to me, God! You cannot snatch this innocent child away.

Mohandas' face had tensed. 'Kastur, let me give this one last try and god shall see us through,' he said earnestly.

I sat quietly with all hope lost. Mohandas undressed the child and wrapped his body in a soaking wet sheet. Next, he covered the sheet with two thick blankets leaving just his head exposed.

'Leave him there, Kastur. Just keep placing cold packs on his forehead. I am going for a walk. I need to get away.'

'Wait, Mohandas,' I held his arm agitatedly and whispered. 'Don't leave me alone with the child.' But Mohandas was gone. I heard a clock strike the hour of ten somewhere in the distance. My clammy hands felt even colder on Manilal's burning forehead.

Half a mile away, on a dark and desolate beach, an anxious Mohandas was pacing up and down, chanting the name of the Lord. His fervent prayer, a repetition of *Ram-naam* that promised to banish all fear and evil, resounded loudly in the still nightsky. After forty agonizing minutes, he headed back to the house. His nerves had somewhat steadied after the intense and continuous chant, but his heart still pounded in his chest as he made his way home.

Back in Manilal's room, I had witnessed a miracle. Just half an hour after Mohandas left, the child began to sweat profusely. I could see that his fever had come down and his delirious rambling had stopped. He had opened his eyes and a faint smile played on his lips. Relieved, I stroked his moist forehead with trembling hands, holding back my tears.

It was Manilal who first spotted his father entering the room.

'Get me out of these blankets, Bapu.' His feeble voice was barely audible. 'I'm drenched.'

Mohandas rushed to his son's bed and sat down in a heap on the floor. I looked into his eyes and saw tears brim over as he pulled the blankets off and cradled Manilal in his arms.

'Thank you, God. Thank you, Kastur, my beloved. Thank you for having faith.'

I squeezed his arm gently. He moved Manilal's head onto my lap and both of us wept.

'God is kind,' I mumbled into his ear.

❊   ❊   ❊

Soon after Manilal recovered from his tryst with near-death, we decided to move out of our dark and dingy house in Girgaon that had begun to suffocate me. We located a bungalow in Santa Cruz, in the outer suburbs of Bombay. It was roomy, airy and had a pretty little garden that was bathed in sunlight all day long. There was a market close by and a school where I imagined Manilal could be enrolled as soon as the next session began. Everything appeared so picture-perfect.

Mohandas also got accustomed to his daily commute by the local train from Santa Cruz to the city. Travelling on a first class ticket, sometimes as the only traveller in the compartment, he felt a sense of pride at being able to indulge in such luxury.

Life for us was on the upswing. Even though Mohandas did not get many court assignments or legal cases, he was earning enough money from chamber-work that enabled us to live comfortably. He often attended High Court trials while enjoying the cool sea breeze that wafted in through the windows, even as he listened intently to the routine proceedings in the halls. His benefactor, Gopal Krishna Gokhale was ever helpful, and kept a constant check on his protégé, visiting his office several times a week with friends and referrals, though he never stopped identifying "party work" that he desired Mohandas to undertake.

In the meantime, I settled comfortably in my new home. Despite my long stints in a foreign land, deep down I was a traditionalist and enjoyed mingling with my neighbours, most of whom were Gujarati-speaking Hindus from Kathiawar. I was finally rid of the pressure of flouting tradition by fraternizing with people from other castes and religions; something I had been compelled to do in Durban, which had aroused guilt pangs in me long after I returned.

But here I was a free bird, naturally adapting to roots that governed my thought and conduct.

'The orthodoxy in which I had been brought up, should never have been violated,' I had often complained to Nandkunwer in Rajkot.

'Our religion has divided the community into inflexible caste groups, with specific duties assigned to each,' she said. 'Our wise sages must have done that for a very good reason. Who are we to challenge them? But you must stop fretting, Kastur. In South Africa, you were simply being a good wife. As long as you adhere to the *dharma* of being a good wife, you can do anything that isn't forbidden by society. Your soul is pure. No sin shall accrue you.'

My sister-in-law's words had felt like balm to my anguished soul. Now as the mistress of the manor in my little abode in Santa Cruz, those painful memories, that agonizing guilt and those ethical compulsions had vanished. For the first time in many years, I felt happy and free.

✄   ✄   ✄

1902

Early in November, an urgent cablegram arrived for Mohandas from Durban with a short message.

Chamberlain expected here. Please come immediately.

Mohandas instantly understood the portent of the brief message. I learned that this was to be the first trip by a British Secretary to South Africa after the end of the Boer war, in which the Empire had been victorious.

The Indians in Natal, who had come to depend on Mohandas for all communication with the authorities, feared that Chamberlain's visit would not augur well for them. They needed Mohandas to negotiate with the government on their behalf and called upon him to honour the promise he had made before leaving South Africa.

I was in a state of near collapse. We had just about settled down to a regulated life in our new home in Bombay with Mohandas well entrenched in his legal practice. The thought of moving house all over again unnerved me.

'No, we cannot go, Mohandas! We cannot keep upsetting our lives every time there's a faint tremor in South Africa. We owe a duty to our children and I can't bear to think of disrupting their education now. Please! We cannot go. Surely there is someone else who can negotiate with the government?' My pleading voice trailed off....

'It will be a betrayal. I cannot let them down, Kastur. I had promised them, remember? If you are reluctant to come with me, then I shall have to go alone.'

My imploring eyes were fixed on his. He cupped my chin in his palms and said, 'You can stay here in Bombay, while I travel to South Africa. I'll be back soon. I won't be gone for more than a year.'

I realized that there was no point in arguing any further. There was a finite resolution in my husband's words and the matter was deemed closed.

The next day, Mohandas shot off a cable to his friend in Durban saying that he was prepared to leave as soon as they sent him the money for his ticket. Expectedly, the money arrived by return post, and Mohandas agreed to sail back to South Africa. But as the time for his departure neared, the thought of leaving us began to trouble him. He was making enough money in Bombay to meet our monthly expenses and he intended to send back the same amount from there, but what if something untoward were to happen to him? The home in Santa Cruz was on a monthly rent. My jewellery had been sold long ago. We had absolutely no savings. If he died, we would be left on the streets, starving and penniless.

Greatly agitated by the morbid prospect of his hypothesis, he tracked down an American insurance agent and bought a policy from him with a cover of ten thousand rupees. He named me the sole beneficiary of the claim, after which his mental agitation somewhat subsided.

❈ ❈ ❈

'What are you doing to me, Mohandas?' I said, pushing the large yellow envelope away. 'Are you telling me that this vile piece of paper will be my support when you are no more? Can any Hindu woman even think of a life without her husband? All our lives we pray to the almighty to spare us the agony of becoming widows and here you are standing before me, handing me this bunch of papers that promises to reimburse me with money, should you die? That too, on the eve of your departure, which has wrecked my peace?'

I burst out crying and let the file of papers fall to the ground. Mohandas stood before me, rooted to the floor. On his face was a tenderness that had never failed to assuage my ruffled nerves. He pulled me gently into his arms and turned my face upwards.

'Look here, Kastur. Look into my eyes and stop crying. I am not being cruel. Nor am I trying to scare you. But you have to live alone and look after the children while I am gone. Be practical, my beloved.'

He was stroking my damp, chafed cheeks with his fingers as I buried my face into his chest.

'Death does not warn before it strikes. It can happen to anyone, anywhere and I cannot be a fool, living in denial, leaving you here alone and unprotected like this. Keep this file carefully and do stop crying. You are weakening my resolve. Now…now, Kastur. All will be well.'

Mohandas brushed my eyes with his fingertips. I pulled away. Mohandas smiled. He handed the policy papers back to me and left. I sat there on a divan in the living room, clutching the envelope that held the lifeline to my security, should destiny and god decide to play a dirty trick on me. I had to fight hard to refrain myself from tearing it to bits and flushing it down the toilet. I mumbled to myself,

Give me an insurance against WIDOWHOOD if you can. That is what I want! Not this! Give me that indemnity, Mohandas, if you are so prescient! Not this silly piece of paper that guarantees me a tidy sum to tide over my widowhood should you die!

During the last days before his departure, Mohandas was immersed in settling all his pending legal matters. Other problems had also cropped up. Harilal had not adjusted to the school at Gondal. The hostel was below ordinary and the teaching of a very low standard. His long absence from India made him lag behind in class and he missed being with his father and me. As a result, Mohandas had to pull him out of school and pack him off to Rajkot to live at home with his uncle Laxmidas and a houseful of cousins. However, Gokuldas continued with his schooling as a boarder in Benares. A few days later, Mohandas invited a relative to move into our Santa Cruz bungalow to keep me company.

Twenty-three-year old Chaganlal Gandhi, who was working as a clerk in a firm in Bombay, moved in with his wife Kashiben and his son, who was a little younger than my Ramdas and Devdas; so for me it was a full house. I would grow to love Kashiben and my sons got on famously with her son. Also, Chaganlal offered to give tuitions to Manilal in his spare time, which was a great relief for me.

Meanwhile, Mohandas had collected a group of his young relatives to accompany him to Natal. With the hope of finding their fortunes in South Africa, this youthful lot of enterprising Gandhis set off with him to lend him a hand for the Natal Indian Congress. Nineteen-year-old Maganlal Gandhi, the younger brother of Chaganlal, happened to be the first amongst the chosen ones. The two brothers had grown up with us under the care of Karamchand and Putli Ba after their father Kushaldas had been orphaned at a very tender age. Mohandas' parents had brought him up as their own son long before Mohandas was born. Kushaldas Gandhi was the first man in Kathiawar to have completed his high school and always remained a role model for his younger cousin, Mohandas.

That night a familiar restlessness crept up in me again. Mohandas could have easily chosen to take Harilal with him instead. I knew that Harilal would be equally agitated if he heard what his father had done. I spent a sleepless night in my bed, fretting for and commiserating with my absent son who was being inadvertently penalized by his ever-benevolent, self-sacrificing father to whom no one was more equal than the other; or rather everyone was more equal than his own son.

Alas! The seed of discrimination, the very tenet that Mohandas strove to demolish all his life had germinated in his distant, neglected and hapless firstborn. And, that square yellow envelope continued to haunt me as Mohandas slept blissfully in the next room completely oblivious of the conflicting forces that had destroyed my sanity.

In the second week of November 1902, Mohandas sailed out of Bombay harbour, a happy man. Content with all the arrangements he had made for us, he stood on the deck of the steamer watching the receding shore as the cool breeze tousled his hair. He had one thought foremost in his mind…

I'll be back in Bombay before the year ends!

How wrong was he!

※   ※   ※

THIRTY THREE

For us, life in the Santa Cruz home carried on at a comfortable pace. I was happy to be with the boys, Chaganlal, Kashiben and her son, but I missed my Harilal. Living without Mohandas was painful enough and I had accepted that his driving passion for social service would always surpass his need for us. But living away from Harilal was like a throbbing wound.

The thought of my teenaged son, alone and abandoned by his father, separated from me and his siblings wrenched my heart. I longed to hear the peals of his carefree laughter to watch that naughty twinkle in his eyes that so reminded me of Mohandas. He was such an uncanny replica of his father, a miniature of the paternal mould. How was I to know that there was a wound festering deep in his heart that came from a feeling of being discarded by his parents. More so, because the hostel at Gondal had been a suffocating, horrific experience. There was no doubt that he felt better off at home in Rajkot with his Mota bapu— Laxmidas and other relatives, but I knew that Harilal yearned for us. How unfortunate was his lot? The firstborn, eldest of four Gandhi boys, but the most neglected by Mohandas and by default, me.

In January 1903, just a few months after Mohandas had left for Durban, Laxmidas decided to get Harilal engaged. He thought Gulab, the lovely, nubile eleven-year-old daughter of Haridas Vohra was a perfect match for my fourteen year old Harilal. The Vohras were of the Modh-Bania caste and had close ties with the Gandhis, so Gulab's parents readily agreed to the betrothal of their little "Rose" to my son.

Harilal was in Rajkot when his Mota bapu informed him of his betrothal. The *akshat-kumkum* ceremony to formalize the future union of the two, was swiftly organized, much to the astonishment of Harilal. He knew nothing of the girl he was to marry and I wished either Mohandas or I could have been there by his side during the ceremony. But Mohandas, who had been informed about the engagement, had shown no excitement at the auspicious occasion. He wrote to his brother Laxmidas,

Principally, I am against child marriages. Therefore, I am unable to feel any happiness on Harilal's marriage. The question of his marriage is immaterial and of no importance. These days I have stopped thinking of Harilal as my son.

My heart froze when I heard the cruel words of that missive. Sitting in faraway Bombay, the innocent face of Harilal, his imploring eyes, loomed into my head. I dreaded to think of Harilal's reaction to his Bapu's letter.

How did Mohandas presume that a young, teenaged boy could comprehend the hidden, albeit altruistic meaning in his father's words? Although I was distraught, I understood that my husband had not meant to be hurtful; that Harilal was indeed his own blood, but Mohandas was driven by a zeal that made him look at several as his own sons.

For the moment I pushed my anguish away and tried to align myself with the joys of a fulfilling and bright future for Harilal, conjoined with his beautiful, Gulab. A warm glow engulfed my heart. I lit a *diya* before my family deity and thanked the Lord profusely.

'Do not despair, Harilal!' I said aloud. 'Ba will be with you soon and cradle your lovely Rose in her lap, to bless the both of you. Don't despair, my son, for I shall always be with you.'

✖ ✖ ✖

By the time autumn descended on the subcontinent, a letter from Mohandas threw everything into disarray yet again. It had been twelve months since he had left us and now we were being summoned forthwith to join him in South Africa. There was no indication of how long we would have to stay there or if we were to return to India at all. I was instructed to leave Harilal behind so as not to disrupt his studies. Moreover, Harilal had just about adjusted to the school in Rajkot and I took pride in the fact that most people regarded him as an intellectually gifted boy. His new-found keenness to study pleased me and somewhat took the edge off my earlier anxiety. I consoled myself,

Laxmidas will be a good father to him. There is no point obstructing what destiny had ordained.

In the days before we were to set sail, I was gripped by the painful realization that I would be parting with Chaganlal and Kashiben. I did not know when I would see them again. As Kashiben helped me with my packing and the time for our departure grew closer, the thought of abandoning her family and my Harilal grew more intense. Other uncertainties began to plague me. Travelling alone with three boys across the seas was daunting enough and Mohandas' letters made me aware that South Africa had rapidly changed since we had last been there. I would no longer be living in Durban or Natal as he had set up practice in Transvaal, a place that was known to be hostile to Indians. The thought of leaving my comfortable nest in Santa Cruz for Transvaal was forbidding. I braced myself and collected my wits about me, all set to board the ship that would set sail in the next few days for the second time – to commence yet another tumultuous phase of my life.

Harilal's absence bore a painful hole in my heart.

Forgive me, son! Ba has no choice in this matter, but she loves you the most of all...

Alas! My silent plea could not touch the heart of Harilal. Were all mothers cursed with a lifetime of worry? Like a torch handed down by generations to blaze the trail of human frailties and fret over the welfare of our produce, was mine also to be a life-sentence of pain?

I sailed for South Africa with a heavy heart!

❊　❊　❊

Thirty Four

1904

I reached the familiar shores of South Africa this time with the three boys in tow. The tiring journey during which Ramdas had fractured his arm playing board games with the Captain, felt nothing like the stormy one we had encountered the first time. The doctor on the ship had put his arm in a sling and had told me to get it attended to by a competent doctor, as soon as we landed.

This sparsely populated place held no fascination for me that day. My mind was filled with apprehension about the broken arm of little Ramdas who bore a stoic grin on his innocent face.

Johannesburg was a city I had never visited before. A city inhabited by alien people who spoke an alien language that was not English. As soon as we set foot in the city which was carved onto the slopes of Witwatersrand Mountain, some 300 miles north-west of Durban, I was stupefied. To me the memories of Bombay, my secure little bungalow on the beach in Santa Cruz with its familiar sounds and a landscape that reflected in the soft patina of its artistic vista, were in sharp contrast to the unfinished gold-rich mountains that gripped the pulsating city in its rugged bosom.

Mohandas had rented a large eight-bedroom house in Kensington, the European part of the city. It would be a while before I could give up my independent life to settle down in my new home. But first, Ramdas needed medical intervention.

⁂

Harilal had first set eyes on Gulab when he was sixteen years old. They had been engaged for two years, but he had never met her before. He had only seen her photograph on the day of their bethrothal. Dressed in a rich brocade turban, a silk kurta and a sparkling white cotton dhoti with a narrow red border, he looked a fine replica of his father, thin-faced, intense, and bubbling with the exciting prospect of being wed. Laxmidas, Mota bapu to him, and Aunt Gokiphoi were conducting the rituals like adoring surrogate parents. Gulab's father placed a coconut in Harilal's lap and a silver coin in his hand. He draped an intricately woven silk *chaadar* around his shoulders, applied vermillion on his forehead with his right thumb and stuck some dry rice grains on it. Harilal's eyes lit up with joy. The attention he was getting was a rare thrill and his heart filled up with sweet longings to be with the pretty girl, Gulab, whom he would not see for a long time. The absence of his Bapu and Ba stabbed at his heart. He would have wanted them to conduct the most crucial ritual of his life, and he yearned to be with his younger siblings that day, but the thought of Gulab wiped out all other misgivings and he surrendered to the ecstasy of the moment.

Laxmidas and Gokiben had acted on their own accord. They were the elders, I had no say in the matter, and Mohandas did not have the time to worry about things back home in Rajkot, least of all Harilal's marriage. I swallowed one more bitter pill like many others in the past, wishing him well, blessing my sweet Gulab whom I had only seen as an infant from afar. I consoled myself,

It won't be long before we shall all be united.

'Harilal is a lucky child,' Mota bapu said to Gokiphoi, 'Kastur and Mohandas should be happy.' The ceremony ended and the matter closed.

For two long years, Harilal had been engrossed in a strange new world of his own; one that was filled with merriment, laughter, colour, romance and his lovely Gulab. He had often walked past the Vohra home, loitering near the gate, sneaking a peep inside the house to catch a glimpse of his beloved and then laugh loudly at his impatience!

I won't even recognize her if she came before me—there are so many girls in there....

But the fire in him burned on, passionately. Cousin Gokuldas had once shown him a framed photograph of Gulab, in which she sat on a straight-backed, high chair, flanked by her parents. She held a flower in her hands and wore a long chain around her neck. Harilal gazed at the innocent girl in the frame for a long time. He stared deep into her kohled eyes that were fringed with long lashes, his heart hammering inside his chest.

'Look, Gokulbhai—Gulab flutters her lashes when I look at her. Her eyes talk to me, Gokulbhai!' Harilal pressed the frame close to his heaving chest and closed his eyes. In that moment, he felt Gulab's tiny, slender arms wrap around him. It was a moment that he wanted to stretch into eternity.

A few months later, Harilal was struck by a severe bout of typhoid. He ran a very high fever that did not break for many days and he became delirious. Gokiphoi and Mota bapu decided to move him into the Vohra home as they believed he would get better nursing by his in-laws, since there was no one else competent to tend to him at the Gandhi household.

⁂

When I reached our rented house in Johannesburg, Ramdas was in severe pain and the temporary sling on his arm had fallen off. The overhanging anxiety of setting up a new household again, sharing it with strangers and adhering to Mohandas' weird notions of schooling for the boys, their diet, self-devised tips for good health among other things, was compounded by Ramdas' excruciating pain.

'We need to show him to a good doctor,' I told Mohandas nervously. 'He is in unbearable pain and I fear if it is not set right immediately, the broken bone will make his arm crooked.'

But Mohandas already had other plans in place.

'I am going to treat him myself, Kastur. The mud pack treatment is a foolproof method, remember? We had used it on Manilal when he was critically ill.'

My heart lurched into my dry mouth and I felt my hands tremble, but I was silent. Each day thereafter, I held Ramdas tenderly while his father unwrapped bandages off the broken arm and after applying freshly-made poultices of mud, bandaged it up again. To my amazement the pain gradually eased away and my skepticism vanished. Ramdas' arm had begun to heal. My trust in Mohandas' home remedies was reinforced yet again.

By now I had settled into my new home, set up my kitchen, located the best markets in the neighbourhood and made friends with a few other Indian women. What was most reassuring was that plans to find schools for the three boys were underway and even though the gnawing pain of being far away from Harilal never left me, I found myself settling comfortably into a routine.

While dusting the rooms one day, my gaze travelled to a framed photograph that I had brought with me from Bombay. It had been a sultry September day. Just a few days earlier, Mohandas had sent word that he would not be returning to India and he wanted me to come with the boys to South Africa. All three except my Harilal were told to be there. I had put on my best Parsi silk sari with a narrow embroidered border, a long sleeved blouse with pretty lace cuffs, brown buckle-up shoes and knitted socks and the boys were dressed in formal black, button-down suits, shiny shoes and socks. We had traipsed off to the best photography studio in the Fort area of Bombay to capture a family portrait that would freeze that "happy family" moment for posterity.

The frame had me in the centre, my eyes serene and posture erect. On the left was three-year-old Devdas, perched on a high wooden pedestal wearing a white cap. My right arm rested on his knee. Eleven-year-old Manilal, staring into the camera intently, stood in front of a carved pedestal on which Devdas was seated. On my right sat five-year-old Ramdas on a stool. His head came up till my upper arm, and standing right behind him, wan-faced, intense and sober, was Harilal. The photographer had captured each person in the frame, perfectly. The sight of Harilal in the picture sent a stab into my heart. The resemblance to his father was unmistakable but his wistful eyes had a sadness that resonated with the pain I was feeling in that surreal moment.

Oh Mohandas! If only you knew how painful it is to be denied the love of a father. If only your heart could beat for Harilal the way mine does!

❃   ❃   ❃

Thirty Five

South Africa had changed drastically. The British victory in the Boer war had failed to bring any relief for the Indian community. Even though they had been staunchly loyal to the Crown and had been hailed as "Sons of the Empire", the cruelties and indignities heaped on the Indians by the British, showed no signs of abating.

As soon as Mohandas arrived in Durban he was whisked away by his friends to meet Joseph Chamberlain, the British Colonial Secretary.

'We do not interfere in the affairs of the colonies,' Chamberlain had said dismissively. 'If you choose to live amongst the Europeans, you must try and win their confidence yourselves.' His abrupt response dashed the burgeoning hopes of the Indian community to the ground.

Shaken up rudely, they confronted Mohandas—'Just look at them,' they ranted. 'You had said they will be more sympathetic towards us if we cooperate with them.'

Clearly Mohandas had erred. He had misjudged the attitude of the British bureaucracy but his faith in British justice was undeterred, so he resolved to take up the cause of his fellowmen, this time in Transvaal.

He set up a legal practice in the pulsating city of Johannesburg, which was inhabited by over twelve thousand Indians, and applied for admission to the Supreme Court, which was accepted. His progress thereafter was rapid and encouraging.

Some time later, dining at a vegetarian restaurant in the city, Mohandas came across a number of like-minded people that made his life in Johannesburg comfortable and trouble free. It was here that a deep friendship grew between him and

Hermann Kallenbach, a wealthy, German Jew. An architect who was a liberal thinker, Kallenbach was a vegetarian, a theosophist and a scholar of Buddhism. With so much in common, their friendship flourished and for Mohandas, a deep emotional dependence developed subsequently.

Kallenbach indulged Mohandas. Through his good office he met a very influential property agent called, Louis W. Ritch who was a senior leader of the Theosophical Society of Johannesburg. Ritch helped him to locate office premises in the legal quarters of the city, a privilege that no Indian had had so far, in the imposing precincts of Risik Street.

By now, Mohandas was all poised to commence his onslaught on the authorities in Transvaal. He gradually made successful inroads into their bastion by exposing the ill-treatment meted out to Indians and after a few judgements in his favour, the Indian community reposed complete trust in him. They were now overly confident that the firebrand young barrister from Bombay would not fail them; he would steer them out of their misery after all.

Very soon Mohandas gained the reputation of a leading lawyer at par with any of his European counterparts. His practice was booming and was far more lucrative than it had ever been in Durban.

❇   ❇   ❇

Although life in Johannesburg was on the upswing, Mohandas was torn between his familial responsibilities and his commitment to public service. Thoroughly immersed as he was in his spiritual and intellectual pursuits, as well as professional obligations, he had to postpone his plans to return to India indefinitely. He continued to live in a tiny, sparsely furnished apartment behind his office, redirecting all his energies and his surplus funds towards his impassioned cause.

A little while later, Madanjit Vyavharik, a Gujarati businessman in Natal, the proprietor of the first Indian printing press in South Africa, asked him to start a weekly newspaper for the Indian community. Mohandas had always believed in the supreme power of the printed word, and jumped right into the venture promising to write and also lend financial support. That gave birth to the *Indian Opinion* that made its debut in June 1903. In order to enhance its initial outreach, four different language editions in English, Gujarati, Hindi and Tamil were set into motion, which later petered down to just English and Gujarati. Thereafter, the newspaper managed to spearhead Mohandas' innermost ambitions.

At last, the Indian community had found a voice to express themselves and a platform to share their grievances and the *Indian Opinion* succeeded in uniting them further for a common goal.

Thirty-four year old Mohandas who was at the peak of his career as a practicing barrister, a revered Indian leader and part owner of a widely circulated newspaper, had become a name to reckon with across South Africa. It was time to be united with his family that constantly hankered to be with him, so he rented that plush eight-bedroom bungalow before shooting off a cable that summoned all of us except poor Harilal, to Johannesburg.

⚥ ⚥ ⚥

In the dusty bylanes of Rajkot, dotted by lush green trees and clusters of white houses that packed an exploding Gujarati populace, romance was blossoming in the adolescent heart of Harilal. Egged on by cousin Gokuldas, Harilal could barely contain the thrill of knowing that not too far away in another part of the city dwelt a nubile, pretty little rose, who was betrothed to him barely a few months ago. They had never met but those haunting eyes in that mesmerizing photograph had sucked his soul right out of his body.

'Gulab—my Gulab,' the intonation of those two syllables sent his pulse racing to a dizzying pace. His heaving chest would rise and fall in resonance, till he became one quivering mass of sound and emotion. Gokuldas would egg him on—'I know what you are thinking, Harilal. But she's not going to be yours just yet.'

Or sometimes—'I saw Gulab today, Harilal. She's so innocent, so beautiful, but she won't even recognize you,'—slapping his back in jest, Gokuldas would scamper out, with Harilal racing behind him.

'Show me where, Gokulbhai? Where was she? Can I see her too? Please take me to her, will you?'

And so the banter carried on.

But each night in his dreams, those dark smouldering eyes, fringed by a row of long curling lashes, would flutter like butterfly wings and stir the deep recesses of his mind. In that instant Harilal would forget that he had been abandoned by Ba, Bapu and his brothers who had left him in the care of Gokiphoi and Mota bapu to fight his private demons. For now, that sweet throbbing painful space had filled with the ever smiling image of his darling Gulab.

Till typhoid struck!

Thirty Six

Mohandas had a hectic routine in Johannesburg. Setting out early morning for work on his bicycle, or sometimes on foot, he would return in time for dinner, often accompanied by colleagues or friends to enjoy my home-cooked Gujarati meals. Each night after dinner, he stayed up preparing his briefs, writing articles for the *Indian Opinion*, which were regularly sent off to Durban, for publishing. Most often he slept alone on his office divan, and I found him to be distracted and somewhat aloof. The sad realization had long dawned on me that I was no longer the centre of his universe and the sexual power that most women hold over their men, had in my case, grievously diminished.

Mohandas' commitment to his cause was solely focussed on the *Indian Opinion*, an enterprise that had him stretch his resources to a breaking point. He was determined to turn it into a profitable venture for he dreaded the humiliation the Indian community would face in the wake of a closure. I had no way of knowing that most of his savings had been sunk into the *Indian Opinion* and he was paying a sum of seventy-five pounds sterling every month, to sustain it.

One balmy March evening, a few months after we had settled into our home in Johannesburg, I got a message from Mohandas that left me bewildered. He wasn't coming home for dinner and would only return the next morning. Something did not sound right. A mild anxiety arose within me but I pushed it aside, had an early dinner with the boys, finished with the day's chores and went to bed. For a long while, sleep eluded me. The unsettling thought of Harilal, all by himself in Rajkot, haunted me. The all-consuming guilt of being a mother in absentia was eating at my vitals.

✂ ✂ ✂

The dreaded Black Plague had broken out in South Africa, about which Mohandas had learned from his associates at the *Indian Opinion*. He came home the next day, grim faced, to tell me of the disaster that had befallen the Indian community. Twenty-three people were already stricken and given the highly contagious nature of the disease that struck and killed with the speed of lightning a lot more were likely to be afflicted. Moreover, bad sanitation, rotting garbage on the streets and the cities' overflowing gutters were ideal breeding grounds for the looming epidemic. The situation was compelling enough for Mohandas to swing into action and all of us got sucked into the need to check the spread of the incurable and terrifying pestilence.

The Black Plague breakout of 1904 had a deep impact on Mohandas, the boys and me. It also touched several Europeans whose lives overlapped with ours and that drew them onto a common platform to address the travails of the local Indian community.

Little Manilal and I found ourselves a vital part of the core community service group. He would accompany me to the affected areas where I would speak with all the women, instilling in them the awareness of how to combat the contagion and prevent its spread. We occupied an empty building that was converted into a makeshift hospital, and then quarantined the premises for the safety of others, thereby working closely with Mohandas.

Perhaps for the first time in all these years, Mohandas saw a woman in me that he had failed to recognize before. He could no longer overlook the unique ability I possessed to work with and inspire other women on my own. He could no longer deny that I was also a force to reckon with and was as committed to his cause and ideals as he was, and with the same zeal.

But sadly, he had missed the point. I was not emulating him in his predefined passions and goals, I was merely being loyal to the essence of my calling and soul, a truth that he would never know.

❊ ❊ ❊

Life returned to normal after the plague abated and the family settled back at home. It was time to focus on the boys' education. Mohandas continued to be adamant about teaching them himself.

He believed that he could impart better education than any school in South Africa and so prevailed his unconventional methods, as before.

Every morning Manilal and Ramdas accompanied him on a five-mile walk to his office during which they were given tuitions. Even in their father's office, the boys were kept engaged with reading and writing assignments while Mohandas went about his business. The trek back to the house in the afternoon was utilized to review all that they had learned that morning. Although I was far from happy with this unconventional system of education that Mohandas had devised, it was reassuring to see that the boys spent a good part of the day in close proximity to their father.

Mohandas was a strict disciplinarian. On one occasion when twelve-year-old Manilal had forgotten to carry his spectacles to the office, a need that had arisen after his bout of smallpox five years ago that had impaired his vision, Mohandas ordered him to walk back home those five miles to fetch them. At midday I saw the tired, bedraggled boy stomp into the house, almost in tears. He crumpled on to the sofa breathing heavily, without uttering a word. 'Bapu is cruel, Ba!' he blurted out after a while. 'Would anyone be so heartless as to make his son trek five miles to fetch a pair of glasses that he had forgotten? So what, Ba? Anyone can make a mistake. Don't you make mistakes? And Bapu…he's not perfect…either.' His voice trailed off into a long chain of sobs as I cradled his head into my bosom, wiping his tears with my sari's *pallu*.

'Manilal, you are a big boy now. You are strong like your Bapu. And he means well, son. Now stop crying and have your lunch. I have made your favourite *daal* and *dhokla*. Come now! Eat it before it gets cold. And hurry. You have to get back to the office or Bapu will be cross.'

I sat across him on the dining table, while he gulped down his favourite food, wiping his eyes on his shirtsleeve.

'Manilal! I know Bapu is sometimes too demanding of you. But son, never forget that Bapu loves you very much and would want only the best for you.'

Manilal looked up at me. The pain in his eyes had not receded and I doubt if my pleading words had penetrated his senses at that moment.

I told him at length about Mohandas' fastidiousness with me. I narrated the horrific chamber pot incident after which I had nearly been thrown out of the house. I told him how I had lashed out at his father, provoking him to an even more violent outburst and how I had finally backed down because I had realized the gravity of his convictions.

'Your father is a good man, Manilal. He wants you to be a good son and that is why he is hard on you at times.'

I pulled Manilal into my arms, and stroked his untidy hair.

'You are a good son, Manilal. Your father knows that and expects a great deal from you. Now go, hurry up. Wash your face and run back to office. Your father will be anxious if you are late.'

Manilal sprang out of my lap, rushed into his room and a few minutes later darted out of the front door.

'Don't forget your glasses, son!' I lilted after him, but he was gone.

I leaned back onto the sofa, my thoughts trailing Manilal's steps as he sprinted back to his father's office. The little boy's pride had been bruised. He would need tender and careful handling all the time, which would not be difficult for me. I was always around. But my Harilal? Far, far away, living alone without his brothers and parents; how was he coping with the savage onslaught of life? I had no way of knowing. Letters from India took as long as sixty days to reach us. That he had changed schools since we had left India was the last thing I had heard. Apparently he was lagging behind in class so it had been necessary, but there had been no news after that. I consoled myself in my ignorance.

He's a very bright child. God watches over him when his mother can't. All should be well!

Yet my anxiety never lessened.

How was I to know that Harilal had been stricken by a bad bout of typhoid fever.

❈   ❈   ❈

THIRTY SEVEN

As planned by Gokiphoi and her brother, Laxmidas, Harilal moved into the Vohras' home to recuperate from typhoid.

In the distance he spotted her. The sweet, innocent, doe-eyed beauty, shy and diffident, was hiding behind the dense profusion of colour and fragrance. The miniature bells around her ankles jingled sweetly as she darted from side to side, unaware of his penetrating gaze. Harilal stood rooted to the spot. The pretty gazelle pranced in solitary abandon, her dark billowing hair cascaded to her knees, swaying in rhythm with her silent song. Harilal moved forward slowly. Captivated by the serene beauty of his sweet Gulab, he was pulled towards her by a force that only love can steer. The fair countenance, her ruby-red lips, those shell-shaped ears and her tiny upturned nose could not have been more perfect. The thrill of being so close to his beloved stirred the core of his heart. He held his arms up and called out to her –

'Come to me, my sweet Rose – your rightful place is in my arms and I enclose in my reach the immortal rush of eternity.'

All of a sudden she spotted him and froze. Her cheeks flushed a shade of red. She lowered her eyes and covered her face with her bright yellow "chunni". Harilal was beside her. He swirled her around and pulled her into him, placing his parched lips onto her half-opened mouth. It was their first kiss. He looked at her closed eyes and kissed her again.

'You are burning with fever,' she uttered in broken gasps. He pushed her head back and planted another deep, lingering kiss on her lips again.

'Oh Gulab, how I had yearned to taste the sweet nectar from your lips, to hold you, to hold you in my arms, to feel your milky white

skin against mine…but you are sweeter than the sweetest rose, softer than the softest white lily. I shall never let you go…'

A cool hand on his brow awakened him. He opened his eyes and saw Gulab by his bedside, looking deep into his eyes. 'What were you mumbling? I heard you call my name…'

But Harilal was too delirious, both with the thrilling touch of Gulab's hands on his feverish brow and the beautiful apparition that stood before him, bending over his bed. Her silky long tresses caressed his gaunt cheeks. Harilal was ecstatic. He had to fight the strong temptation of crushing her to him that instant.

'I do love you, my beloved,' he mumbled. Harilal had become a slave to those smouldering eyes. 'You shall soon be mine, my lovely rose!' Gulab blushed. She shrank into herself, lowering her thick eyelashes that had fanned out on her reddened cheeks. A smile played on her lips as she turned her face and stole away. The lingering scent of Gulab's body stayed with Harilal all day, and his fever never abated.

It was the typhoid which had drained him. His eyes had sunk into their sockets and the skin of his face had turned morbidly ashen. Yet this was the first time in his life that the absence of his Ba and Bapu had not flung him into a lonely abyss of despair. For once Harilal felt overwhelmed by the exploding love he had received from his future in-laws. And the thought of Gulab, who tiptoed into his room every hour just to touch his cheek or brow or bring in a tray laden with bland semi-solid food cooked by her mother, was enough for him to hang on to his thread of life—the life of an adolescent who was maddened by the love he felt for his sweet Gulab.

Gulab would come to him several times each day. She would sometimes just smile and stare at him. Sometimes she would speak a few words and place her palm on his burning forehead. One night as Harilal lay on his bed, staring out of the window, he heard the rustle of her footsteps and her sweet voice wafted into his ears.

'Are you awake?'

Harilal was scared. What if someone saw her with him at that hour?

Gulab smiled again, that sweet unrestrained infectious smile.

'I'm going to be your wife…who can say anything to me?'

She pouted as her voice trailed into a melody of tinkling sounds and she placed her hands on his mouth to silence him.

'Bapu says you will be going back home soon. Will you?'

Harilal couldn't tear his gaze away…he felt his illness vanish.

'I am alive because of you, Gulab. Your nursing and prayers have saved me.'

'No no, don't say that. I am your slave, my lord. I shall wait for you forever. You are my moon and I pray to God to unite us soon.'

Gulab was startled by a sound at the door. She quietly darted away.

Indeed she was a divine gift from heaven for she had eased his aching solitude. The endless hours of yearning to be with his Bapu and me had now been replaced by the tinkling sounds of Gulab's laughter; the heady fragrance of the jasmines in her hair and the sweet words she uttered every time she saw him.

'You will be well….and I shall be beside you, never fear…'

It was that reassurance, that spring-well overflowing with pure love that nursed him back to life. A new Harilal had emerged from this cocoon of his childhood, unshackling his demons, a free and fearless young boy dyed in the vibrant colours of virgin love. Life looked beautiful and rosy and walking hand in hand with his sweet Gulab, he would surely conquer the universe.

✄ ✄ ✄

I had been unduly restless the week before the letter from Rajkot had reached Johannesburg, informing us about Harilal's illness. I had woken up many times during those nights with unexplained bouts of cold sweat. I paced up and down the hall, not knowing what had disrupted my peace, but deep down inside I knew all was not well with Harilal.

It was a bit of a relief when I heard that he was down with typhoid and had been shifted to Gulab's home. The sweet little bride-to-be could take my place and nurse him out of his agony. The infinite power of love was stronger than the mightiest power of the universe and I never doubted for even one moment that she would lead him out of his living hell. I prayed fervently,

God be with them. Let my Harilal grow up to be the man he is meant to be.

The firstborn son of Mohandas was made for excellence. He would do his Bapu proud. I reassured myself.

Harilal left the Vohra home in the pink of health, with lightness in his heart and a new spring in his step. Every moment of his day was spent in replaying the sweet nothings that Gulab had whispered into his ears. He played back every little occurrence, every trivial exchange, every touch, every glance of hers that drove him to dizzying heights of ecstasy, all day long. His school and books had no place in this continuing cloud of euphoria and all he could do was pine for and write long passionate letters to his lady love, to which she responded with matching vigour.

I cannot sleep a wink. My mind is filled with the scent of your body. The time since I kissed you last seems like an aching stretch of passion and longing. The sun sets and rises again and I wait. My heart fills up with more longing and pain. The distance between us is strangling me. I can't breathe. Every time I close my eyes, I yearn to wake up in your arms. Those love-tinted doe-eyes haunt me endlessly. When I think of you and the first time I set eyes on you, I want to fall in love with you over and over again…Come to me, my little Rose, your Harilal is nothing without you…

The wait to be united with her was torturous and he counted each day aching and longing to hold her again in his arms as his wife.

But life has a savage way of smashing dreams and disrupting plans.

❃   ❃   ❃

'I am sending for Harilal,' one morning Mohandas said to me. 'He should come to South Africa since he is lagging behind in his studies and has no interest in school. It may do him good to be with the boys and us, Kastur.'

I was seized by instant lightness in my heart. At last those restless nights of vigil, of constantly worrying about Harilal would come to an end and I would be at peace, united with my precious son.

But outside the secure confines of our home, things were anything but peaceful. Disturbing reports about the poor management of the *Indian Opinion* had been pouring in and the newspaper had run up enormous debts. The co-founder of the newspaper had quit and was on his way back to India. Mohandas had to take immediate steps to salvage the situation.

While boarding a train to Durban, his newfound friend Henry Polak came to bid him goodbye and presented him a book by John Ruskin titled *Unto this Last*.

This book was to drastically alter Mohandas' life thereafter.

Mohandas sat up all night in the train devouring Ruskin's book that had him totally enthralled, and by the time the train chugged into Durban station twelve hours later, Mohandas was a converted man. Determined to change his life in accordance with the ideals of John Ruskin's book—which not only reflected his innermost thoughts but also laid out the precepts of the Hindu *dharma*—his mind travelled back to life in the quiet little model village that he had seen in Natal many years ago. The idyllic peaceful settlement with its own gardens, mill, school and even a printing press where everyone would work like one harmonious family, became his new dream.

So inspired was he by the "Ruskin Model", that he decided to move the office and press of the *Indian Opinion* to the countryside. He dreamt of a perfect cooperative—a self-sufficient village community that would be drawn upon to fulfill his socialistic dream. Not everyone in the staff of the *Indian Opinion* however, shared Mohandas' enthusiasm, but the key handlers of the press were as excited as he was, so they agreed to go along with the plan.

Soon a landowner in the vicinity of a railway station in Durban was identified. He had a sugarcane field just eighteen miles outside the city, in a place called Phoenix and offered Mohandas twenty acres of fertile farmland with a natural spring and orchards of orange, mango and guava trees for a total cost of one thousand pounds. Some eighty-odd acres of adjoining uncultivated land was also thrown in with the offer and the deal was sealed.

Barely two days after reading John Ruskin's book, Mohandas' dream, a rare combination of pragmatism and idealism, had come to fruition.

The news of Mohandas' efforts to rescue and save the *Indian Opinion* spread like wildfire throughout the community and help began pouring in from all quarters. Working tirelessly from dawn to dusk each day, living out of makeshift tents amongst snake-infested trees and wild grasslands, the sheds were completed in a record time of three weeks. Thereafter, the next phase of laying out roads, digging canals for irrigation and cultivation of the land began.

In the month of November in 1904, the printing press was moved to Phoenix and after a host of usual teething problems the first issue of a newly-launched *Indian Opinion*, all neatly folded and stacked in bundles, found its way two-and-a-half miles down to Phoenix station. With the printing press functioning officially, it was time now for Mohandas to focus on the development of the settlement.

❈ ❈ ❈

Right from the time the community of simple mud huts with thatched roofs had been conceived, Mohandas had planned to gradually retire from his law practice in Johannesburg and move his family to Phoenix. But since the running costs of the press were solely dependant on the subsidies donated by him, he couldn't afford to wind up his legal practice just yet. He divided most of his time between frequent visits to the settlement, where he worked on the construction of a simple dwelling for himself, and his law office in Johannesburg. And for months, I kept the home running while he struggled to turn his dream into reality.

Meanwhile Henry Polak, who was astounded by the effect Ruskin's book had had on the young and spirited Mohandas, also moved to Phoenix and took charge as editor of the *Indian Opinion*. Mohandas' joy knew no bounds. I felt that his infinite capacity to inspire, influence and win loyalty from strangers had set him a class apart from others of his ilk. It made my chest swell with pride to think that I was indeed the wife of an extraordinary man, but the niggling thoughts of an abandoned Harilal, dampened my euphoria yet again.

Not long after, our house in Johannesburg filled up with friends and associates whom Mohandas had invited to stay with us. I was accustomed to sharing space with young Indian law clerks, but now Henry Polak, who had earlier left Phoenix to work in the law firm, and his wife Millie also moved in and I found myself quite happy and comfortable in their company.

Language problems notwithstanding, Millie Polak was warm and affable. She shared the household chores and kitchen-duties, with Mohandas often acting as our translator. She soon began teaching me some conversational English and we became one happy family with an efficiently running household.

❋   ❋   ❋

Back home in Rajkot, Harilal was gripped by exhilaration of another kind. Mohandas' missive had sent him into a trance. He couldn't believe his Bapu had actually asked him to come to South Africa, but he was torn between his deep yearning to be with the family and the prospect of parting with his beloved Gulab. How tenderly she had nursed him and brought him back from the jaws of death. A sweet pain and longing resurfaced in his pulsating chest. On the one hand was Bapu's call, the fructification of his heart's desire. And on the other, the maddening compulsion of love that he felt for his Gulab. The conflict was disturbing and there seemed no solution in sight.

Gulab's father was equally perturbed by the news. Harilal being summoned to distant Africa, the other end of the world, did not please him. These were changing times; he would be far away in a foreign land, with alien people who had different perspectives and value systems. In the case of Mohandas it had been different. He was above sin, but Harilal was an impressionable child and Gulab was besotted by him. Letting him go away indefinitely would be terrible for the young couple and not without risk for Gulab's family.

An easy formula was worked out by Laxmidas. 'We shall get them married before he leaves,' he announced triumphantly. 'Choose an auspicious day for the wedding and start the preparations. I shall write to Mohandas and inform him of our decision.'

Harilal's joy knew no bounds. His stars seemed to be smiling on him. All his dreams were coming true. The past years of his loneliness and rejection were becoming a faint memory. All he could think of was the countdown to the day of being united in holy wedlock to the love of his life—the singular purpose of his being and then the subsequent sailing off to Africa, to be with us.

He held a folded piece of paper inside his moist palms on which Gulab had written him a letter when the date of their marriage had been finalized. A long sweet letter in poetic verse, in her own hand, carried the promise of her passion and the undying declaration of her love and surrender. Harilal had read it over and over several times. He unfolded the paper for the hundredth time that day, touching the surface, scanning it with dreamy eyes once more –

Dear husband… the basis of my life,
Salutations
My heart adorned with virtue
Resplendent like the moon
Shines in the beautiful land of Porbandar

An ocean of truth, born in a high family
I am blessed to have him as my husband
It takes many lives of good deeds to get such a man
I Gulab, offer from Rajkot my Pranams
I have not had a glimpse of you for so long
Not even in my dreams
Yet the Gods know that our hearts are one
The thought of our union is nectar to my mind
Accept the love that I offer you
How I wait for the eighth day of the sukla paksha of Vaishakha
How I wait for the moment of our union

Come soon my spring, my soul Harilal
Like a night without a moon I long for you
My beloved, the moon has risen in the sky
The moonlight is resplendent
My mind is enthralled with thoughts of you
My heart filled with only you.
Beauty, youth, virtue, character, and knowledge unite in you

I am blessed by the Gods, my being is fulfilled.
Your virtues flow as a river and surround me
They envelop me like the fragrance of musk and sandalwood
Overlook my shortcomings, consider me your slave
Oh free me from the pangs of separation, my beloved
I pray you are in good health. God willing we shall meet soon.
I plead forgiveness for this late letter.
You may give me the punishment I deserve.

Written by one in love, craving for the moonlight and longing for her moon-like lover,
Gulab

✄ ✄ ✄

Mohandas and I had no knowledge of either the preparations, or the forthcoming ceremony. The letter informing us about Laxmidas' decision had not even reached South Africa, and the wedding ceremony was already underway in Porbandar. The auspicious day was set in May 1906. The Vohra and Gandhi homes were magnificently decorated with ceremonial lights and flowers. The sun had set over the horizon and a rosy glow had enveloped the two who were united in holy wedlock. The bride and groom conjoined by a thread of burning passion and love, waited impatiently for the rituals to begin.

Little Gulab made a beautiful, coy bride. Covered from head to toe in a bright saffron silk sari, and a gold-bordered veil that screened her face, she had been anointed with sandal oil and turmeric earlier that day. The little teenager, exploding with the anticipation of being united with Harilal, trembled as she ascended the stage where her beloved husband-to-be stood, dressed in an ivory white, silk kurta and dhoti and a big orange turban tied around his head. She strained her eyes to look at him through the translucent mesh of her veil and a ripple of excitement stirred her.

Loud chants of Vedic mantras, the beating of drums, the swaying *shehnais* and a fusion of music and colour swallowed them. Her gaze moved shyly to the little bridegroom who did not seem that little to her, any more. She placed the marigold garland around his neck with trembling hands and he around hers as he whispered in her ear—'At last you are mine my love, my Gulab.'

The drummers and the singing women surrounded them, lifting them off their feet into an ethereal world of song and dance. They glided through, circumambulating the ritual fire seven times hand in hand, following the priest's intonations, following the ritual of flinging dry rice into the leaping flames and then bending down to seek the blessings of the elders.

The newlyweds bound together by the nuptial knot, fastened by his shawl and her *dupatta*, touched their heads to the feet of Laxmidas first and then Haridas Vohra. Harilal's eyes had misted over. This was the act of reverence he would have ideally bestowed first on his Ba and Bapu. How he ached to see his Bapu and me that day. A painful lump rose in his throat but the touch of Gulab's arm and her innocent gaze gradually eased it.

While far away, on the other side of the southern hemisphere, an empty restlessness had gripped me.

✷ ✷ ✷

It was in the wee hours of the morning that Harilal led his blushing bride into their garishly decorated bedroom in the Gandhi home. Their bed had been decorated with strands of marigolds and a thick layer of rose petals was strewn all over. He held her trembling hands and sat down on it, crushing the rose petals underneath. Gulab's heart was beating wildly. Despite the gruelling hours of the innumerable marriage rituals, the freshness on her face had not diminished. A sweet smile played upon her lips. Harilal leaned towards her and pulled the *dupatta* back from her head to uncover her face. Her parted hair, tied back in a plait that caressed her waist was scented with the fragrance of rose *ittar*. He deftly undid the large jewelled pendant that was dangling on her forehead. Her red *bindi* smudged right across her brow staining the end of his kurta sleeves. His turban lay undone on the floor. He placed his hands onto the small of her back, took her into his arms and rocked her gently, their bodies vibrated in unison with the celestial sounds of the universe.

'I do love you my precious Gulab. And God knows how much I have pined for you all these days. We are man and wife now, my beloved—and no power on earth can take you away from me.'

Her virginity surrendered at the altar of love, Gulab had crossed over from the threshold of childhood into the intractable world of womanhood while Harilal had crossed over from his carefree days onto the first step of full-grown manhood. There could be no turning back for either of them.

The temple bells chiming in the distance lulled the heady pair, locked in a passionate embrace, to sleep.

THIRTY EIGHT

By now Mohandas' law practice had surpassed that of any European barrister in South Africa and his towering capability and unassailable integrity was recognized throughout the land. Mohandas however wore his success with great unease. Feeling trapped in the pursuit of material gains, his conscience was burdened by the violation of the teachings enshrined in the Bhagavad Gita which stressed on non-possession and detachment as a soul's prime spiritual goals. But he was positioned on a path totally at variance with either of those. He was singularly focussed on making me and our children self-reliant, to lead a life of simplicity. Soon Manilal, Ramdas and little Devdas were also drawn into his experiments of frugal living.

While wholly participating in his new methods which included hand grinding flour to bake bread each day, a task that was routinely assigned to Henry Polak, Millie, the boys and me, I was not happy with the haphazard education of my sons. Mohandas' work left him no time to teach the boys and the walks to the office had practically stopped. His retort that his sons were learning more valuable lessons of good living at home, did little to appease me. I was slightly relieved when the Polaks began conversing with the boys in English and Millie volunteered to become their governess and teach them reading, writing and simple arithmetic. With that the peace and harmony of the house was restored once again. Mohandas however was restless again. I was the first one to spot those signs of anxiety—his outward show of calmness was a veneer. I was convinced that some grave inner turmoil was wrecking his peace.

It did not take long for me to comprehend that the laurels of his being a highly successful attorney had only heightened the feeling of his failure as a public servant. His tireless efforts to reverse the unjust laws of South Africa had borne no fruit and he was burdened by a deep sense of guilt. The only salvation for his inner conflict was to undertake a vow of poverty, which entailed not merely simple living, but also directing his private income entirely towards social work.

I was not surprised by Mohandas' drastic proclamation that followed soon after. I had been expecting a far greater upheaval. The fact that he was renouncing all wealth by undertaking a vow was slightly alleviated by the fact that he had not sworn to stop earning money. He was merely pledging to keep nothing for himself except what was essential for subsistence.

Back home in Rajkot, on hearing of his latest vow, all hell had broken loose. Laxmidas and the family reacted violently when they heard that they would not be getting any more remittances from South Africa. Mohandas conveyed to them that if the brothers believed he still owed them some debts, they should understand that those had long been settled. Naturally the blame of Mohandas' drastic step was flung onto me.

'Kastur, the greedy selfish wife, from a more affluent family than the Gandhis,' became the easy target for the censure. I was the bad one and worthy of damnation.

What followed was a long and angry exchange of accusatory letters from both sides, but Mohandas remained intractable. The brothers finally conceded that his vow of poverty was self-imposed and I had not been instrumental in pushing it. They took refuge in the belief that Mohandas had gone mad, for no one in his right mind would renounce the world and part with all his earthly possessions. Disregarding all the furious criticism from his family, at thirty-seven, Mohandas stayed resolute in his decision; his vow of poverty was intact and the matter closed.

❇ ❇ ❇

On 2 June, the Gandhi family boarded a train at Johannesburg station to finally move to Phoenix. Mohandas felt a heady lightness. We were all embarking on a new life; one which conformed with his newly established ideals of poverty, detachment and public service in a settlement that would propagate his vision of the ideal, self-sufficient village.

As we swayed from side to side with the motion of the fast moving train, my thoughts raced ahead. I did not know how drastically life was going to change for me in my new home, but the thought of being united with my Harilal made my mind soar high above the clouds. We were going to be one happy family at last!

❇ ❇ ❇

In Rajkot, the newlyweds in the throes of their passionate fairy tale romance were totally immersed in themselves, oblivious of the time ticking by for Harilal's departure to South Africa. When the day arrived he was overcome with sadness. He had spent the whole night in Gulab's arms not wanting to let her out of his embrace.

Harilal knew it was a long journey over the seas, to the distant land that beckoned him. He missed his Bapu. He yearned to be with his brothers, but above all he needed to rush into my arms to tell me all about his little Gulab, and how much he had missed us at his wedding.

The memory of a nasty incident crept back in his thoughts. Bapu had written a terse, angry letter to Mota bapu that reached just before the wedding day. Those cruel words had scorched his soul. The scars were deep and old wounds opened again.

Harilal's marriage has not made me happy...These days I have stopped thinking about Harilal as my son!

While Harilal burned all alone in the agony of his Bapu's hurtful words, I was going through my own private hell. How would I ever be able to let him know that I ached for him as much as he did for me and that in my mind, Gulab was the perfect bride for him? If only I could fly down into his heart and kiss his pain away. If only he could believe that his Bapu was an extraordinary man—a man different from all others and being his son should be enough reason to glorify him eternally.

The next morning when it was time for Harilal to leave, Gulab came out to the verandah where the elders had assembled to bid him goodbye. He touched each of their feet in reverence, to seek their blessings and then turned to Gulab. Her smouldering doe-eyes were swollen and red. She stared at him silently. There was nothing more to say. She had spelled it all out the night before.

I'll wait for you as the earth waits for the moon, my beloved.

Harilal had kissed away each tear that fell from her eyes, stroking the back of her head and whispered, 'I will call you to Africa, my sweet Gulab, sooner than you know. And Ba and my brothers shall shower you with all the love you deserve.'

Her sobs eased away as she nestled her head on his chest and he did not stop kissing her till she fell asleep.

It would be their last night together in a long time, the night that Gulab conceived the first grandchild of our glorious Gandhi lineage.

THIRTY NINE

Harilal stood on the deck of the steamer that was sailing majestically towards the South African continent. On the swirling waters of the Indian Ocean he watched the receding shores of his beloved homeland feeling bittersweet pangs of separation. The last time he had sailed on the high seas was some years ago when he had left South Africa. It was precisely five long years that he had been away from his Ba and Bapu and just a few days since he had kissed his little Gulab farewell. Harilal's eyes misted over. The thirst for his Gulab marred the joyous anticipation of being united with all of us. If only he could have brought her with him, but the thought of meeting his brothers stirred up an excitement in him yet again.

Harilal looked out at the rolling waves of the ocean. The thick black smoke billowing out of the ship's funnels mingled with the muddy waters that reflected the dark sky. He had been married for three months. His mind conjured up the doe-eyed image of dear Gulab once again. Her sweet smile touched his lips and a faint euphoria engulfed him.

How could Bapu have been so heartless? Bapu's letter and his harsh words gnawed at him.

These days I have stopped thinking of Harilal as my son...

The sharp message that had severely wounded his innards reverberated time and again in his head.

'Really Bapu? You really don't think of me as your son? And your wonderful, innocent daughter-in-law, my sweet Gulab—will you think of her as your daughter-in-law or will you be as cruel to her as you are to me?'

Flooded again as he was with the thought of Gulab, his dejection somewhat eased away. For now, the rolling waves of the vast ocean stoked up his long suppressed dreams. He looked forward to a life in Phoenix with the family and pushed away the pestering slight of Bapu's harsh words. He was eager to live in the settlement that his Bapu had created. Manilal's letters describing it had fascinated him.

There are abundant trees of oranges, mangoes and plums. A beautiful stream runs through it where we go swimming. A sweet lark sings sweetly to us each day. The tall grass is infested with snakes and you never know when a fearsome snake may appear…

The snake, the sweet melodious lark, the fruit-laden trees and the tall unruly grass had Harilal mesmerized. The scenic beauty of Bapu's creation enticed him. It was just a few days away. Manilal continued,

Bapu has named it Phoenix. And do you know why? The Greek mythological bird, Phoenix immolates, and dies and then it rises up again from its ashes to a new life.

Harilal understood the correlation. Bapu's battle against the British for the rights of his fellowmen was likely to destroy him and in that event we would all be reduced to ashes, but would we rise like the grand bird and be reborn to fight for the truth? I had my doubts, but I was sure Mohandas understood the symbolism of rising from ashes to the divine light of truth.

The rolling ship was steadily taking Harilal away from his beloved to the unknown land and a commune dominated by his Bapu. He did not know what to expect. The pangs of separation from Gulab had become even more painful.

'Wait for me, my beloved,' he mouthed a silent plea as he stood by the railing of the deserted deck of the ship that was moving forward, under the overcast monsoon sky.

❄ ❄ ❄

When the ship docked after an exhausting twenty-day journey, an unusually harsh winter sun was blazing down on the city of Durban.

Harilal, lugging his two tin trunks and a holdall, made his way intrepidly through the noisy crowd. He looked around for a familiar face. Bapu had been informed of his arrival. Someone should have been there to receive him, if not his Ba and Bapu. 'Harilalbhai!' a voice rose from over the din.

He saw the familiar face of Paragjibhai, an associate who had been involved with his father's work. He had seen him the last time he was in South Africa. Harilal could not conceal his disappointment. 'Where is Bapu, Paragjibhai? How come you are here? Is Ba well? And my brothers? Are they okay?'

Harilal bombarded his father's appointee with a million questions. He had expected one of us to be there to receive him.

'Your Bapu is in Pretoria, caught up with his work. Ba informed me of your arrival. So here I am.' Paragjibhai smiled, but Harilal's face remained grim, unable to share his joy. He hauled his heavy tin trunks, the mattress and rug and followed him through the crowd without uttering a word.

✁ ✁ ✁

The days and nights preceding my son's arrival had been most agonizing for me. Mohandas' outburst after learning of Harilal's marriage was still fresh in my mind.

Harilal and Gulab are married! Do you hear that? Motabhai took it upon himself to arrange everything without my consent.

The deep agitation spilled out like fiery embers from his eyes. His angry words had stunned me, yet deep down somewhere a light and heady euphoria had lifted the gloom from my heart.

Acting in the boy's interest... How dare he?!

For a fleeting moment, I was flooded with relief as the object of Mohandas' anger was not my hapless Harilal, it was Laxmidas. But the pain of being denied the greatest joy for a mother, of witnessing the wedding of her son was tearing me apart. That Harilal had been married without my consent was another painful reminder of my irrelevance in his life.

'When did it happen?' I had barely been able to slip in a word during his unending tirade.

'Early last month. And do you know that everyone was there? Everyone, but the people who matter the most—his brothers and the two of us.' He read out the list of invitees from Laxmidas' letter that infuriated him even more.

'Everyone except us, Kastur! Laxmidas knows how I feel about child marriage, yet he acted against my wishes. Gulab and Harilal are too young. He should have known that Harilal has a lot to learn before he even thinks of starting a family. This is absolutely unforgiveable.' Mohandas had slumped over on the chair, holding his head between his palms. Deep frown lines criss-crossed his brow. I came close to him and took his hands into mine. It came to me in a flash. Of course Gulab and Harilal were in the throes of a passionate romance, and the relatives recognizing the risk of the unpardonable sin of sex before marriage had thought it best to get them married. Of course it was in their best interest. My heart melted and a warm glow rose upwards in my chest. I sent out a silent blessing laden with love to my beloved children, the two innocent and beautiful newlyweds.

'Perhaps Harilal wanted it.' I offered hesitantly.

'Nonsense!' Mohandas spluttered. 'How can Harilal know what he wants at this young age?'

Mohandas' forceful words silenced me. I dared not speak aloud the thoughts that raced through my head.

Our son does know what he wants, Mohandas. You don't. Alas! You never will. My Harilal, eager, impetuous, strong-willed and single minded certainly knows what he wants. And you Mohandas, impulsive, rigid and persistent, how can you not be aware of the attributes of your son? Have you forgotten how driven you were by lust at his age? It was impossible to deny you your carnal demands. And how you have struggled all these years to conquer your sexual desires? Can't you see that Harilal, who is your own flesh and blood, may also be driven by a passion as intense as yours? And little adolescent Gulab—what about her desires, the child gripped by insane love for your son? Indeed getting them married was the wisest thing to do...

But I said nothing. Not even when Mohandas shot off that bitter note to his brother. A missive that was sealed by my silence would be one of the last letters to pass between the brothers for a long time thereafter. I prayed to god that Harilal would not misunderstand his Bapu's harsh words.

❌ ❌ ❌

I had been waiting impatiently that day. Pacing up and down I had stepped out of the doorway several times, gazing at the dusty road that led to the settlement. Little Ramdas and Devdas stayed by my side clutching on to me—awaiting the arrival of their brother.

Harilal arrived and came straight up to me, and touched his forehead to my feet. My eyes brimmed over as I stroked his head and lifted him up from the floor. 'Oh how much I have missed you, my son. How I have yearned for this day,' I mumbled, choking on my words.

I held him in my arms for a long while, not wanting to let go. He stood silently, whilst I, the aching mother who had pined for him all these years, had burst open a dam of unspoken grievances and un-exchanged missives of love. We wept.

'Where is Manilal?' he asked, noticing only the younger two who were also crying.

'He goes to a dispensary nearby to nurse the patients. Bapu has assigned him this duty. He should be back soon,' I said, wiping his face with the *pallu* of my sari. 'He sponges them, dispenses medicines and assists in their care.'

Harilal looked bewildered.

'You don't need to be a doctor for that.' I added quickly, sensing Harilal's confusion.

'And what about the two of you?' He had circled his arms around the younger boys. 'Are you going to school? Or are you still being taught at home by Bapu?' There was a slight sarcasm in his voice.

'Bapu teaches us when he's here, but it's been a holiday these days, Motabhai,' they quipped. 'In Bapu's absence, we don't study. But we have other chores to do. We collect letters, we work the pumps in the orchards, we till the land and sometimes we do carpentry.'

I could see Harilal's face contort in frustration.

'Come Motabhai, let's go out.' Ramdas was tugging at his brother's sleeve. 'There are lovely oranges in full bloom in Phoenix. You will be thrilled to see them.'

The boys traipsed out to the fruit orchards. I could hear their merry twittering and laughter streaming into the kitchen while I heated up the food.

Harilal's anxious face disturbed me, but somewhere in my mind I wanted to believe that all would be well.

FORTY

By the evening, Harilal had been updated on most happenings at the settlement by his brothers and me. His eyes lit up with pride when we told him that the untiring efforts of his Bapu had transformed the settlement at Phoenix and the *Indian Opinion*. He appeared extremely thrilled about the prospects of getting involved with the work.

When Mohandas returned later that day, Harilal saw the face of a much leaner, tired man. Harilal touched his forehead to Mohandas' feet and looked up at him reverently.

'How are you young lad?' he enquired, a twinkle had lit up his eyes.

'And how is little Gulab?'

Harilal answered in monosyllables expecting his father to talk to him about the marriage.

'I suppose your Mota bapu and Gokiphoi are in good health.' A barrage of inanities came flowing out in the matter-of-fact exchange that followed.

'I'm disappointed that your studies are not progressing like they should. Now you must give up the yearning for this unnatural education that has driven you all these years. True education is all about character building, son—not what you have been taught in schools so far.'

Mohandas patted the boy's head and walked away. 'You shall join the office from tomorrow, Harilal. It will make you understand the problems of our society and expand your vision…,' his voice trailed off. Harilal stood silent, rooted to the spot watching his father's receding form through the doorway.

Those brief casual words that had fallen on his ears were incomprehensible. He had never understood his father's unpredictable moods, or how working with him in the settlement or even at the newspaper office would enhance his character. This was one of Bapu's many enduring mysteries that Harilal had stopped trying to unravel, but the fact that Bapu had made just a fleeting mention of his precious Gulab, hurt him. The pain of Bapu's cruel message resurfaced and he looked towards me for solace. My heart went out to the hurting child and I took him into my arms.

'Don't misunderstand him, *beta,* your Bapu really loves you. Come on now, the *puran-poli* will get cold. I've made your favourite *shrikhand* for you with my own hands. Come on.'

I know my words rang hollow on those ears that would never be able to forgive that deep emotional assault.

I went to bed after completing the day's chores. The excited chattering, streaming from the boys' room till the wee hours, comforted me.

⁂

Harilal started work very early the next day. He was awestruck by the discipline in his father's office, where a constant flow of visitors were dealt with utmost efficiency. He looked forward to becoming a part of the organization with great enthusiasm. The pain of Gulab's absence notwithstanding, he dived headlong into the work making serious efforts to learn English and try his hand at his father's newly acquired typewriter. Carefully pouring over copies of the newspaper, he began to sort out and arrange other files, sometimes even studying legal matters to get a deeper understanding of running a newspaper.

Life in Phoenix was not easy. The settlement stood for simplicity, unity and equality. The food was basic and eating sugar was strictly prohibited. Breakfast was a staple of black tea and bread. Sometimes on a holiday, everyone ate only oranges and plums from the orchard. Harilal marvelled at the way his father swallowed the bland and sugarless food, relishing it as if it were his most adored delicacy, but he could tell that the other residents were suffering. They were forced into silence in front of his father, but behind his back it was different.

The worst hit by this deprivation was little Devdas. He wailed and cried every time he was given his meals. He hardly ate a few bites preferring to remain hungry rather than suffer that inedible fare. It made me miserable to see him hungry and the days he didn't eat, I went hungry too. Once I gave him a few spoons of sugar to entice him to eat and my heart melted when I saw him wolf down his meal as he drooled over the sugar *katori*. After that day I began feeding him one pint of sugar with each meal, unmindful of Mohandas' decree and the wrath I would incur, should he find out.

Mohandas found out in just a few days. While checking the expense accounts at Phoenix, an inmate tattled to him.

'Mrs. Gandhi serves Devdas sugar every day, Bapu. It is her extravagance that has caused this increase in daily expenditure,' he blurted out.

Mohandas' face clouded up. A deep furrow etched across his forehead. He felt hurt and betrayed.

That evening after the customary prayer meeting, Mohandas sat grim-faced. I had no idea what was coming.

'The money at the ashram belongs to the community, and every single penny is to be spent for the welfare of the community alone,' he said sombrely, glaring at me. 'If we misappropriate public wealth for our personal benefit, temptation or taste, then we forfeit the right to serve the public.'

There was a pindrop silence. The boys and I sat on the floor amongst the inmates listening to Bapu's speech. It still hadn't occurred to me that the lecture was aimed at me.

'Today Ba has favoured her son...and I have been shamed. I am shamed at the deliberate disobedience of my order. I am ashamed by this blatant indulgence.'

The sharp censure hit me like a gunshot. I could not believe I had been the object of this cruel public humiliation.

'Today it is Devdas,' he continued, 'tomorrow it shall be others. This amounts to stealing...'

My eyes had brimmed over. There was a suffocating lump in my throat as I felt a hundred pairs of eyes piercing me. I gripped Devdas' little hand and bowed my head. Harilal sat beside me, looking intently at my face. I could see his eyes had also filled up with tears. He glared at the whistleblower sitting smugly beside his Bapu. His entire body had turned into a quivering mass of rage. He sat there long after the prayer meeting was dispersed and Bapu had vanished into the crowd without as much as a fleeting glance towards us. He did not see me rise, scoop Devdas up into my arms and rush into the house.

A deep conflict of varied emotions racked Harilal's mind, while I spent a painful night clinging to Devdas as sleep eluded me. Weakened in body and spirit after the birth of my last two sons, and the fatigue of repeatedly moving homes, I had begun to suffer prolonged bouts of menstrual bleeding that made me acutely anaemic.

That night, totally drained in spirit, I felt my life was ebbing out with the blood that did not stop oozing out of my body.

I wept. I wept for Devdas and for Harilal. That terrifying disquiet in his eyes, that icy aloofness, that piercing gaze, haunted me.

❊ ❊ ❊

The Zulu rebellion in Natal had turned into a full-scale war. Unmindful of the raging conflict that had seared my soul and re-opened Harilal's old wounds, Mohandas plunged headlong into tending to Zulu warriors. He inducted a large team of volunteers as members of the Indian Ambulance Corps, men who spent long periods nursing the wounded tribesmen on the battlefront. They cleaned and dressed their festering wounds even as the white soldiers jeered and cursed at them from the other side of the stockade fence.

The days that followed were nothing short of a nightmare. The atrocities perpetrated by the British against the Zulus, mounted each day with the natives being dragged out of their huts or even hunted down like animals and then beaten, flogged or kicked mercilessly before being shot. Some were hanged publicly as a warning to deter others from fomenting further rebellion. Never had the barbaric character of the white man been more evident. The Zulu rebellion was declared as suppressed only when the news of these brutalities became public, the expedition finally abandoned and the Indian Ambulance Corps was sent home.

Deeply scarred by the torture and senseless carnage, a peculiar revelation came to Mohandas during the war. On the long and arduous marches through mounds of torn limbs, watching mangled bodies hanging from trees, he saw a parallel between the nature of armed violence and human sexuality. The outrage perpetuated on the black natives by the white colonizers aroused in him a deep empathy with those who were maltreated and abused. A strong aversion against male brutality swept his senses. He viewed sexual sadism to be a prime symbol of male prepotency and cruelty and in that moment, he took a vow of celibacy—a strict imposition of abstinence from sex for the rest of his life.

Feeling deep pangs of guilt at the constant demands he had made on me for the satisfaction of his carnal needs, he began questioning and blaming himself for victimising me, and my failing health a result of his relentless self-indulgence. Harilal, Manilal, and the other two were all conceived in the throes of sexual passion. The difficult childbirths I had to undergo were enough to convince him to not father any more children. He feared that his failings would reflect in their lives. Harilal's early marriage to a prepubescent girl made him suspect that his son, who himself was a product of sinful passion, was beginning to reveal a pattern chillingly similar to his.

For years Mohandas had pondered upon the meaning and purpose of life on earth. The raging conflict within him, the battle between his duty towards his family and his calling to serve humanity had ripped him apart. The human brutality he had witnessed during the Zulu rebellion, the bloody carnage that it precipitated and the suffering that he was striving to alleviate had finally crystallized the real truth within. His was a battle between the spiritual and the physical and the only way he could restore his inner peace was by a complete detachment to worldly pleasures. He sought to attain that absolute state of desirelessness to facilitate his transcendence to a higher spiritual plane beyond the cycle of life and death. The revelation brought about a certain exaltation within him. It also opened up unlimited vistas for the service of mankind.

How ironic was it that while this violent upheaval that had deluged Mohandas' soul and was morphing him into another human being, a tiny embryo of the same gene pool had taken root inside the body of little Gulab. A new soul was being nurtured within the innards of the sweet Gandhi bride.

✷ ✷ ✷

Mohandas informed me of his vow of *brahmacharya*, a complete abstinence from sex, with a deep sense of uneasiness. The only person to be directly affected by his vow, he felt nervous facing me for he had pledged lifelong fidelity to me in front of the sacred fire at the time of our marriage. This time around, the crucial moment of the disclosure passed without any kind of reaction from me. I could sense his awkwardness and then the incomparable feeling of relief that followed. I was neither provoked nor surprised. I had become accustomed to Mohandas' eccentricities. I had also understood that as a faithful Hindu wife, I would have to blindly follow in the footsteps of my husband, no matter how much it violated my sensibilities.

'I have no objection and we shall live like brother and sister,' is all I said without the slightest inflection in my voice.

What I did not say was,

it was your decision to ravage my body at will; now it is your decision to ravage my mind. So be it Mohandas, so be it. Brother and sister we shall be!

The niggling suspicion that this embargo applied solely to me and not to other women, crept up in my head, but I held my tongue, and instead, consoled myself,

He's an extraordinary man, my husband. And it is my dharma to follow him, whichever direction his conscience dictates.

I did not allow Mohandas' attitude towards me to create any discord in our lives. In fact I made an extra effort to sweeten it, but time and again it did cross my mind that the circumstances in which you are born have a compelling pattern of repeating themselves. I feared for the future of my poor Harilal.

God have mercy on my child!

My earnest plea rang out in the still of that dark night while Gulab retched due to her early pregnancy nausea in the distant shores of my beloved Rajkot.

FORTY ONE

Harilal was getting accustomed to his austere life in the ashram at Phoenix. The tiny rooms with log-wood walls and floors were sparse and the amateurish construction had visible flaws. At night after the inmates retired to their rooms, occasional sounds of nocturnal birds and the soft murmur of the brook outside stirred up the air and a deep sense of calm descended upon the settlement.

Harilal lay on a blanket spread out on his makeshift cot outside his room. There was a slight nip in the air. All inmates were given a set of two blankets each, one to lie on and the other to cover themselves. The absence of a pillow irked him. He tossed about on his cot trying to find a comfortable position for his weary neck and shoulders. Most times after a long day at work, he would fall asleep as soon as he lay down on the bed, but that night sleep eluded him. He tossed and turned restlessly till daybreak and tumbled out of bed hurriedly to go to office.

Harilal had totally immersed himself in work at the printing press where he spent most part of his day. It thrilled him to see copies of the journal being bound and parcelled out each night. But the restlessness in him resurfaced after his encounter with a former clerk in his father's office who was now a full-fledged barrister. This man who had once worked in a lowly position at Bapu's office, now engaged with him in a discussion like an equal! The air of supreme confidence, that heady feeling of success and that utterly enviable European accent astounded Harilal. He suddenly felt small in his presence.

'Good to have you back, Harilal,' he boomed. 'We desperately needed a hand at Bapu's office.'

Harilal barely understood his words. Slighted and embarrassed, he shuffled around nervously and mumbled. 'Ah! Mr. Ritchie. You have changed. Totally changed!'

'Yes, Harilal,' Ritchie beamed. 'But for this I can only thank your father.' He looked at Bapu adoringly, the gratitude pouring out of his eyes. 'It was he who inspired me to go abroad and study for a law degree. I am so grateful to him. As a barrister I can serve the people just like he does. Or else I would have been a mere volunteer all my life.' His loud laughter boomed into Harilal's ears. He felt foolish standing there before them, not knowing what to say.

'And what about you, Harilal? You must have also obtained your law degree in India by now?'

Harilal was dumbstruck. He felt as if a hundred bricks had fallen on his head. He stood silently with his head bowed and eyes fixed on the floor as he heard the noisy footsteps of Ritchie walking out imperiously.

At dinner that night Harilal brought it up again. 'Bapu, I feel that some arrangement should be made here for our education. I have no education, but why should my brothers suffer the same plight? I see that they are almost as bad as me. And just look at Ritchie! How tall he stands! His arrogance comes from his English barrister's degree. And look at us. We are a bumbling bunch of uneducated yokels! I feel ashamed of myself.'

Mohandas looked up at his distraught son and set his spoon down. In an even voice he spoke, 'What nonsense do you speak, Harilal? How can you say this? You are not inferior to anyone in any manner. The training you boys are getting in Phoenix, by being closely connected to the movement cannot be compared to any textbook learning perpetuated on us by the British. These, my son, are the lessons that shall mould your character, not a school education.' I could see the irritation rise on Mohandas' face.

I gathered some courage and butted in. 'You can build their character and instil in them a spirit of service as much as you like, but do they need to remain illiterate? Are you forgetting that even your friends Polak and Kallenbach have stressed on the need for a good education for them? As it is we have no savings for their future and we are also depriving them of a proper education. How wise it that? What will become of them? Have you ever given this a thought? Will they become beggars?' I blurted out in one breath. My voice quivered and eyes brimmed over.

'You are the victim of evil temptation, Kastur.' Mohandas said sharply. 'Both your son and you are in the grip of this disease that shall lead you to your doom. If these children are made from the essence of my spirit, they shall never need these meaningless degrees. They shall be far superior to all those who have been to formal schools.' Mohandas pursed his lips for a while before he resumed eating. Everyone on the table fell silent.

The air was heavy with the hostile confrontation that was threatening to turn ugly. Manilal spoke for the first time, 'Bapu! Everyone asks us where we go to study. And also which class we are in. I feel ashamed of myself, for I have no answer.'

Mohandas looked at the younger boy piercingly and said, 'No Manilal. Don't be ashamed. Raise your head high and tell anyone who questions you, "I study in Bapu's class!" Never be ashamed of the truth.' A wistful look appeared in Mohandas' eyes as his voice trailed off and he rose from the dining table to wash his hands.

Manilal and Harilal were quiet. I shifted nervously as I picked up the plates and carried them to the kitchen. A violent storm raged on in Harilal's head.

Why couldn't that pompous clerk have been schooled in Bapu's class instead of us? Why was he sent abroad by Bapu for his law degree? Wouldn't we have been better off if we were the children of his servants?

Burning thoughts pierced Harilal's mind like poison arrows chipping away at his peace. The pain of being so far away from his beloved Gulab had suddenly become unbearable. He did not know that a sweet surprise awaited him the next day.

✄ ✄ ✄

The morning mail brought a letter addressed to Harilal that he tore open, recognizing Gulab's handwriting on the envelope.

A new life breathes in my womb. I wait impatiently for the moment when I can place our baby in your arms. Oh how much longer will I have to bear the torture of waiting for you?

Gulab

The letter from Rajkot couldn't have arrived at a more opportune moment for Harilal. Ravaged by the rejection that he was feeling by his father's unyielding conduct, the news of his child growing in Gulab's womb yanked him out of his melancholia.

'At last the God's are smiling upon us,' he murmured as he kissed the familiar handwriting over and over again. He carried that precious piece of paper close to his chest, savouring the delightful news all day, till he fell asleep.

That night he dreamt of an exciting new life with Gulab and her yet to be born child. Theirs was an unbreakable bond of pure, unselfish love. He promised himself that his baby would never suffer the emotional torture that had been meted out to him by his cruel father. He would ensure his child acquired an English barrister's degree and only then would he feel vindicated for life's injustices, once and for all.

A couple of days later, Mohandas returned from Johannesburg to Phoenix. Without removing his collar and tie or asking about the welfare of the residents as he usually did, he came straight into the kitchen where I stood preparing his dinner and called out to me.

'Where are you, Kastur?' A wide smile played on his face. 'Look at me. I have some exciting news for you. Listen to me, will you?'

'You seem happy,' I said while I continued with my cooking. There was a rare lilt in his voice. I looked up at his eyes that twinkled with merriment.

'What happened? Has the British government agreed to all your demands?' I asked, trying to humour him. It had to be something connected to his work. Nothing else could have made him that happy. 'There's news from Rajkot! Come out of the kitchen now and sit down.' He took an envelope out of his pocket and held it in the palm of his hand. His eyes had lit up with joy, as had mine.

'Gulab is pregnant! Kastur! We are going to be grandparents! Do you hear?' Those three delightful words struck me like a bolt from the blue. Never in my wildest dreams had I expected to hear such joyful news from Mohandas. And just then, Harilal entered the room. Mohandas put his hand on Harilal's shoulder. It was a rare moment of tenderness between father and son. Harilal had a shy smile on his face.

'This means more responsibility for you, son,' he said softly, ruffling his hair.

I grabbed Harilal's hand and looked at him adoringly, joy radiating from every pore of my body. He sat down on the sofa, close to me, looking out of the window as if in a daze. I stroked his head gently and whispered into his ear, 'You are going to make me a very proud grandmother, son, and your baby shall wipe away all your worries! Your good days have begun!' A warm silence engulfed all of us. Mohandas sprang up from the chair and added, 'Let's celebrate Gulab's *seemant* here in Phoenix. The puja for a *bahu* in the seventh month of her pregnancy cannot be performed anywhere but with her in-laws. You are going to be a grandmother Kastur! And what could be better than ushering our first grandson into the ashram and making him an inmate from the moment of his birth?' Mohandas was ecstatic. I had not seen him like this in a long time. I willed the vibrating cheer to seep into Harilal who sat with his head bowed, silently beside me.

'Tamey shoo kahi rahya chho?' I interrupted. *'Hoon kaayado maara putri eka chokari janma apay chay te jova mate prema karasay?* I would love to see my daughter-in-law give birth to a girl. I want to welcome a *Laxmi* into the home and we do need a *Laxmi* for good fortune and happiness here, don't we Harilal?'

Everyone perked up with gay laughter that rang out in the air. The new soul growing in Gulab's womb thousands of miles away, had succeeded in spreading cheer in the ashram even before it had taken birth.

It is a lucky sign! Thoo! Thoo!

I spat twice on the floor to ward off any evil spirits that might be hovering in the vicinity. I sent a silent blessing to both mother and child. It would be an impatient wait before I could welcome my little Gulab.

'All right then, Kastur. I am going to write to Motabhai and Gulab's father to find an escort to bring her to South Africa. It's time we met our daughter-in-law and nurtured her with our own hands.' Mohandas' words enveloped Harilal in joyous disbelief. He could not believe that his Gulab would soon be with him in South Africa and never part.

I'll wait for you impatiently, Gulab. Each moment is a long agonizing wait, my precious. And I send a long deep kiss to my baby that breathes in your womb. Be careful when you board that ship! I am waiting.

Harilal mouthed a silent message to his wife as he stepped out to the verandah with a new spring in his step.

Phoenix was going to celebrate the arrival of its *bahu* and the forthcoming Gandhi grandchild with ardent fervour!

Forty Two

Barely sixteen years old, travelling to an unknown land amongst strangers made Gulab nervous. Although the foremost thought in her mind was to be re-united with her beloved Harilal, she was troubled by the prospect of being in Africa that seemed so different from her safe haven in Rajkot.

Gulab was aware of the fierce zeal that Mohandas had instilled in the people of South Africa and the devotion that they had for him. She knew how under the leadership of her revered Bapu, they fought fearlessly for their rights against a cruel dispensation. She had learnt of the violence and conflicts from Harilal's letters that had made her tremble with fear. So, when Mohandas' letter had arrived asking her father to send her to South Africa, Gulab was terrified. She had no idea how she would adjust in that strange land, also dominated by English-speaking people. She had browsed through a geography book to locate the country that she would be sent off to shortly. Her father had told her it took twenty days by steamer to get from Bombay to Durban. That unsettled her even more because she had no idea where Bombay was!

Gulab reached Phoenix on a clear and bright day. The sky was a soft blue, interspersed with a few wispy, white clouds. The children of the inmates were frolicking in the open, picking ripe plums and oranges from the trees laden with a bounty of fruit. A sense of gay merriment had pervaded the air as everyone waited impatiently to welcome the new bride.

Like every new bride arriving for the first time at the home of her in-laws, Gulab was nervous. She was particularly apprehensive about meeting Mohandas, whom she imagined to be a strict patriarch. And she desperately wanted to make a good impression on me, her new mother-in-law.

All of Gulab's fears vanished the moment she set her eyes on Bapu and me. Fully covered with her sari *pallu*, she bowed down and touched her forehead to Mohandas' feet. Overflowing with a novel tenderness and joy, he patted her head, held her by the shoulders and raised her from the floor. He pecked her forehead tenderly and in a cheery voice said, 'Chanchi *dikri*, just remember that your Bapu welcomes you in this home not as a daughter-in-law, but as my daughter.'

Mirth rang though the residents of the settlement. I could see Harilal's eyes light up and Gulab's brim over with tears. No one other than her parents addressed her as Chanchi and the sweet sound of her nickname from Bapu's mouth instantly eased her apprehensions. She felt wanted, loved and at home with all the people who mattered. 'You are not faraway from home, *dikri*,' Mohandas continued, 'and never forget that here you are our eldest daughter, elder than everyone else around.'

Gulab's mind was filled with the love that her Bapu was unabashedly showering on her. It took her little time to embrace everyone as her own kin, the impish Devdas, playful Ramdas and of course, her adoring husband, the elusive Harilal.

❈ ❈ ❈

Harilal's reunion with Gulab that night was a passionate outburst of pent up emotions. The long days of separation had deeply intensified the longing they felt for each other and now that she was with child, he felt more intensely in love with her. This time it felt like a bitter-sweet throbbing in his heart. Harilal took his doe-eyed wife in his arms gently and held her close. For hours they stayed locked in a tight embrace, reliving the longing and pain of the days gone by. Gulab was consumed by a euphoria that spread deep into the folds of her womb. She was secure in the arms of her lord and in the knowledge that their baby would be delivered in capable hands.

'My lord is beside me and all's well with the world,' she cooed in Harilal's ear, nestling contentedly on his chest.

❈ ❈ ❈

10 January 1908

It was an unusually hot day. A blazing sun was beating down on the city, while everyone waited anxiously for the arrival of Mohandas who had been away to Johannesburg. All eyes were fixed on the narrow weather-beaten track that led to the railway station. All preparations were in place for the *seemant* ceremony that was to be conducted with great fanfare, but strictly according to custom, as per Mohandas' orders.

Unlike the bland meals that were fed to the inmates everyday at Phoenix, everyone was looking forward to a grand feast, but only after the ritual blessing of the mother-to-be and her unborn child. Mohandas' favourite dishes were being prepared and a rare treat of sweets, *farsaan, puran-poli, dhokla* and *methi-na-gota* was on the menu.

I had happily broken all the austere rules and restrictions that Mohandas had imposed in the kitchen. It was a day to rejoice and nothing was going to stop me from demonstrating my eagerness to pamper my adored daughter-in-law.

An excited Gulab sat bedecked in a ceremonial pink and silver sari on a low stool, waiting for Bapu and the rituals to commence. But there was no sign of Mohandas. The train should have arrived two hours earlier, and the two men who had gone to the station should have brought him home by now. The long wait felt even longer that morning and I became restless. I feared that little Gulab would be completely exhausted squatting on that low stool on the floor, so I ordered everyone to feed all the children as well as little Gulab.

'Let the young ones eat. We can wait for Bapu,' I said.

Soon dark clouds appeared in the sky and the sun disappeared behind the cover of darkness. This did not augur well. My anxiety was beginning to rise with each passing moment.

Devdas had perched himself on the branch of a tall tree in the front yard to look out for his father.

'They have come!' he shouted. And everyone ran out to greet Mohandas.

'It's not Bapu. Wait.' Devdas said. 'There's someone else approaching. But where is Bapu?'

Many of the other children had scampered up the trees around the entrance to get a vantage-point view of the road outside. A few ran down the path excitedly to greet the people who were nearing the house.

'Bapu's not with them, Ba,' Devdas' eyes grew wistful as he looked at me. 'Who are these people and where is Bapu?' My heart raced. I was in panic. This certainly was cause for alarm.

The two men who had gone to fetch him entered the gate looking worried and blurted out. 'The police have arrested Bapu. He's been sent to jail.'

I crumpled to the floor in a heap. Harilal, Manilal, Devdas and Ramdas huddled around me and Gulab came running out to the verandah, her large eyes stricken with fear and face bereft of colour.

Mohandas along with twenty-six of his colleagues, all prominent in the boycott campaign that he was ardently pursuing, had been arrested. They were to appear before a magistrate's court in Johannesburg the following day.

For over six months these men had been protesting against fingerprinting and the obtaining of certificates of registration that was made mandatory for Indians in all prominent townships and cities of Transvaal. With strict instructions from Mohandas to avoid any kind of provocation or violence, they had been working on a carefully mapped-out strategy of peaceful resistance.

Even as the *Indian Opinion* gave the *satyagrahis* extensive coverage, the government had waited patiently for the movement to die a natural death. But when it failed to abate, they had stepped in with harsher measures. This had led to Mohandas and his co-protestors appearing voluntarily in court, where they impetuously demanded from the bench the heaviest penalty to be awarded to them. They were sentenced to two months of imprisonment and their petulant demand ignored.

Mohandas' co-worker who had carried the ominous news, stood quietly before all the assembled residents with his head bowed. The evening shadows had lengthened over the settlement, plunging it into darkness.

✄ ✄ ✄

The arrest of Mohandas couldn't have come at a more inopportune time. All the earlier jubilation ceased and a pall of gloom descended on the residents. The foremost thought in everyone's mind was 'who will lead the *satyagrahis* now and what will become of the movement?' I gathered all my courage and looked up at the messenger of the ill-omened missive.

'Naidubhai, in which jail has my husband been imprisoned?' I asked him anxiously. 'Who else is with him? How long is he going to be held captive? What about his food?'

I bombarded Naidu with a volley of questions, my voice interspersed with sobs.

The nonplussed Naidu faked a smile on his sullen face.

'I have never been inside a jail, so I cannot say, Ba, but those who have, tell me that they serve a sticky, sugarless gruel made of maize flour for breakfast, a small portion of rice, salt and ghee for lunch and the same maize gruel with some vegetables for dinner.'

With the enticing aroma of freshly made *puran-polis* wafting in the air, the thought of my husband eating that horrific prison food made my stomach knot up. I looked at the table laden with mouth-watering dishes that had been cooked for the revellers. I imagined Mohandas locked up in a dark cell wearing coarse, dirty clothes, gulping down boiled vegetables, bland rice and a ghastly cornmeal porridge. I moved away from the table and said, 'I cannot share my husband's hardships in jail, but I can at least share his punishing diet. So until he is released, I pledge to eat nothing but unflavoured sugarless cornmeal. This shall be my contribution to his *satyagraha*.'

All the women of the ashram, dressed in their finery, carrying gifts for the expectant mother, stared at me in silence.

'But that should not be our worry, Ba,' Naidu, the South Indian co-worker of Bapu, managed to say a few words in his laboured Hindi. 'What is of greater concern is that in Bapu's absence we are without a leader and our battle is doomed.'

I heard Harilal shuffling around. He stood erect with his eyes focussed straight on Naidu's face.

'Do not worry, Mr. Naidu,' he said. 'In Bapu's absence it is my duty to carry on his unfinished task. I shall join the *satyagraha* and carry on the fight against the atrocities of the British government.'

There was a resolute ring to Harilal's voice. He did not bat an eyelid as everybody stared at the reticent lad.

My heart leapt into my mouth. My chest filled with pride. I glanced at Gulab who was standing beside me, her glowing eyes fixed adoringly on her heroic husband. Looking resplendent in her pink sari, flush with the glow of pregnancy, Gulab watched her husband become the cynosure of all eyes. I held her elbow gently and drew her to me. She moved into the crook of my arm absorbing all the tender warmth that exuded from my body.

'Will you also go to jail, Motabhai?' It was the quivering voice of Devdas. He was tugging at Harilal's arm. Panic had overcome all the children as much as it had swamped the elders.

'Yes,' he said placing his arm around Devdas' shoulders. 'Yes I will if it comes to that. But you and Ramdas are big boys now. You will be here to take care of Ba and all others. Won't you?'

Devdas looked agitated. 'But Ba says that *Laxmiji* is coming to our house in a few days, Motabhai... It will not be right for you to be in jail when she arrives.' The innocence of Devdas' remark sent a ripple of laughter through the people collected there.

'Motabhai, I have an idea.' It was Ramdas. 'You stay here and wait to welcome *Laxmiji*. Devdas and I shall take on the fight with the British government. We can go to jail instead of you.'

The boys embraced each other and Gulab joined them.

The child-like banter of Ramdas and Devdas continued for a while later. Lightness descended on the ashram and the earlier gloom somewhat dissipated. Everyone dispersed for the night.

❈ ❈ ❈

Forty Three

In the dark cover of that grim night, when all the guests had returned home, Harilal and Gulab lay in a close embrace in their room. Gulab's head rested on his gently heaving chest, her breath intermingling with his. They lay there for a long time together, the air thick with the deep love they shared with each other and their unborn child.

'Are you awake, my sweetness?' Harilal whispered. 'Our little one is listening to every word we speak. I need to ask the both of you something. What will you do if I go to prison? What will the two of you do without me?'

Gulab moved closer into the space between them and looked at him adoringly. Her wide, child-like eyes had become even wider and her breath more rapid.

'What do I say, my beloved?' she replied shyly, looking away. She had placed her soft palms on Harilal's cheeks. 'I only know that you will do what is right.'

'And suppose the government sentences me to a long term in jail? I shall be forced to live away from you, Gulab. Then how will you manage without me?'

Gulab fell silent for a few moments. When she spoke, her voice was steady.

'All I can say is that I shall abide by whatever you say, my lord. Don't you see how unquestioningly Ba supports Bapu? How resolutely she stands by him in all his pursuits. That is exactly what your Gulab will do. That is what you would expect from a Gandhi daughter-in-law. I support you blindly. So stop fretting, my beloved. Stop fretting about me and....' Gulab's voice trailed off mid sentence into a whisper.

'You stopped, Gulab? What were you going to say? Come on speak fearlessly, my little rose.'

Harilal kissed Gulab on her parted lips, a long deep passionate kiss that took her breath away.

Gulab's face was glowing. Her coyness reflected in the colour of her flushed cheeks.

'Stop worrying about me and our child,' she murmured into his ear.

'Oh Gulab! I do love you so much. And that is just what I wanted to hear. All I need is you, your trust and your love. And then I am invincible.' Harilal's voice was laden with tenderness.

'Shhhh!' She said placing her lips on his trembling mouth.

'Go to sleep now. Our little baby needs to sleep too. Go to sleep, father and child…I am not a separate entity from you, my beloved. My soul is fused with yours!'

With each of her caressing strokes on his furrowed brow, Harilal's anxiety eased away. The sweet song Gulab hummed sent him into a trance…

Nazar na jaam chalkavi ne
Chaliya kya tamay,
Jigar ne aam tarsavi
 Ne tamne bolave pyaar,
Tamey ubha rahyo…
Ubha rahyo…Ubha rahyo, yaar…

(You tricked me with the wine
Overflowing from your eyes
Now you make me pine for you
By making me fall in love
Stay on, stay on, stay on, my love…)

The tiny little Gandhi inside her womb kicked and frolicked about in tune with her melody and then became still. All three were lulled into a beautiful and peaceful, romantic slumber, while in a far corner of the quiet settlement, I spent a sleepless night in astral travel, knocking on the formidable doors of a dark prison cell in Transvaal.

❋ ❋ ❋

The weeks ahead were filled with fear. Even though I had learned to accept Mohandas' long absence from home and I knew his work required him to be away for extended periods, but this time it was different. He was a convict, locked up with hardened criminals in the custody of a hostile government that was determined to punish him for his role in the battle of Indian resistance. Each day I waited anxiously for a translation of newspaper reports that were our only source of information of the developments in Johannesburg.

To my relief, I discovered that Mohandas was not alone. All his colleagues who had appeared with him in the magistrate's court had also been sentenced to two months in jail. I also learned that within a few days, close to one hundred and fifty protestors had been rounded up and thrown into jail. The prison that was built to accommodate fifty prisoners, was now crammed to three times its capacity and what made it worse was that no one knew what was happening inside.

Ridden by my mounting terror, I had no choice but to surrender to God. It was not in my nature to wallow in self-pity, nor did I allow myself to fall into the trap of doubt, so I sought refuge in prayers. I gathered my wits about me and regained my composure, calling upon my undying faith in the Almighty.

God will watch over him…

The thought was both reassuring and empowering, and I went back with renewed vigour to looking after the affairs of the settlement, taking charge of all that ought to have been done in the absence of my husband.

❋ ❋ ❋

The pineapple harvesting season that everyone looked forward to had arrived and hectic activity was underway. Even with my limited knowledge of arithmetic, I had devised a memory for numbers and every evening I would report the figures to whoever was in charge of bookkeeping. Other than the fully pregnant Gulab, everyone was involved in picking and harvesting of the ripened pineapples that were crated and sent off to the market to be sold. Taking a break from my kitchen chores one hot afternoon, I wandered into the fields where all the four boys were engrossed in their work along with others from the settlement.

Manilal was the first to read it. He had stopped his work and grabbed the day's newspaper eagerly. His eyes lit up with joy and he ran towards me waving the paper wildly in the air.

'Ba! Ba!' he shouted. 'There's good news!' Gulab, Devdas, Ramdas all came running to him.

'Bapu has been freed, Ba! Do you hear? Bapu has been freed!'

A wave of joy lurched up from my stomach. I couldn't believe my ears.

'Are you sure, Manilal? Read it again. What you are saying is not possible. Bapu had been given two months in jail, it's only been three weeks. There must be some mistake!'

I learned later that Mohandas had been summoned to Pretoria, under police cover. After what seemed like a convincing argument before General Smuts, a release order was signed for him and his co-workers, and they were let off. Mohandas would walk free. I rejoiced more because his release meant freedom from the self-imposed pledge of a bland, cornmeal diet that I had undertaken the day he was arrested!

With Gulab's help I prepared a grand feast the night Mohandas returned. It was a feast that was to be shared with the family, the neighbours and all the inmates of the settlement, but above all, this time it was a feast for me.

❃ ❃ ❃

Life soon limped back to normalcy in Phoenix. Mohandas plunged headlong into his cause once again, working frenetically with his fellow protestors all day long.

It was no secret that the Indian community was incensed over the compromise that had secured Mohandas' release from prison. Their faith in the British government had been shaken and the feeling of betrayal had aggravated.

One morning a disgruntled Pathan called Mir Aslam, seized by a fit of rage, struck at Mohandas. He pummelled him with a stick mercilessly and left him lying in a pool of blood on the road, for dead. To be assaulted, not by a ferocious white mob, but by a man belonging to the very community for which Mohandas was fighting the government, was more shocking than the attack itself. Mohandas was rescued by a Christian priest who administered first aid to him and kept him in his home till he was well enough to travel back to Phoenix.

Once again clouds of gloom gathered over the settlement. It left me panic-stricken, but I fought the urge to rush to Johannesburg to be by his side, fearing it would incur unecessary expenditure, since every penny was needed for the running of the settlement.

In a few days a letter arrived from Henry Polak that relieved me of my anxiety. Mohandas was safe and recovering from his injuries that fortunately had been no deeper than surface wounds. The baptist clergyman, Reverend Joseph Doke had summoned a doctor to treat him. On his regaining consciousness, the police had waited to record his statement, which Mohandas had declined. The assailant was let off in the absence of any criminal charges.

I was not surprised by Mohandas' action. It was reassuring to know that my husband was still the obstinate and unpredictable man I had known him to be.

Mohandas' return however was not yet ordained. His homeward journey was marred by fresh threats of violence. He had stopped at a railway station in Durban to address a crowd and enlist the support of Indians in Natal, when an angry mob of Pathans incited by feelings of betrayal stormed the platform where he stood. His supporters had to whisk him away to safety. It was only after a great deal of persuasion from his people in Durban, that he returned to the settlement, ruing that it was impossible for him to live in constant fear.

I kept as calm as I could while Mohandas sat beside me, narrating the events that had led to this ugly episode. I noticed the raw scars of the wounds on his body. The fresh gauze dressings on his scalp that had been shaved in several spots disturbed me. I tried not to imagine the force of the cruel blows that the savage Pathan must have rained on him and how dreadful the pain must have been.

'I am prepared to face the worst; you never need worry about me or the family. We shall be all right,' I said in a voice that belied my fears.

I could see the tension ease away from my husband's face. His eyes dimmed over with gratitude. He took my hands into his. 'That was just what I needed to hear, Kastur. You read my mind. That was just what I needed to hear you say.'

Late that night, in the quiet of my room I lay on my bed alone and wept.

❧ ❧ ❧

She was named Rami. The girl born to Gulab on the ninth day following fasting and feasting, in the run-up to the birthday of Lord Rama, was a pretty little thing. She arrived late in the evening while the inmates of the settlement waited impatiently outside a makeshift labour room for the wonderful news.

Earlier that day, Mohandas had called for a magnificent feast to celebrate the festival of Ramanavami and bring alive the moments of Gulab's seventh-month puja that had got disrupted by the news of his arrest.

'Prepare a grand feast, Kastur,' he said, 'and invite everyone in the ashram to join us. Make your famous *puran-polis* for all and let's rejoice the birth of Lord Rama while we countdown to this baby's arrival.' And the celebrations had begun.

'Make this a day for everyone to rejoice. Never mind if my fasting does not permit me to savour your delicacies, Kastur. Feed all the others and let them pray for an easy delivery and a healthy child for Chanchi. She can deliver any day now and I can be picked up by the government anytime, so I don't want her to feel that her father-in-law does not pamper her.'

Mohandas laughed out loud; a cheery laugh that vibrated the core of his being, which reverberated off the walls of our home and wafted out to the clear blue sky.

'And don't forget to give Chanchi an extra dollop of ghee, Kastur. It will be good for her. It will make her labour short and easy.' There was love pouring out of his words as he glanced at Gulab who blushed, lowered her eyes and shied out of the room. A faint smile flickered in her eyes.

Mohandas and Harilal were both at the printing press when a young girl came running up to them. Panting hard as she climbed the steps, she shouted out, 'She's arrived, Bapu! She's arrived. Ba's wish has come true. *Laxmiji* has arrived. Chanchiben has had a baby girl!' On hearing the news, a loud cheer rang through the ashram. A cool breeze blew on Harilal's face as he stood still, drowned in a wave of ecstacy. He closed his eyes and murmured a silent prayer to thank the Lord. His mind filled with the face of little Gulab and the heady scent of her body diffused in the air.

Thank you, my beloved Rose. Thank you for this wonderful gift that shall bind us together in an even tighter bond. I love you, my precious flower and can't wait to hold our baby in my arms.

He could hear his Bapu's sing-song voice somewhere in the distance.

'What an auspicious coincidence! *Laxmiji* has arrived on Ramanavami. She is indeed a gift from Rama. We shall call her Rami. Isn't that a fine name, Harilal? Rami, the gift of Lord Rama!'

But Harilal was not listening. He was consumed by the novel exhilaration of fatherhood and the new surge of passion he felt for his beloved Gulab.

It was the 10th of April, 1908.

✖ ✖ ✖

During the week that Phoenix had been celebrating the joyous birth of Rami, thousands of miles away in Rajkot, death had struck the Gandhi household. Gokuldas, Raliatben's newlywed son, was killed in a freak accident while playing cricket.

Earlier, Gokuldas had expressed his intention of rejoining us at the ashram in Phoenix, along with his bride, but fate had ordained otherwise. The news of Mohandas' beloved nephew's untimely and sudden death plunged the family into gloom. Mohandas was devastated. He had always envisaged a long life in public service for his promising nephew, but more than him it was Harilal who was stricken with grief. Gokuldas was closer to him than his own brother, and his death affected him deeply.

A few weeks later, a shattered Harilal left Gulab and Rami at the ashram to join the *satyagraha* movement with his father and I felt a sense of relief. Harilal was always sensitive to the suffering of others, so I felt that he might find solace in public service and come to terms with the death of his older cousin.

The news of Harilal independently leading a group of *satyagrahis* was greeted with fresh vigour in the settlement. Before leaving for his mission, Harilal went to bid goodbye to Gulab. He held the three-month-old Rami in his arms who gurgled and smiled when she saw her father. Gulab however was agitated, but Harilal's zeal somewhat alleviated her anxiety and she let him go.

Harilal came to me and touched his head to my feet, seeking my blessings. He sported a bright red *tilak* on his forehead and a garland of fresh flowers around his neck that one of the inmates had put on him. I blessed him, kissed his forehead and saw him leave, comforted in the knowledge that he was now one with his father.

Harilal assembled with his team near the Transvaal frontier. The *satyagrahis* were shouting slogans loudly, 'Junior Gandhi *zindabad*! Junior Gandhi *amar rahe!*' Long Live Junior Gandhi... The air reverberated with continuous cheering that day and an extraordinary fervour was felt by each protestor on the streets.

In an instant, Harilal ceased to be himself. He had transformed into a larger than life "Junior Gandhi", the proud son of an illustrious father whom the world had come to deeply idolize and emulate. It was a watershed moment in my son's life, but alas! Frittered away.

⚸ ⚸ ⚸

On 24 July, Harilal was picked up by the police for selling fruit on the streets of the city without a mandatory hawker's licence and thrown into jail on the charge of illegal trading. The next morning, Harilal was pronounced guilty in the magistrate's court. He was ordered to either pay a fine of one pound, or serve a seven-day sentence of rigorous imprisonment. With his head held high and defiance burning in his youthful eyes, Harilal opted for the prison sentence.

Mohandas who had been present in the court was beside himself with joy. He embraced his son in full view of all those present, congratulating him for his courageous spirit.

'Today you have made me the happiest person in the world, Harilal. You have proved that you are a worthy son and a true *satyagrahi*. You have done me proud.'

The bond between the father and son had never been this strong. It instilled a deep sense of optimism in me for I believed that the birth of Rami had indeed ushered in good times for Harilal and us.

For Harilal it had been a first—a hitherto unknown experience of being in custody. Later standing in the defendant's box in a courtroom packed to its capacity, he saw his Bapu in a black robe acting as his counsel for defence.

'My Lord, I request you to award the severest punishment possible to the *satyagrahis!*' He pleaded.

Mohandas' scathing words boomed across the silent courtroom that broke into a loud murmur.

Harilal was stunned, his face shadowed by bewilderment—

What had got into his Bapu! Why was he saying this? Wasn't he supposed to be pleading his son's case?

'I say this, my Lord because they will repeat their earlier actions and get arrested again and that will cause a waste of the precious time of this Hon'ble court. To save both parties from wasting time, I appeal to you to give them the longest term possible.'

The courtroom erupted with a long continuous applause. The British authorities and the magistrate were dumbfounded for never had they witnessed such a peculiar plea. The *satyagrahis* led by Harilal were awarded a short, rigorous imprisonment and set free a few days later.

Harilal emerged from prison a stronger man. The abhorrent jail food had failed to break his spirit. In fact it made him impatient to break the law and court arrest yet again, just as his father had.

I was ecstatic. What greater joy could a mother have desired? It far exceeded the exhilaration I had felt at becoming a grandmother on the birth of Rami!

❈   ❈   ❈

16 August 1908

On the precincts of the Hamid Mosque in Johannesburg, a congregation of 3,000 Hindus, Muslims, Parsis and Christians had converged for a peaceful demonstration. In the centre of the front yard, on a raised platform was a large African cooking pot with a jerry can of kerosene oil placed beside it. More than 2,000 Registration Certificates lay stacked alongside, ready to be thrown into the fire. It was the largest *satyagraha* ever planned by Mohandas, who by then had completely abandoned his law practice to devote all his time for the movement.

As the deadline given by Mohandas to repeal the draconian Black Act imposed by the government neared, the crowd got restive. At 4 pm, a messenger riding a bicycle arrived at the mosque carrying a telegram from the authorities. The stiffly worded missive was read out to the agitated crowd—

The Black Act shall not be repealed. No change in the government's stand.

The frenzied crowd surged forward and began hurling the certificates into the cauldron. Someone poured kerosene oil into the pot and a burning matchstick set the bundle on fire, amidst loud continuous cries of 'Burn them! Burn them!' Tall flames leapt out of the cauldron and the crowd began to clap wildly. From somewhere amongst them Mir Alam, the Pathan who had assaulted Mohandas, appeared onto the platform and Mohandas embraced him. Loud cries of cheer and applause rent the air again.

The next morning, all the newspapers carried reports of the massive *satyagraha*. The *Daily Mail* compared the certificate-burning episode by the Indians of Johannesburg to the famous Boston Tea Party of the American Revolution. For the *satyagrahis* and Mohandas, this was a momentous victory.

Forty Four

I had been neglecting my health for sometime now, consumed as I was with the goings-on in the lives of Mohandas and Harilal. The violent clashes with the authorities, and the attempt on Mohandas' life had taken a heavy toll on me. Also, since the birth of Ramdas and Devdas I had been suffering from bouts of heavy menstrual bleeding, which had made me anaemic. But I didn't want to be a source of stress for Mohandas, so I went about my daily chores uncomplainingly.

My rapidly deteriorating health went unnoticed even by Mohandas during his visits to Phoenix, for his singleminded focus on the *satyagraha* had left no room for much else. The grim truth was that the *satyagraha* had made little headway. The much publicized certificate-burning protest to demonstrate the resentment of the Indian community against the newly-enforced laws hadn't changed anything. This hung heavy on his mind.

Early in October, after two weeks of hectic preparations at Phoenix, Mohandas left for Johannesburg to campaign against the newly-introduced Immigration Act. Determined to bolster the movement by courting arrest once again, he sent a telegram to the settlement,

Keep absolutely firm to the end. Suffering is our only remedy. Victory is certain.

Those cryptic words brought little solace to me. My mind was emotionally drained, as was my worsening, failing health. Outlining his plan, a special mention was made on the front page of the *Indian Opinion* the next day.

On 10 October 1908, Mohandas was awarded a sentence, whereby he would either have to pay a fine of twenty-five pounds, or go to jail for two months. Eighteen days later, Harilal and Hermann Kallenbach met a buoyant, rebellious and utterly committed fighter in prison, with his spirit intact and a mind completely consumed by the cause.

⚹ ⚹ ⚹

The news of my ill health came to Mohandas in prison. An urgent letter from Albert West, a resident of the settlement who edited the *Indian Opinion*, informed him of my excessive bleeding and the need for immediate hospitalization. West urged him to pay the stipulated fine and rush back to Phoenix.

The letter must have delivered a sharp jolt to Mohandas. It suddenly dawned on him that in his preoccupation with his punishing work schedule and commitment to public service, he had totally neglected me. Torn between the two, he wrote me a letter, in an attempt to appease me or perhaps to allay his own guilt.

My dearest Kastur,

Mr. West has just given me the news of your ill health. Though I feel anxious about your health I am not in a position to come and nurse you. I hope you will understand that I have renounced everything in life for the sake of the struggle. If I come to you now I will have to plead guilty of breaking the law and pay the fine to secure my release from jail. You know this is not possible. I shall be reducing the struggle to a farce.

However, I am sure you will feel better if you remain strong in your mind and eat well. And if it is destined that you shall die, I think it is better for you to go before me. You know that I love you very much. And you must know that I shall continue to love you just as much even after you are gone. Even if you die, you will be eternally alive because your soul is deathless.

On my part I would like to assure you that I do not intend to marry another woman after your death. And this I have told you many times. You must have faith in God and set your soul free. Your death shall be deemed to be another great sacrifice for the cause of satyagraha. My struggle is not merely against the authorities, but against nature itself. I hope you understand this and don't feel offended. That is all I ask of you.

Yours, Mohandas

P.S. Manilal and Chanchi; I want you both to read this letter yourselves and then aloud to Ba. I feel very worried but I am helpless. Please keep me updated of her health regularly, look after your younger brothers and I shall pray that Ba is up and about soon.

Blessings from Mohandas

The cold, matter-of-fact letter from my husband hit me like an avalanche of ice. I couldn't decide if I was angry or sad at the stark revelation that in his mind Mohandas was ready for me to die. He had indeed prepared to deal with my dying, long before death would actually consume me. The insensitivity of his words masked by a presumptuous audacity, the so-called resignation and reassurance of his commitment to me even after I was gone, seemed frivolous.

To come to terms with the truth that it made little difference to Mohandas' life, whether I was dead or alive, was painful. All my life that I had spent waiting on him, pining for him, supporting him when he was struggling, had come to naught in one stroke. Did I mean nothing to this man?

My insides ravaged by continuous bleeding, my body frail with anaemia and my mind outraged by his letter, I sank back in my bed trying hard to hold back my tears in front of Gulab and Manilal. It would be a long time before Mohandas could redeem himself in my eyes again.

✄ ✄ ✄

In the next couple of days I did somewhat recover in body, but my spirit which had taken a cruel blow, was taking longer to heal. When Mohandas returned after his release from prison, he was shocked to see how worn-out and frail I had become. Whether he was burdened by guilt on writing that letter or not, I was unable to say, but his attitude appeared a bit more sympathetic. And when we heard of Harilal's arrest a few days later, I saw him visibly disturbed, particularly when he saw how flustered I had been.

Finally, he insisted on a thorough medical examination for me.

✂ ✂ ✂

A month later Mohandas and I were on a train to Durban to consult a Parsi physician by the name of Dr. Nanji, who was also one of Mohandas' trusted friends. Dr. Nanji was of the opinion that my haemorrhaging could only be controlled by surgery that needed to be done immediately. My physical condition being what it was, I would be unable to withstand anaesthesia, so he suggested on a curette procedure that would be painful, but was the only option.

The procedure went off well. I bore the piercing pain courageously after which Dr. Nanji and his wife, who was a trained nurse, requested Mohandas to let me stay on to recuperate in their home instead of going back to Phoenix.

'We'll take good care of her,' he said, 'and she'll get all the rest she needs. You can go back to your work in Johannesburg with a free mind.'

Mohandas was fully aware that his absence from the *satyagraha* was costing him dearly, and after consulting with me, he set off on a train to Johannesburg, leaving me in the care of Dr. Nanji and his wife. I had expected nothing more from him, so his going away had little impact on my ravaged mind. It did occur to me however that had he been ill, would I have left him in the care of strangers and vanish into a wilderness for the sake of my elusive cause?

My forebodings were not unfounded. The procedure had failed in controlling my bleeding and I continued to haemorrhage as before. Heavy doses of painkillers had made me weaker and more lethargic each day. Two weeks after he had left, a panic-stricken Dr. Nanji telephoned Mohandas in Johannesburg.

'Kasturba is very weak,' he said. 'She's losing too much blood and unless she is fed a healthy non-vegetarian diet, she will not regain her strength. She must be given beef broth or else her life is in danger.'

Mohandas was appalled. 'That is preposterous, Dr. Nanji. I cannot allow you to feed my wife beef broth! Under no circumstances can we do that. What does Kasturba have to say? Have you spoken to her about this?'

Dr. Nanji hadn't mentioned anything to me. He believed I was in no condition to decide anything for myself. He insisted that the best and only remedy to get me back onto my feet was beef broth.

'I fear for her life,' was the last thing he said to Mohandas who boarded the first train to Durban to intervene in the matter.

When Mohandas reached Durban he was shocked to learn that Dr. Nanji had already given me a bowl of the broth without my knowledge. Despite the doctor's noble intentions, Mohandas was furious that he had been betrayed by a trusted friend, and even more that I had been an innocent victim of this betrayal. Dr. Nanji however, was unrepentant. As a doctor he had done his duty and saw no reason to be apologetic, as he had only acted in the best interest of his patient. 'It is a matter of life and death and I need not consult a patient in my care on the course of treatment I choose,' he said emphatically to my irate husband.

Critically ill and extremely weak to even react on hearing that I had been fed beef broth, I reached out for Mohandas' hand. In my trembling voice, which was barely audible, I said, 'Take me home now. I know I'll get better if I am in my own home.'

Unmindful of Dr. Nanji's vehement protests we decided to leave for Durban as early as possible.

'I promise I shall be fine,' I said to a very perturbed Mohandas. 'Just take me home.'

❃ ❃ ❃

Nothing could have been more embarrassing for me than have Mohandas carry me out himself to board a rickshaw that would take us to the station. Having been reduced to just skin and bones, he easily bore my weightless body in his arms, with a grave expression on his countenance. I shrank within myself at the impropriety of being seen in public in my husband's arms, but drained of all my strength I had no option but to be propped up like a child on his back through the streets of Durban in broad daylight. Even at the station he carried me across the length of the platform to my seat on the near empty train that gave me ample room to sleep through the journey.

At Phoenix, some men from the settlement were waiting to receive us. I was fed a glass of warm milk and then placed on a makeshift stretcher fashioned out of an old hammock to navigate the two-mile arduous trek home. The sugarcane fields through which I was carried back by Mohandas and the other two were soaking wet and slippery after it had rained that morning. But strangely my spirits lifted as we approached the ashram and the mere sight of my family and friends made me feel better.

The next day I was put through a rigorous schedule of mud packs and nature cure remedies. Never before had Mohandas' health fads been more regimented and all my skepticism notwithstanding, I saw a remarkable improvement in my health. As the news of my grave illness and the horrific beef broth betrayal spread amongst the Hindus of Natal, a religious preacher appeared at our door one day. He held forth on the tenets of Hindu philosophy and quoted from the scriptures to dispel the notion that Hinduism prohibited the consumption of flesh and alcohol. The long debate between the swami and Mohandas carried on endlessly in the presence of Manilal and Ramdas, with no conclusion in sight. Mohandas argued vehemently against the eating of meat and consumption of alcohol and the swami would not stop citing religious verses to refute him, until I finally intervened.

'Swamiji! Say what you will, but I would rather die than eat beef, even if it is the last and only cure on earth! You may discuss this for as long as you want with my husband and the children, but please do not trouble me again. I have made up my mind!'

The swami beat a hasty retreat, the matter closed and I went back to my nature cure regimen even more resolute in my faith. The treachery of Dr. Nanji's violation of my *dharma* soon faded away.

❄   ❄   ❄

FORTY FIVE

Outside the cosy cocoon of the ashram-home in Phoenix, the world was convulsing with tumultuous changes, even as the sundry arrests of Mohandas and Harilal continued unabated. In the span of one year post my surgery, I had got word of their arrests, no fewer than eight times. They served sentences, sometimes together in the same prison and sometimes separately, which I reckoned must have been doubly harrowing for Harilal. The government however, was hell bent on breaking the resistance and crushing Mohandas. They transferred him from Volksrust, where a number of his fellow *satyagrahis* had been imprisoned, to the dreaded Pretoria Central Jail.

Allowed to write only one letter each month, he shot off a lengthy five-page message to Manilal, who had just turned sixteen and had been entrusted with the responsibility of being the man of the house. Filled typically with a list of moral instructions, the long letter was a detailing of the dos and don'ts for his son, and the need to imbibe purity in thought, word and deed.

On 23 June 1909 Mohandas was released from the Pretoria Central Jail. He had barely stepped into the settlement, when he was sent off to England on behalf of the Indian community to negotiate for an autonomous federal government, which would enjoy Dominion status within the British Empire. Meanwhile Manilal, enthused by his brother's commitment to the cause, expressed his keenness to join the resistance in Johannesburg and court arrest. Much to my relief, Mohandas shot down the idea and wrote Manilal another long letter that pointed out the virtues of living in Phoenix, where its placid serenity induced a natural search for the soul and promoted the quest for truth.

Back in England, Mohandas was up against a wall with no resolution in sight. He asked Henry Polak to go to India and seek advice from his mentor and friend, Gopal Krishna Gokhale who had become a member of the Viceroy's Legislative Council. Mohandas felt that it would build further pressure on the authorities in London. Even though Polak was met with warm and encouraging responses from the leaders in India (who sent strongly-worded messages to the negotiators), when the Union of South Africa Act was passed by the parliament four months later, no concessions or guarantees had been included to protect the rights of Indians in South Africa.

On 13 November 1909, Mohandas set sail from England for Cape Town aboard the S.S. Kildonan Castle, a saddened, frustrated and disillusioned man. On the homebound voyage that lasted seventeen long days, Mohandas locked himself in his cabin and gave vent to his rage by penning a 30,000-word manuscript titled, "Hind Swaraj"; while I, the silent, suffering, and eternal companion of this maddened fighter for civil rights, had no option but to wait for his return. The few letters that he wrote to eleven-year-old Ramdas did little to ease my anxiety.

This was not the first time it occurred to me that even though Mohandas had completely submerged himself in his peculiar experiments with truth, the real brunt of its pursuit had fallen onto me.

⚘ ⚘ ⚘

In the early months of 1910, with far more at stake than just my health, I began feeling an increased sense of restlessness. Although I had become accustomed to Mohandas' long absences and his undying devotion to the cause, which I had come to accept, to suffer the same travails for my sons was getting unbearable for me.

In the past eighteen months, Harilal had spent less time in Phoenix than his father. He had been imprisoned for a total of fourteen months with hard labour, a thought that disturbed me deeply. I constantly fretted about Gulab and my little Rami. Gulab's personality had undergone a change. She was no longer the happily dispositioned, vivacious girl I knew. I could understand the poor girl's plight. My own years of loneliness as a young wife kept haunting me and no amount of my cajoling Gulab could bring her out of the shadow of gloom that had enveloped her. What was even more terrifying was that Manilal had also been arrested repeatedly after he had joined the agitation and the thought of him undergoing the harshest prison terms, three so far, was heart-rending. I feared the day when Ramdas and Devdas would also follow their calls of duty and join their father's *satyagraha*.

But for me there was going to be no respite. The struggle in South Africa had taken another dimension. Thousands of coal miners who had called a strike on Mohandas' advice had been rendered jobless and it had fallen upon Mohandas to provide food and homes for them. As a result, he decided to lead a march to Transvaal to protest against the law that prohibited free movement of the native labourers. He hoped that if they were arrested, the government would have no choice but to provide them food and shelter. If not, then they would continue to march right up to a property donated by his old associate Hermann Kallenbach, where Mohandas planned to establish "Tolstoy Farm", a settlement to rehabilitate unemployed coalmine workers and their families. I would also have to move bag and baggage and set up house all over again.

The news of Harilal's arrest and imprisonment, once again in the harshest of prisons could not have come at a more inopportune moment. I had last seen Harilal six months before Mohandas had declared his intention of moving to Tolstoy Farm. Try as I did, I could not extricate myself from the despair that engulfed me. I knew that Harilal's feelings of dejection were dangerously high and I had no way of allaying them. Had I known that that was going to be the cruelest blow of destiny to fall on my son, I may have tried to shield him, but even my best efforts were powerless in the battle against his stars.

✼ ✼ ✼

It was a cool, breezy evening at the settlement in Phoenix when Henry Polak arrived without prior notice. Mohandas had not returned from his trip to London and I was eagerly awaiting to hear some news about him. All the residents had gathered around Polak to hear about Mohandas' whereabouts. After an extensive briefing, he turned to me and said earnestly.

'I have special news for you, Mrs. Gandhi.'

My heart skipped a beat.

'Oh don't get me wrong, Mrs. Gandhi,' Polak beamed. 'I have some news that shall make you very happy. You have always been worried about your children's education, haven't you? And that Mr. Gandhi has never done anything about it. Well, all that is about to change. Mr. Gandhi has written to me that our old friend Dr. Pranjivan Mehta, has been very helpful to him in England.'

The bewildered expression on my face must have amused Polak for he broke into a throaty laugh.

'Mrs. Gandhi, Dr. Mehta has proposed that one of your sons be sent to England to study law for which he is prepared to underwrite all expenses and make the necessary arrangements.'

Polak's words were like manna from heaven. I held his hands and thanked him profusely.

'You have made me a very happy woman today, Polakbhai!' I gushed as I clasped Polak's arm.

At last my innermost desires were going to fructify. At last my precious Harilal would get what he had been wanting all his life, and together we could dream of a bright future for him as a barrister with a grand English degree.

For the first time in months, I slept peacefully that night.

✼ ✼ ✼

Unlike me, Harilal did not sleep a wink. It had been almost three years since he had quit school and left India. The burning need for a formal education had somewhat died down in Phoenix, particularly in the company of his little Rami and beloved Gulab. His total involvement in the *satyagraha* with his father had scotched all those desires, but the sudden prospect of going abroad to study law, rekindled his hopes and jolted him out of his delusory state. All those phantoms came rushing back and the dreams of his future as "Barrister H.M. Gandhi, Bar-at-Law" resurfaced.

That night, lying in the tight embrace of his beloved wife, he bared his soul to her.

'If Bapu does send me to England for my education, Gulab, we shall be separated again. How will I ever live without you?' he whispered. 'I am torn between my desire to study in England and my love for you. Every moment I have spent away from you impales my heart like a million arrows and yet the maddening need for that education overpowers me.'

Harilal held her close and kissed her passionately. Her eyes had welled up with tears. He cupped her cheeks in his palms and said, 'Look at me, Gulab. You love me so much that it scares me.'

Gulab's tears fell from her eyes onto his hands. He kissed her again and again. Then she spoke: 'Are you scared of love? Don't be, my lord and master. Never speak like this. Love that weakens you, cannot possibly be mine. You must go to England with a happy heart and fearless mind. Don't worry about Rami and me....' Her voice trailed off into a broken sob and she clung onto him. Both of them wanted that moment to last till eternity. It was a passion that would linger on for hours. It was the night she conceived their second child.

❋ ❋ ❋

'No, never. I will not hear of it!' Mohandas' stern words ripped through the air. They struck Harilal and me like a shard of glass, piercing our minds painfully as we came to terms with his obdurate decree.

I knew right then that Mohandas would remain unyielding in his decision and Harilal's dreams would come crashing down that instant. No amount of coaxing by the boys or me worked and it was decreed that the privilege of availing Pranjivan Mehta's offer would be bestowed on Chaganlal Gandhi.

Mohandas was fanatic about showing any kind of favouritism towards his family, so Harilal or the other two did not stand a chance, and a stunned, and heartbroken Harilal returned to Johannesburg in a huff, to court arrest all over again.

We moved to Tolstoy Farm in the summer of 1910. It was an exhausting change for me. It was the year that I had suffered another bout of haemorrhaging and had become a shadow of my former self. It was also the year that ushered in the birth of a soul who was to grow up in a Maharashtrian home as a rabid Hindu nationalist; allegedly a closet homosexual and a staunch, self-styled "patriot" who would be globally abhorred for the most shocking political assassination, the world had ever known.

Far away from the verdant shores of South Africa, thousands of miles across the turbulent southern Indian Ocean, at the Nativity Mission centre in the district of Poona, on the steamy night of 19 May 1910, Nathuram Godse was born to Vinayak Vamanrao and Laxmi Godse.

Positioned on totally divergent paths, Mohandas and Nathuram Godse's lives would collide in the not-too-distant future, in a macabre explosion that would shatter the world!

Forty Six

The chugging sounds of the train that picked up speed as it raced out of Phoenix station aggravated the searing rage in Harilal's heart. His father's cruel words had driven a stake into his heart that wrecked his peace.

...I have made up my mind. Chaganlal will leave for England to study law under the sponsorship of Pranjivanbhai. And there shall be no further arguments...

Harilal's vehement protests had drowned in his father's emphatic words that hung in the air like frozen icicles. Although this wasn't the first instance, he failed to understand how Chaganlal was a more deserving student than him and why his Bapu was being so cruel and discriminatory towards him, yet again.

The prospect of losing Harilal after the confrontation between father and son had terrified me. And the rancour I felt against Mohandas began to mount. I fought hard not to use Harilal's angst to attack his father, but the wounded look on my son's face drove me to a frenzy.

Each time I closed my eyes, my mind travelled back to the point where my pain had taken root, and I was submerged into the torturous drift of time. I couldn't block the grim revelation that being the son of Mohandas Karamchand Gandhi had perhaps become the greatest curse for my son, Harilal.

❃ ❃ ❃

Tolstoy Farm was a gift from Hermann Kallenbach. A tall thickset, square-headed German Jew, he was a man of strong emotions and child-like simplicity. He had bought eleven hundred acres of land twenty miles outside Johannesburg at Lawley, and gifted it to Mohandas and the *satyagrahis*, after which he and his family moved in with us.

Kallenbach and Mohandas became close friends and often shared the task of teaching the children geography, history, mathematics and theology. So great was the affinity between the two and so synchronized their commitment to the cause, that Mohandas virtually cut himself off from the other goings-on in the world and his family. He spent hours in Kallenbach's company doing various chores at the farm, learning carpentry, cooking, baking bread, walking ten miles each day back and forth from Johannesburg; so much so that even I at times felt that Kallenbach had completely possessed my husband's mind and soul and created a greater distance between him and me.

Meanwhile Harilal, freshly released from prison was undergoing severe emotional churnings of another kind. His flagging spirits did not revive even after he reached Tolstoy Farm with Mohandas, who had come to receive him on his release from jail. He had not forgotten his father's betrayal, in sending Chaganlal to study in England. However, on reaching Tolstoy Farm, Harilal was pleasantly surprised. It was completely different from the Phoenix settlement. At the sprawling expanse that housed more than twice the population at Phoenix, he saw Indians of different castes and religions co-existing harmoniously as one big family.

That night in his room he lay in the arms of Gulab on a comfortable new cot, staring at the ceiling of his new surroundings wistfully. His jail cell, his hard bed, that rough blanket and a raw wood plank for a pillow, seemed so far away.

'You had a terrible time in jail, didn't you?' she murmured caressing the scars on his weather-beaten arms with her fingertips.

'Oh! how I yearned to be in your arms, my sweet Rose, how I missed you.' Tightening her into a suffocating embrace, he placed his head onto her frail shoulders and closed his eyes.

After what seemed like an eternity, she spoke softly into his ear. 'I am with child. You are going to be a father again.'

Harilal was stumped. His grip slackened as he sat up on the bed beside her. With his life in turmoil, filled with uncertainties, it was not the right time to have another child, but he said nothing.

'My father wants me in Rajkot for the delivery this time and Bapu says he shall send me as soon as he can find a suitable escort.' Gulab continued.

'Oh my sweet Gulab! You are the mother of my child and the pulse of my being. If you go away, I shall be all alone again!' said Harilal.

'My love, my lord and master,' Gulab whispered. 'I'm not going away forever. And I am never far from you. Never! Not even when I am away.' She snuggled up closer and pulled his hands onto her stomach. 'Now don't despair. This baby shall be upset too.'

Harilal stroked her belly tenderly with his eyes closed. A sweet melody that Gulab had sung in her childhood played on her lips.

Haala karoon hoon, vaala karoon hoon
Ghanshyam tamnay, vaala karoon…

She sang the words of that soothing lullaby softly, rocking both father and the unborn child to sleep.

❉ ❉ ❉

Harilal went back to Johannesburg and was arrested again, this time with a big group of *satyagrahis*. By now I was sure that he somehow sought a release from his angst by suffering the hardships of a prison life, all the while relaying the underlying message to his stonehearted father that he was competent, committed and truly worthy of the scholarship that had been denied to him.

This time around when he returned to Tolstoy Farm, he felt even more alone. With Gulab's departure to India, an agonizing void gripped him, pushing him into a deeper abyss of misery. He missed her terribly, but a ray of hope kindled his sagging spirits. While Tolstoy Farm slept in a peaceful slumber, he tossed and turned in his bed waiting for daybreak, to make one last plea to his unyielding father. He watched the stars twinkling in the nightsky and waited restlessly for his last encounter with Bapu that woefully, would culminate in the total breakdown of their relationship.

❊ ❊ ❊

'Bapu,' he said the next morning, seeking the opportune moment when Mohandas was with Ramdas and Devdas. 'I have heard Chaganlal has returned to India without completing his studies in London. If Dr. Mehta's sponsorship still stands, would you allow me to avail of it this time?'

Harilal watched his father's face cloud over. His small eyes shadowed with pain as he rubbed his palms on his temples. Harilal stood rooted to the spot and after what seemed like an eternity, he heard his father speak.

'What are you saying, Harilal? Have you not overcome your obsession for taking undue advantage of an offer of charity by any means, fair or foul? When will you ever understand that I would rather die than favour my family in any way? I have already written to Pranjivanbhai. I shall be sending Sohrabji to London and all the arrangements have already been made. I should have known it was not in Chaganlal's destiny to become a barrister.'

Harilal was dumbstruck. His face turned an angry red. His forehead lined with beads of perspiration, and his lips trembled with rage. His brothers looked at their father, aghast. Sohrabji Shahpurji Adjania, a Parsi co-*satyagrahi* from Natal of all the people? He was the chosen one? How could he do this?

Harilal decided to break all ties with his father once and for all and disappear into oblivion.

That ominous day on 8 May 1911, Harilal left Tolstoy Farm in the cover of darkness leaving behind a note for his father without disclosing anything about his future plans. Harilal did return to Tolstoy Farm six days later, persuaded by Kallenbach and Mohandas after they had located him in Johannesburg. He spent all night walking up and down the orchards with his father, arguing and spelling out every grievance. But they arrived at no truce—both stood their ground and parted ways, which would have far reaching consequences.

Harilal finally left Tolstoy Farm two days later, a broken, frustrated man. His parting words scorched through my head over and over again.

'He just does not care for us, for any of us, Ba…!' he said bitterly. Carrying with him just his tin trunk, a copy of the Gita and his Bapu's photograph concealed between some old clothes, he trudged out with despair in his heart, till he receded into the cover of the dark night.

I did not want my faith in the Almighty to waver, but I couldn't prevent the cloud of anguish that engulfed me. My eyes filled with tears as the two younger boys held on to the corner of my sari and stared at me helplessly. All three of us huddled together on the floor and wept. But Harilal was gone.

FORTY SEVEN

1912

The year marked the beginning of many a metamorphic changes in the lives of those whose destinies were inextricably linked with mine. Harilal had left South Africa, but had not reached Rajkot. In Rajkot, Gulab had given birth to a boy who they named Kanti. Ashamed of his successive failures, Harilal could not bear to face his wife or her parents so he had travelled to Ahmedabad. He was determined to resume his studies and unshackle himself from the yoke of being the son of the illustrious Mohandas Karamchand Gandhi, before he would set eyes on his wife again.

By now, Mohandas was even more consumed by the *satyagraha*, and totally absorbed in the company of Hermann Kallenbach, and that had left me feeling cordoned off from them. They spent hours together in their quest for truth and I felt isolated, unable to decipher their philosophic exchanges and intense conversations in English. Feeling more alienated from my husband than ever before, I turned my attention to my duties at the farm tending to and caring for the other three boys and the families of inmates. It was my effort to run away from the futility of the role I was playing in Mohandas' life. But the gaping hole in my heart made deeper by the pain of an absent Harilal, never went away.

❈ ❈ ❈

Life in Tolstoy Farm was governed by a set of extremely austere rules laid down by Mohandas. All the residents were tied together by a common thread of *satyagraha* and they were expected to live like one family with a common goal. There was a community kitchen where simple food was cooked for all; "Equal labour for all" was Mohandas' diktat, so the chores were shared equally by the residents in turn. Even the rooms were not permanently allotted to anyone. They were shared by rotation and often a series of mattresses spread out on the floor served as their beds.

The children of inmates were given the same set of rules. They had a regimented routine, which included a swim in a stream that flowed through a scenic, secluded area within the farm, surrounded by a lush green forest where they could enjoy a few hours of noisy revelry every morning. The joy of the excursion, and the free mingling of boys and girls, from the ages of seven to twenty years, was a part of their leisure activities, after which they returned to the farm to resume their duties.

No one noticed that Manilal, now twenty years old and the oldest in the group, had become a tall, handsome young man with sexual stirrings that are natural at his age. To be drawn to a beautiful woman in a wild forest, with a host of children splashing around in water, like dancing fish on a bright summer day, was expected. And the nubile and beautiful sixteen-year-old Lalita had him completely enthralled. Bursting with the passion of youth, this sharp-eyed, olive-complexioned girl with long, black, hair cascading down to her rounded hips, held him in a trance.

Full of verve, this vibrant and chatty adolescent girl was everyone's darling. There was never a dull moment with her around and she had managed to draw even the quiet and aloof Manilal into a dialogue with her coquettish, flirty manner, and he just couldn't tear himself away from her.

One day, after the swim, everyone had emerged from the stream and were scattered around the bank sunning and drying themselves. A cool breeze had stirred up the leaves and the warm rays of the sun felt heavenly for all those who were drenched to their skins. Lalita was standing a few yards away from them with her back to the others, drying her long hair.

A few children were still splashing around in the water and Manilal dived back in to bring them out, as it was time to return to the ashram. One of the boys slipped out of his grasp and darted towards Lalita. Manilal ran after the little boy, but when he set eyes on Lalita he stopped just a few feet away. Her fair smooth back partly covered by her thick tumbling hair, her shapely shoulders, long willowy arms and her slender legs had transported him into a surreal land of *apsaras*.

She looked like a glistening, celestial creature; a little mermaid, perched on a rock on the beach, enticing him, teasing him, inviting him and compelling him to embrace her. Everything else in the background faded away that moment. Manilal lost track of all space and time as he slowly moved towards her.

'Lalita! You are so beautiful,' he mumbled as he came near her. He placed his hands on her back, moving them down the length of her wet hair.

Lalita blushed. She lowered her eyes to the ground. He continued stroking her tresses.

'Your hair is so beautiful, Lalita, so beautiful. You are like a dancing fairy, descended straight from heaven.' He had lifted a section of her lengthy strands and kissed her neck. Her dark tresses curled around his fingers, their fluidity and heady fragrance snaked up his nostrils. He stood there for a long time unmindful of several pairs of eyes that were watching this lustful exchange.

But Manilal was unperturbed and went home in a cloud of heady euphoria. He had never been so enthralled before. The two reached the settlement a bit later than the others, but soon resumed their duties as if nothing had transpired between them. That night Manilal stayed wired up, reliving his erotic encounter again and again, impatient to see Lalita at the river the next morning, and every day, thereafter.

A few days later, the swimming group was at the stream once again, with the older girls bathing on one side and the younger ones on the other, squealing and splashing around in the water noisily. Manilal dived into the deeper end, his muscular body and sinewy arms slicing the surface like a skilled athlete. He dived under the surface and came up on the other side where Lalita was swimming along gracefully, her long hair billowing behind her. It had spread out over the surface like a sheet of shimmering black silk, dancing along, enticing him, calling out to him. He felt that compelling ache to touch her again. He moved swiftly in that direction, picked up those strands and drew them close to his face. The girl bolted, jerked her head and flailed her arms to get out of the water. Manilal stared at her as she recoiled in horror. He let go of her hair, and raced back to the shore.

Manilal had mistaken Chanda for Lalita. A terrified Chanda emerged from the stream trying to steady herself after the unexpected "under-water" encounter. She had seen Manilal and Lalita that day, holding each other's hands. She had seen Manilal kissing her, touching her shoulders inappropriately and playing with her hair just a few days ago. She cringed. His behaviour was unpardonable. She hurried back to the ashram without drying her clothes, while Manilal stood staring at her in terror, dreading the aftermath of his blunder.

That evening after dinner and the routine night-time prayers, Mohandas summoned Manilal. With trembling steps and beads of perspiration shining on his brow, he entered the room. He paled to see his Bapu seated on a straw mat on the floor with Chanda and Lalita sitting on either side. Their heads were bent and their hair cascaded around their shoulders and fell to the ground in a neat circle. He felt drawn to those dark, silken, tresses again. That strong compulsion to touch them overcame him, but he steeled himself and turned his eyes away.

He looked at his Bapu leaning on a round cushion with his legs folded under him. He looked at Chanda, Lalita and then at Mohandas again. He could see that every muscle on his father's face was contorted and a deep frown creased his brow. Mohandas' lips quivered as he glared at his son. His cold gaze made Manilal freeze in his shoes.

'Manilal!' his voice trembled as he addressed him. 'I wish to hear from you, what happened today between Chanda and you. I want to understand, *beta,* where I have failed in my duty or my dedication.' Manilal felt as if he was struck by a bolt of lightning. He felt gagged. His whole body shuddered.

'Since both Chanda and Lalita have felt that you have committed a grave sin, at least tell me which sin of mine has sullied your character.' Mohandas' voice broke. His anguish poured out of his eyes.

Manilal knelt down. 'Bapu,' he sobbed, tears falling down his face. He was convulsed with remorse and fear. 'Chanda is right. I have committed a sin. Please punish me. These girls have not done anything wrong. I am to blame. Don't punish them, Bapu. Please!' His pitiable cries could have melted the stoniest of men. 'Give me a double punishment—but don't punish them!' he kept pleading with Mohandas.

Mohandas' face clouded with anguish. He held his son's hand and made him sit down beside his mat on the floor. 'No Manilal! It's not your fault. The fault is mine. It is I who has failed to instil high values in you. I have failed to groom your character. Not you, not Chanda, not Lalita, not any of you; it is I who should be punished.'

All the three children in the room were aghast by Bapu's pained utterances.

Chanda looked up. Her face was sullied with tears that had dried in black streaks across her cheeks. Her eyes brimmed over again and her mouth trembled. In a quivering voice she spoke, 'I am the culprit, Bapu. I should have ignored Manilal's silly moment of weakness and not come running to you to complain.'

'No child,' Mohandas quietened her. 'You did the right thing. We must always nip sin and disease in the bud. It should be stopped before it gets out of control. But the question before us is, what was it about both you and Lalita that seized Manilal thus? What made him turn into a beast, so blinded by his lust that he could only see you two girls who are like his sisters, as objects of his unholy desire?'

Manilal was silent. Lalita's tantalizing drenched body accentuated by her damp clothes and her streaming, lustrous hair played back in his mind. It was that captivating mane that had driven him to dizzy heights of desire. Oh! How he had lusted for her wet body and long silken hair. Manilal bit his lip, fearing that his face would give him away in his father's court, where he was on trial.

'Speak up, Manilal. What is it about these girls that drove you to such madness? Pushed you on the vile path of sin? You must confess your sin right now, for avoidance of confession is a far greater sin than the sin itself.' Mohandas had pursed his lips and his hollow cheeks looked gaunter than before.

Manilal cried out. 'Bapu, please don't punish these girls. They are both innocent. They did nothing! It was their long black hair that enticed me. I became blind, Bapu.'

Lalita was trembling and Chanda began to weep.

Mohandas shut his eyes. Everyone fell silent and only the sounds of sobbing, sniffing and deep breathing could be heard in the room. After a long time, Mohandas opened his eyes. The anguish on his face had not diminished.

'You are right. I cannot punish you. I have no right to. Your repeated transgressions only reflect my shortcomings and failures. I shall have to do a penance for my weakness. I have decided to go on a long fast. May God grant good sense to all of us.' Mohandas closed his eyes again.

'No Bapu! No!' Both Lalita and Chanda cried out.

Manilal looked drained. 'Please Bapu. Why should you go on a fast of penance? It is I who has sinned. I shall fast for as long as you decide.' His voice quivered as he spoke.

'Manilal, only fasting shall not serve to cleanse your soul. You will have to take a vow of celibacy for twelve years. You will have to leave Tolstoy Farm and completely immerse yourself in your work. You should not have even a moment's respite, so that your mind is never idle. It is empty minds that breed sin, son. You cannot stay here any longer.' Manilal stood with his head lowered, absorbing his father's harsh decree.

'Please Bapu!' Lalita had mustered up her courage to speak. 'Why Manilal? He did nothing; it was I who seduced him. Punish me, Bapu. Don't send him away.'

She broke into a loud sob that racked her body. Chanda looked at her helplessly, with tears falling from her eyes too.

'Please don't go on a fast, Bapu. We shall do just as you say,' she said. 'We shall not fail you, Bapu. We shall abide by the punishment you decide for us, without question.'

Mohandas silenced them with a gesture of his hand.

'Neither of you shall be punished, but the root of sin needs to be removed immediately. The long, devilish hair that enticed Manilal shall have to be sacrificed so that no one else is ever lured in its trap again.'

Three anguished cries rang out in the still of the night: 'Bapu!'

Lalita and Chanda clasped each other's hands and wept. Manilal was told to fetch a pair of scissors and both the nubile girls were rapidly shorn of their gorgeous locks in less than ten minutes.

❊ ❊ ❊

When I entered the room, I gasped loudly at the sight of those long tresses on the floor. The tonsured heads and terrified faces of Chanda and Lalita made me recoil in horror. Manilal was nowhere in sight and the two girls were weeping loudly. Mohandas was holding the scissors, his face devoid of any emotion. I grabbed his hand and snatched the scissors away. Over the noise of my deafening inner street, only Mohandas' low monotone could be heard.

'You have become purer now by sacrificing the root of this temptation. This act shall serve to cleanse your souls. After this, you should feel lighter. You should feel that you have embarked on a path of penance. From now on, even the shadow of sin shall not fall on you.'

I took both the wailing girls into my arms. My eyes blurred with tears as I bundled them out of the door.

The sinister dark night had turned even darker as we made our way to their quarters. I knew that nothing, no power on earth could have balmed their bleeding souls that moment. They had been scarred for life.

Manilal was banished from Tolstoy Farm to Phoenix the next day after being coerced to take a twelve-year vow of celibacy. Everyone knew that he had been caught fondling and kissing Lalita and later Chanda, by the stream that morning. This was a serious violation of the ashram rules and he had to be awarded the harshest punishment according to his father's decree.

When Harilal heard of the cruel incident, old wounds opened up again and plunged him into deeper despair. As for me, I had begun to fear that I was about to lose my second son.

❊ ❊ ❊

FORTY EIGHT

While time raced on with a velocity that none could either slow down or obstruct, tragedy had struck an ocean liner in the Atlantic Ocean. The unsinkable, luxury ship "The Titanic" collided with an iceberg and sank to the bottom of the sea on its maiden voyage from Southampton to New York, killing over 1,500 people aboard. It sent ripples of terror in the hearts of people across the world, particularly those like us who frequently travelled across the oceans on ships. I felt a sense of foreboding. It was an ominous start to the year.

Outside Tolstoy Farm the resistance movement had been reduced to a mere in-and-out-of-jail routine with little progress. The spirit of the *satyagrahis* had flagged, but Mohandas remained as fiery and committed to the cause, never once doubting that there would be victory in the end.

On 20 October, Mohandas' old associate and mentor, Gopal Krishna Gokhale arrived in South Africa on a month-long tour. Having witnessed him fight against the South African government to protect the rights of Indians, he believed he could groom Mohandas for leading the fight against the British, back in India. As a high-ranking member of the Viceroy's Legislative Council, Gokhale was given a warm reception by the South African authorities. He was assured that they would repeal "the Black Act", lift the discriminatory ban on immigration and abolish the annual labour tax levied on Indian workers.

A buoyant Gokhale emerged from his two hour-long meeting— 'All has been settled, Mohandas. And you will be able to return to India within twelve months,' he said. 'I shall accept no more excuses from you.'

Mohandas however was skeptical. He shared little of Gokhale's optimism.

'I don't trust them,' he said. 'Do you have a written agreement?' His sombre voice drew a loud laugh from his mentor. 'What I have told you, will happen Mohandas.' But Mohandas' face remained clouded with doubt.

'You don't know these white men, Gokhalebhai!' he said. 'I am not as hopeful as you are. Many, many more Indians shall have to go to jail before I can return to India.'

Those words proved to be prophetic. An upbeat Gokhale returned to India, but the South African government rescinded on every promise made to the ageing leader. The official understanding was reduced to mere verbal assurances and even more stringent measures were put into place soon after. After returning to India, although Gopal Krishna Gokhale was deeply saddened by his South African experience, he was now even more convinced that Mohandas indeed was the right man to lead the fragmented freedom struggle in his homeland. To a packed audience at a local congregation in Bombay he proclaimed, 'Gandhi has in him the marvellous spiritual power to turn ordinary men into heroes and martyrs.'

I winced at the irony of Gokhale's words. Yes Mohandas did possess the enviable power to turn ordinary mortals into glorious martyrs and heroes, but only if they were not his own sons. The disconsolate faces of Harilal, Manilal and the two teenage girls, shorn of their tresses, never stopped haunting me.

⚬ ⚬ ⚬

Early in 1913 Mohandas decided to move the base of his operations from Tolstoy Farm back to Phoenix. Even though this meant the drudgery of packing my bags and moving house again, the prospect of returning to Phoenix was like going back home and I approached it with keen enthusiasm. A few months later, the Supreme Court of South Africa ruled that any marriage that hadn't been solemnized according to Christian rites would be deemed illegal, thereby rendering the existing marriages of thousands of Hindus, Muslims and Parsis of Indian origin invalid. The children of such marriages were declared "illegitimate" and not liable to inherit property and such women could even be subjected to deportation.

The ruling shook up the Indian community throughout South Africa and an extremely agitated Mohandas declared that he would protest against this draconian law. He said that it was time for the women to rise in revolt and if necessary court arrest, to avenge the insult meted out to them and their children. All my arguments against his diktat fell on deaf ears. The last thing Mohandas said to me was, 'You can fast-unto-death if the jail authorities ill-treat you, Kastur. And if you die in jail, I shall worship you like a Goddess.' And the matter was closed.

Tempers ran high in the settlement and everyone's nerves were wrung out. I had long acknowledged my husband's total commitment in fighting for the rights of his fellowmen, but for the first time it dawned on me that this had become my fight too. However, for the *satyagrahis* the most crucial moment had arrived. If the peaceful resistance movement did not succeed now, it never would. The government's breach of promise to Gopal Krishna Gokhale, their failure to repeal the "Black Act" and the invalidation of non-Christian marriages had evoked unprecedented waves of anger from our fellow Indians. And clearly, the government was in no mood to offer any remedial measures. Mohandas seized the opportunity. Realizing that a new tactic had to be put in place, he urged the women to become proactive *satyagrahis* and court arrest. The campaign took off almost instantly. All the women from the settlement took to the streets and began hawking fruit without trade licences in contravention of the prevalent ban, but the police, wary of a violent public outcry against the arrest of women, had no choice but to ignore them.

On 23 September 1913, putting aside the fear of imprisonment and the hardships of jail life, I boarded a train to Transvaal with a group of twelve Gujarati-speaking men and four women from Phoenix. This highly charged group of newly-inducted *satyagrahis*, of which Ramdas was the youngest, was on a fearless mission. Mohandas saw us off somewhat sombrely that day without any of the customary ceremonial fanfare.

On reaching the border, all of us were taken into custody and produced before a magistrate who pronounced us guilty of violating the law and we were sentenced to three months of rigorous imprisonment. As a group, we had succeeded in achieving our goal quite effortlessly; as an individual, I became one of the first women *satyagrahis* to be arrested. But watching my fifteen-year-old Ramdas being escorted by uniformed policemen to the men's cell, wrenched my gut. Head held high, eyes gleaming with pride he walked erect, right into the fearsome iron-grilled door that led to his jail cell, without as much as one glance at his panic-stricken mother. We women were bundled off to Maritzburg jail where we would serve our harsh sentence for ninety long days.

News of the arrests of peaceful women protestors spread like wild fire amongst the Indian community. It stoked deep emotions of frustration and anger particularly when they learned that among the protestors who had been jailed were Mohandas' wife and fifteen-year-old son. Waves of unrest gripped the community and large groups of *satyagrahis* stormed the streets to break the laws peacefully with an intent to get arrested.

Meanwhile at the Maritzburg jail we were subjected to constant harassment by the authorities. Sick prisoners were ignored, the food served at most times was rancid and worm-infested. Several inmates contracted a fever that had led to severe emaciation. A few even died.

I bore the brunt of prison life with courage, never letting my spirits sag for fear of demoralizing my colleagues. I continued working on the arduous chores assigned to me and never once missed the evening prayers, but the truth was that I was wearing down and the other women inmates had begun to notice. Rattled by the imprisonment of Ramdas of whom I had no news, I became deeply depressed. I had heard that Manilal had also been imprisoned in Transvaal and Mohandas had been arrested and awarded nine months of rigorous imprisonment in a faraway place, that I had never heard of before.

Harilal's life was already in shambles. Now that Mohandas, two of the boys and I were locked up in different jails, with no communication with each other, there couldn't have been a greater hell for the Gandhis.

❊ ❊ ❊

By the time his ship sailed into Bombay harbour, Harilal had somewhat regained his composure. Throughout the tiring nineteen-day-long journey, Mohandas' words echoed through his numbed mind.

Son if you feel your father has been unjust to you, then please forgive him…

Harilal had steeled himself to shut out the pathos in his Bapu's voice. His heart had hardened way too much after his father's repeated cruelty. He did not want to allow any weakness to chip away at the wall that he had built around himself. His love for Mohandas had been leeched out of his soul and he felt no desire to forgive him.

Disembarking from the ship with heavy footsteps and a heavier heart, he felt lost and alone. He yearned to be in the arms of his Gulab, the only place in the world where he could find solace but he was ashamed to face her and his little daughter. His eyes lit up at the thought of Rami, frolicking in his lap and the newborn Kanti. If only Gulab hadn't left him alone in South Africa, he wouldn't have been so lonely and depressed. If only he had stopped her from going away, all his burdens would have eased. But now things were beyond his control.

He stepped off the gangway peering at the people crowded on the quay. There was not a single familiar face. No one had come to receive him. No one really cared. He could have been dead or lost forever. No one would miss him. Harilal felt wretched.

All kinds of emotions stirred within him—he needed to resume his studies at any cost for once he attained a degree, he would get a respectable job to support his family and earn the dignity he deserved; he needed to be recognized as Harilal, and not as the son of Mohandas Gandhi. Being his father's son had only caused him grief and humiliation.

He boarded a train to Ahmedabad to enroll in a school to earn a Matriculation degree.

But sadly for Harilal, the yoke of his family name was not destined to be eased off his back just yet.

FORTY NINE

The day after Harilal reached Ahmedabad, he met the principal of New English School and submitted his application for admission into the Matriculation class. The bewildered college principal sized up the tall, self-effacing man who looked far too old to be a student.

'I was forced to abandon my studies, sir,' Harilal stammered. 'My father was in Africa, so he wanted me there.'

The principal's eyes lit up.

'Africa did you say? What did you say your surname was? Gandhi? Are you the son of that famous barrister who is the champion of Indians in South Africa?' The awe-struck principal could barely conceal his admiration. Harilal shrank into himself.

'Oh! We shall be proud to admit the son of Gandhi in our school,' he continued.

The mention of his father's name infuriated Harilal, but in his desperation to get admission into the school, he just lowered his head and nodded. 'I am quite happy to take you in, Harilal,' the principal persisted. 'But will you be okay sitting amongst boys half your age?'

Harilal's embarrassment mounted. He bit his lip, his eyes filled with anger as he turned around and walked away.

Wandering aimlessly on the dusty streets of Ahmedabad, troubled by nagging thoughts of the challenge that lay ahead, he spent a sleepless night before arriving bleary-eyed to school the next morning. The classroom was filled with chattering boys who appeared to be between the ages of fourteen and seventeen years. It would be a tedious if not a humiliating task adjusting to them, but he had no choice. He swallowed his pride to ready himself for the lot that fate had dealt him.

The next day he began his search for a house and a job. The little money that he carried with him was running out. He desperately needed something that would sustain him and restore his self-esteem. But, wherever Harilal went, his Gandhi lineage followed. He found a place owned by one Miya Khan in the suburbs of the city, who on learning he was Gandhi's son gave him a room free of cost. 'I have a firm in Durban that has a long standing relationship with your father. The doors of this house are always open for you, bhai...' he said.

Harilal was stumped. Taking advantage of his Bapu's goodwill was the last thing he wanted, but he accepted Miya Khan's generous offer and moved in the next day. With each passing day, Harilal's desperation to earn money intensified, but the enthusiasm to acquire the Matriculation degree had begun to wane.

❆ ❆ ❆

In class, Harilal felt alienated by the younger boys who looked upon him with an air of disdain. The studies also taxed him. Having been away from school for over five years, what came effortlessly to his classmates was a cause of anxiety and confusion for him. Harilal felt dejected; he felt a greater burden of failure than before. He blamed his sorry plight on his cruel father for whom he could feel only a ferocious loathing. Alone, jobless and dejected, he spent hours playing chess in Miya Khan's house with some other unemployed boys his age, whom he had befriended; till one day all his resources dried up.

Harilal had told no one of his whereabouts in India. He had not bothered to write home to us either, and I was sick with worry, more so when I learned that he had not even contacted Gulab. And she poor thing, suffered the same anxiety in greater measure. Harilal pined for Gulab endlessly. Wallowing in self-pity with an exaggerated sense of antipathy towards his heartless father, he had nowhere to go, till he met with Pranjivan Mehta's brother, Reva Shankar.

Reva Shankar had been informed by Mohandas of Harilal's return to India and had been instructed to take care of his needs. By the time he offered to sponsor his studies in Bombay, the humiliation Harilal had experienced in school at Ahmedabad had destroyed all his ardour to attain that degree. Reva Shankar's words however, touched him. That was the first act of kindness he had encountered in a long time.

'Harilal, you are Bapu's son. Don't hesitate to tell me if you need anything. I am here to support you, until you can take care of yourself,' he said amiably.

Harilal felt like he had been slapped across his face, but given his penurious circumstances, he silently accepted Reva Shankar's benevolence.

That evening Harilal and his friends gathered at his place to play their routine game of chess. Boisterous backslapping and loud laughter rang out into the farthest end of the quiet neighbourhood till the wee hours of the morning. The revelry continued unabated with snacks and drinks and animated chatter after which Harilal felt lighthearted and happy. His problems seemed far away and the thought of seeing Gulab and his two children soon, had made him heady.

Just as Harilal entered the lane after seeing off his rowdy friends, the deep voice of one of his elderly neighbours jolted him.

'Harilal! To kill time with this bunch of ruffians until such unearthly hours does not quite become you. It is nothing but cruel fate that the son of such a great man is leading a waster's life!'

Harilal was dumbstruck. His heady euphoria came crashing down that instant. He shut himself in his room smarting in the agony of those words. He would go to Rajkot in the morning to bring his family back with him.

⁂

Across the turbulent seas, far away from the corroding pain that pierced through the heart of my beloved son, I spent another restless night on my hard prison bed. I needed to know that he was safe and well and I felt my tormented soul soldered to his, in the invisible chasm of hell's courtyard. My heart ached to hear his voice just once. I prayed to the Lord for peace for my Harilal, the tragic victim of his father's self-righteousness. I prayed to the Lord to forgive his Bapu for killing the simplest desires of his son that had catalyzed his emotional breakdown.

Alas! My prayers dispersed unheard into the air of the still dark night at Maritzburg prison, while Harilal burned in the agony of the scorn and humiliation that continued to plague him.

❋   ❋   ❋

In the meantime, Harilal reached Ahmedabad and embarked on a new phase of his life with Gulab and the two children.

However, it was a gruelling effort for him to curtail his carefree ways and lead a regimented life with his family. His interest in studies had completely waned, as he could not bear the mockery he had faced in a classroom filled with boys who were years younger than him. There was a continued shortage of funds and the pressure of earning a livelihood weighed heavily down on him, whenever he set eyes on Rami and Kanti.

Gulab understood his plight. Even though she had not approved of the manner in which he had parted with his father and left South Africa, she had merged her identity with that of Harilal on the day of their marriage. In keeping with the high ideals of the Gandhis, she believed in surrendering to her husband unquestioningly. Gulab hated her life in Ahmedabad. She often thought about the wonderful days spent with the family in South Africa. Even though she remained troubled deep inside her heart, she said nothing to her husband.

Much to the disappointment of his wife, Harilal failed his Matriculation examination. He had not expected any different, but Gulab was in utter shock and fell ill on hearing the devastating news. Harilal did not return home that day for fear of facing Gulab. She waited for him patiently, burning with a fever that ravaged both her body and mind. Late that night while she lay tossing and turning in her bed, she heard the front door open and faltering footsteps of someone tiptoeing into her room. Harilal, dejected and forlorn collapsed on the bed beside her and buried his face into her bosom. She held him tight and remained silent for a long while. He looked up at her pale face. His parched lips and sunken eyes broke her heart. Then she spoke. Her soft whisper stirred him. 'My precious one,' she whispered, 'how can we go on living like this? How long will we have to take the beatings of your attempts to run away from reality?'

Harilal felt a growing lump in his throat. He tightened his arms around her and shut his eyes, unable to face his latest failure in a series of misfortunes that just would not let up.

'We have a new life breathing in my womb now. We shall soon be a family of five for you to sustain.' She murmured shyly.

Harilal's grip slackened. A third child in his days of penury was the last thing he would have wanted.

'Let's go back to Ba and Bapu in Africa. It will be good for us and for the children...' Gulab's voice trailed off. A cold chill descended on them and silence engulfed the two entwined bodies even as the little unborn foetus slept blissfully inside the cosy womb of its despairing mother.

Harilal was dumbfounded. He shuddered at the prospect of returning to the terrible days spent under his father's dictatorial dispensation in Johannesburg after the unpleasant parting he had been put through. He glanced at Rami and Kanti sleeping in their cots beside him. His heart ached for them.

'We shall return to Ba and Bapu, Gulab. Don't fret. We shall go back to South Africa,' he mumbled.

That night after long painful deliberations, Harilal penned a letter to his father. The pain in his heart did not reflect in the words he wrote...

> *Bapu I am impatient to see you and Ba. Will you allow me to come back to South Africa with Gulab, Rami and Kanti and join the movement once again?*

Gulab wrote to me separately to tell me that she was pregnant with their third child.

The letters had vastly different impacts on all of us. While Gulab felt elated at Harilal's decision and the prospect of leading a normal life all over again, Harilal was in the depths of despair. Returning to his father was an admission of defeat. He feared that he would become the laughing stock of the inmates at the settlement, but Gulab's gentle insistence had left him with no option. He eagerly awaited a reply from his father that would help ease his growing awkwardness.

The reply came not too long after.

...Harilal, come with Chanchi only if you can forgo your desire for a useless education and meaningless degrees. And come prepared to go to jail. You must also overcome your lustful desire for Chanchi, till such time that you can fend for yourself. I have learned of your mistake and do not feel confident that you are willing to sacrifice this carnality and can truly serve the cause...

Mohandas' letter had come at a time when Harilal's morale was at its lowest ebb. He had heard of the horrific hair-cutting episode of Lalita and Chanda and Manilal's shameful humiliation. He couldn't believe that his "chaste" father was deriding him for the natural stirrings he felt for his own wife! Neither could he believe that in his father's hypocritical decree, the innocent child sleeping in Gulab's womb was becoming a hapless casualty.

He winced at the thought of poor Manilal's exile and that humiliating vow of chastity that had been forced upon him and he was even more determined not to fall prey to his father's tyrannical ways.

He had no way of knowing that we had moved back to Phoenix and would leave South Africa forever in just about eight months. He swore never to reach out to his father for help again and stopped all communication with him thereafter.

Mohandas' letter buried deep within the smouldering cinders of Harilal's turmoil, remained unanswered, while I had begun my final countdown to return home.

✂ ✂ ✂

Fifty

1914

The First World War broke out on 28 July 1914, the tremors of which were felt in every corner of the globe. As if in resonance with the global strife, the turmoil of Indians in South Africa had assumed mammoth proportions. Massive protests had shaken up the seat of power in England. After long deliberations, the Crown communicated its displeasure to South Africa for its inefficient handling of affairs, and ordered the immediate and unconditional release of Mohandas, along with Henry Polak and Hermann Kallenbach.

Three days later, a grim Mohandas emerged from prison before a milling crowd that had gathered in Durban. The man who was to soon to be deified as the Mahatma, in solidarity with his oppressed fellowmen, had shed his European attire. Wearing a plain knee-length cotton kurta and dhoti with his feet bare, he stood erect, with his head held high. His bare head and unshaven face symbolized his state of mourning for ten fellow Indians who had been killed in clashes with the authorities in and outside prison. When he spoke, a quiet stillness descended upon the electrified congregation.

'Prepare for an even more gruelling process of purification, for no justice is coming to us.'

The next day, accompanied by Kallenbach, the Polaks and several other *satyagrahis*, Mohandas reached the gates of Maritzburg jail, where my three-month long incarceration had come to an end.

I emerged from jail, a mere shadow of my former self, a frail weather-beaten woman weakened in spirit, but not in my resolve.

I travelled back to Phoenix with the other women who had been set free along with me, leaving Mohandas to continue his peaceful protest with the unyielding authorities.

A couple of weeks later even as intense negotiations with Generals Smuts and Botha were underway, I fell gravely ill again and Mohandas had to be urgently summoned to Phoenix. For six weeks Mohandas stayed by my side day and night, preparing himself for my imminent death. He obsessed over my suffering, blaming himself for the pain he had inflicted upon me all these years. He wrote to a friend,

> *I don't know what evil resides in me. I have a streak of cruelty in me that compels people to attempt the impossible in order to please me.*

To his relief, I did not die and he travelled to Cape Town to resume talks with the hostile government.

After a series of setbacks in the following months that sparked off more protests and several arrests, an agreement was hammered out between the opposing parties and the Union Parliament which passed the Indian Relief Bill as a compromise measure. The bill proposed that the three-pound tax (which entailed that any Indian in South Africa had to leave after a period of five years or be re-indentured for a further duration of two years) would be abolished; non-Christian marriages recognized and the import of indentured labour be discontinued within the next five years. This settlement rendered some relief for the Indian community and was a victory of sorts for Mohandas. More importantly for him, this triumph was achieved by his non-violent methods of peaceful resistance. For once Mohandas felt the pressure on him ease up and he thought of returning to India, to fulfill his promise to Gopal Krishna Gokhale.

I spent my last days in Africa in a whirlwind of celebrations. As the news of our departure spread, a spate of farewell parties, banquets and receptions were held for us. I felt a tinge of pride, reflecting on the days gone by and Mohandas' relentless struggle that had changed South Africa irreversibly, but only I knew how much South Africa had really changed him.

On 18 July 1914, we finally boarded the R.M.S. Kilfauns Castle at Cape Town onward to London. General Smuts heaved a sigh of relief on our leaving the South African shores. In his parting shot he imperiously said to his colleagues, 'The saint has left our shores, I hope forever!'

But not even Smuts could have anticipated the real power of Mohandas' doctrine of non-violence and the forces it would unleash in our homeland.

Fifty One

The nineteen-day sea voyage in the cramped third class cabin that was Mohandas' preferred means of travel, offered a much-needed respite for the homebound travellers. Completely exhausted by the turmoil of the past few months, Mohandas and I confined ourselves to our cabin, eating only a special diet of fruits and nuts. Mohandas spent most of his time sorting papers, writing letters and reading. A part of the day was alloted to me for reciting verses from the Bhagavad Gita and Ramayana. And Hermann Kallenbach, my husband's precious soulmate, who had accompanied us on our journey to India after the ship made a brief stopover at London, was given a one-hour lesson everyday in Gujarati. Although I needed this long awaited break from my household chores in South Africa, my mind wandered restlessly not allowing me even a moment's peace.

Undoubtedly for me, South Africa had been a life-changer, but I had no regrets leaving it. I looked forward to my maiden visit to England where Mohandas had gone to study for his Bar-at-Law many years ago. But more than anything I waited impatiently to be re-united with my Harilal, Gulab and the three grandchildren, the youngest of whom I had not yet seen. Little Rasik—oh how I pined to cuddle him in my arms and never let him go.

The thought of Harilal opened up old wounds again. I dreaded to think of how he might have reacted to his father's scathing letter. If only I could have softened the impact of those cruel words.

❈ ❈ ❈

Returning to India on that last voyage deluged me with some grim truths that I had been dreading to face while I was in South

Africa. We were returning to our homeland after many of our dear relatives had passed on. Mohandas was now the sole surviving son of Karamchand and Putli Ba. Each time news of the death of one of Mohandas' brothers was brought to us, the triple wedding of the three Gandhi men in Porbandar would come alive in my mind. But the fast paced life in South Africa and the intensity of the *satyagraha* left little time for anyone to grieve.

Between the years 1913 and 1914, Karsandas and Laxmidas had died. My brother Kushaldas Kapadia, his wife and daughter had also succumbed to the virulent typhus fever that year. The only surviving Kapadia now was my youngest brother, Madhavdas. Alas! life had slipped away while we had been fighting for the oppressed Indians of South Africa.

Late in July, when R.M.S. Kilfauns Castle docked at Madeira, off the coast of Morocco, menacing war clouds had gathered over Europe. It took us two long and fearsome days to reach our destination at Southampton during which our ship had to be towed through a maze of submarine mines spread out below the sea in the English Channel. When we finally disembarked on British soil on 6 August 1914, we had landed right in the midst of a country facing a full-blown war.

I saw London the first time like a rustic, awestruck child. The streets were festooned with colourful buntings and wide banners streamed across them. Vibrant bands were playing patriotic tunes on bagpipes. There were newly enlisted volunteers parading to military training camps and hordes of onlookers lined both sides of the streets, waving the Union Jack that had me in raptures.

The arrival of Mohandas and his entourage however had not gone unnoticed. The local newspapers were full of stories about the firebrand, enigmatic Indian leader. Many carried anecdotes of the *satyagraha* and its aftermath in the Imperial South African colony. Some even lauded me, the wife of Gandhi as a pro-active revolutionary, who had also endured infinite hardship and imprisonment in support of the Indian community.

A grand reception of welcome was held in our honour at the Cecil Hotel, which was attended by many of Mohandas' English and Indian friends. Even though our trip to London had been at

Gopal Krishna Gokhale's behest, the elderly leader could not attend the reception as he was in France being treated by the miraculous waters of Lordes for his chronic diabetes. Mohandas felt that we should wait in London till Gokhale arrived, and much to my relief he rented a room for us in an inexpensive hotel in Kensington.

Meanwhile with the prevailing atmosphere of Germany's aggression in the ongoing war, Hermann Kallenbach was met with an unexpectedly hostile treatment in the UK. Mohandas realized that it would be hazardous for him to accompany us to India as planned, because he not only risked being mistaken for a German spy, he could have even been arrested for the transgression. Thereafter, Mohandas urged Hermann to return to Johannesburg.

After a tearful farewell, Mohandas and Kallenbach parted ways, and he returned to South Africa a heart-broken man, to resume his career as an architect.

✳   ✳   ✳

It was while spending a few days in the hotel room at Kensington that Mohandas conceived of forming an Indian Ambulance Corps in Britain, just as he had done in South Africa. Seized once again by his loyalty towards the British Crown, he felt compelled to assist the government in the prevailing times of war. He issued appeals to all Indian resident doctors to volunteer for the cause and received an overwhelming response from them. With dozens of his compatriots including doctors, lawyers and students joining in, he sent a letter to the Under Secretary for the State of India pledging their loyal cooperation with the British. I also volunteered my services and signed on the letter, following which a special plea by the wives, daughters and sisters of diplomats and other high ranking Indians was circulated, offering their unconditional support in Britain's war effort.

The cold damp English weather however, took its toll on Mohandas. He came down with pleurisy that confined him to bed and me by his side, nursing him in the best way possible. All attempts at following a strict vegetarian diet and nature-cure remedies failed. What made matters worse was that I had also caught a bad cold while Mohandas' condition deteriorated.

An Indian physician was called in to look at the both of us, who advised us to leave England as soon as possible. He feared that the onslaught of the harsh northern winter would only aggravate Mohandas' condition and endanger his life.

It was time for us to go home.

✄   ✄   ✄

The news of our return to India reached Harilal long before we had set sail from South Africa. He was no longer bitter with his father, but his restlessness had not subsided. He desperately wanted to believe that despite that cold, cruel, steely exterior, his Bapu did love him and that had made him even more anxious to meet Mohandas and me.

Harilal fretted about me constantly. He always believed that I was a harassed, servile wife to his overbearing, insensitive father and there was no one with whom I could share my feelings. But the thought of being united with his brothers, Bapu and me after so long somewhat eased his troubled mind.

Harilal was delighted to see Manilal, Ramdas and Devdas who reached India a few days before our arrival. Manilal was the reticent and serious one, Devdas the agile and impish wiry teenager, and the tall Ramdas' maturity was far beyond his years. He re-lived the happy times he had spent with them in Phoenix. Recollecting every little detail of the fruit orchards at Durban, to the fun-filled revelries at the settlement, he played back those delightful adolescent moments with his siblings.

He learned from Manilal that his Bapu and I had planned on staying in Bombay with Seth Narottam Das for a few days, after which we were to go on condolence visits for the deceased brothers to Rajkot and Porbandar. Seth Narottam Das, an old time associate of Mohandas, was a wealthy mill-owner of Bombay. Harilal was certain that his Bapu would have no problems staying at his home but he travelled to Bombay a few days prior to our scheduled arrival and through Reva Shankarbhai reached Narottam Das' home to wait for us.

✄   ✄   ✄

On 9 January 1915 when S.S. Arabia sailed into a packed Bombay harbour we saw a milling crowd in the blazing midday sun that had gathered to welcome us. Somewhat revived in spirit, Mohandas and I clambered down the gangplank completely overawed by the multitudes that were waiting to greet us.

A heady euphoria seized me. The crowd was eager to receive "Mohandas the revolutionary" who had fought tooth and nail for his fellowmen in a foreign nation, racked with racial abuse. They had lined up for a glimpse of their new messiah, who they believed would now deliver them from their plight. It was perhaps the first real validation of how deeply the Gandhian principles of peaceful agitation and non-violent war had impacted the collective consciousness of India.

I was the first to spot the face of a beaming Harilal in the crowd. His piercing eyes that scanned the disembarking passengers lit up when he saw Mohandas and me. Through my teary eyes I saw him approach us and touch his head first to Mohandas' feet and then mine. Mohandas was smiling benevolently. He placed his hand gently on his son's bowed head and said, 'Harilal! Son, you look well! I am so happy to see you. How is Chanchi? And my two grandchildren? How are they? Rami and Kanti must be big now.'

I looked on as a wave of tenderness washed my insides. It was as if a frozen wall had just melted between a father and son and nothing unpleasant had ever happened between them. Harilal straightened. The sight of his father's pale face, gaunt cheeks and emaciated body unsettled him. He turned his bewildered gaze on me and then back to his father's face.

'You look tired, Ba. And Bapu looks so frail? Are you not well?' His lips quivered as he held me by the elbow and led us out to cars waiting outside.

'Stay with us for a few days, Harilal,' Bapu said to his son.

My spirits perked up at Mohandas' words.

'Yes , Hari.' I said. 'It's been such a long time. Don't go away just yet.'

That evening at Seth Narottam Das' home it was a happy reunion of sorts. I felt at ease being with Harilal. If there was any trace of the humiliation that he had felt when he left Africa in a huff, he was doing a fine job of concealing it.

❈ ❈ ❈

The city of Bombay stirred by the homecoming of Gandhi, the great Indian champion from South Africa, was in a celebratory mood. The colonial government that had not so long ago grievously insulted Mohandas was now bending over to felicitate him, and a meeting had been arranged with Lord Willingdon, the Governor of Bombay. Mohandas was dressed in his simple Kathiawar cotton dhoti and turban. And I, hailed as the enduring heroine, wore a plain *khadi* sari and no jewels other than my red glass bangles when we were presented to the hosts. We mingled with the elitist gathering at the governor's house with ease, even though I heard Mohandas protesting from time to time that both of us were complete rustics who felt more at home with the indentured labour of Natal than the well-heeled gentry of Bombay.

Soon after, we left for Rajkot with Harilal who had agreed to accompany us after his father prevailed upon him.

'It's vital that you come to Rajkot, Harilal. Mota bapu has passed away. We need to condole with the family and also settle property matters,' he said.

Harilal sat with his head bowed, his eyes lowered to the floor. He had hoped that some portion of the ancestral property would come to him. Given his current financial position, and a growing family, it would help him tide over his difficulties, even if temporarily.

'Harilal,' Mohandas continued, 'while I have been abroad, Mota bapu and your other uncles have been taking care of the family here. It was he who educated me and sent me to Africa. He got you married to Chanchi and always extended his support to us. I am deeply indebted to him, son, but I cannot carry on accepting obligations now. I feel guilty that I have done nothing for the family. And I will be in no position to do anything in the future, since I shall dedicate my life to the service of my people. So I think it is about time the family property matters are settled.'

'You must have made the right decision, Bapu,' he mumbled. 'Who am I to comment on this?'

'Okay, listen to me carefully. I have decided to forgo all my rights on the ancestral property. Since I am not in a position to give anything to anyone, I shall not be accepting anything from them now onwards. And after I hand over the houses in Rajkot and Porbandar to your uncles' families, you will not be able to have any financial dealings with them either. It is imperative for me to be totally clear on this. Do you understand?'

Harilal stiffened as I tightened my hand on his wrist. He could not believe what he had heard his Bapu say. In a way his father was hitting at his failure, warning him to stay away from borrowing money from members of his family and not to expect any income from their properties. Harilal's face clouded over and he froze.

Once again he felt mocked at for his failure to obtain a degree. The humiliation of taking a charitable allowance from his Bapu stirred up his wounded pride again. Convinced that Mohandas was deliberately trying to show him down, Harilal burst out.

'Bapu!' he shouted angrily. 'I cannot remember ever disagreeing with you in any situation. I have never disobeyed your command. But today you have made me realize that I have no choice but to succumb to your diktats, no matter how cruel or unreasonable they may be.' I dug my nails into Harilal's arm in an attempt to quieten him. My heart raced. I was unable to prevent the unprecedented verbal war that was escalating before my eyes. Mohandas' face had become grim. In a voice laden with sadness he said, 'Harilal my son, if you can rid yourself of this deep malice in your heart, I shall be the happiest person alive, but I see you move fast on a path that shall bring you neither success nor peace.' Mohandas wiped the sweat from his creased brow.

After a moment of awkward silence, Harilal spoke, 'Unfortunately our ways have already parted Bapu, we have no meeting point at all, but you still have time. Set the lives of my younger brothers in order. Don't drive them away like you have done me, I beg of you. It is still not too late for you to give them a better future than the one you forced upon me, for if you don't do so now, I dread to think of what they shall become.'

Mohandas winced. The words spewing out of his son's mouth pierced him like a blazing spear.

'Have faith in god, Harilal,' he said trying hard to keep his composure. 'His path is always that of well being. Don't lose faith, *beta*. It is only when our faith wavers that we have to face sorrow.'

Mohandas closed his tired eyes and fell absolutely silent. He placed a hand on Harilal's head and said, 'My blessings go with you, Harilal. May happiness and success adorn your path. Now go—my blessings are always with you.'

Harilal felt the blood rush up to his temples that had begun to throb. He held my feet tightly with both his hands and placed his feverish brow on them. Then he rose and left the room.

What choice do I have but to obey your orders, Bapu? What choice?

Harilal's lament wafted into my ears as he trudged out. I felt sick at the thought of losing my Harilal again. Never had hatred and anger been more apparent to me. And no amount of consoling myself that hatred originates from the same glands as love, could alleviate the pain in my bleeding heart.

FIFTY TWO

While we left on our journey to Rajkot and Porbandar, Harilal had packed his bags and returned to Ahmedabad. He was a completely forlorn man, broken in spirit; a man who had no direction in sight. The poor boy had really believed that his father would take cognizance of his pitiable finances and the needs of his expanding family and his days of misery would come to an end.

Alas! Mohandas had snuffed out all such hopes. Even the ancestral property, a share of which was rightfully his, had been cruelly snatched away. The property of his forefathers would only benefit his cousins and the other useless hangers-on of his Bapu. He could not help ruing over the bitter irony of his fate. Once again he was racked by the hatred he felt for his cousin Chaganlal whom he blamed for having obstructed his English barrister's degree. Once again he found himself filled with a deep rancour towards his father for having shut all doors on him. He was convinced that this final blow would fuel further speculations about the rift between his Bapu and him and leave no doubt in anyone's mind that Harilal was indeed a black sheep, unworthy of the Gandhi name.

❃ ❃ ❃

It was a dark night when we reached Rajkot. I was deeply disturbed to see my once vivacious sisters-in-law, living under the grim shadow of widowhood. How time had ravaged their faces and forms and I dreaded to think how difficult it must be for them to live as widows in a cruelly oppressive society. I hugged them and wept. I recalled the happy days we had spent together, and how these women had shaped my life. The frustration of not being able to offer any succour weighed me down. As I left for

Porbandar, I was racked with the fresh wound of Harilal's plight and the unending grief of my loved ones.

It was a relief when we left Porbandar for Shantiniketan in Bengal, a school for the study of fine arts started by Rabindranath Tagore that had become home to many of the Phoenix inmates who had travelled back to India with us. A small self-contained township near Calcutta with its own dairy farm and hospital, it housed a hundred and twenty-five pupils who were taught singing, dancing, painting, music, poetry and literature.

Mohandas was pleasantly surprised when he saw that all the Phoenix settlers at Shantiniketan continued to live by the principles of self-reliance and simple living that he had practiced and preached. He immediately felt at home in Tagore's abode of peace. Unfortunately, just two weeks after we had reached Shantiniketan, a telegram from Poona brought us the dreadful news of Gopal Krishna Gokhale's death. It plunged Mohandas and me into gloom.

I began to reflect on the days gone by, where we had been caught in a whirl of cataclysmic events that had drastically altered the course of our lives.

�֍   �֍   ✖

It was the year 1915. Mohandas was forty-six years old. For more than twenty-three of those years he had lived outside his country. It was Gopal Krishna Gokhale who had been instrumental in getting him to return to India and it was on his insistence and support that Mohandas had dedicated himself to the service of his homeland. In a way, it was Gokhale who had predicted that Mohandas was destined to be a great national leader. Finding little synergy between Mohandas' methods of service and the prevailing political climate, he had wanted us to tour around the country to first witness, observe, and then modify our views to suit the needs of an India that was struggling to unshackle from a cruel colonial regime. But now Gokhale was gone, and with him much of the vigour that he had so carefully instilled in his protégé.

We boarded an afternoon train to Poona with Maganlal, to attend the funeral. Grief stricken and stunned beyond belief after having met him just a few weeks ago in London, it was hard to think of Gokhale as one deceased.

Resigned to my fate with the overhanging anxiety of Harilal, his wasted life, his angry oath to never see his father again, his cruel words in an open letter to publicly humiliate his father, returned to trouble me yet again. I tuned-out of the picturesque landscape racing before my eyes on the moving train, to block out the pain of Harilal's latest assault and fell asleep.

❈ ❈ ❈

Thus began Mohandas' extensive travels nationwide. To reacquaint himself with the people of his homeland and their struggles, he embarked on a journey with the dual purpose of locating a suitable ashram for himself. Whenever possible, I accompanied Mohandas on these expeditions, and the more he toured India the more convinced he was that the most suitable place for us to settle was our native state of Gujarat.

The beautiful city of Ahmedabad, with its ancient mosques and medieval ruins that had housed the handloom weavers for hundreds of years became the natural choice. In keeping with Mohandas' dream of reviving weaving and spinning as a cottage industry, to promote the welfare of millions of his countrymen, it seemed just perfect. More so because Ahmedabad had become the hub of India's fastest growing textile industry, and he felt that he could easily persuade the wealthy owners of these mills to support his ashram and the cause.

Eventually a local attorney offered to donate his bungalow in Kochrab, a village few miles outside the city of Ahmedabad, to Mohandas. The house was comfortable, but not large enough to accommodate a community. The additional space around the bungalow however lent itself to building several rooms, so finally, Mohandas decided to establish his ashram there and initiate his activities as planned.

❈ ❈ ❈

Meanwhile Harilal, the desolate and abandoned wanderer, vacillating between deep love and overpowering hatred, was hankering after his *bona fide* legacy that was so cruelly being denied to him. He was beset with intense churnings felt by a "neglected son" and dreaded the dark future that he would have to battle alone. The conduct of his cold-hearted father, he could never understand, much less forgive.

How paradoxical was the situation! The entire nation revered Bapu as the chosen one, as the greatest liberator of the oppressed classes, but the injustice that his own family faced at the hands of their messiah, needed to be exposed. He felt it was his duty to tell the world how cruel his Bapu had been to him, to Ba and to his younger brothers. Harilal was faced with a conundrum—on the one hand was his Bapu's teachings of following the path of truth and fearlessness, which he would be violating if he did not do anything about exposing his father's true character, and on the other, was the much-revered Bapu whom the world had come to worship as a living god. After much deliberation Harilal decided to write an open letter to his father to lay some of those phantoms to rest. He sat up all night spewing venom on those sheets of paper. The long-simmering feeling of oppression felt somewhat lighter after his torrential outburst. He felt vindicated.

Harilal looked at the folded pages of the lengthy, open letter he had so painstakingly written. He sealed the envelope and wrote in a neat straight line on top:

My open letter to my father M.K. Gandhi. Bar-at-Law.

He wanted the letter to reach his father before he left from Calcutta. Next, he took out a separate sheet of paper and began listing the names of his relatives and public figures to whom he would send copies, the next morning.

As planned, the letter did reach Mohandas while we were still in Calcutta. Mohandas tore open the envelope and removed the thick bundle of pages that were contained within. With trembling hands, he began to read his son's ramblings and with each passing second I saw his face cloud over and eyes fill up. I felt as if my heart would explode.

Then he began to read it aloud, translating each line as he proceeded. It was a very long letter of accusations, detailing all that Harilal had been through in his life.

In the service of Pujya Pitaji,

A worm enters the body of a wasp and flies away having assumed the form of the wasp. I believe something similar happened to me. I have received much from you, I have learnt much, I was formed by you and my character emerged unblemished. The only difference is that I lacked the patience and endurance of a worm and ran away even before I could become a wasp.

I separated from you with your consent. In so doing I followed the dictates of my conscience. This too I learnt from you.

It is usually not possible to distinguish the Phoenix Institution from you. And hence I left that too. We spoke much. You said much; you also did all that you could. I also said all that was possible for me to say. It was destined that we be separated.

When I experienced the desire to write to you at length, the following thoughts came to my mind.

Your life has been a public one. Even your personal life is no secret. All are naturally curious to know more about your life. Many would have asked you questions about the sudden change in me. I have been unable to say all that I wished to say to you.

For such reasons I considered it proper to write this public letter to you.

The thoughts expressed in this letter are my own.

Our differences are not of recent origin. We have had differences for the past ten years. They stem from one subject. You are convinced that you have given me and my brothers necessary education. You are convinced that you could not have given us a better education than what you did. In other words you have given us necessary and sufficient attention. I believe that with your preoccupations and engagements you have unintentionally paid us no attention at all. It affected me and that is what I shall describe in this letter. I believe that due to your overwhelming desire to provide us education and care, you have experienced the illusion of having done so.

For ten years now I have been crying and pleading with you. But, for the wasp, the worm is insignificant. That is, you have never considered my sentiments. I believe that you have always used us as weapons. 'Us' in this context means me and my brothers—Manilal, Ramdas and Devdas...

....If you have no knowledge of our sentiments, then there is no possibility of you paying any heed to what we have to say to you. You have oppressed us in a civilized way....Thus oppressed I have remained melancholic, anxious and, as a result, sick. You have instilled fear in us, of you, even while we are walking, ambling, eating or drinking, sleeping or sitting, reading or writing, and working. Your heart is like a 'vajra'. Your love... I have never seen; so what can I say about it...?

....As your political life became full of hardships you have changed your ideas, and along with that you have also twisted our lives. I believe without any hesitation that our lives hitherto have been irregular and uncertain....We might be foolish; but allow me to add that you have kept us foolish. You have never considered our rights....

....Pitaji, you have not paid any attention to us even when we sought it. God grants a newborn child mother's milk. If the child is given any other food, it has indigestion and falls incurably ill.

It is necessary to narrate my life story in support of what I have said earlier. The period to which I refer is from 1906 to 1911. In the end I ran away from you in 1911. This is the second time that a similar incident has taken place.

In 1906, at the age of nineteen, I implored and beseeched you, I made innumerable arguments and pleaded that I should be allowed to chart the course of my life. I wanted to study, to gain knowledge; I had no other desire. I demanded that I should be sent to England. I wept and wandered aimlessly for a year but you paid no heed. You told me that character building should precede everything else....

....I was told that I should leave Johannesburg and live in Phoenix to build my character. The 'Indian Opinion' is published from Phoenix.

Phoenix is regarded as a place for those desiring a simple life. No one can question the objectives of Phoenix...I was asked to build my character in a place like that. But who was I? Was I of any consequence there?

But, the plight of my mother was much worse than mine at Phoenix. I saw that she was being insulted often. What I saw was like witnessing a thief admonishing the sentry. People brought complaints to you...If you had maintained records of all the complaints it would certainly fill a small notebook.

....It is beyond my capacity to describe the hardships that my mother had to undergo. All this I could not bear. If we ever brought complaints to you, your response would be, 'He is a good man. He desires your welfare. And such and such is a jolly fellow.'

It was then the idea that you were using us as weapons took root in my mind.

In 1907 the satyagraha commenced. I joined the struggle. I had the opportunity to think freely in jail. When I was out of prison I shared with you my ideas about how and what education we could acquire. But you deprecated my thoughts. I remained oppressed. I considered myself a lost cause. I stopped expressing my views.

Finally after pleading with you for five years, in accordance with your teaching I obeyed my conscience and ran away after writing a personal letter to you....

Despite leading an unhappy life in Ahmedabad I do believe that I learnt much, experienced much.

Now you have returned to India. I spent some days with you. My effort to rejoin the Phoenix Institution has failed. My views remain unchanged. You remain steadfast in the choice of your path and consider it to be just. When I complained to you that you did not allow me to go to Lahore and asked me to stay in Ahmedabad, you responded by saying, 'Why did you not remain firm in your views then?'

Now I am firm in my views and will remain so. If I were to die doing so, I shall die a satisfied man. I know that my conscience is free of sin....Even after hearing and reading all this you would say only one thing, and that I know: 'I have always loved my sons to the extent that I have not allowed them to do anything that I have considered wrong.' Pitaji, the facts given above contain my response to your justification. One more thing remains to be said here. It is so subtle and delicate that it cannot be said fully, nor can it be expressed through words. Nevertheless, I consider it my duty to write about it.

You admonish me that I married 'against your wishes'. I accept that. Given my circumstances I feel that my action should be pardoned. I believe that no one could have acted differently under those conditions.

You know that I got engaged while I was still a child...Please allow me to state that ever since the marriage, we have remained captive to your wishes. We have been married for nine years. We have spent six of those years apart, pining for each other.

I dissociated myself from the Phoenix Institution because I witnessed hypocrisy there. I consider the objectives of Phoenix to be most superior; but with respect to what I have seen, you are the only one who leads his life according to those objectives...It is often asked, 'Where are the restrictive impositions in the Phoenix Institution?' Such a contention is unacceptable to me. Because whatever I did there and saw others do, I felt their conduct was enforced by fear. It was as if everything was based on one principle: 'Let the groom die, let the bride die, but do as Bapu says.'

And it is a fact, Pitaji, that those who believed so became dear to you and those who did not were despised. This was especially true for us; and among us, it was I who was so despised.

...Pitaji, whenever we told you 'We do not benefit from the Phoenix Institution' or 'We have not seen others gaining from the Phoenix Institution', you told us to follow the example of Murabbibhai and Shri Chaganlal....We should keep them as our ideals.

I have been bewildered whenever you have said so; because, I have neither been able to bear it nor have been able to express what I have observed...Their example teaches us to nurture our self-interest....

Pitaji, I have not been able to say even one-fourth of what I have to say. The letter has become very long. Printing is expensive. From where will I find the money to pay for it?

Before I conclude, Pitaji, if I have unknowingly expressed rash and immature ideas I seek your forgiveness from the depths of my conscience. At the age of twenty-eight I have been forced to write to you like a young child; this pains me, but I had no other choice. My conscience dictated the letter and I merely wrote it. Whatever I have said about the Phoenix Institution I have said because of my blood relations with it. Therefore, I have pointed out only its shortcomings. The virtues of the Phoenix Institution are known to the world.

My entire letter stresses one point—you have never been generous and patient with our failings. You have never considered our rights and capabilities; you have never seen the person in us. Your life and actions are very harsh. I consider myself unsuitable for a life such as yours. To you a son and others are equal. If there be two accused— one of your sons and someone else—you have considered it unjust to regard the other as guilty. It is justice that a son must suffer, but unfortunately I have not been able to bear such suffering.

Moreover, whether it is right or wrong, I am married. God has granted me four children. I am caught in the web of worldly relations, in its delusions and enchantments; I cannot acquire the detachment of an ascetic and renounce the world like others.

Therefore, I had to separate from you with your consent. I feel that I must earn my own livelihood. Even after this I am willing to join the Phoenix Institution at your command. You know that I have not disobeyed you on purpose. It is possible that my views are wrong. I hope that they prove to be wrong—if I realize that they are wrong I shall not hesitate to reform myself. In the deep recesses of my conscience, my only desire is that I be your son— that is, if I am good enough be your son.

Your obedient son Harilal's Sashtang Dandvat

Chaitra Sud Purnima
Samvat 1971
31 March 1915
Mumbai

Mohandas' lips quivered and pursed into a downward sneer. He remained pensive for a long time and I could not contain my painful sobs that just would not let up. The bitterness expressed by his son had hit him hard. With trembling hands he folded the pages and put them back into the envelope. Then in an aching voice he spoke. 'Harilal must be quite relieved after venting his anger. I am glad he has made it public, but one day he shall realize his mistake and will regret his deed. I feel no anger towards him; only an overwhelming sense of pity.'

Try as I did I couldn't muster up the courage to advocate my son's cause that day. Deep down in the folds of my aching heart I knew there was no element of untruth or exaggeration in what Harilal had written, but blinded as I was for my child, the fact that he had become so defiant and had so shamelessly humiliated his father, found no justification, even to the mother in me.

The letter lay in Mohandas' pocket for many days and the gloom that surrounded him did not lift. The news of Gokhale's death had only partly diverted that sadness onto another plane.

This had been the most punishing moment in the life of Mohandas, the hapless father of a recalcitrant son. And once again my heart bled for both.

Fifty Three

Life at Kochrab Ashram was even more austere than it was at Tolstoy Farm or Phoenix. Mohandas had devised a stringent code of conduct listing nine rules that every inmate solemnly swore to adhere to. Most of the vows were the tenets that he practiced in his own life; truth, non-violence, celibacy, palate-control, avoidance of stealing and to be devoid of any possessions. Three new vows had been added to the existing list in keeping with the need of the prevailing situation in India; to wear or use nothing foreign-made, to be fearless in order to fight the injustices of the Imperial rulers and to accept all "untouchables" as one of our own.

The first lot of twenty-five permanent members of the Gandhi Ashram who arrived at Kochrab were a group of devoted men, women and children. It was a new beginning for us, a time to lead a peaceful life once again as one large happy family. I found myself immersed in the hustle and bustle of the settlement, and felt quite at home.

Mohandas' keen desire to induct some untouchables into the precincts of the ashram soon bore fruit. One of Gopal Krishna Gokhale's colleagues in Bombay had identified a schoolteacher, his wife and child, who were willing to join the ashram.

Dudhabhai, Daniben and their little daughter, Laxmi, arrived from Bombay to be welcomed by Mohandas into the Kochrab Ashram family. After the initial awkwardness, things became normal and they soon merged with the commune comfortably.

Outside the ashram however, the orthodox Hindu community was appalled by the inclusion of untouchables into the home and property of a staunch Hindu. At first there were mild threats of the water supply being disconnected, but later the growing number of protestors in Ahmedabad threatened to force the withdrawal of financial support from the wealthy textile mill-owners on whose benevolence the ashram survived.

'This is no ashram. It's a colony of untouchables,' ranted the furious protestors. The danger of a complete social boycott and prevention of all access to community service loomed large before us. Mohandas however was unperturbed. Firmly believing that the work we were doing was in the service of god, he was certain that they would be shown the right path.

'All right!' he said indignantly, 'If that is the case, then we shall all move to the untouchables' quarters in the city of Ahmedabad and subsist on whatever we earn by manual labour, but our spirit shall not be broken so easily!'

A timely intervention by Ambalal Sarabhai, one of the wealthiest textile mill-owners, who had donated an annual sum of twenty-five thousand rupees to cover the running costs of the ashram, diffused the crisis. And Mohandas resumed his activities with the same fervour as before.

Inside the Kochrab Ashram similar rumblings had already taken root. A subtle discrimination was being inflicted upon the newcomers by some of the residents. I too was having a hard time, allowing free access to Dudhabhai's family into my home and kitchen. All those years of conditioning during my childhood had made it impossible for me to ignore the aversion I felt for them.

It was not long before Mohandas got wind of this. He had noticed that Daniben was never allowed to help with the cooking and I always stopped Dudhabhai outside the kitchen, whenever he wanted to even get himself a glass of water. When little Laxmi strayed into my kitchen one day, he saw me scrub the utensils she had touched and wash the kitchen floor, after she had left.

That evening after the regular prayer meeting, a sombre-looking Mohandas addressed all the assembled residents.

'I have noticed some disturbing things happening at the ashram. It is bad enough for me to battle adverse reactions to our principles from the world outside, but I am shocked to see that the inmates here have violated a vital ruling laid down by me,' he said.

I squirmed. I knew his simmering anger was directed only at me.

'Acceptance of untouchables is the first ethic of our home, and all those who are unable to comply with this rule are welcome to pack their bags and leave.' He said firmly.

I was seated on the floor, right in front, inside the hall where we had collected for the evening prayers. I felt Mohandas' piercing gaze on me and I didn't have the nerve to look up at him. I knew he was furious. Who could have known that better than me?

Later that night, several inmates flocked to Mohandas to apologize for their behaviour. Some even offered to apologize to Dudhabhai and his family for the humiliation they had inflicted on them.

My reservations however, remained and deeply disappointed Mohandas. He had presumed that after years of living abroad and working for the socially oppressed, I would have been more accepting. For several days thereafter, I avoided all contact with Mohandas fearing an admonishment. I went about my daily chores silently, hoping that things would settle down with time.

One morning I was sitting in my verandah, watching little Laxmi frolicking alone in the courtyard. She was dancing unabashedly to her own song, unaware that I was staring at her. What a lovely, happy child she was. So appealing and radiant! The melodious peals of her laughter and song touched the chords of my heart. Mohandas had been right.

She is also God's child. A sweet messenger of God's truth.

I felt a cloud lift from my mind and I rushed out to the courtyard, scooped up the squealing child into my arms and hugged her tight till her breath nearly stopped. All barriers broken, all prejudices gone, I took her into my bosom with the same fervour that I would have felt for Rami or any other grandchild—and in that overpowering moment I felt I had been touched by the hand of god.

❃   ❃   ❃

For Harilal, the lengthy, angry and accusatory letter to his father had had the desired effect, but only for a short span of time. It had been his moment of self-redemption, his sweet revenge. In the public eye however, it had done little to tarnish Mohandas' image and neither did Mohandas harbour the embarrassment for long. Dismissing it as Harilal's heightened irritability and personal failure, he chose to ignore it as one more in the long list of his son's faults.

In the meantime after having lost all hopes of receiving any monetary support from his father, Harilal approached Seth Narottam Das once again for a job at his textile mill in Bombay. The textile king was delighted to see him, and after extending a warm welcome, he enquired about his Ba and Bapu. Harilal's face clouded as he spoke, 'Seth, you must be aware that Bapu and I have parted ways and I need to find a job to support myself.'

'There should be no dearth of jobs for a bright man like you, Harilal. Where do we find trustworthy and hardworking people these days?' He beamed. 'You can begin your training immediately at Sholapur, after which you can take over as my key person at the Calcutta office, if that suits you.'

Narottam Das' words were like manna from heaven. The persistent gloom he had been feeling, dissipated.

'I assure you, Seth,' he said, barely able to contain his excitement, 'I shall never betray your trust and shall go to Sholapur and then to Calcutta, just as you desire.'

With a new spring in his step, Harilal returned to Ahmedabad to break the happy news to Gulab. He revelled in the feeling that he would need nothing from his Bapu ever again.

But how terribly wrong he was!

❈ ❈ ❈

In the months that followed Gopal Krishna Gokhale's death, the growing unrest in the country was threatening to shake up the very foundations of British rule. The man on the street felt a surging rage which had deeply impacted Mohandas. Having spent most of his adult life in a foreign land, fighting for the rights of his oppressed fellow Indians, he now felt compelled to reinvent and align himself to the complexities of his homeland.

In the winter of 1915, Mohandas attended the annual meeting of the Indian National Congress. With the intent of merely being an observer to formulate his own agenda, he found to his surprise, a firmly united front in the making. Nationalist leaders of all faiths had come together on a common platform to devise methods of capitalizing on Britain's involvement in the World War to their advantage. To harness these diverse energies to fight on a united platform for freedom was not going to be as difficult as he had imagined, mused Mohandas. He now waited for the right opportunity.

An impressive orator, whose candid outpourings targeted the top leaders of the Indian National Congress, members of the Indian royalty, as well as British officials, Mohandas soon became the darling of the media and the masses. His rhetoric managed to strike a chord even amongst the Indian youth and he found himself always on the move, motivating people across the subcontinent, with his fiery speeches.

Meanwhile there was news from Calcutta. Gulab was pregnant again with Harilal's fifth child. Here Maganlal and his wife had returned to Kochrab and were ready to undertake the vows to be inducted back into the ashram. Dudhabhai had left for Bombay with his family after a teary farewell. Parting with Laxmi was heart-wrenching, for it was only when I said goodbye to her that I realized how deeply attached I had become to the little girl in such a short span of time.

I often travelled out of Kochrab Ashram with Mohandas on his cross-country trips for that was the only chance I got to be alone with him and discuss family and ashram matters. From an anonymous traveller in the third class compartment bound for several destinations across India, Mohandas soon became the most revered and recognized face of the Indian freedom movement. Wherever he went, he found hordes of people waiting at train stations to greet him amidst cries of 'Long live Gandhi', 'Gandhi *amar rahe.*'

Mohandas' speeches were simple. He advocated the revival of Indian values and stressed on the need for character building. He preached his time-tested principle of non-violence as an unfailing alternative to senseless killings and discouraged inflammatory speeches. He continuously promoted the supreme power of *satyagraha* as the only means to achieve freedom. The simplicity and purity of his message permeated to the poorest of the poor which resulted in more and more people being drawn to him and the cause.

One day in the early spring of 1917, a peasant named Rajkumar Shukla arrived at Kochrab. Hailing from Champaran, an area in Bihar known for the cultivation of indigo, a plant that yields natural blue dye, he had been trailing Mohandas on his nationwide tours in the hope of finding an answer to the problems that ailed the farmers of his native village. Moved by the magical stories around Mohandas and his commitment to the cause of oppressed fellowmen, Shukla believed that only the *Mahatma* could rescue the farmers of Champaran from their sorry plight.

Mohandas was planning to visit Calcutta for a conference in a few weeks' time, and I was to go along to be with Gulab during the birth of her child. Mohandas heard Shukla's tale of woe patiently and agreed to travel to Champaran with him, after the conclusion of the Calcutta conference.

❊　❊　❊

Harilal's life had taken a different turn after he accepted the job at the Sholapur office of Narottam Das. He had written to his father with elation about his new assignment, his likelihood of settling in Calcutta and his apprehension of keeping his family with him till he was able to rent a house. Believing it to be the best option, he said he had decided to send Gulab and the children to be with us at Kochrab, till such time that he was in a position to keep them with him either at Sholapur or Calcutta, wherever he was posted.

Gulab was deeply troubled at the thought of living away from Harilal again.

'I cannot live without you!' She was weeping as the words tumbled out of her mouth. 'Not a single moment can I be at peace! Please don't send us away.'

Nestled like a baby in his arms, she hid her face in his chest and cried. Harilal drew her closer and stroked her head till her heaving chest eased and sobs quietened.

'You think I can live without you, Gulab? You think I can be happy for a single moment if you are not by my side? Now quiet! Don't cry. I promise I shall call you back as soon as I know where I am posted and am able to rent a house for us. Until then my sweet Gulab, you stay with Ba. She loves you dearly and will be happy to see the children. You will be happy too!'

'How can I be happy without you?' Gulab persisted, her large doe-eyes brimming with a fresh burst of tears.

'Come now, Gulab.' Harilal kissed her forehead gently and crushed her into a suffocating embrace. 'Look at me. If for even one fleeting moment you are unhappy in Kochrab with my mother and Bapu, just tell me and I shall come running and take you away.'

A hesistant smile played on Gulab's lips. She closed her eyes as Harilal kissed her tear-stained cheeks till she drifted away into a troubled slumber.

✖ ✖ ✖

Mohandas read out Harilal's letter aloud with a marked indifference in his voice. He sat down at his desk on the floor, and took out his pen to write him a fitting reply that was despatched without any delay.

Harilal opened his father's letter that reached him a few days later. No blessings, no happiness at his new assignment, no good wishes for his success; nothing! All he said was,

I am not happy that you are planning to live in Calcutta. It is the city where innocent animals are slaughtered every day at the Kali Mata temple. You should abandon the thought of settling in a place where there is so much violence.

Harilal was stunned. He was in no position to heed Mohandas' ridiculous advice, nor did he have the will to debate it. By that logic all the citizens of Calcutta should have made a mass exodus to another land rather than breathe the polluted air of a city besmirched by the bloodshed of hapless animals.

Without bothering to reply to his father's preposterous note, he packed off his family to Kochrab the next day and boarded a train to Sholapur, as soon as they left.

And two days later, Harilal was summoned by Narottam Das to take charge of the office in Calcutta.

✶ ✶ ✶

Calcutta infused an unknown and rare enthusiasm in Harilal. For the first time in years he felt alive, and the prospect of a much-coveted financial independence, excited him. The cruel words of his father's last letter were pushed away from his mind and he eagerly looked forward to his first day at work. Even though the salary he was being offered was not very high, Harilal thought it was enough to sustain his family and hoped that in due course of time he would be able to start his own business in the highly profitable field of textiles.

Harilal rented a small house not too far away from his workplace, but gradually, the fearsome ghost of loneliness overpowered him and he would often find himself reliving his miserable days in Ahmedabad without Gulab and the children. In the evenings while his colleagues and new-found friends converged at cheap bars around the red light area of Sonagachi, Harilal would trudge home with a heavy heart, pull out his tattered, dog-eared copy of the Bhagavad Gita, and seek solace in its verses of wisdom.

But the day-to-day survival in the bustling city created a number of problems for Harilal. To his dismay, he soon realized that his salary was barely enough to cover his rent and daily expenses. There were no savings, so nothing could be sent to his family. His days were spent immersed in his work that left him with little time to think of anything else, but the dark nights brought heavy feelings of loneliness. He missed Gulab and the children immensely. How long would he be able to carry on like this, he did not know. Even though Gulab's frequent letters alleviated some of his misery, his will was wearing thin. The desire to be united with his family gnawed at him constantly, but he lacked the means to sustain them, a fact that pushed him deeper into a pit of gloom.

As a last resort he wrote an imploring letter to his brother Manilal, describing his desperate financial condition, asking him to help with some money that he promised to return as soon as he was in a better position. He beseeched him to bring Gulab and his children to Calcutta.

Manilal's heart melted at the sad plight of his elder brother and with the consent of Mohandas and me, he accompanied Gulab and the children to Calcutta, in keeping with his brother's wish.

Once in Calcutta, Manilal began to hear rumours about his elder brother's wayward ways—he had fallen prey to the vagaries of cheap women and alcohol. Manilal was more than aware that his father was strictly against anyone extending any sort of financial support to Harilal. But his brother's piteous plea had shaken up Manilal to such an extent that not only did he give him a neat sum from his personal savings, he also bought some kitchen utensils and furniture for his home, when he saw how miserably he lived.

Fifty Four

On 7 April 1917, Mohandas left for Champaran with Rajkumar Shukla, while I stayed back in Calcutta to be with Gulab who was in the last stages of her fifth pregnancy. In the following week she gave birth to a baby girl whom we named Manu and I found myself totally absorbed in caring for both mother and child, cooking, cleaning, attending to household chores and tending to the older children.

However, my Harilal continued to worry me. I could see he was deeply in love with Gulab and now had a secure job, but his constant anguish and overwhelming financial burden was depriving me of the joy I should have felt at being with my beloved children and grandchildren.

❌ ❌ ❌

Arriving in the distant backwaters of Champaran, Mohandas was quick to gauge that the plight of the farmers was much more *serious* than what Shukla had conveyed to him.

For over fifty years, the British who had unleashed cruelty on the poor peasants, owned most of the arable land. The poor local peasants and their families either worked in the fields for paltry wages or rented tiny plots from the landowners on which they were allowed to raise their own crops. The system mandated that the farmers cultivate "indigo", a plant of high value in the international market, but also hand over fifteen per cent of their yield to plantation owners. The landlords used the revenue thus collected under a completely illegal form of private taxation system, for frivolous hunting parties or the wasteful purchase of expensive goods.

This ruthless exploitation that was being practiced for nearly five decades was highly profitable for them even as they unleashed tyranny upon the hapless peasants of Champaran. To make matters worse, the farmers had become progressively poorer after the Germans developed a similar synthetic dye that was much cheaper, and the worldwide demand for indigo took a beating.

Totally unaware of this development, the poor peasants had accepted in good faith a seemingly generous offer from their wily British landlords who offered to relinquish all claims on personal indigo harvests, in exchange for an enhanced rent to be paid to them.

It was only when the farmers tried to sell their crop in the open market that they realized that it was worthless and they had been cheated. A few bold peasants like Shukla resorted to legal action, but ultimately had to give up, owing to the high lawyers' fees and a slow movement of their cases in courts. However when the World War broke out and the supply of synthetic dyes from Germany was blocked, indigo prices in India soared again, but the landowners quickly swung into action by not only reinstating the old system, but also in continuing their demand for a higher percentage of rent from the peasants.

A reign of terror was unleashed upon those who refused to sign the new contracts. They were tortured mercilessly, publicly beaten, arrested on false charges, their houses were burnt down and their crops confiscated.

When Mohandas arrived in Champaran, the air was thick with hostility and rage. Within a week, he formulated a plan, similar to the one he had practised to perfection, not so long ago in South Africa.

❊ ❊ ❊

I returned to Kochrab a few weeks after Manu was born. Harilal's anguish continued to haunt me. The newborn baby girl had done little to lift his gloom and I feared he would be pushed deeper into the terrible vices that had gripped him.

Barely had I stepped into the ashram when I saw a letter from Mohandas waiting for me. It was his first communication since he had left Calcutta. He described in detail the need for him to take-up the cause of the tortured peasants of Champaran and said that he was recruiting volunteers to camp there; how he needed teachers to spread awareness through education in the region; he wanted all the ashram workers to join him, but most of all he wanted me to reach there as soon as I could, to begin working with farmers' wives and daughters. He somehow thought that I would be able to help them become enlightened individuals to fight against the atrocities that they had tolerated for the last fifty years.

Mohandas also wanted our seventeen-year-old Devdas to accompany me to Champaran. He wrote,

He can help in teaching the children, that shall be his duty and service to his motherland.

Mohandas' earnest call to action stirred the people of Kochrab Ashram as much as it did outside. From across the nation people converged at Champaran to join in the fight for the rights of those destitute and oppressed peasants and leading the battle was I, along with my youngest son. My heart swelled with pride and for the moment that nagging concern about Harilal faded away.

✄   ✄   ✄

Throughout the long blistering summer months in Champaran while Mohandas plunged himself in finding suitable legal recourse for the poor peasants, I took up the district's social and health problems, assisted by a band of volunteers and my son. Amongst those who formed the core group were the familiar and comforting faces of Henry Polak and Chaganlal's son, Prabhudas, who had also participated in the struggle in South Africa.

Moving around the area with a team of workers, I spent hours in each village educating the inhabitants about public sanitation, the use of toilets, collection of garbage and the need to stop spitting, defecating and urinating in the open. It was a task that I could perform effortlessly and tirelessly.

It wasn't long before our efforts bore fruit. A small medical clinic manned by a volunteer-doctor from Poona opened in the district. Several thatch-roofed classrooms were constructed with the help of enthusiastic villagers and the local children began attending classes run by volunteers including Devdas and Prabhudas. A district-wide sanitation and awareness programme had also been successfully introduced.

As the involvement of the local people began to increase in the campaign initiated by Mohandas, a sense of unease began to grow amongst the British landlords. The press was rife with provocative articles on the trouble stirred up by *outsiders* and any peasant found to be giving hostile statements to lawyers was threatened, witch-hunted and beaten up. We even had government spies trailing us, watching our every little move, but slowly the volunteers led by Mohandas befriended them and they crossed over to support the cause.

Meanwhile, Mohandas vowed not to leave Champaran until basic peasant reforms were in place. He had been labouring tirelessly for twelve months during which time he was persecuted and arrested, but ultimately his efforts bore fruit when the Agrarian Reform Law was passed in the province of Bihar in 1917.

The Bill abolished the draconian "share-cropping" system, which had long burdened the poor farmers. It prohibited the increase of rents at the whims of the landlords, refunded some percentage of the extra money that the farmers had paid towards the last increase in taxes and finally paved the way for the exit of most of the British landlords from the region forever.

Freed from the cruel yoke of the colonial masters who had exploited and tortured the farmers for over half a century, the peasants of Champaran could breathe easy at last.

And Mohandas would be catapulted to the highest echelons of heroic splendour, bestowed with the title of "Mahatma" that would stick to him for posterity.

✼ ✼ ✼

The summer of 1917 brought with it torrential rain and floods in Gujarat, followed by a virulent outbreak of the dreaded plague. The deadly epidemic spread its tentacles right up to Ahmedabad. The air was thick with disease carrying organisms and the streets of the densely populated city were strewn with dead rats. The menace was compounded tenfold due to the lack of proper civic amenities and sanitation. The death toll continued to rise and the disease spread rapidly to the outskirts of the city, engulfing several villages in its morbid reach.

When the news reached us at Champaran, we rushed back to Kochrab to take stock of the critical situation. Mohandas decided that it was imperative to move the ashram to a safer location without wasting any time.

Four miles north of Ahmedabad, on the banks of River Sabarmati, was a treeless, roadless inaccessible tract of land that was large enough to accommodate Mohandas' growing colony of "ashramites". Ironically, the land that appealed to him was barely a mile away from Sabarmati Central Jail. Afterall, imprisonment was an integral part of every *satyagrahi's* life!

Within a span of seven days, the purchase of land and other formalities were swiftly executed and by the middle of August, Sabarmati Ashram, under the supervision of Maganlal Gandhi, was ready for us to move in.

⁂

Some weeks earlier, a letter addressed to Manilal had fallen into Mohandas' hands. Tucked amidst the bundle of correspondence that he sifted through every morning, Mohandas recognized Harilal's handwriting on the envelope and tore it open. Harilal's one-page note to his brother shook up Mohandas, and as he read and re-read those lines over and over again, it opened up old wounds and his whole body trembled with rage.

He spent a sleepless night ruing over his vagrant son's uncontained greed for material comforts. His persistent pursuit of an illusion, his wayward behaviour and sinful habits were tortuous enough, but what pained him even more was that despite his stern directive against any sort of help, monetary or otherwise to Harilal, Manilal had defied him. Not only had Harilal shamelessly asked his younger brother for help, his brother had provided him financial aid.

Mohandas summoned Manilal to his room immediately after the morning prayers. The letter from Harilal lay open on a low desk before him. Manilal's hands trembled as he read it, with trepidation writ large on his face. Mohandas was quiet; a deep frown creased his forehead. He spoke with a voice laden with pain.

'What is this, Manilal? Is this true?'

Manilal lowered his eyes to the floor. He tried to steady his trembling hands, but in vain.

'Yes, Bapu,' he said. His low voice could barely be heard.

Mohandas looked at him, his piercing gaze was directed straight at the petrified boy.

'You are guilty of not one, but two breaches! You have helped Harilal despite my specific instructions not to do so, which is bad enough, but what you need to explain is, where have you collected so much money from? What is going on behind my back?'

Manilal trembled as he spoke, 'Bapu! Do you think I have been swindling money from the ashram expenses? No! This is my money. It is the money I earned and saved in South Africa.'

But Mohandas was not appeased. 'Don't you know that anyone who enters public life and joins the ashram has to abide by its rules. Don't you know that no one is allowed any private savings because all earnings belong to the people we serve? Manilal, you are guilty of committing a terrible sin.'

Manilal was reminded of that horrific day at the Tolstoy Farm. The day he was brutally shamed and two innocent nubile girls were mercilessly shorn off their locks. Mohandas' face bore the same fury as it did on that fateful day.

'Don't you know how reckless your brother has become? Don't you know that everyone from the ashram has been forbidden from lending him money? And don't you know that the money you have slyly taken from the ashram to help him will be spent sinfully, wasted on brothels or gambled away?'

'Bapu!' Manilal pleaded. 'Please believe me. My conscience is clear. I am not lying. I have not used a single paisa from the ashram's funds to help Motabhai. You can have the accounts checked, Bapu!' Manilal was in tears.

'No, Manilal, this is not a matter of accounts. This is a serious matter of ethics. You are definitely guilty, but more than you, it is I who is to blame. We must repent for your actions, both you and I.' Mohandas blurted out in one breath.

Manilal sank to the floor. His sobbing did not stop.

'Yes, we must both repent,' his father continued. 'You shall be relieved of the management of the ashram right away and proceed to Madras. You will have to live there by yourself on whatever you can earn as a labourer. You cannot take any money from here and are forbidden to disclose your identity to anyone there. There is a weaving organization in Madras and if you wish you can stay there like a simple servant and learn to weave. And I,' he paused, 'I shall fast for three days, as penance for my failure. Now go, Manilal! Leave the ashram with a happy heart and think of the work you shall be doing, as service to god.'

Manilal's tear-streaked face was drained of all colour as he left the room and the ashram.

The news of Manilal's ouster from the ashram and the events that led to it, reached Harilal within the next twenty-four hours. Harilal was in shock. His father had been cruel to a point of villainy for a trivial exchange between his brother and him. He clenched his jaws fiercely and bit his lip till blood trickled out onto his unshaven chin. He felt a deep revulsion for his cruel father. His whole body contorted as he slammed his fist on the table before him. A loud scream emanated from his constricted throat that reverberated off the walls of his empty home, into the balmy night.

✂ ✂ ✂

FIFTY FIVE

Harilal sat holed up in his office all day in a numb stupor. The news of Bapu undertaking a three-day fast as penance had spread like wildfire and when he did step out, his colleagues bombarded him with questions regarding the need for his father's sudden *atmashudhi*. Harilal felt irritable. He had no answers and he felt disgusted that Manilal had been thrown out of the ashram. His poor brother was being penalized for lending a paltry sum of money to a desperately needy elder brother. Manilal's action did not warrant such severe punishment. Filled with bitterness he lashed out in anger at his colleagues, compelling his manager to intervene.

'Mr. Gandhi! Your behaviour has become intolerable,' he ranted. 'If your father's fasting is disturbing you so much then it is better for you to leave the job and go back to the ashram. If you can't think about the welfare of the mill that employs you, go and join the *satyagraha!*'

The manager's harsh words made it worse for Harilal. He stepped out of the mill premises that evening, not wanting to go home to face Gulab. He was in no mood to answer her piercing questions about Manilal's expulsion and Mohandas' preposterous *atmashudhi*, a deliberate act of self-loathing by his father to punish the family. While lumbering aimlessly in the lane that led out of the factory, he spotted an old Bengali acquaintance who sidled up to him and whispered, 'Come with me, Gandhi *Moshai*,' he boomed. 'I have just the cure for your troubles. Just two sips and all your worries will vanish. Come, you shall be my guest…'

Perhaps for that one brief moment, Harilal did feel repulsed by the thought of going down that vile road of self-destruction. But then he felt a rush in his veins, a fresh surge of anger and loathing for his father. He needed something to soothe his burning soul. He narrowed his eyes and reached out for the outstretched hand of his old friend, who was beckoning him into a land of fantasy, with the promise of total exhilaration and no abiding vestiges of the gloomy life he was trapped in.

⚘ ⚘ ⚘

When Harilal staggered home, it was well past midnight and Gulab was pacing up and down the street looking out for him. He had left at eight that morning, without having eaten a morsel. She was gripped by panic, fearing terrible consequences. The children lay blissfully in deep slumber untouched by the frenzy of their mother and the recklessness of their missing father. Harilal collapsed into her arms and stumbled on to the floor. His unsteady steps and the smell of liquor on his breath, terrified her. She helped him up from the floor with great difficulty and led him by his arm to the bed. Her eyes filled with tears as the putrid stench of alcohol crept up her nostrils. She ran to the sink and retched.

Harilal blabbered continuously. His slurring rhetoric strung with indecipherable words would not stop. She heard him swear at Bapu and then cry out for his mother. She feared that his loud clamouring would wake up the children, so she tiptoed into the room and placed her hands gently on his forehead. The touch of Gulab's cool, moist palms must have soothed Harilal for he turned over, curled up in a foetal position and fell asleep. Gulab sank to the floor. She stayed wide awake all night, her thoughts racing wildly, watching the sad state of her husband. Copious tears flowed down her face as she closed her eyes and prayed.

Help my beloved from tumbling down this pit of self-destruction,
God almighty! Help him find his peace and forgive him his sins.

She knew that no amount of fasting by his self-righteous father could ever redeem Harilal's pain. And what a tragic irony that was!

Who could have known better than me that in his relentless pursuit for perfection, Mohandas had injured the core of his most loved ones; those he sought to make perfect. I was also aware of my own limitations in being able to either obstruct his plans or change him. In the process I had devised my own silent form of *satyagraha*, a prolonged and non-violent protest against his emotional atrocities towards me and my sons by which I sometimes succeeded in making him retract his steps.

❈ ❈ ❈

A few weeks after Manilal had been banished from the ashram, I found Mohandas writing a letter to a well-known publisher in Madras requesting him to give a suitable job to his son. The publisher hired Manilal at the printing press, which eased a bit of my anxiety and the burden of Mohandas' guilt for the unduly harsh treatment he had heaped upon him.

Several months later, when Albert West who looked after the publication of the *Indian Opinion* at Phoenix, expressed his desire to recuse himself and return to England, Manilal was dispatched to South Africa, to take charge of the ongoing battle against racial discrimination and also to oversee the publication of the newspaper. News of his recruitment at Phoenix reached me while I was still in Champaran. Manilal's sudden departure for South Africa made me restless. I fretted about his going away, not knowing when I would see him again.

The only consolation was that at twenty-six, my Manilal, after a series of serious confrontations, had succeeded in regaining his father's confidence and had earned a position of trust and responsibility in a foreign land. And that meant a lot to me.

❈ ❈ ❈

March 1918

I left Champaran in the spring of 1918, a proud and contented woman. My persistent efforts had brought about significant changes in that primitive village of Bihar. The streets had been cleared of all waste. The earlier stench of decaying garbage had vanished. Flies and mosquitoes had been exterminated. People had imbibed basic habits of cleanliness and hygiene and I was hopeful that these changes would endure over time.

When I arrived at the new settlement on the banks of the Sabarmati, I was somewhat bewildered. I felt like a visitor in an alien place as I wandered around aimlessly, watching the various activities which were underway. The neat rows of fruit trees, brick-covered pathways, simple whitewashed houses under construction, the familiar sights of a school, library and a weaving shed were coming up rapidly amidst a cluster of modest cottages for the residents. I saw a flight of stone steps leading down to the river that gave way to a wide patch of green, where the morning and evening prayers were held. A sense of calm descended over me. I shut my eyes as I leaned back against a tall tree. I mused,

Soon this will be my own haven and these new faces that inhabit the ashram shall become my family, all engaged in a common dharma; the quest of truth.

❇ ❇ ❇

Back in their home in Calcutta, after that long miserable night during which Gulab had kept vigil on her husband lying in a drunken stupor, Harilal had regained his consciousness. He had woken up to a sunny day, with no visible hangover from his binge the night before. He avoided Gulab and crept out to the verandah without hugging and greeting his children as he usually did. Gulab, with her tear-stained face and swollen eyes, meekly followed him out. He looked at her guiltily as she stood quietly beside him, just staring at his blood-shot eyes and bedraggled clothes. Tears pricked up in her eyes again and fell onto her face. She made no attempt to wipe them.

'Forgive me, Gulab. I am sorry I have hurt you. Will you please forgive me?' Harilal implored.

His painful pleading prompted a fresh bout of tears that trickled on to her cheeks. Harilal wiped her face gently with both his palms.

'Who am I to forgive you?' Gulab could barely speak. 'I must have committed some grave sin that has made you do this. But forget about me, I dread to think of what Ba and Bapu shall say? Can you even imagine their plight?'

Harilal was stunned into silence. He closed his eyes and tightly curled his fingers around Gulab's wrist. He hugged her and wept. The moment passed while they held each other in a tight embrace, and the sad incident was swiftly forgotten. Each one hoped that it would never happen again and that pain would never revisit their home.

Alas cruel life! It had yet to dole out more blows onto the unfortunate duo.

❋ ❋ ❋

Harilal's innumerable vices, some grossly extravagant, were proving to be unsustainable. There were no extra perks or promotions from Narottam Das and due to his reckless spending on parties and alcohol in the company of his new-found Bengali friend, he was living hugely beyond his means.

At that time, the First World War had led to a tremendous upheaval in the textile industry. Since the government had slapped strict checks on production and distribution of cloth, a few astute businessmen had exploited the situation to their advantage and made thousands of rupees in a span of just twenty-four hours. Harilal felt tempted by the prospects of easy and quick money that would realize his long-awaited dream of starting his own business.

Every evening he drowned his sorrows in alcohol along with his ever-benevolent friend and then staggered home to creep into bed, hoping Gulab would not notice. Lying in her bed, pretending to be asleep every night, she watched her husband totter into their bedroom and sneak into his side of the bed. Then she would cry herself to sleep.

One night Harilal poured his heart out to her.

'If only I had some money, Gulab,' he whispered. 'There are enough opportunities to make us rich without any risk or much effort. I know the textile trade well. In the prevailing condition, I am certain I will earn a huge profit. If only…!' His voice trailed off and touched a chord in Gulab's heart.

She took his face into her palms and pulled him to her bosom. 'Don't lose hope,' she said softly. 'My mother has saved up some money for her old age. She has three thousand rupees. I can ask her for you and then your problems will be solved.' Harilal froze in her arms. He couldn't believe his ears.

'Oh Gulab! That is just what I need,' he gasped. 'I shall continue to be in this job, so do not fear. I can pay her the interest she gets on this saving. And I shall return the amount to her as soon as I can.'

With the prospects of his dream coming true, Harilal slept like a contented child, locked in the arms of his beloved Gulab. He knew he was going to be a rich man.

❈   ❈   ❈

The next day, a carefully drafted letter to Gulab's mother was sent off to Rajkot.

'Be careful, my beloved,' Gulab whispered lovingly. 'In your obsession to become a millionaire, don't lose this money or we shall never be able to show our face to anyone ever again.'

Harilal laughed loudly. His excitement bubbled over in his booming voice.

'Stop worrying, Gulab!' He said. 'You watch now, my sweet Rose. Just watch me fill your home with tons of jewels and gold.'

Somehow his words didn't convince Gulab. She looked at him sadly, and said, 'I want no gold or jewels, my lord. Can't you see? Your happiness is my only treasure!'

The feeling, that she was going to be of some source of relief for her depressive, alcoholic and wayward husband, had kindled a ray of hope in her heart. She would be able to sleep easy after a long, long time that night!

❈   ❈   ❈

FIFTY SIX

Harilal was exhilarated when he found a letter from Gulab's mother by return post. She had written saying that nothing could be of greater importance to her than her daughter and son-in-law's happiness, so she would gladly send him that sum of three thousand rupees. She wrote,

> *Keep faith in God and march ahead. But please send me the interest in time. I am handing over to you, every paisa I have.*

With a handsome three thousand rupees at his disposal, Harilal felt a new surge of energy in his veins. He plunged headlong into the textile trade and bought cloth that was at the time in high demand, but short on supply. He had made prior arrangements with some merchant-mediators who promised to buy it from him immediately. However, these prospective buyers had given no advances to Harilal, who in his enthusiasm to make his three thousand into thirty, had not even indemnified himself against any possible mishap.

Unfortunately, even before the transaction could be completed, the government flooded the low-on-supply market with large quantities of its own stock of textiles. Harilal was caught in a cleft stick! The mediating firm not only refused to pick up his stock, they also reneged on returning the advance to him. As a result, he kept borrowing more money to honour his commitment of sending the interest amount to Rajkot each month.

Soon creditors began hounding him, demanding their money back and all hopes of him recovering even the initial three thousand rupees came crashing down. Harilal was panic-stricken. He could neither go to work nor face Gulab. Angry creditors accosted him at odd hours and soon everyone discovered Harilal's dirty financial mess.

Meanwhile, the manager wrote to Narottam Das apprising him of Harilal's waywardness, warning him not to trust him in the future. Narottam Das wrote back a stern note telling the manager to keep an eye on Harilal's activities and if his waywardness persisted, transfer him to another branch. Shrouded as he was in his blanket of woe, he once again sought refuge in his Bengali friend; the saviour who had initiated him into alcohol and fuelled his carnal vices. But even he was not in a position to fund Harilal's addictions, and deserted him.

Groping around in a drunken stupor one day, Harilal bumped into a goldsmith from Porbandar who was visiting Calcutta on some business. The goldsmith, beholden as he was to the Gandhis for bringing so much pride to his hometown, was delighted to meet Harilal and offered help in whatever way he could. Harilal took a loan of two thousand rupees from him with the promise that he would pay it back in installments every month from his salary.

'You are a very well-known man, Harilalbhai,' said the goldsmith, while handing over the wad of currency notes to him. 'Just by the mention of your father's name, lacs of rupees would rain down on you. And that is an adequate guarantee for me.'

Feeling upbeat with the freshly borrowed sum, Harilal dived back into the cloth market, but unfortunately, some unscrupulous traders who had preyed on his weakness, duped him yet again and even that last chance to realize his "get-rich-quick" dream was cruelly crushed. Falling deeper into debt, once again he drowned himself in alcohol that temporarily blocked his insurmountable pain. For Harilal there was only darkness.

✀　✀　✀

Meanwhile, Gulab's mother panicked, as did the hapless goldsmith who had been undeservedly betrayed. Shortly after, two letters addressed to Mohandas arrived at the ashram. In the first, Gulab's mother had made an appeal to him to come to her rescue. She detailed the circumstances that had compelled her to hand over every penny of her life's savings to Harilal and the decrepit state he had reduced her to. She wrote to Mohandas, pleading,

Help me recover my money. I have nothing else to live by.

The goldsmith from Porbandar had a similar grouse.

I acted in good faith. Where was the need to have cheated me?

Mohandas was in shock. I was more than agonized.

Then more complaints came pouring in. Harilal's greed for money, his obsession with easy gains, his disregard for the family name and honour, the erosion of all his moral values....Mohandas had had enough. He wrote to him:

Harilal Beta, your character is your wealth. Worship it, nourish it and cherish it. Understand this truth. It is the only wealth that you should pursue and treasure.

Harilal glanced at his Bapu's letter with disdain.

'Empty words, Bapu! Just so empty!' he murmured. 'Your words can't balm the festering wounds on my soul. And what good is character when you have creditors baying for your blood—hammering at your door, waiting to strangle you? Keep these canons to yourself! Don't try preaching godliness to a dying man.'

Harilal reached out for the half-empty bottle of cheap liquor that lay on his table, took a long swig till he had emptied it, leaned over and and rolled it on the floor.

'Don't teach me the value of character... You have worked persistently to destroy it. Don't teach me to become "you",' he slurred.

Harilal fell back on his bed, clutching the half-torn letter close to his chest and passed out.

✼ ✼ ✼

All doors had finally closed on poor Harilal Gandhi. Overcome by a feeling of failure, ashamed to face Gulab, he began staying away from her, recoiling violently at her touch, taking refuge in his drunken stupors. The liquor addiction gave way to uncontrolled carnal desires and Harilal became a frequent visitor to the infamous lanes of Sonagachi, where the flesh trade flourished after sunset.

Gulab was devastated. She spoke with no one about her wasting, philandering husband. All she could do was weep copious tears, beg for mercy before her god, and pray for good sense to redeem her self-destructing husband, whom she could neither stop nor rescue from the den of vice. This, along with insufficient funds to run the house, the constant insults from sundry creditors and her neglected brood of five helpless children, pushed her against the wall. She had had enough. Her mind and body caved in, putting the balance of her fragile household in jeopardy. Gulab collapsed under the sheer weight of the physical and emotional burden. She became seriously ill.

Gulab's deteriorating health jolted Harilal. He could see that she was sinking rapidly and feeling both guilty and responsible for her condition, he began tending to her all day. He stopped going to work, his business or whatever was left of it, took a beating and things only got worse. With no resources to even buy medicines for Gulab he had no hope in sight. One morning, he held her hand and wept inconsolably like a child.

'I failed you, my beloved,' he sobbed. 'We have nothing and you are so ill. Why don't you and the children go to stay with Ba for sometime after which I shall send you to be with your mother in Rajkot? A change of climate will help you recover and I may be able to save some money while you are away.'

Gulab was too drained to object. 'Your happiness is my happiness...' she said feebly. 'I pray to Goddess Amba to show you the path of righteousness. I pray for peace and success for you.'

Harilal took his frail wife into his arms and rocked her to sleep. His tears mingled with hers as they fell on her cheeks, down her neck to her heaving chest.

Gulab, the ever obedient, servile wife slept like a baby in his arms. Neither one knew that these were the last moments of their turbulent lives together. Harilal would never set eyes on his beloved Rose again.

�֍   �֍   ✖

Fifty Seven

For days, rumours of Harilal's scandalous pursuits had been trickling in to Sabarmati Ashram. His proclivity to frequent change of jobs, mounting debts, waywardness, dependance on cheap liquor and general debauchery had angered Mohandas beyond repair and unnerved me. I constantly fretted about Gulab and my grandchildren, wishing I could either bring them to Sabarmati or go to Calcutta.

Late in June 1918, perhaps as a result of my fervent prayers, Gulab arrived unexpectedly at Sabarmati, with her five children in tow. I moved them into a new hut, overjoyed that my deepest desires had actually come true. I could not wait to pamper my five adorable grandchildren and be the doting Ba to them once more.

Ten year old Rami, the three boys Kanti, Rasik and Shanti and the youngest, twelve-month-old baby girl Manu, filled my heart with abounding cheer. The memory of the days I had spent pining for them faded away. Gulab however, was a cause of worry. I was shocked to see how frail she had become. Her pale, weather-beaten face appeared to have aged far beyond her twenty-six years. There was no trace of that vivacious sixteen year old, doe-eyed, beautiful bride, whom I had welcomed at Phoenix ten years ago.

Emboldened in my comforting presence, the ailing, emaciated girl poured her heart out to me and spoke candidly about her husband's hopeless condition. She confirmed all my fears about Harilal's wrongdoings, dispelling every doubt I may have had about him.

'He is growing more bitter with life and even more disillusioned with himself,' she said. 'Most of his angst is against Bapu. He can never forgive Bapu for being so utterly cruel to him. He's ashamed, Ba; ashamed that he cannot even provide basic essentials for the house and his children.'

Gulab burst into tears.

'He shuns me, Ba. He's become aloof, and quiet,' she continued. 'He only wants to be in the company of his horrible friends. What more can I say? He's picked up so many evil habits. He goes to Sonagachi almost every day.' Her voice had dropped to a whisper. 'I am so terrified. I just don't know what to do. And now he's lost his job, Ba... People say he gambled away the firm's money so they sacked him. Luckily some friends took pity on us and bought us train tickets to Sabarmati. What is going to become of him? We are doomed.' Gulab was inconsolable. She rested her head on my lap and continued to weep for a long time. My eyes filled up as I watched her cry. Crazy thoughts zigzagged through my head. I was infuriated by Harilal's reckless behaviour. How dare he put his family through this! How dare he venture on this trail of self-destruction! For the first time in my life I felt something harden inside me – I felt a growing rancour towards my son. He had no right to destroy these six innocent lives that were so closely interlinked with his; even if he believed he owed no debt of gratitude to his mother!

I spent the next few weeks totally engrossed in Gulab and the children, trying to assuage their pain, making them rise to the joys of being with their hitherto absent grandmother. I sang to them while I bathed them, told them endless tales from Hindu mythology, taught them new songs and washed and combed Rami and Manu's beautiful hair. I cooked for them and fed them delicious food and my favourite sweets, taking them for long walks where Gulab would vent her grouses and fears. Gradually, just by watching her children come alive again, Gulab's spirits began to soar. A slight pallor returned to her face. The hollow of her cheeks filled out just a wee bit. The dark circles around her soulful eyes became lighter and her long hair regained some of its earlier shine.

When it was time for them to leave for Rajkot, Gulab bade me goodbye cheerily after touching her forehead to my feet.

'We'll be with Ma in Rajkot for a short while, Ba, and then I'm sure we will be called back to Calcutta, soon.' she said.

My eyes trailed her as I saw them off at the railway station. She still looked frail and her shadowed eyes that reflected the shattered fragments of my own world continued to unsettle me.

I stared wistfully at the train chugging out of the station till I could no longer see Gulab and Rami's waving hands and their heads leaning out of the window. Their visit to Sabarmati had filled a void in my life, but their going away left a gaping wound inside me that was not going to heal for a long time.

Gulab's eyes disturbed me. The uneasiness gnawed at me all night. Had I known this was to be our last meeting on earth, my farewell would have been scripted differently. I may not have let her go at all. Poor Gulab! A passive victim of her untiring devotion to an emotionally gruelling husband was on a morbid countdown to her last day on earth.

❈ ❈ ❈

Harilal felt alone and even more miserable after his family left Calcutta. With Gulab and the children away there was no check on him and the empty house terrified him. No longer could he come home to unwind after a weary day at work, so he sought solace in overdoses of alcohol that drove him every evening to the shady lanes of Sonagachi where he found temporary release.

Feeling hemmed in from all sides with a debt of over fifteen thousand rupees, he became acutely depressed. The guilt of not being able to send any money to Gulab preyed on his conscience and he drifted around like a rudderless ship, looking for some miracle that would set him back on track.

It was on one such dreary evening that a broker gave Harilal an irresistible business offer. The investment needed was astronomical, but he promised quick and huge returns, so Harilal succumbed.

As was well known, Harilal was one of Narottam Das' most trusted employees who had been given charge of most of his cash transactions. And despite his excessive indulgence in gambling and alcohol, Narottam Das was aware of his impeccable account-keeping skills.

A while later, a regular trader from Madras handed Harilal a sum of thirty thousand rupees in lieu of some goods he desired. The sum was just what Harilal needed, and the timing right. He mused excitedly,

> *It will only be two weeks before I deposit the money back into the company account. No one will notice and my dream will finally be fulfilled.*

With a wildly racing heart, his mind filled with renewed hope, he handed over the money to the broker who reassured him that not only was this operation risk-free but in a matter of a fortnight, all his all woes would vanish, with no one any wiser!

Meanwhile the trader from Madras informed Narottam Das that thirty thousand rupees had been handed over to Harilal, and Narottam Das in turn, issued directions to Calcutta to despatch the goods to him. But all hell broke loose the next day. The manager, who had been instructed by Narottam Das to dispatch the goods, found that Harilal had deposited no money on account of the Madras shipment, while the goods had already been despatched.

Harilal was immediately summoned to the office for an explanation. He had no choice but to admit that he had wrongfully kept the money for a personal business venture and that there was no way he could get it back. His cover blown, Harilal stood disrobed and maligned in the eyes of all, a cheat and a thief. Narottam Das was faced with a serious dilemma. Had it been anyone other than Harilal, he would have handed him over to the police without a thought, but this was Mohandas Karamchand Gandhi's son and if he were to be tried and convicted for embezzlement, the entire country would convulse in shock.

He wrote a letter to Mohandas detailing the terrible misdeed of his son, asking his advice on how to deal with the matter. Mohandas was devastated. It was a crippling blow to his already weary mind. With a heavy heart and trembling hands he penned a painful reply to his friend.

> *The fact that Harilal is my son should not deter you from the path of justice Narottambhai. If he has committed a crime he should be*

treated accordingly. Hand him over to the police and let the law take its course. Let the matter be judged in a court of law.

The reply put Narottam Das in a greater quandary. He understood Mohandas' principles, but it was unthinkable for him to follow his advice. He cleared up the papers in the Calcutta office and buried the matter once and for all. Harilal lost his job and was on the streets again.

Advised by his friends at the office, a cowering Harilal wrote a letter of confession to his employer before he left. Still unable to swallow the harsh words of his father, he handed his last letter of apology to Narottam Das and stormed out of office, reeling in shock. That night in a fit of bitter rage he wrote a brief note to his father.

You are a cruel man, Bapu! Which father would recommend handing his son over to the police in the darkest hour of his life? Yes I know I am a failure. I have embezzled money from my employer and I hang my head in shame. But instead of holding my hand and steering me away from darkness you have thrown me into a burning pit of hell.

Indeed Harilal was burning with fury in the most treacherous fires of hell. He boarded a train from Calcutta to search for a job in some other city like a no-where man, wandering and lost once again.

❈ ❈ ❈

Once again destiny threw father and son on each other's path at a railway station. Mohandas was informed that Harilal was also seated in a train that had halted at Nadiad, en route to Calcutta. Mohandas got off to look for him and found him crouched on a three-tier berth in the third class compartment, dishevelled and exhausted. Harilal was aghast coming face-to-face with his father. He bent his head in shame, unable to utter a word.

Mohandas was shocked to see Harilal. His face was wrinkled and ashen, his hair that had greyed considerably looked scruffy and his eyes had sunk deep into their sockets. His hands trembled as he stood still with his head bowed. Mohandas was overcome by grief. What had Harilal done to himself? His eyes filled with tears and with a heavy heart he said, 'Son, I don't have any money to give you. I can only hand over to you a legacy of character. If you preserve and cherish this, god will always be with you.'

Mohandas failed to say anything more. His voice choked and tears fell from his eyes.

'When I am not around, look after your mother, Harilal…look after Ba!' he quivered as he turned around and stepped out of the compartment.

Harilal burst into tears. He watched his father ambling across the platform, his shoulders had caved inwards and he kept wiping his eyes as he shuffled away.

'Ba is my responsibility, Bapu! I shall look after her as long as I live,' Harilal cried out. 'But your legacy of character? Your legacy is not good enough to pay my debts and who knows whether I outlive you or you outlive me!'

He cried inconsolably like a child. He couldn't wait to down a large peg of his "panacea" to numb his pain.

Whereas, Mohandas wrote a heart-rending letter to Devdas when he returned to his train:

Devdas!

Harilal has lost all his tenderness, Son. Do not be pained by it, but watch out to see how much a man falls once he starts falling!

Meanwhile in a distant corner of Rajkot, Harilal's little boy Shanti was seriously ill. He had contracted the dreaded Spanish flu.

⁂

After bidding farewell to Gulab and my grandchildren, settling back into the ashram routine was not going to be easy for me. Their absence made me so miserable that I sent word to Mohandas that I desired to be with him during his countrywide travels. On

17 July 1918 a letter arrived from the headquarters of Mohandas' recruiting campaign at Nadiad, in the district of Kheda.

Beloved Kastur, I know you long to be with me, but the work must continue at all costs. Therefore it is best that you stay where you are. If you are missing the children just consider all the children of the ashram as your own and you will stop missing them. As you begin to love others and serve them like you served your own you shall feel joy welling up in your heart...

And another followed two days later...

...Your unhappiness makes me unhappy. If it were possible to take ladies along I would certainly have taken you with me. Kastur! Haven't we learned to find our happiness in separation? We will meet again if God wills so...

Mohandas' letter only deepened my misery. I had allowed my identity to completely merge with his and had expected my mind to resonate with the same intensity as his. Over the years I had watched him agonizing over moral dilemmas, riding brazenly over most emotional crises, but I had expected a little more than those brief, unfeeling words that gave me no solace.

I was often whipped by a feeling of guilt and self-doubt, but what unsettled me the most was the deep despair Mohandas was suffering and I could do nothing to assuage him.

To add to all his woes, the intensive recruiting campaign that he had begun at the instance of Viceory Maffey proved to be a non-starter; Mohandas had agreed to initiate an enlistment drive for Indians to fight for the British during the World War. In return they had promised to grant Home Rule as soon as the war ended. Certain Indian nationalists who had a more aggressive stand against the British, like Bal Gangadhar Tilak and Annie Besant, also front-runners in the anti-imperialist struggle at that time, ridiculed this posture as being self-deluding.

I saw Mohandas when he arrived at Sabarmati Ashram in late August that year. I stared in horror at that gaunt, emaciated man. His eyes had sunken deep into their sockets, and there was an air of gloom around him. I knew he was ill and depressed. He dismissed my apprehensions with a wave of his hand.

'It's just mild dysentery, Kastur! I am fasting and shall soon be well.'

I nursed him with all my energy to bring him back to health, urging him to stay on in the ashram till he became stronger, but Mohandas left for Nadiad barely after a week, where he suffered a near collapse after his dysentery worsened.

The doctors diagnosed it as acute exhaustion and a nervous breakdown, which was common those days, but Mohandas attributed it to overeating in Sabarmati, at the hands of his indulgent wife.

'She tempted me with my favourite foods and I succumbed,' he complained to the amused doctor.

When I heard how acutely ill he had become, I panicked. I had been told that he had refused all medicines and food and was becoming weaker by the hour. I wanted him to come back to Sabarmati as soon as possible since I knew that there was no one who could look after him in Nadiad.

But Mohandas was too ill to withstand the train journey. Luckily Ambalal Sarabhai, the leading industrialist of Ahmedabad who had supported the ashram with generous donations, came to his rescue. Along with his wife he drove Mohandas in their car to be nursed back to health in the privacy of their home.

The Sarabhais availed the services of the best doctors in the city and I visited them daily, urging Mohandas to accept medical assistance. I also ensured that he ate proper food. Although Mohandas responded to the good nursing and care in Ahmedabad, his recovery was slow, and soon he began agitating to be taken back to Sabarmati.

'I want to die in my own ashram, Kastur. Take me back,' he pleaded. His gloomy words struck deep in my heart, and I moved him back to the ashram, soon after.

❈ ❈ ❈

Meanwhile a virulent outbreak of Spanish Influenza had ravaged every corner of the globe. Even as the World War continued unabated in its brutal destruction of humanity, the devastation unleashed by this pandemic disease was incalculable. Nowhere was the death toll more staggering than it was in India and in the month of October alone, it had crossed twenty million.

A terrifying premonition began hounding me and I constantly fretted for the safety of my sons and their families. While being with Mohandas in Sabarmati was a great relief, I prayed to god to protect Harilal and his children from the dreaded curse.

But in Rajkot, riding the garb of the dreaded flu, the grim reaper had already infected three-year-old Shanti. The fourth child and youngest son of Gulab and Harilal was in the throes of the deadly disease that would rapidly slay him.

Gulab was beside herself with grief. She cradled her son as he burned with fever in her arms all night, and wept. She kept placing cold towels on his tiny forehead, but his fever did not let up. His breath sounded raspy and shallow and soon he became delirious. Her feeble heart lurched into her mouth as she watched him sink rapidly, his eyes roll up in their sockets and his breathing suddenly stop.

She convulsed. A loud shriek escaped her lips. Calling out loudly to her mother, she fainted. It had been a long night's vigil. She wished Harilal had been with her, to hold his son in his dying moments.

Crying inconsolably she held his lifeless body in her arms all night, praying to God to bring him back to life.

At dawn, she lay the lifeless little body on the cold floor and steadied herself. All the blood had drained out of her head and she trembled with the agony of watching her dead child crumpled up and blue, lying still, on the floor. She could not bear to watch them pour a few drops of the holy *Ganga-jal* in his mouth and begin preparing for his funeral.

Gulab broke into a cold sweat. Deafening chants of *Ram-naam* drowned the noise around her. A strong trembling racked her body and she felt the ceiling of the room turn round in circles. Her heart raced and her head felt like it would burst. No one knew that she had also been burning with fever all night. Her tear-filled eyes were fixed on the corpse of her three-year-old child. She swayed and keeled over on the floor. By the time her mother and sisters came close and tried to revive her, Gulab was dead.

Weakened by years of malnourishment, her successive pregnancies, and extreme emotional exhaustion, she had contracted the raging flu from her son and succumbed to the dreaded disease in a matter of twenty-four hours.

The Gandhis lost two of their kin in one cruel stroke. It was 18 October 1918.

A distraught Harilal, on a train from Calcutta, his four wailing children clinging on to their dead mother, the grieving mother and sisters of poor Gulab and a completely wrecked me, all bound together in this hour of insurmountable grief, wept copiously.

With both Gulab and Shanti gone, we huddled together to perform the funeral rites of our two loved ones. We were joined by hordes of mourners from the neighbourhood who unmindful of the contagious flu, had assembled at the home of the bereaved, to bid them farewell.

✄ ✄ ✄

Harilal's world had come crashing down. Gutted with the pain of losing his beloved Gulab and little boy Shanti, he was beside himself. He clung to his four children all day weeping and mourning his youngest child and his lovely Gulab.

'If only I had known she was so broken in body and spirit, Ba, I would never have let her out of my sight. Alas! I shall never see her again. If only I could have told her, how much I loved her.'

It could not have been a more agonizing time for me than to watch my four innocent grandchildren and an inconsolable son withering away in their sorrow. No words could assuage Harilal's pain or compensate their loss. Gulab and Shanti were both dead and they would have to come to terms with this brutal truth sooner or later.

So would I!

✄ ✄ ✄

FIFTY EIGHT

From his sick bed, emaciated and demoralized as he was, Mohandas *did* send a letter of condolence to Harilal. It was written in the neat hand of Mahadev Desai to whom it had been dictated, but I was truly appalled when I saw the slip-shod, half-hearted attempt he had made to commiserate with his son. I dreaded to imagine what effect those stinging words would have on Harilal.

> ....*The only thing that pleases me is to be ever occupied with the activity of the utmost purity. One will find true happiness in the measure that one understands this and lives accordingly. If this calamity puts you in a frame of mind in which such happiness will be yours, we may even regard it as welcome...*

Harilal read out those acrid words to me as I reeled in shock. How could a father be so cold, so savage, when his son was at his lowest, hit by the worst emotional tragedy – the death of a loved one? But the incongruity of Mohandas' spiritual advice at a time of unbearable grief and his remorse over the widening rift between him and his son could not have been more evident. The unbridgeable chasm between father and son was squeezing out a bit of my life with each breath. And I had no means to put it back together again.

I acceded that it was my karma and I had to bear it. I eased Harilal's head on to my lap, and stroked his hair gently, till sleep overcame him. To him the façade of Mohandas being holier and nobler than all his fellowmen was being slowly peeled away, layer by layer, exposing the rot that lay beneath.

❦ ❦ ❦

Once again I stood, alone and abandoned, at a challenging crossroad of my life. I could not block out Mohandas' emotional fragility nor could I ignore Harilal's cry for help. After the thirteenth day when the period of mourning ended, I sat down with Harilal to make some hard decisions about his children's future.

'Hari,' I said to him tenderly. 'Look at me. I am ready to take care of the four children. To keep them in my home, to tend to them for as long as you wish me to. You do realize that this burden is too cumbersome for Gulab's sisters or her widowed mother to bear. But my son, I cannot stay in Rajkot any longer. I must go to Sabarmati where your ailing Bapu needs me desperately.'

I could see Harilal stiffen at the mere mention of his father's name, which made it even more punishing for me. I was faced with a choiceless choice—whether to stay in Rajkot and take care of the four innocent toddlers and their broken father, who needed me like never before, or to return to my ailing husband, who I would like to believe, needed me too?

I left Rajkot with a heavy heart. The fear of pushing my son into a deeper pit of gloom and the remorse of abandoning those helpless, motherless children in the care of their maternal grandmother had deepened the wound caused by the deaths of Gulab and Shanti. But on reaching Sabarmati, I realized how ill Mohandas had become. Depressed and emaciated he had lain in bed for days, refusing to eat or be treated by the doctors. He had been in excruciating pain due to an anal fistula caused by uncontrolled dysentery and been experimenting with all sorts of alternate treatments that had failed.

So despondent had he become with his deteriorating health that one evening, wallowing in self-pity he had summoned all the ashram-inmates and delivered a disturbing pre-death speech. The panic-stricken ashramites were only too relieved to see me back, to take charge of their ailing leader.

A few days later, a senior Congress functionary, Vallabhbhai Patel came to Sabarmati with the news that the World War had come to an end. Germany had surrendered. A peace treaty had been signed and the British had made an announcement that no recruitment of soldiers would be required to be made from

India in the future. The news that should have made Mohandas delirious with joy had little, if any, effect on him. He treated it with uncharacteristic apathy—overcome by the exhaustion and pain that was rigging his mind and body.

The morbid depression and the persistent ruminations of his death had not eased even after I had returned and resumed my job of nursing him.

Unbeknownst to me, there were other conflicts raging in Mohandas' mind. While I fretted about his ill health and an extremely fragile mental condition, I did not know that he had begun to resent my very presence around him. Pouring out his innermost feelings to his secretary, Mahadev Desai, who painstakingly took notes to record every word he said, the rancour against me soon became common knowledge.

'I can't bear to look at Ba's face,' he burst out one day. 'She behaves like a meek cow at all times. I have realized that there is an element of selfishness in the suffering she reveals in her eyes. But then she overpowers me with her patient gentleness. I am compelled to ease up.'

Clearly Mohandas had begun to despise me. Of all the nasty probabilities that life was about to throw in my face, I was least prepared for this. My patience was also wearing thin. His obstinate refusal of food and medicines and his own quack diagnosis was getting to me. I could see that he was withering away, mocking at and playing with death, but I could do nothing.

How ironic was it that a man who could alter the minds and conduct of thousands of people by his message of peace and non-violence, was deliberately inflicting a surfeit of violence on his own body. It was clear... Mohandas was resigned to embrace death. I had just about extricated myself from the gloom of two tragic deaths and dreaded the thought of facing another one so soon. I resolved to pull my husband out of his depressive abyss at any cost.

Driven by the excruciating agony of his festering fistula, with no hope of any relief at Sabarmati, Mohandas finally agreed to travel to Bombay to consult a doctor.

❄ ❄ ❄

In mid-December we met an orthodox surgeon in Bombay who was of the view that surgery was Mohandas' only option. However the patient's seriously emaciated condition was not conducive to immediate surgery and he advised building up his strength by proper dietary changes, and a frequent intake of milk. Mohandas was indignant. Having vowed not to drink cow's milk in protest against the prevalent method of cruelly milking the animal, he made it clear that under no circumstances would he break it.

My mind was seized by the urgency of the moment.

'What about goat's milk?' I asked diffidently. 'Surely you can't object to that?'

I could see I had stumped Mohandas, and from that day goat's milk became his staple diet.

Mohandas went under the surgeon's knife soon after and stayed on to convalesce at Mani Bhawan, a spacious and luxurious mansion on Laburnum Road in Bombay that belonged to Pranjivan Mehta who three decades ago, had given shelter to the young law student in London.

It was an old association that had transcended the passage of time.

❊ ❊ ❊

In the early months of 1919, Mani Bhawan became a home of joy, and fervent activity. With Mohandas almost fully recuperated, Harilal had returned to Calcutta and the four children were sent to Mani Bhawan in my care. They filled my home again with their innocent laughter and it wrenched my heart to imagine the suffering they had undergone on the loss of their mother and a sibling, just a short while ago. Only Rami, the eldest of the four looked like the pain had shadowed her face. She hardly spoke and had a glazed look in her once-sparkling eyes.

Their sad plight was not lost on Mohandas either. He indulged the younger two and became completely engrossed in tending to the older ones. I could see that he revelled in the company of his grandchildren. A tiny crevice seemed to have opened up in his cold heart for he wrote an unusually tender letter to Harilal,

> *….plump Manu's radiance is ever growing brighter. Kanti and Rasik, the two boys are always playing around my bed. The scene takes me back to your childhood…*

I thanked the Lord. Perhaps in the aftermath of a great tragedy, we were being compensated with a surfeit of happiness that had been missing from our lives for as long as I could remember.

It was as if the children had transformed their grandfather! I saw Mohandas take special delight in bantering with six-year-old Rasik. He scribbled a limerick for him one evening that seemed like it had crystallized my long-awaited dream of familial love:

> *Rasiklal Harilal Mohandas Karamchand Gandhi*
> *Had a goat in his keeping*
> *The goat would not be milked*
> *And Gandhi would not stop weeping*

The children rolled over on the floor, while we laughed loudly at the nonsensical rhyme. I revelled at the restored bond between us; and I saw long elusive happiness that had finally descended on the hitherto star-crossed Gandhis.

❈ ❈ ❈

However all the mirth and filial love at faraway Mani Bhawan failed to lift Harilal's spirits. The singular reason for the painful void in his life was Gulab. Maddened by the guilt that he had been openly unfaithful to her and had fallen short of his basic duties as a father and husband, he felt tortured every waking moment. Every little thing in his house screamed out at him—accusing him of having neglected her, numbing him into a melancholic stupor. The thought of his four children separated from him by circumstances, and one by death, racked his heart. When the pain became unbearable, he sought refuge in his bottle, for only that could alleviate his suffering unquestioningly, faithfully and silently.

He sat stone-like in front of Gulab's photograph and wept all day. And when his tears would dry up, he would turn it over, place it with his father's photograph that he had carefully carried back from South Africa and drown himself in his bottle all over again. Despite the melancholia he was aware that he had a life to lead and one that was anything but pleasant—his unpaid rent, the borrowings for his liquor bills and the duty to send some money for his children who were to soon leave Rajkot for Sabarmati, hounded him.

Harilal was stirred by the need to work and earn a livelihood all over again. With the end of the World War, there was a false sense of stability and for a while the markets had steadied and the demand for raw materials from Asia shot up again. A host of opportunities for trade and business floated around. He was acquainted with many Europeans during his stay in South Africa, and having made several contacts while he was employed with Narottam Das, he began dreaming of setting up an import and export business. Then fate threw him back on the path of an old associate, Paragjibhai—the one who had been waiting at Durban to receive him when he first landed there. After spending a couple of years with Mohandas in Phoenix, Paragjibhai had relocated to India.

Harilal met Paragjibhai who was shocked to see him. It wasn't as if he hadn't heard unsavoury rumours about him, but his heart went out to him nevertheless.

'I know fate has been cruel to you, Harilal,' he said hesitantly, 'Do not worry, I shall help you. But first you need to become stable.'

He offered to support Harilal's import and export venture and help him set up an office in Bombay.

Harilal felt his spirit soar for the first time in months.

'It shall be our partnership, Paragjibhai,' he beamed as he hugged him heartily, 'and since we are true soldiers of the *satyagraha*, we shall call our firm "Satyagrahi Brothers".'

Paragjibhai held out both his hands to Harilal in a firm handshake. A new venture based on past friendships and goodwill was beginning to take shape.

✄ ✄ ✄

Convalescing in the comfortable confines of Mani Bhawan, early one February morning while browsing through the day's newspapers, Mohandas sat up in alarm. A new legislation was ready to be passed by the Imperial Legislative Council in Delhi. It made him realize how rapidly the political situation had changed during the period of his illness. Unlike what Harilal had imagined, Mohandas was prescient enough to understand that there was a great unrest in the aftermath of the World War. Prices had skyrocketed; there was economic instability, unchecked black-marketeering and widespread unemployment. Scars of the catastrophic Spanish flu epidemic were still fresh and the country was on the brink of a disaster.

However India was still under the rule of the British and several leaders of the national movement were struggling to attain complete freedom. This made the Crown uneasy and fearing violence and terror attacks from Indian activists, the government of Great Britain appointed an English jurist, Sir Sidney Rowlatt to assess the danger of revolutionary uprisings. What followed was a draconian legislation, the Rowlatt Act which allowed the government to retain wartime emergency powers; any Indian accused of sedition could be tried in secrecy without a jury and condemned without the right of appeal; dissidents were to be denied the right to free speech and the mere possession of printed matter of seditious nature, could entail imprisonment upto two years.

To Mohandas this was the suppression of a fundamental right and a downright betrayal on the part of the Imperial rulers. Although he had not fully recovered from his illness, he shot off a telegram to the Viceroy denouncing the Rowlatt Act as:

> *unjust, subversive of the principal of liberty and symptomatic of a deep-seated disease in the ruling class.*

A few days later, we left for Sabarmati with the four grandchildren and a frisky goat in tow.

❊ ❊ ❊

On 24 February 1919, Mohandas convened an urgent meeting of his co-workers at the ashram. He sounded frantic—there was no time to waste, the battlelines were drawn and he had to chalk out a careful strategy to protest against the passage of the oppressive

Rowlatt Bill. Scores of Mohandas' followers signed pledges of peaceful defiance against the Bill and Mohandas set out on a nationwide tour to garner more support for his mission.

The news came to him on 18 March while he was campaigning in Madras. Unmindful of the unanimous wave of resistance by its Indian members, the Imperial Legislative Council had passed the Rowlatt Act. Mohandas spent the rest of the day in a series of conferences with his colleagues to devise some ways to delay or forestall the law and its partisan provisions.

After a restless night Mohandas announced that he intended to ask people across the length and breadth of the country to call a one-day peaceful strike against the Act. The *hartal* was to be much more than merely a day of "no work". It was meant to be a solemn day of national mourning whereby Indians of every caste, creed and faith would abandon all other pursuits and spend twenty-four hours fasting and praying. The message spread like wildfire and the entire nation galvanized to join in the peaceful protest.

The sun rose on 6 April 1919, to an electrified India and millions of people gathered peacefully to confront their oppressors without resorting to any violence. It was as if the entire nation had come to a grinding halt. The fields were bare, neither bullocks nor farmers in sight. No carts moved through the countryside. The villages and towns bore a deserted look. All shops had their shutters down. Schools and government offices were closed and there was an eerie silence in the streets as all the people had stayed home to fast and pray.

In the cities there were mass meetings and processions of both Hindus and Muslims, all bound together by the voice and will of Gandhi, in a mammoth movement of peaceful non-cooperation.

In Bombay Mohandas himself led the peaceful *hartal*. At the crack of dawn, hordes of men, women and children, all dressed in white as a sign of mourning, gathered on Chowpatty beach, near Mani Bhawan to chant, pray, and take a symbolic dip in the waters of the Arabian Sea. The swelling crowds later marched in silence through the streets of the city, stopping occasionally for speeches and prayers. Hindus and Muslims displayed unprecedented signs of fraternity and tolerance. In some places,

Hindus led by Mohandas were even invited into the mosques where speeches were delivered to the congregation.

That evening Mohandas and a co-worker, an old-time Congress liberalist Sarojini Naidu, drove slowly in an open car through the streets of Bombay followed by a massive crowd of *satyagrahis*. Along the march, they sold thousands of copies of the *Hind Swaraj* with a message from Mohandas, written specially for the occasion. All this was in grievous violation of the newly-ordained Rowlatt Act, but the Bombay police acted judiciously; hence no arrests were made and the day ended on a peaceful note.

The Empire was visibly shaken with this show of unprecedented unity and perceived it as a grave new threat to the Crown. On the streets of Delhi, police squads forcefully obstructed a huge procession of peaceful marchers by opening fire on them. Five Hindus and four Muslims were killed on the spot.

The situation had become volatile.

❈ ❈ ❈

FIFTY NINE

On 13 April 1919, a crisp, bright Sunday morning greeted the people of Punjab. It was the day Punjabis celebrate *Baisakhi*, the booming season of harvest. The province was under martial law to curb any kind of local rebellion and strict restrictions had been clamped down on civil liberties, with a complete ban on the assemblage of people at a public gathering.

Defying the ban, about ten thousand people had gathered at the Jallianwala Bagh in the city of Amritsar to protest against the recent arrest of two prominent national leaders. The protestors, many of whom were pilgrims that comprised men, women and children, had converged peacefully at the park that was enclosed on all four sides by an eight-feet-high stone wall.

The British military Governor of Punjab, General Reginald Dyer, riled by this abject violation of his orders, marched into the garden with fifty armed Gorkha soldiers. Infuriated on seeing the large crowd that had collected there, he ordered his soldiers to open fire on them. The troops took their positions, blocked the single narrow exit, and rained bullets into the crowd.

Hundreds of gunshots shattered the silence of the early morning air. The firing continued non-stop for ten agonizing minutes. It was only when all their ammunition had been exhausted, did the troops stop firing.

Within an hour, 386 men, women and children lay dead, their mangled and bloodied bodies strewn across the grassy patches of Jallianwala Bagh. Over 1,600 were seriously injured. But the cold-blooded General Dyer had not yet finished. He then decreed that no one should attend to the dead or wounded for the next seventy-two hours, to ensure the maximum number of casualties.

A pall of gloom descended upon the city. The festival had turned into a black, bloody Sunday, sending ripples of shock across the length and breadth of the nation. The gory incident deeply saddened Mohandas and the shock and horror of the brutal massacre spread to every corner of the world.

The Imperial government was disgraced internationally for having perpetuated this unprovoked and savage slaughter of innocent, peaceful marchers. This incident would finally pave the way for the ultimate collapse of the Empire in India.

And the cruel General Dyer would meet with divine retribution right in the heart of his homeland, sought by a gun-wielding martyr seeking to avenge this genocide, not too long into the future.

❃   ❃   ❃

In the aftermath of the dastardly massacre where the blood of innocents had been shed on the soil of Punjab, the wounded nation rose up in rebellion. Hordes of people turned out on the streets to protest against the brutalities of the British government and a mass movement to boycott all foreign-made goods was set into motion. Mohandas toured the nation, preparing for a new and more strident confrontation with the authorities. His message however, continued to embody complete non-violence. He urged the people to lay down their heads before the oppressors till such time that they were exhausted of crushing them. A ferocious energy was building up, and all eyes were glued on Mohandas with renewed hope and expectations.

But there were impassioned churnings of another kind that were making Mohandas restless. For the past two years he had been in the throes of a spiritual romance. The object of his infatuation was a feisty Bengali revolutionary, Sarala Devi Choudhurani who was the wife of a Punjabi musician, who lived in Lahore. Her father was the secretary of the Indian National Congress in Calcutta, and by virtue of her singing and crusading for civil liberties against the British, Sarala Devi had been nicknamed Bengal's Joan of Arc. Sarala Devi's husband R. D. Choudhury, also a freedom fighter, had been in jail for eight months during that period, but he had no objection to his wife's closeness with this gentle prophet of non-violence. Both the men strongly believed that Sarala Devi was the incarnation of Goddess Durga, the "most revered female *Shakti*" on earth and hence beyond reproach. Mohandas travelled to Sarala Devi's home in Lahore and they toured the country together after the massacre, quite enthralled with each other.

Mohandas treated Sarala Devi as his *spiritual wife* after an *intellectual wedding,* and he openly claimed that *he bathed in her deep affection as she showered her love on him in every possible way.*

For the homespun and handwoven garments that he had made his signature style, Sarala Devi had become his most adored model for donning *khadi,* and they flitted around openly like lovelorn teenagers with stars in their eyes.

Sarala Devi was aristocratic, gorgeously dressed, sensuously beautiful, and imperious. She had everything that I with my earthy rusticity lacked. But even though she was clearly besotted with him, unlike me, Sarala Devi did not bow to Mohandas' authority in any way. She vehemently opposed his non-violent methods and believed that to attain independence, a violent revolution was essential. She felt that Durga's *shakti* was always accompanied by violence, and that was the only and best way forward in this battle for freedom; an ideology which eventually led to their parting ways.

Much as I should have liked to believe that this relationship full of sensuality, was asexual, and my husband's romance with Sarala Devi was entirely platonic, a large component of their eroticism was openly flaunted by them and the demarcation between sexual, sensuous, erotic and platonic had long been erased.

Like all such liaisons, this one too came to its natural end, but my husband's guilt if any, of having wronged me, was never expressed by him.

One thing however was certain. He looked upon her with desire, a kind that I had never seen in his eyes before, not even when I was the sole object of it, after we were wed.

Wasn't this a violation of that vow of celibacy? Or was I the only victim of that pathetic vow? I wondered.

Meanwhile a twenty-three-year-old spirited and ambitious boy of Bengali origin was studying for his Civil Service examination in England. Born in Orissa, to Janakinath Bose and Prabhabati Devi, the ninth amongst fourteen children, Subhash Chandra was a brilliant young man with strong patriotic sentiments. Sitting in the imposing confines of his college, like many others of his ilk, he was shaken up by the brutal massacre of innocent Indians at Jallianwalla Bagh, by the very people he was interning with.

Compelled by a deep nationalistic calling, Subhash Chandra cut short his apprenticeship and returned to his homeland, determined to help in liberating his fellowmen from the Imperial tyrants. He sought an appointment with Mohandas, became a member of the Indian National Congress and began working in earnest to fulfill his duty towards his motherland.

Earlier that year in Chauri Chaura, a village near Gorakhpur in the United Provinces, a large group of protestors participating in the non-cooperation movement had suddenly turned violent and the police had been compelled to open fire on them. In retaliation, the demonstrators had charged at the police station and set it ablaze, resulting in the death of all the occupants including twenty-three policemen. The British declared martial law in the province, carried out several raids and indiscriminately arrested hundreds of people thereafter. Mohandas was appalled at the outrage. He called off the movement immediately and commenced a five-day fast of penance to make amends.

❈ ❈ ❈

Meanwhile Harilal's latest ill-fated business venture had badly bombed. Plagued by unending misfortunes, he was wrongly accused of theft, cheating and fraud. He suffered a huge monetary loss and an even greater loss of face before his mentor and saviour, Paragjibhai and incurred serious ill-will from my brother Madhavdas, who had also entered into some transactions with him.

Jobless, penniless and disgraced once again, Harilal lost all interest in his firm, Satyagrahi Brothers that by now was defunct. Stirred by the loud reverberations of his father's ongoing anti-British activities and the horrific Jallianwala Bagh massacre, the *satyagrahi* in him awakened and he felt compelled to join the nationwide movement headed by his father once more.

❈　❈　❈

It was evident to me that Mohandas had undergone another radical transformation. He had always been driven by one single mission, but was now like an unstoppable fireball in pursuit of complete freedom from the British. He travelled tirelessly, writing articles everyday for his new journals, *Navajivan* and *New India* that left him no time for Sabarmati Ashram.

I knew it was time for me to step in.

By the summer of 1920, in close cooperation with our loyalist Maganlal Gandhi, I had taken charge of all the day-to-day operations at Sabarmati. I had garnered enough experience in handling routine matters, conducting the early morning prayers and mediating in family problems that occurred amongst the "ashramites", a task that had hitherto been Mohandas' brief.

Drawn as I was, completely into the vortex of *satyagraha,* mine had also been a process of complete transformation. Aware of the urgent need to galvanize every single Indian into the movement, I had surrendered to the cause, working relentlessly to awaken the oppressed soul of India and make freedom from the British, a reality. Moreover, this was in the background of Mohandas' call that embodied his newly-proclaimed goal of "*swaraj* in a year", which had shaken up the very soul of India during the last twelve months.

The untimely death of Bal Gangadhar Tilak and the waning influence of an increasingly irresolute Annie Besant, both of whom were prominent leaders and reformists of the national movement, had created a huge vacuum in the country's politically charged atmosphere. Annie Besant's founding of the Home Rule League, which advocated self-rule by Indians, and her open criticism of the British government's policies, had led her to be accused of sedition and she was sent to prison. This, coupled with his unique and unbeatable non-violent form of protest, had catapulted Mohandas onto the frontlines of the battle. In the eyes of his fellowmen, he became the holy messiah who had descended on earth to rescue India from the torturous yoke of Imperial rule.

Although my ashram duties were time-consuming and made it difficult for me to join Mohandas on his sundry travels, the few times that I did accompany him, I carried my *charkha*, representing the kernel of his philosophy to India's multitude, and particularly to its women, to teach them to be self-reliant. Emboldened by the sight of me spinning the *charkha* silently by Mohandas' side during his public meetings, hordes of women who had never ventured out of their homes, began appearing at meetings carrying offerings of homespun yarn as donations towards the cause.

At one such gathering Mohandas launched a scathing attack on the use of foreign goods calling for a nationwide boycott of anything which was not manufactured in India by Indians. A series of public bonfires were lit where stacks of foreign-made clothing was set aflame. I too gave away my favourite silk sari, an expensive gift from a friend and now-departed mentor, Gopal Krishna Gokhale, to be burnt. I think I saw a flicker of sadness in Mohandas' eyes as the hungry flames crackled and devoured the beautiful sari reducing it to ashes, in a matter of seconds. Thenceforth, *khadi*-clad women showed up at such meetings in huge numbers, proudly sacrificing their prized items of clothing to be thrown into the ceremonial fires.

So powerful was the impact of Mohandas' message that no village, street or home remained untouched by it and the number of activists swelled rapidly. It was time for the nervous British officials to swing into action.

⚜ ⚜ ⚜

On 10 March 1922 at 11.00 pm, under the cover of darkness, a police jeep pulled up at the entrance of Sabarmati Ashram. The Superintendent of Police of Ahmedabad trooped into Mohandas' hut, waving an arrest warrant at him. The ashram residents who had retired for the night converged anxiously at the door. They watched Mohandas collect his meagre belongings; a loincloth, two blankets and a few books and stride fearlessly out to the waiting police van.

Later, the residents took their positions on the floor outside my hut and we began to sing the evening hymn.

Jai Ram Ram...
Vaishnav jan toh teney kahiye je
Peer paraayi jaaney re
Par dukkhe upkaar kare toye
Mann abhimaan na aaney re
Jai Ram Ram...

The echoes of the hymn floated out into the moonless night as Mohandas was swiftly driven away.

Mohandas' sudden arrest had not come as a surprise to anyone. After the tumultuous events of the last six months and the confrontation with authorities, this was bound to happen. The non-cooperation movement had turned cyclonic. The British who had earlier been dismissive about the threat and effectiveness of a silent revolt precipitated by it, were compelled to intervene. Invoking the hitherto dormant provisions of the Rowlatt Act, they clamped down on the people with renewed vengeance, banning all public gatherings, gagging the press, conducting massive midnight raids on Congress offices and arresting thousands of dissidents, across the nation.

Three weeks later in a crowded courtroom at Ahmedabad, the air was heavy with an eerie silence. Mohandas' trial began. Charged with sedition, he proudly accepted full responsibility of his "so-called" crimes and then proceeded to deliver his fiery defence. It was a carefully-crafted and a deeply personal explanation of what was raging within him.

At what was later termed as the "Great Trial", he proclaimed that he had no option, but to oppose the evil and draconian Imperial rule. Upholding his conviction in the tenets of non-violence and non-cooperation that he intended to pursue regardless of any obstacles, he asked the presiding judge to award him the harshest punishment and maximum penalty possible. Justice C.N. Broomfield, who had a long-standing career in the Indian Civil Service and a favourable disposition towards Indians, was caught in a bind.

'My own task is the most difficult one that anyone in my position would ever have to face,' he said.

Acknowledging before the packed courtroom that in the eyes of millions of his countrymen the accused was a great patriot and a man of lofty ideals, he awarded Mohandas a sentence of six years of simple imprisonment.

I was numb as the words of his judgement echoed inside the courtroom. Six years was a long time. Everyone rose as the judge stood up and left, after which a loud murmur broke out. Some wept, some rushed to touch Mohandas' feet and a few came forward with offerings of gifts. I moved close to him, following him out, as the officers led him to a waiting police van and whisked him away to Sabarmati Central Jail.

I collapsed on a bench outside the court. As I watched the cloud of dust behind the racing police van, my insides had turned to lead.

That night at the ashram, I dictated a long message to the people, which was published in *Young India* the next morning –

March 23, 1922

My dear Countrymen and Countrywomen,

My dear husband has been sentenced today to six years simple imprisonment. While I cannot deny that this heavy sentence has dealt a severe blow to me, I have consoled myself that it is not beyond us to reduce it and have him freed by our own efforts long before his term ends.

I have no doubt that if India rises to carry out the constructive programme of the Congress we shall succeed not only in obtaining his release, but also solving the issues we have been fighting for.

The remedy lies with us. If we fail, the fault shall be ours.

I appeal to all men and women who feel for me and have regard for my husband to whole-heartedly concentrate on the programme and make it a success. Our success will free us from our political bondage and solve all our economic problems thereafter.

According to the will and message of Mr. Gandhi

a) *All men and women should give up wearing foreign cloth and adopt khadi.*

b) *All women should make it their religious duty to spin yarn every day.*

c) *All merchants should cease to trade in foreign piece goods.*

Kasturba Gandhi

✄ ✄ ✄

Sixty

While my husband, confined to solitude in Sabarmati prison was contemplating his role in the destiny of his nation, I was constantly fretting about the fate of my family. There was no respite for me at the ashram. I had to preside over the daily activities of the ashramites, and most importantly, keep their morale high.

Harilal remained a deep wound in my heart. His failed business ventures, his weakness for carnal pleasures, his addiction to alcohol and his never-ending demand for money had hurled me into a pit of gloom. The other three boys were still unmarried. With their father locked away indefinitely, I took it upon myself to find suitable matches for the younger three, who were all well past the age of marriage.

Manilal was foremost on my mind. Far away and alone in Phoenix, he was managing the *Indian Opinion* efficiently, but there had been reports of him being restless and miserable. Even at the age of thirty, there were no prospects of his betrothal in sight, a thought which constantly troubled me.

The day after his arrest, Mohandas shot off a letter to Manilal from his prison cell at Sabarmati.

March 11, 1922

.....Tomorrow I shall be sentenced and my desire to write shall diminish. I have not received any statement of accounts from you for sometime. Do send them immediately. Ramdas tells me that I should write to you about marriage and that deep down you are eager to get married, but feel free to do so only when you are released from your vow of celibacy. Do not forget you have taken that vow on your own, so only you can release yourself. In

my opinion you are at peace with yourself only because you took that vow. You can be free of your past misdeeds as long as you keep away from thoughts of marriage. I can vouch for that. I am at peace because Ba has embraced celibacy and accepted me as a friend. I shall be committing the gravest sin if I exercise my sexual right on her as a husband now. My work would suffer badly and I would destroy everything I have strived for in a single moment. I want you to decide for yourself. I write to you as a friend, not as a father, who is ordering you. If you cannot live without getting married, by all means get married. I hope you write to me about your innermost feelings.

Bapu's blessings

The hard-hitting letter from his father made Manilal sad. His loneliness intensified as those discomforting words of clinical counsel resounded in his head. I felt equally disturbed, but somewhere in the folds of my heart, I felt a deep anguish for Mohandas. It tore me apart to think that along with grave apprehensions about his own uncertain fate, how several other burning conflicts were being doused by him under that mask of composure, of a certain detachment.

My thoughts hauled me back again to Harilal. At thirty-four he was aimless, jobless and wayward. He suffered from all the vagaries of a wasting vagabond, yet his ego and obstinacy prevented him from coming to live at Sabarmati. To him, the asceticism of an ashram life was far worse than incarceration in a prison cell. And living with his Bapu? Another hell!

Nevertheless, my heart bled for Harilal. A virile, once able-bodied man, he must surely miss the times he shared with Gulab. Periodically, rumours of his desire to remarry had been trickling in. He had first broached the subject a few months after Gulab's death. Claiming to remarry for the sake of giving his four young children the care of a mother, he argued his case fervently, but his plea was shot down by both Mohandas and me.

Mohandas would hear nothing of it. He said it was immoral of him to even think of remarrying and the matter closed. I had a different reason. Gulab's face had not stopped haunting me even after her death, and keeping in mind the tender romance the two had shared, I just couldn't bear the thought of another woman occupying Gulab's place in her husband's life, so soon.

But now the guilt of a mother denying her son his basic needs stirred up yet again. It made me sleepless and restless. The fiendish irony of Mohandas' oft-repeated words jolted me.

Remember, when he was born I was totally blinded by sensual pleasures and you were a party to my approach. Therefore we are both responsible for what he has become. How can we blame Harilal?

And as a mother, I wanted to scream at my husband, saying:

No! I wasn't blaming him, Mohandas! I was only weeping for him!

✄ ✄ ✄

On a cold December morning in Calcutta, three months before the "Great Trial" that resulted in a six-year sentence for Mohandas, Harilal was arrested and sent to jail for a period of six months. Stirred into action by his renewed patriotic zeal that had become pandemic to the entire nation after Mohandas' rousing call for non-cooperation, Harilal had once again been drawn into the *satyagraha*. Addressing a crowd of Muslims, who were fighting to save the Khilafat Movement that had been crushed by the British after the end of the World War, he seized the opportunity to share his father's sentiment. But there was no doubt that he also wanted to desperately rebuild his tarnished image and self-esteem.

Emboldened by the frenzied reaction of the Muslims to his speeches, he re-lived those glorious days in South Africa where he had been hailed as "Junior Gandhi", with hordes of supporters shouting loud slogans in his praise.

Harilal looked at the teeming crowd of Muslims as he took centre stage. All eyes were fixed on him. He heard someone announce his name on the microphone and the gathering came alive with a deafening round of applause. His ears rang with loud cheering sounds of "Mahatma Gandhi *zindabad*", and he felt a warm flow of energy in his veins as he began to speak.

His voice was clear and loud. He spoke straight from the heart, uninhibited by his lack of knowledge about the Khilafat Movement. Every word he uttered was met with a thundering applause; every sentence was interspersed with the cheering crowd shouting slogans in support of Harilal and the Khilafat. He felt blood surging in his veins like never before. And he knew that the people were showering adulation upon him because he reflected a man who was the Mahatma for the crowds gathered in front of him—Bapu. It was his moment of absolution.

The restive crowds, however, impelled the government to swoop down on Harilal, who was sent to prison for a period of six months. Holding his head high before the magistrate, he proclaimed, 'What in your view constitutes a crime, to us the citizens of this country, is our birthright. Our first duty as humans is to fight injustice, cruelty and slavery, and if that is a crime then I plead guilty, with millions of my fellowmen. But we shall continue to engage in such crimes.'

Harilal's face remained impassive during the trial.

The first thing he did when he reached the prison in Calcutta, was to write a letter to Mohandas and me. But even before the letters reached us, the prison warden handed him a telegram from his father.

Congratulations, son. You have done me proud. My blessings are with you.

With trembling hands, Harilal folded the telegram and touched it to his forehead. He was gripped by a rare sense of joy. At last he had redeemed himself in the eyes of his Ba and Bapu. No one would ever look upon him as an aberration in the glorious life of his father.

✼ ✼ ✼

Harilal was released from prison in June 1922. He went straight to Poona to meet his father who had by then been shifted to Yerwada Central Jail. He thought it was an opportune time to bring up his desire for his second marriage, but Mohandas was adamant. After some arguments between father and son, Mohandas relented, but put forth a condition.

'If you can find a widow, who has as many children as you and if both of you mutually agree to love and accept each other's children as your own, you can have my consent.'

Once again Harilal felt that despondency and frustration creep up in him. Nothing had changed. *"Marry a widow?"* How abominable! How could he even think of marrying a woman, who had been with another man? Dejected, he returned to Calcutta and continued wallowing in self-pity, till I arrived with his four children and Ramdas, to visit him a few months later.

I sensed a simmering resentment in Harilal the moment I set eyes on him. He spoke his heart out to me, reiterating his natural desire to get married again and his father's unreasonable stand. Although I supported Mohandas in his views of re-marrying a widow, I believed that more than his aversion to marrying a "non-virgin", Harilal was in no position to take on the burden of an additional family if she came with children. I quietly backtracked and the subject closed for the time being.

❇ ❇ ❇

Mohandas was released from prison on 13 January 1924 after having served barely two years of his six-year term. He had taken ill after a bout of acute appendicitis for which he had undergone surgery, but his recovery was alarmingly slow. Fearing widespread violence and demonstrations in case of his death in-custody, the authorities had decided to set him free.

Mohandas travelled to Bombay at the invitation of one of his wealthy Parsi supporters and spent a few weeks recuperating on his secluded estate at Juhu Beach. The solitude in the serene seaside home was however short-lived as he was besieged by thousands of visitors—his followers, friends and supporters, who were celebrating his early release. Mohandas returned to Sabarmati as soon as he regained his strength and was back to work as usual at the ashram. Nothing had changed—simplicity, frugality and self-reliance were strictly followed at the commune. I felt as if we were back at the Tolstoy Farm in South Africa.

A few days later, the ashram had an unexpected visitor—a young Punjabi Brahmin boy called Pyarelal, who was fresh out of university. He was keen to volunteer his services even as his family had opposed losing their only son to the Gandhi ashram. They had expected him to join the Indian Civil Service as per the family custom and secure a lucrative government job. But so drawn was Pyarelal to Mohandas and his commitment to freedom that he managed to prevail upon them. Eventually, Pyarelal went on to become one of Mohandas' most trusted secretaries. He would serve him faithfully till the day Mohandas died.

⚸ ⚸ ⚸

April 1926

Early in spring that year, Manilal was in the throes of a passionate romance. He had fallen in love with a Muslim girl, Fatima, whose family was known to us for many years. After much deliberation, he picked up the courage to write to his brother Ramdas about his desire to marry her. Manilal wanted his advice on how to broach the subject with their father—a formidable task indeed!

I was getting more and more restless with each passing day. The future of all my sons hung in uncertainty. There was little I could do about Harilal who was in trouble again. An advocate from Peshawar had complained to Mohandas about his son's wrongdoings, the familiar litany of his failed business ventures, his addiction to alcohol and cheap women.

Subsequently, on the front pages of *Navajivan,* Mohandas publicly denounced Harilal's latest business venture when he discovered that he had taken money from investors, invoking the Gandhi name. And not only had he lost all that money in his failed businesses, once again there were rumours that he had squandered much of it on alcohol, women and gambling.

With a heavily burdened heart, Mohandas dictated a strongly-worded denouncement to Mahadevbhai, who typed it and sent it for publication in *Navajivan,* the following day.

It is true that Harilal is my son, but we have been estranged for many years and I am not involved in any of the ventures he undertakes. He should not reap the benefits of my name. For all those who have been cheated by him, I express my sympathy. If

Harilal has even one iota of morality left in him he will return their money. That is the path of truth. In this world, there are limits even for a father when it comes to helping a son. Hence only God can help him. Those who have been cheated are advised to be careful in future.

The public shaming of my son had singed me as much as it had wounded him. But I decided that I was not going to waste any more time weeping for Harilal. Instead, I urgently needed to go about looking for a suitable match for Manilal.

Meanwhile Manilal's letter, declaring his love for Fatima and his desire to marry her had been forwarded to his father by Ramdas. Mohandas was aghast. He scribbled a note of strong dissent almost immediately, without even consulting me.

I have read your letter to Ramdas. You follow the Hindu religion and Fatima follows Islam. Your desire to marry her is against your religion. It would be like putting two swords in one scabbard. What religion will your children follow? Who will hold a greater influence on them? Your marriage to her cannot happen. It will be a great jolt to Hindu-Muslim relations nation-wide. This issue cannot be solved by inter-marriage. And you cannot forget you are my son. Society will not forget it either. If you go through with this you cannot serve the people and you shall be unfit to work for the 'Indian Opinion'. For this I cannot seek Ba's consent —she will not give it. Her whole life will be embittered. I have no courage to tell her about this. May God show you the right path.

Bapu's blessings

Manilal was heartbroken. Unable to take their passionate romance forward after his father's stern rebuke, he parted with his childhood sweetheart after a teary farewell never to meet again. And poor Fatima, the victim of an accidental hex, disappeared into oblivion as if she had never existed.

I was not even consulted in the proposed betrothal of Manilal and Fatima. Although the topic was never broached again, my heart continued to bleed for my disconsolate son and his unrequited love.

Meanwhile destiny intervened. It played out its predetermined hand and the daughter of Nanabhai and Vijay Laxmi Mashruwala, prosperous textile merchants, whom I had met on many occasions, was offered for marriage to Manilal. The Mashruwalas were not only ardent followers of the *satyagraha,* they had renounced the world to devote their lives and wealth to public service. Their home, some two hundred miles northeast of Bombay, in Akola, was an open house that always welcomed travellers from the Gandhi ashram.

Sushila, one of their three daughters, was a beautiful twenty-year-old girl with a deeply artistic temperament. To my mind, I couldn't have found a better match for Manilal. Things moved rapidly thereafter and on 6 March 1927, Sushila and Manilal were married in her native city with much fanfare. The newlyweds were made to take the mandatory vows of austerity and poverty, before leaving for the ashram.

The bride and groom along with the *baraatis* boarded a train back to Sabarmati soon after the ceremony. A rare feeling of triumph had engulfed me. Revelling in the joys felt by a mother-in-law that had long eluded me, I was taking the newlywed bride of my second son, home; a thrill that had been denied to me when Harilal had married Gulab.

The nervous newlyweds took their separate places at opposite ends of the coach, far away from each other. I looked at the shy bride adoringly. Then I called out to Manilal.

'Why are you sitting so far away from your *dulhan,* Manilal? Come and sit beside her. Look at her. She is dying of nervousness, the poor child. Talk to her Manilal, won't you? Comfort her, *beta!* She doesn't know anyone here.'

In a stark departure from protocol, Manilal moved forward shyly and took his seat beside Sushila, who did not raise her eyes from the floor.

The train gathered speed as it raced onwards to Sabarmati. Liberation from societal norms and outdated customs was a novel feeling for me. A thrilling upliftment engulfed me.

❄ ❄ ❄

Sixty One

The newlyweds left for South Africa a few weeks after we returned to Sabarmati. Manilal resumed his charge of publishing the *Indian Opinion* and tending to Tolstoy Farm.

Mohandas' harsh public dressing-down meanwhile, had made Harilal even more enraged and bitter. His creditors had become doubly ferocious and they closed in on him like a pack of hungry wolves. Feeling hemmed-in from all sides, he found unexpected solace in an associate, Chittaranjan Das, whose father was a prominent member of the Congress party from Calcutta. Chittaranjan Das sympathized with Harilal and felt sorry for his wretched condition.

'Calcutta will kill you, Harilal,' he said. 'How long can you stay here like this? My advice to you would be to go back to Gujarat.'

But Harilal was in no mood to go back to his father's dreary abode.

'Easier said than done, Chittaranjan Babu,' he sighed. 'How can I leave without paying off all my creditors? And here I am, dying of stress; worried sick about my children, the poor creatures. Abandoned by me, they are being looked after by my wife's sister in Gujarat. And I can contribute nothing for them. Can you imagine how rotten I feel?' At that moment, it was as if some divine power had taken hold of Chittaranjan Babu's mind, and some celestial angel had taken cognizance of Harilal's unfortunate plight.

'Don't worry, Harilal,' Chittaranjan Das reassured him. 'I shall pay off all your debts. Give me the details and inform your creditors to collect their dues from me.'

Harilal was stunned. He could barely speak. He began to tremble. He steadied himself and in a shaky voice said,

'Chittaranjan Babu! What are you saying? You will pay off my debts? How will I ever repay this?' But Chittaranjan Das had decided to bail him out.

A burden lifted from Harilal's heart. There was indeed a god above. With all his dues paid off by a benevolent benefactor, he made his way to the station to board a train to Rajkot a few days later. He hadn't seen his children in a long time. He was worried about Rami who was of a marriageable age. Gulab's sister, Baliben had lined up a few proposals for her and they awaited his approval. The thought of his children deepened the hollow in his heart.

How he missed them!

⁂

Life in Rajkot seemed so beautiful; so free of turmoil. Harilal was transported into a world filled with laughter and merriment. Baliben had put her heart and soul into tending for her dead sister's children who looked happy and secure. All four of them hovered around their father and he rejoiced in their company. Manu climbed onto his lap, and played with his hair, while Rami shied away. She looked so much like her mother and had grown to be a beautiful young lady. Harilal felt a lump in his throat. The thought of sending her away was unbearable.

Baliben looked despairingly at her brother-in-law who had become a bag of bones; his face haggard, bones protruding out of his shabby, ill-fitting clothes, his eyes sunk deep into their sockets and skin which had turned a deathly black.

That night Harilal sat with his sister-in-law reviewing all the prospective grooms that she had identified for Rami. Finally, they chose Kuverji Parekh, for whom Harilal sought his father's approval in a letter detailing the boy's suitability.

However, Rami's marriage alliance had only brought momentary happiness for Harilal. When he thought of his desperate financial condition, he was flung into an abyss of despair all over again. He desperately wanted to buy some gifts for his children before he left from Rajkot, and the fact that he had no home to call his own, made him even more dejected.

Harilal racked his brains trying to recall the names of people he knew in Rajkot; people from whom he could borrow some money. But things had changed. No one would risk lending him money, particularly after Mohandas had publicly shamed and disowned him. Asking for a loan would only bring him more ignominy. After long deliberations, Harilal approached Thakore Sahab, the King of Rajkot to whom the Gandhis had rendered many years of loyal service.

Harilal plucked up the courage to speak out his mind to Thakore Sahab. Driven by the power of truth, he spoke to him with sincerity and candour about his wife's untimely death, his failed business ventures and how he needed money for his daughter's marriage. He confessed about his strained relations with Mohandas and his inability to raise funds on his own, because he had been branded a crook, cheat and defaulter in the eyes of the world.

By some stroke of good fortune, Thakore Sahab agreed to loan Harilal the required sum from his treasury.

'Your forefathers have served us, Harilal,' he said smiling benevolently, 'and it will be shameful if we do not help you in your hour of need.'

Richer by ten thousand rupees, Harilal had collected enough to splurge on Rami's wedding like a doting, dutiful father, as well as tide over his day to day existence comfortably, till he could find another job.

'I have done it my darling Gulab!' He said aloud that night. 'And you would have been a proud woman today. Your daughter shall be sent off in the grandest style that any father should desire. If only you could have been here with me for our Rami's *kanyadaan*. If only you had not left me like this, my sweet Gulab!' Harilal's throat choked with remorse. He clutched at his heavy heart and wept.

❊　❊　❊

Rami Harilal Gandhi and Kuverji Parekh were wed in Rajkot amidst great fanfare and a no-holds-barred celebration.The extravagant show put up by Harilal raised many doubts within the family regarding the source of his money, but no one spoke a word about this to him and neither did Harilal disclose his borrowing from Thakore Sahab to anyone.

He felt a deep sense of satisfaction after Rami left her natal home to begin a new life with her husband. Even his other children had never felt closer to their father the way they had this time around. But Harilal was faced with yet another problem; his sister-in-law, Baliben, who made him feel extremely uneasy in her presence. Although she had done a remarkable job of raising her dead sister's children, she was openly hostile towards her brother-in-law. It was also a fact that at one time, Harilal had felt a fleeting sexual attraction towards Baliben, but that was many years ago, and now the woman made no pretense of her loathing for him. A few days after the wedding ceremonies were over, Harilal decided to leave for Bombay, for it was no longer possible to suffer Baliben's overt hatred.

Harilal had often fought the temptation to come and live with us in Sabarmati, but life at the ashram did not suit him. He had moved too far away from the austerity it demanded and the wounds from his father's last assault were still raw. At Sabarmati he believed he would be compelled to live a life of failure and humiliation, even if his Bapu miraculously forgave him.

Moving to Bombay on the other hand was filled with hope. With the money left over from Thakore Sahab's benevolent loan, he hoped to survive in that land of opportunities till he could find himself a job.

Harilal found an inexpensive room at the Kashmir Hotel, in Dhobi Talao. Nestled in the heart of the city, it was surrounded by hordes of low-income settlements and promised enough avenues for entertainment. With a decent sum of money in his pocket, his daughter settled, no creditors at his throat and not a care in the world, his self-control snapped and he went back into the murky pit of alcohol, gambling and cheap women.

Walking alone for miles in the city of Bombay, taking the occasional tram in search of that elusive job, he would invariably end up with a bottle, in a cheap brothel.

But both peace and a means for his livelihood were not coming to him just yet.

� ✽ ✽ ✽

After many lonely and wasted hours wandering around Dhobi Talao, on the streets of Bombay, providence granted Harilal one more chance to redeem his fate. At a commemoration function to mark the death anniversary of a renowned Parsi leader, Dadabhai Naoroji, whom Harilal had deeply admired, he chanced upon a Parsi gentleman, Ardeshir Godrej, who immediately took a liking to him, on learning that he was Mohandas Gandhi's eldest son.

He offered Harilal the job of promoting the sale of Godrej soaps, which he reasoned was not a losing proposition, since Gandhi's nationwide call of boycotting foreign goods and adopting *swadeshi* products had met with a rousing success. It was as if a gateway of new opportunities had suddenly opened up for Harilal. The Godrej Company welcomed him to its office the next day as a sales representative. And Harilal undertook to popularize the soaps in the entire subcontinent.

Harilal's enthusiasm soon bore fruit. The soap sold well and with money in his pocket, the cloud of depression slowly dissipated. He began dreaming of bringing his children to live with him in Bombay, but the desire for domestic bliss was soon vanquished by his passion for other things that had now become part of his life. Even while touring the country on his sales promotion trips, his vices followed him unsparingly. He would often absent himself from work, spending days and nights on drinking binges in his room at the Kashmir Hotel, but because of the extraordinary sales boost that the company had registered after he took over, Ardeshir Godrej continued to pay him his monthly salary and ignored his lapses. In a rare moment of lucidity, Harilal wrote a letter to Baliben expressing his desire to relieve his children from her custody, requesting her to make the necessary arrangements for sending them to Bombay. He wrote another letter to Mohandas, telling him about his job with the Godrej Company and his capability to take care of his children at last.

✽ ✽ ✽

Harilal was getting impatient. The simmering resentment he had been harbouring against Baliben flared after he received a curt reply from her, questioning his ability to look after his children. In the short but strongly-worded letter, she had accused him of being a lowly character, given to vile addictions. She said that she feared he would corrupt the minds of his innocent children. She also wrote that the children were no longer with her, but were in Sabarmati with their grandparents.

A similar reply from Mohandas had further stoked his rage. His father had written that while Harilal had full authority on the lives of his children, the decision to choose where they wanted to live should rest with Kanti, and if he chose to live with his father, Mohandas had no objections.

Harilal felt his head was going to explode with hatred towards Baliben for her dismissive and humiliating behaviour and at his father's meanness.

The following morning, Harilal began drinking from the moment he woke up, completely submerged under a cloud of depression. Late evening, and by now totally inebriated, he staggered out of his room and boarded a tram from Dhobi Talao to the enticing Foras Road's red light area, where he sunk himself in the numbing pleasures of the flesh, till he passed out.

Earlier that day, Harilal's benevolent boss, Ardeshir Godrej, worried by his frequent absences from work, himself had gone looking for him at the Kashmir Hotel. To his utter horror, he found Harilal completely wasted and drunk. His sparse, unclean room was strewn with empty bottles of alcohol, soiled clothes and some stale food that lay all over the bed and floor. With great difficulty, a visibly embarrassed Harilal reeking of alcohol, rose to his feet to greet Godrej, but fell back on the sofa, his shaky legs barely able to hold his weight.

'What have you done to yourself, Harilal?' Ardeshir Godrej cried out. He stretched out his arm and sat beside him. 'Is it good to consume so much alcohol?' Harilal rolled his hooded eyes, pointed a finger towards the ceiling and laughed loudly. The fiendish sounds of his laughter bounced off the walls of the dingy room and wafted into the mid-morning sky.

'Don't forget you are the son of Mohandas Gandhi,' Godrej continued. 'Why are you doing this to yourself and to your father? How will you ever get back to work if this doesn't stop?' Godrej's voice was laced with concern.

Harilal winced at the sound of his father's name. Whipped out of his stupor, a terrible rage flashed from his bloodshot eyes. 'I do not wish to work for your damn company, Mr. Godrej. Please accept my resignation immediately.'

Ardeshir Godrej was stunned. He sat silently beside Harilal, his head bowed, for a long time. He realized there was no point in coaxing the senseless man any longer. He rose and left the room quietly with sadness in his heart.

'How can you help someone who is hell-bent on destroying himself?' He mumbled as he walked away.

Poor Harilal was jobless again. He had foolishly axed his own feet. The words of Ardeshir Godrej had yet again scarred his benumbed soul. Being the son of Mohandas Gandhi was his worst mortal aberration. If he could, he would have taken a scalpel and sliced off that part of his life forever. He put his mouth to the half-empty bottle, took a long draught and slammed it hard against the door.

As the burning liquid trickled down his parched throat, the sound of shattering glass fell on his deaf ears. He had passed out.

❈   ❈   ❈

Sixty Two

Harilal had no one to turn to. Mohandas had become impenetrable and Baliben loathed him. He knew that both were convinced that he had strayed on to the path of depravity and had wronged them; whereas the truth was that it was his Bapu, who had repeatedly been unfair to him and ill-treated him.

The only way he could avenge himself was by seeking justice from the people. He decided to publicly humiliate his father by writing articles against him in different newspapers, so that everyone would see the duplicity and cruelty their "messiah" was meting out to his own wife and sons.

In a series of highly emotional and damaging articles titled "Our Rebellion–Mahatma's Buddhavtar", Harilal began pouring out his litany of woes. Emphasizing on how his father's dictatorial behaviour had crippled him right through his life, he accused him of destroying the lives of his mother and brothers as well. These were sent to *Hindustan Prajamitra,* one of the most widely read Gujarati newspapers of the time.

An exhilarating lightness overcame Harilal when he saw the first article in print. He felt vindicated after months of restlessness, and slept peacefully that night.

But the next morning his mind had fogged up again. That momentary triumph had vanished and reality struck. He was jobless. Luckily for him, Ardeshir Godrej in his kindness continued to send him his remuneration even after he had resigned from the job.

Harilal managed to survive in this manner for some more time, but soon that supply of money also stopped and like growling demons, his problems began hounding him all over again. He decided it was time for him to go and visit his children.

✻ ✻ ✻

Totally oblivious of the violent political rumblings that had racked the entire nation, Harilal set off on a train to Rajkot with his belongings stuffed into a soiled cotton *jhola*. A shabby pair of pants, one shirt, a pen, a brass bowl, a personal copy of the Bhagavad Gita, and Gulab's photograph were shoved into that bulging bag that he slung over his shoulder. He also pushed in his last two bottles of alcohol and pulled the string tight to close it.

With no money in his pocket, a weary and defeated Harilal settled into the seat of a moving train. The clanging sound of the two bottles in the bag reassured him. The thought that he would soon be with his children was comforting.

All through the journey, Harilal was gripped by an uncontrollable fury towards Baliben and Bapu. He opened one of the bottles and began drinking greedily from it till it was empty. The more he drank, the more impatient he became to see his children.

At dusk, the train reached Rajkot. Harilal draped his faded shawl on his shoulders over a jacket that was tattered at the cuffs, put on his worn-out *chappals* and stepped out, making his way straight to Baliben's house. His fists were clenched into a tight ball, his jaws tightened and he began to slur incoherently. Overpowered by the deep hostility he felt towards his sister-in-law, he staggered unsteadily, waving his shawl in the air, mouthing loud invectives directed at the world at large.

When Harilal reached Baliben's house, it was quiet. The clock had just struck ten. Everyone had gone to sleep and the lights had been turned off. Harilal knocked at the door rousing a startled Baliben from her slumber. Manu, who had been sleeping beside her, rubbed her eyes, turned over and went back to sleep.

'Who is it?' asked Baliben, her voice laden with apprehension.

'Open the door. It's me, Harilal.'

Harilal's trembling voice sent her heart racing. She was scared.

What could he want at this hour?

By this time Manu had also woken up. She came close to Baliben and grabbed her arm. Her face had turned white with fear.

Baliben pushed open the door slightly. She saw Harilal leaning against a pillar at the entrance, his hand still on the doorknob. Reluctantly she let him in. A strong odour of stale alcohol singed her nostrils.

'Are you all right, bhai? What brings you here at this time of the night? And in this condition?'

Manu's eyes widened with horror when she saw her father reeling drunkenly. He flopped helplessly into an armchair near the door. His gaunt face, bloodshot eyes, dishevelled hair and torn clothes terrified her. She crouched behind Baliben, clutching her arm in a tight grip.

'Baliben! Where is Kanti? I have come to take him. Bring him to me. I have to educate him. I shall make him a doctor. And this one! My little Manu…' he stretched his arm to pull Manu towards him. Manu was trembling. She had shrunk into herself, and was hiding behind her aunt. Harilal rose unsteadily on his feet and lurched at her. Manu let out a deafening scream. She ran backwards almost tripping over the furniture, screaming and crying hysterically.

Baliben stood in front of Harilal, blocking his advancing steps towards the screaming girl. 'Stop it, bhai! Stop now! Get a hold of your senses.' She had crossed her arms in front of her and was trying to push him back.

'You are drunk and have no business to come here like this, at this time of the night. Just look at Manu. She's terrified of you. What have you done to her? Get out this minute…or I shall…' Baliben was trying to sound brave, though her quivering voice belied her confidence.

'You will what…?' He leered! 'I am not drunk, you mad woman. I am totally in my senses and I will not allow my daughter to stay with you any longer.'

Harilal pushed Baliben roughly to one side and staggered menacingly towards Manu.

'Come now, Manu. Come to me, child. I am your father…' he beckoned her. There was a lopsided grin on his face.

'No!' Don't come near me!' Manu screamed. 'You smell so bad. I know you are drunk. I won't go anywhere with you. Don't dare come near me…' She ran to Baliben and clung to her, weeping loudly.

'You have to come away with me, Manu,' he continued. 'This vile aunt of yours is tutoring you against me. I am your father. Do not listen to this filthy woman. She is a cunning *woman!* She wants to take you away from me.'

Baliben had had enough. She pulled Manu into a tight embrace and stood firmly before the drunken man. Harilal lurched out again and grabbed Manu's arm.

'Don't cry, my child,' he slurred. 'Come now, come to your father Manu!' He pushed Baliben aside and dragged Manu towards him. 'I shall free you from the clutches of this evil aunt of yours…'

Before he knew, Baliben had shoved him forcefully to one side. Harilal lost his balance, fell on the floor and vomited all over the threshold.

He staggered up once again, but Baliben moved forward with the speed of lightning and slapped him hard across the face.

Harilal stared at her in silence, stunned by the slap. Manu screamed hysterically and burst into loud wails. Baliben was trembling, her eyes flashing with anger. She slapped Harilal again and again, grabbed him by the shoulders and pushed him out of the door with all the strength she could muster.

'Go away, you drunken lout and don't ever show us your face again,' she screamed loudly slamming the door in his face.

Baliben then turned around, took the hysterical girl in her arms and burst into tears. They sat on the cold floor, locked in a tight embrace all night, but Manu's sobbing did not stop. By the next morning, Baliben had somewhat regained her composure and Manu, still shaken up from the ugly confrontation sat down to write to Bapu.

With trembling hands, she poured out the horrific experience of the night before, in the letter to her grandfather. She sealed it, handed it to her aunt and crept back into bed to relive the nightmare that would scar her for life.

Perched delicately between childhood and youth, this ugly ordeal would wound her soul irreparably, yet deep down inside, her heart bled for her destitute father who was beyond any solace or reform. She pulled the cover over her head, wiping her eyes that had filled up with tears again.

The letter reached Sabarmati Ashram a few days later. The nightmarish incident described in Manu's shaky handwriting, outraged Mohandas and shattered me. I looked up with teary eyes at my husband. His stony face was set in a grim sneer. He was silent. He had shut his eyes. It was a long time before he spoke.

'Let us not abandon hope for his improvement, Kastur. Poor, innocent Manu should not have witnessed this ugly incident. But if Harilal is lucky, he may emerge from this a better person.'

My heart ripped apart as I imagined the plight of a frightened Manu clinging desperately to her aunt in the middle of the night and a deeply humiliated, and drunken Harilal, looming menacingly at her.

'My poor boy! My poor poor, Harilal!' I broke down. 'Bali threw him out in the middle of the night after slapping him. Where else could he have gone with no money and no place to stay…?' My voice quivered. My tears fell unchecked onto my face as I tried coming to terms with the shock.

'She did the right thing, Kastur. Don't cry for Harilal, think about the little girl!' Mohandas said sombrely. 'Maybe Manu should write to her father now, telling him to give up drinking or else forget about her existence. It may just have some impact on him…'

Mohandas' altruistic sermon could do little to placate my torn soul. I continued to weep in the far corner of the room where I sat with my head bowed, while he quietly resumed spinning his *charkha*. The clicking rhythm of the spinning wheel felt like sharp blows on my chest.

✳ ✳ ✳

Sabarmati

12 March 1930

All eyes were focussed on Sabarmati that crisp, bright March morning. In response to the call for a "Salt March" by Mohandas, the ashram had been buzzing with brisk activities for weeks and hundreds of new volunteers had turned up each day, offering to participate. The march was to protest against the draconian Salt Act that had been imposed by the government on the people of India. It prohibited the production and sale of salt by anyone other than the British and doing so was deemed a serious criminal offence.

A few months earlier, Sushila and Manilal had returned from South Africa with their one-year-old daughter, Sita. I was overjoyed to see them after a long gap of three years, but like most of us, both Manilal and Sushila had been sucked into the civil disobedience movement and were engrossed in preparations for the Salt March.

Mohandas had meticulously planned this non-violent protest of civil disobedience, and so great was the power of his word and so devoted were the people that an astonishingly large number of volunteers had assembled at the ashram that day, even before daybreak.

I rose, bathed and finished all my chores at 3 am on that warm day, to be greeted by a swarm of reporters and photographers at the door. Camping overnight in the open fields that surrounded the ashram, they were waiting to catch the first glimpse of the rebellious marchers led by Mohandas.

I felt a peculiar stirring in me that morning as I made my rounds of the ashram, rousing everyone for the morning prayer and supervising the preparation of food for the marchers.

The morale of the volunteers was at an unprecedented high. Wired with hypnotic zeal, they lined up behind Mohandas, with jubilant smiles on their faces.

The night before, Mohandas had taken a solemn vow after the prayers.

'We shall not return to Sabarmati until India is free!' he had pledged and all the ashramites had repeated after him.

At the set time, seventy-five impassioned *satyagrahis* led by Mohandas, began moving towards the seaside village of Dandi in the Gulf of Cambay. They planned to navigate a two-hundred-and-forty-mile trek, in violation of the new law, by manufacturing and selling salt after reaching the village of Dandi. And what would turn out to be the most potent symbol of people's resistance that day, would eventually pave the way for total *swaraj*, bringing Mohandas' dream to fruition.

Even though I was driven by the intensity of Mohandas' zeal, I failed to understand how collecting one pinch of salt could help us get freedom from the British. A crippling fear gripped me. Three generations of Gandhis were marching to Dandi that morning: Mohandas, Manilal and Harilal's eldest son, Kanti who was barely nineteen years old.

The thought of Harilal reopened an old wound. Even though there were more pressing demands on me that day, I couldn't push him out of my mind. How I wished he could have walked shoulder to shoulder with his father in this glorious mission like the other two. But poor Harilal was trapped in his own pit of drunken gloom and no one but god could now rescue him from its depths.

The chilling sound of Mohandas' parting words to the gathering, rang out in the crisp air, breaking my reverie.

Today you carry your death on your shoulders my friends. Be prepared to die. The British may use guns, but we shall not fight back. If you choose to surrender before them with the fear of being killed, I shall feel disgraced…

The fear of losing their loved ones had swept over the women and children of the ashram. I watched Sushila's tear-stained face as she said goodbye to Manilal. Trembling with an outburst of emotion, she ran to me and rested her face on my shoulder.

'No Sushila, you must not cry.' My comforting words did little to contain her loud sobs. 'You don't want your husband to carry the last image of a weeping wife with him?' I stroked her head tenderly and pointed to the others around me. 'Look Sushila! Just look around you,' I said to her. 'All the women are parting from their men. They do not cry like you. You must stop this at once.'

Sensing the need of the moment, I stepped forward briskly and cleared my choked throat. With a strong voice, that belied my own nervousness, I addressed all the members collected there—

Our men are warriors and we are all warriors' wives. It is our dharma to give them courage and strength. If we are brave, so shall they be.

Then I strode towards Mohandas who was wearing a white shawl, cotton dhoti and a pair of rugged, hand-made sandals. He held a long bamboo staff in his hand and his eyes glowed with the pride of a fighter ready to lay down his life in the service of his people. I applied a long vermillion *tilak* on his furrowed forehead invoking the Lord, to bestow victory and protection on him during this perilous mission. Then I moved down the column of marchers anointing a *tilak* on each forehead. The solemn sacredness of the moment permeated the air even as Sushila stood watching me, almost in a trance.

As a soldier of *satyagraha*, faced with the daunting task of keeping the morale of the women and children from sagging, if there had been any doubts in my mind about the genuineness or outcome of this mission, they had vanished. And in that moment, I felt I had become the omnipresent Mother Goddess, myself.

❊ ❊ ❊

Sixty Three

The jubilant marchers led by Mohandas made their way through the gaily festooned streets of Ahmedabad that were thronged by thousands of people, cheering, shouting slogans, and waving flags on either side of the route.

Mohandas, a gaunt and stooped figure wearing just a *khadi* shawl and dhoti, exposing his skeletal torso and thin legs, was watched by the world as he strode along the predetermined route with manic fervour. People lining the paths knelt in reverence as the marchers passed by. Many were perched on rooftops and trees to catch a glimpse of the triumphal parade. Newspapers were plastered with pictures of him addressing massive crowds of onlookers on the way. The progress of the marchers was regularly relayed back to me in Sabarmati, which only heightened my anxiety for I had feared a violent police assault on them. But as the hours ticked by, there was no news of any offensive action from the authorities, and my tension dissipated. I heaved a sigh of relief when the marchers reached Dandi, right on schedule.

On the morning of 6 April after a long prayer meeting on the shores of Dandi, Mohandas along with his supporters waded into the waters for a ritual bath of purification. Then, in full view of a large contingent of press reporters, cameramen and around seventy-five thousand people, he bent down dramatically to pick up a handful of salt-encrusted sand. That moment became the grand call for heralding the peaceful civil disobedience movement in history, and suddenly the entire nation erupted with a mass frenzy, collecting, manufacturing, buying and selling salt, and blatantly defying the law of the land.

The world watched in awe as beaches filled up with thousands of villagers squatting on sand, scooping up the salt-rich soil.

Women and children could be seen wading daringly into the sea, collecting water in pots. Thousands of pamphlets which described "easy methods to manufacture salt", had found their way into the streets of Calcutta. City dwellers boiled sea-water in kettles to challenge the ban and lend their support to Gandhi.

At the base camp near Dandi, Mohandas continued to direct the Salt March plan. Addressing a group of stunned foreign correspondents, he said,

I want world sympathy in this battle of right against might.

Emboldened by the strong public response, he sent a note to the Viceroy announcing his plan to lead a non-violent march to Dharasana, where the government's salt factory was situated. But on 5 May, a nervous and harassed government swooped down on Mohandas and carted him off to Yerwada jail in Poona. He bade farewell to his supporters with a triumphant smile on his face. 'Tell Ba, she is a brave girl...!' he shouted as he was driven away by the police.

Back at Sabarmati, the news of Mohandas' arrest had cast a pall of gloom on the women and children. In the face of fearsome uncertainties, I was duty-bound by my husband's orders to send Manilal to take over as leader of the protest march against the government's salt factory, but to be honest, I was overcome with panic. With Mohandas in prison and Manilal facing imminent arrest or a serious threat to his life, I was reminded of our nightmarish days in South Africa.

On a blistering morning of 21 May 1930, 2,500 unarmed *satyagrahis*, all wearing stark white *khadi* dhotis, shirts and caps, collected at the Dharasana Salt Works. They stopped a few hundred yards away from the giant salt-pans and knelt down to pray. Manilal took the lead. He was followed by a column of twenty-five marchers who began a slow advance across the open field. Ahead of them was a water-filled ditch. A barbed wire fence surrounded the salt-pans that were guarded by a large posse of four hundred policemen, wielding steel-tipped *lathis*. Unmindful of the policemen who barked out stern warnings to the protesters, ordering them to disperse, they continued moving towards the barrier. Suddenly scores of policemen rushed out from all sides, fell upon the silent marchers and began raining blows on their heads. Not one of them raised an arm to defend himself.

Column after column silently marched forward with military precision, taking the blows, falling down with newer ones taking their place. There was no sign of fear nor was there any slackening of their will as they marched steadily ahead with their heads held high, taking the merciless beating on their skulls without a squawk.

In a few minutes, the ground was strewn with hundreds of lifeless bodies. The dark blood that oozed from their heads and limbs, stained their white clothes, making it a nauseating sight.

Finally, when the harsh midday sun beat down on the gathered crowds at 11 a:m, the volunteers concluded their agitation. The wounded had been transported to a nearby makeshift hospital, where they lay in rows on the ground. There were 320 of them with fractured skulls and others with serious injuries. No one had attended to them for over four hours and two were dead.

As if this was not harrowing enough for me, the news that Manilal was untraceable had me in a state of panic. I was sure my son had also been bludgeoned to death.

❆ ❆ ❆

I spent several agonizing days waiting to hear about Manilal, but to no avail. And just when my hopes faded and I had no more tears to shed, a message came from Surat. In a town fifty miles away from the salt factory works at Dharasana, Manilal was reportedly recuperating from a fractured skull at a prison hospital, after which he was to be transported to Sabarmati Central Jail, to serve a sentence of six months. Although it broke my heart, I was thankful that my son was alive and reassured that he would recover fully, albeit in a jail cell.

Sushila and I went to visit Manilal at the Sabarmati prison. I knew Ramdas was also imprisoned there with some other *satyagrahis,* but no one had been allowed to meet him so far. I noticed Sushila's uneasiness inside the jail compound while we waited for Manilal and Ramdas. She had never been inside a jail before and the intimidating walls of the head-jailor's office had made her visibly nervous.

Sushila gasped loudly when she saw the two brothers come into the jailor's office and she began to cry. Manilal had lost a lot of weight. He looked tired and his face was drawn. A nasty scar on his head was a telling sign of the cruelty that had been meted out to him. Ramdas looked emaciated—his face had turned a patchy brown.

I held both of them by their arms and made them sit on the two empty chairs beside me. The sight of my two sons who had been punished for honouring their father's call of duty to the nation, rattled me. I brushed aside my apprehensions, held my head high in pride and patted their heads. My steady voice betrayed no signs of the pain I felt in my heart.

'You both have done us proud, my sons! You have done the nation proud!'

I looked at Sushila's tense face and stroked her cheek. She looked like she was ready to burst into tears.

'Come now, Sushila! You must not cry. You are a very fortunate woman. You have become an integral part of this movement of sacrifice that shall continue to test your strength again and again. You must not cry.'

My tender words must have soothed her as she stopped crying and we both walked out of the jail premises, feeling stronger and calmer.

With most of the men in jail, there was more work for me to do at Sabarmati. I would have to shoulder the additional responsibility of urging the women to take part in the latest phase of the civil disobedience movement. We decided to begin by picketing outside government-owned liquor stores.

After returning from Poona, I travelled to Punjab to visit my youngest son Devdas, who was jailed there. I was stunned to see the milling crowds that had collected at the station to welcome me. I had no idea that the people of India had elevated me to the position of a woman leader, a distinctly different entity from the Kastur who was always seen as the silent, self-effacing shadow of the incumbent Mahatma!

It was a glorious feeling of vindication!

❆ ❆ ❆

The British Prime Minister Ramsay MacDonald was an embarrassed man. He had been deluged with telegrams from all over the world, demanding the immediate release of Mahatma Gandhi. At home, Lord Irwin faced an unrelenting barrage of criticism for the untenable actions of his government. The burgeoning civil disobedience movement had crippled his administration and the police and military had proven inept at maintaining law and order. In the eyes of the stunned world, Britain had taken a humiliating, moral defeat. The ominous Salt March, which had resulted in the brutal beating of unarmed and peaceful marchers, had strengthened the resolve of Indians that they could indeed lift the yoke of foreign rule off their shoulders and obtain complete freedom.

On 25 January 1931, after the intervention of the British Prime Minister, Mohandas along with twenty members of the Congress party, was released from prison. This was to pave the way for a Second Round table Conference to be held in London, after the dismal failure of the first in which not a single representative of the Congress had been present.

In the meantime, the firebrand revolutionary Subhash Chandra Bose had been released from jail after a twelve-month term of rigorous imprisonment. An active participant in the struggle for freedom since his return from England, he had spent several months in and out of jail during the last three years. Bose was deeply appalled by the dastardly hanging of a twenty-three-year-old Sikh revolutionary, Bhagat Singh, along with his two associates—Rajguru and Sukhdev who had been charged for the conspiracy and murder of a superintendent of police three years earlier. The incident had shaken up the very foundation of the British government and infused the entire nation with an unprecedented patriotic fervour.

❈ ❈ ❈

On 29 August 1931, Mohandas set sail for London aboard the S.S. Rajputana accompanied by Devdas, his secretary Mahadev Desai, Pyarelal and a few other co-workers as the sole representative of the Indian National Congress for the Second Round Table Conference. The mood of the people at home was upbeat, contrary to the undisguised rage that had got the authorities in London bristling.

As soon as the ship sailed out of Bombay harbour, I was on a train to Ahmedabad to tend to my assigned work amongst the poor and assist former prisoners in re-adjusting to their families. After working amongst the women for a considerable period of time, I slowly began to recognize that my ability to reach out and teach them, was now an established reality.

In London, the grandiose planning and execution of the Second Round Table Conference came to naught. The hard nosed British aristocrats, who found the sight of the "naked *fakir*" striding up the steps of the palace, nauseating, were in no mood to concede to his demands. Britain's foremost desire to maintain its hold over India was completely at variance with what Mohandas had been demanding unequivocally—*purna swaraj*. Total and unconditional freedom.

Four months later, on 28 December 1932, Mohandas returned to India even more firmly to take his mission of self-governance forward. The news of the failed Round Table Conference had sparked off spontaneous protests nationwide; the imperialistic government used all its might to clamp down on freedom fighters and dilute Mohandas' hold over his people.

Several offices of the Congress party were forcibly raided and their books seized. All their funds were frozen and confiscated. A strict censorship was imposed, journalists were prosecuted and the press gagged. So much so that even a photograph of Gandhi carried by any newspaper was deemed to be a criminal act. The government rounded up and imprisoned 15,000 Indians in January and another 18,000 a month later, of which many were women. The atmosphere had become extremely volatile.

Mohandas was arrested in Bombay just when I had returned to Sabarmati, where the police descended on us and picked up several women. I was the first to be arrested. We were transported to the nearby jail while much of the moveable property at the ashram was seized and taken away. Although I had experienced a jail sentence in South Africa, this was to be my first experience in India. And like the rest who had been arrested with me, I was given a short sentence of six weeks. However, those six weeks in Sabarmati Central Jail were far more torturous and humiliating, but my inner strength kept me and the other women from breaking down.

❋ ❋ ❋

On my release from Sabarmati Central jail, I travelled to Poona to visit Mohandas who had been lodged at the Yerwada prison, but much to my dismay I was informed that he had refused to see any of the visitors.

In a letter to Devdas, who was also in prison, Mohandas wrote:

> *Imprisonment means absence of Rights, therefore I forego all my rights of receiving people or letters to adhere to this requirement. Ba will feel the shock the most, but she is born to endure shocks.*

By mid-summer I had been arrested again and for the second time sent off to Sabarmati Jail; this time for a period of six months. I did not get to see Mohandas even after he had conceded and allowed visitors to call on him.

And then on 20 September 1932 I was informed via a brief handwritten letter from Mohandas that he intended to go on a "fast-unto-death", to protest against the framing of a constitution that had freshly been proposed in London. Not only did it recommend separate electorates for different religious communities, it established the "untouchables" as a separate entity. To Mohandas, this was the greatest assault on his idea of India which strongly rejected a society borne out of religious, caste or class biases. Acceptance of this meant that the Hindus would formalize caste discrimination as decreed by the constitution. He believed that his "fast-unto-death", would 'sting the Hindu conscience into right religious action.'

When I arrived at the formidable gates of the Yerwada Central Jail, I was taken into a large courtyard, by the officer on duty. My heart leapt into my mouth to see Mohandas lying motionless on a metal *charpoy* under the shade of an expansive mango tree. It had been nine months since I had last set eyes on him. He looked pale and malnourished. That "Epic Fast", as it would be later named, was killing him slowly. As I stood there before him, my feet turned to stone. An unnatural calm had subsumed my mind and I felt devoid of any grief.

'Again the same story,' I whispered in his ear as he turned over. My hands felt warm on his moist and cold body. It was time for me to take charge.

Six days later, and despite my intensive nursing, Mohandas' health showed signs of further decline. His life was fast ebbing out. His blood pressure had risen to alarming levels and his frame looked wasted and shrunk. He had dropped almost fifteen pounds and was drifting in and out of consciousness. The authorities were in panic. If Gandhi died in jail, the situation would be unmanageable. That afternoon, the interlocutors finally reached a settlement, the essence of which was, 'henceforth no one is to be regarded as an untouchable.'

The fast-unto-death, punishing as it had been on Mohandas, proved to be a family reunion of sorts. Ramdas was moved to Yerwada to complete the rest of his sentence. Devdas, who had been released from prison, made frequent trips to meet his brother in jail. And Manilal along with Sushila and their four-year-old daughter Sita, arrived at Sabarmati, unexpectedly from South Africa, laden with crates of apples and oranges from Zanzibar. An air of jubilation ran through the Gandhi household.

But Harilal, conspicuous by his painful absence, stirred up my restlessness all over again. I was engulfed by a sense of doom. I had had no news of him ever since the horrific incident with Bali and Manu in Rajkot. I prayed to the Almighty to have mercy on my wayward son!

✂ ✂ ✂

Devdas was thirty-three years old when he married a Tamil Brahmin girl, Laxmi Rajagopalachari, with whom he had been in love for almost five years. Mohandas had been strictly opposed to the inter-caste union as much as the love-match. Being a Modh-

Bania, he believed that inter-caste marriages were never successful and it was imperative for matches to be arranged by parents. But at twenty-seven, Devdas was in the throes of love and his entanglement with the bright-eyed, supremely intelligent Laxmi, the daughter of C Rajagopalachari, only deepened with time.

Compelled by the steadfastness of the young couple, their fathers had stipulated that if the relationship lasted beyond a five-year period of separation, they would be allowed to become man and wife.

On 16 June 1933, Devdas married his beloved Laxmi in the presence of the two beaming fathers and the jubilant families with great pomp and revelry.

Even though I had been imprisoned in January of 1934, the year augured well for me. In the span of just one week, I had become a grandmother of three children. On 14 April, Manilal and Sushila were blessed with their second child, a boy whom they named Arun. Four days later, Usha was born to Ramdas and Nirmala, their third child; and on 22 April, Devdas and Laxmi witnessed the birth of their first child, a girl they named Tara.

By the end of June, I had been released from jail and I set out to join Mohandas with renewed fervour in his work and mission. I was free, but I was homeless. The government had seized Sabarmati Ashram in the last quarter of 1933. Mohandas had commenced his ten-month tour after donating the ashram to a newly-founded society that engaged in the welfare of India's "untouchables". Most of the *satyagrahis* who lived there had left to work on village development projects or had moved away to other ashrams.

By then, Mohandas had also moved to Central India and began living in a mud hut in the village of Sevagram near Wardha. I found him anxious, desperately in need of his hermetic solitude. My being around him would have been intrusive to his mental condition and I could clearly see that he did not need me for his subsistence. For more than two years, I had been living alone, visiting my sons and grandchildren, meeting friends and helping relatives who were needy.

It was a purposeful pilgrimage that took me across the country on missions of charity by providing assistance to special communities. I visited remote towns and villages getting re-acquainted with my people, my sons and my extended family. On some occasions I accompanied Mohandas on his tours outside Wardha, to Benares, where he addressed a large gathering of "untouchables". I travelled to Ahmedabad to be with an ailing Ramdas who was undergoing a series of nature cure therapies. I took his daughter Sumitra to a specialist in Bombay to be treated for an eye ailment. And then I spent some time with Devdas in Delhi, tending to my little Tara who had been ill.

A few times I made it a point to take Manu along with me on these tours. I kept her close to me in an effort to wipe away any pain that she may have carried over after that horrific confrontation with her father in Rajkot, but if there was any trauma festering inside her, she showed no signs of it.

In April 1936, I had travelled with Mohandas to Nagpur to attend an All India Literary Conference, where most unexpectedly, we met our eldest born! Harilal contemptuously announced to his father that several of his Muslim friends wanted to convert him to their religion. I knew right then that that brief and bitter encounter between father and son portended doom.

The last time I had seen him was eighteen months earlier. I vividly remembered that encounter in the small town of Katni where I had accompanied Mohandas on one of his tours.

The tiny station was bursting at its seams as our train halted on the platform. Massive crowds were waiting impatiently for a glimpse of the Mahatma. Loud shouts of 'Mahatma Gandhi *ki jai*' rent the air, even as people jostled around and the sloganeering continued relentlessly. Suddenly, amidst the rising cacophony, the loud cheering from a lone voice streamed into the open window of the stationary train,

'Mata Kasturba ki jai! Mata Kasturba ki jai!'

I peered out of the window, craning my neck to see where this single voice was coming from. My eyes scanned the crowd and settled on an old, bent man dressed in rags, standing on the platform waving his arms wildly; his feeble shouts of *'Mata Kasturba ki jai'* were soon drowned in the noisy outburst of cheering and applause for Mohandas. It was Harilal. I was taken aback.

He staggered up to the window where I sat, wading through the dense crowd, elbowing his way forward, even as he was almost pushed down by the surging masses. He looked up at me, his blood shot eyes had brimmed over. A weak smile stretched across his face. With trembling hands, he held up a stale, shrivelled orange.

'This is for you, Ba, this orange is only for you!' He said as his voice quivered and trailed off. 'And if you are so great Bapu,' he snarled at his father, his mouth curved downwards in a bitter sneer, 'you owe it all to my mother. You are nothing without her!'

Before anyone could react, the train moved forward and thundered out of the station. My eyes filled up, as I watched the sad, forlorn, receding form of Harilal getting swallowed in the sea of cheering faces in the crowd. His faint cries reverberated menacingly in my ears… *'This orange is only for you, Ba!'… Mata Kasturba ki jai…!'*

The orange fell off my lap and with the motion of the moving train, rolled under Mohandas' seat. I saw he had leaned his back against the headrest and closed his eyes, his face contorted with pain.

⁂

Silence stretched between us as I watched the play of emotions on Mohandas' taut face. Some unknown force, the primal shadow that had inextricably tied together the destinies of a father, mother and son was pushing the three onto a predestined path of anguish. Both Mohandas and I shared the guilt of Harilal's anguish. Even though I had always tried to be protective of him, this painful conflict between father and son kept playing out in a fearsome form within me and my heart ached for both.

Seeing him that day at the Nagpur station had sharply jolted me again. It had struck at the bleeding walls of my insides. His struggle against his father's insensitivities had assumed a monstrous form. Harilal was ill, both in body and mind. I could see that his bitterness was festering like sores inside him. He stood at a precarious threshold where for him atonement was possible only if his father was attacked and wounded. His habitual borrowings of money, his bouts of alcoholism and his outbursts of drunken and abusive behaviour were all manifestations of a soul that was dying a slow death. How long would I be able to hold up?

And Harilal just would not relent. The continuous barrage of open letters to his father that had become a public spectacle was distinctly aimed at damaging his image. They purported to validate Harilal's anger and vindicate his stance, but only I knew that they led to further strife between the two men. With great despondency I had heard reports of Harilal's frequent brushes with the law and for the first time that day, I accepted the bitter truth that I had lost my son forever.

In May 1936, a disturbing newsflash was broadcast nationwide.

Harilal Gandhi, son of the Mahatma has become a follower of Islam in a public ceremony in one of the biggest mosques of Bombay. He has adopted the new name Abdullah Gandhi.

In a statement issued to the press, Harilal said,

I have done this to improve myself as a human being.

The newspapers splashed pictures and reports of Harilal addressing milling crowds outside a mosque. Amidst shouts of *'Abdullah Gandhi amar rahe!'…'Abdullah Gandhi zindabad!'* a jubilant and defiant Harilal had fired yet another salvo to injure his benumbed father.

Sixty Four

Mohandas' heart was filled with gloom. It was as if a burning spear had pierced the hitherto unimpeachable fortress of his mind that had never, even in the most trying times, revealed any signs of turmoil. I sat beside him, sphinx-like, not knowing what to say.

'Why do you inflict such pain on us in the twilight of our lives, Harilal?' I mumbled as a torrent of pent up emotions came pouring out of my eyes. It hurt me even more to see that Mohandas had turned to stone. Silenced by the shock of the emotional assault, he retreated to a quiet corner of his room, sat on his mat and began to pray.

It took a while for me to regain my composure. I summoned Devdas and sat down to dictate a letter to my deviant son.

My dear son Harilal,

I have heard that the Madras police arrested you after you were found lying in a drunken state on an open street and a magistrate let you off the next day after imposing a fine of just one rupee. He must have been a very kind man.

Hari, I don't know what to say. All these years I have been pleading with you to stay in check. Just think of the misery you are causing to your ageing parents in the twilight of their lives. You were born as a son to me but are behaving worse than an enemy. In your recent ramblings you have only been abusing, criticizing and ridiculing your father.

Do you realize that you are bringing disgrace upon yourself by speaking ill of him?

Hari, he has nothing in his heart for you but abounding love. He has always been keen to keep you close to him; to feed you, clothe you and even nurse you, but you have never heeded his advise or pleas. He has the burden of so many responsibilities of the world that he cannot do anything more for you. All he can do is lament his misfortune and suffer the disgrace in silence.

But I cannot stand this mental agony any more. Every morning I wake up with a shudder, not knowing what fresh calamity shall befall us. I fear and worry constantly for you. I fear because I don't know where you are, where you sleep, what you eat. I fear that you indulge in forbidden food. I pine to see you but no one knows where you are.

You are almost fifty, Hari. You are my son, my eldest child, but I fear you. I fear to approach you. I fear the prospect of being insulted by you. And now this?

I do not know what has prompted you to change your ancestral religion. It is your business and your choice. Even though I do not approve, it gladdened me to read that you have converted to Islam to better yourself. I felt there was hope and that you would start leading a sober life. Alas! My hopes are dashed to pieces when I see what you have actually become.

I hear that you address massive crowds. You urge ignorant and innocent people to follow your example.

What do you know of religion, Harilal? And what sane judgement can you exercise in your mental condition?

You are playing with people's emotions and lives. Do you realize that they listen to you only because you are Bapu's son? And do you realize that they can be led astray?

Harilal, if you carry on like this you will become a social outcaste, shunned by all.

I beseech you son! Turn back from your folly. Your father has always pardoned you but God shall not pardon your misdeeds.
Ba

It was an open letter "from a mother to a son". Devdas made several copies and sent it to all the leading newspapers for publication. The country woke up to the scandalous development the next morning. The national dailies had carried my letter to Harilal on the front pages. With a mixture of both shock and glee, at every street and crossroad, every home and playground, it became the subject of gossip.

Harilal was in Kanpur when the letter appeared in the newspapers. He glanced at it unenthusiastically and then read it again. A strong skepticism had overcome him as he reflected bitterly:

These could not be Ba's words... she could never have written such a well-structured letter. It had to be Bapu.

He presumed that Bapu was using his mother, to load him with emotional blackmail. He tore the newspaper and threw it in a roadside garbage bin.

At a public meeting that day, he sought it befitting to reply to his mother's appeal.

'I am Abdullah, not Harilal,' he thundered. 'This letter is not for me. It is addressed to Harilal, so I do not accept it. My mother is illiterate. I don't believe she could have written such a letter. I know that someone else is using her to strike at me. Before my conversion I did keep undesirable company, but now, I don't need to learn anything. The only wish I have, is to die a servant of Islam. My mother Kastur Bai has requested me to quit drinking. My reply to this is that I shall indeed give up drinking, the day my father and mother, both embrace Islam!'

In a cloud of exhilaration, amidst thundering applause and loud shouts of *'Allahu Akbar'* and *'Abdullah Gandhi Zindabad,'* Harilal stepped off the podium of a mosque where a huge crowd had collected to cheer him. Wearing a tassel cap, and sporting a scruffy stubble on his unshaven chin, he strode into the milling crowd which was jubilantly shouting slogans.

After a long time that day, Harilal felt a deep thrill, a sweet revenge, for having defeated his father. He had attained his final vindication. 'I am no longer Harilal,' he repeated loudly to himself. 'I am a humble servant of Allah. I have no other God but Allah and no other religion but Islam…'

Uppermost in his mind were the reverberating sounds of the crowds chanting, *'Abdullah Gandhi zindabad! Allahu Akbar…Allahu Akbar.'*

He couldn't wait to get his hands on that bottle of alcohol.

❊ ❊ ❊

Even after my open letter to Harilal was published, I was not at peace. Simmering with hurt and anger, I wondered if Harilal would ever know that as a mother, I felt pained by every groan that escaped his lips, and bled with every wound that was inflicted on him?

I dictated another open letter to Devdas, to be published in the newspapers, in the hope that the voice of a feeble mother would awaken the conscience of the Muslims who were perhaps instrumental in getting Harilal to change his religion.

….I fail to understand your actions…I know and I am glad that a large number of right thinking Muslims and our Muslim friends have condemned this episode. I find this change of faith has made matters worse. Instead of

reprimanding him for his misdeed you have given my son the title of Maulvi. Does your religion permit you to call a person of Harilal's character Maulvi? What pleasure do you find in deifying him like this?

If you truly considered him to be your brother, you would not be doing this, for it serves in no one's interest. Not his, not yours. But if your desire is merely to ridicule us then I have nothing to say. But I feel it is my duty to repeat to you what I have said to my son. You are not doing a right deed in the eyes of God.

Kastur Bai Gandhi

No different from any other day, Harilal had lain alone on his bed, drunk, restless and sleepless. His throbbing head was filled with images of his mother and he felt pained at his impulsive and abusive utterances that morning. He tossed and turned on his crumpled bed all night, overcome by remorse. The slow hours of a tiresome day crawled on painfully, and when he opened his eyes, he was surrounded by darkness, a darkness that terrified him.

He curled himself into a foetal position and passed out.

✄　✄　✄

Mortified of his own shadow, Harilal's will was cracking. He left for Kanpur the following morning with a dull ache in his heart, his head throbbing with the hangover of the previous night. The euphoria of sweet revenge that had surged in his veins was on the wane and he found the task of propagating Islam onerous and hollow. His needs were being taken care of by the people who had pushed him on to this path, but he began to see ulterior motives behind their actions. He was being exploited and used. The promise of a reward of remarriage after his conversion was forgotten by his mentors and the unlimited flow of wealth was nowhere in sight.

Above all else, communal tension in the country was mounting. The final straw was when they conspired to use him for the heinous crime of destroying a Hindu temple. 'You must strike the first blow, Mian Abdullah,' was the fiendish chorus. 'This shall be a victory greater than Mehmood Ghazni's destruction of the Somnath Temple. You shall become an instant hero. And what an impact it shall have! Can you imagine? "Gandhi destroys a Hindu temple!"'

The loud chants of 'Abdullah Gandhi *zindabad*', that rent the air this time made him nervous.

Harilal was rudely shaken. His drunken stupor had vanished. He stood up and waved his hands to silence the ranting crowd. 'Friends!' a hush had descended upon them. 'I don't remember a single instance of Islam that teaches you to destroy places of worship of other religions. I shall not be a part of this.' Then, amidst a ferocious uproar from the crowd assembled there, Harilal strode out. No longer the grand "Abdullah Gandhi", he had become a lowly pariah in the eyes of his Muslim brethren who felt he had betrayed them. The words of my open letter had blistered his heart again. He knew he had to make amends.

Harilal left for Bombay the next morning where on the advice of the reformist Hindus, the Arya Samajis, he reconverted to his original religion. From Abdullah Gandhi, he became Heeralal Gandhi who was made a missionary for the Bharatiya Shradhananda Shudhi Sabha, a Hindu outfit committed to protect people from forcible conversions.

❊   ❊   ❊

The scandalous developments that had led to Harilal's conversion and the subsequent reconversion soon became a matter of household gossip. Tales of his misdemeanours trickled into the ashram constantly. I too was bombarded with regular snippets about Harilal and his sins, but I dared not voice my fears to Mohandas. How ill advised had my Harilal become? And I had no safeguard against the humiliation and defeat that deluged me. Harilal's hatred for his father had assumed demonic proportions. It had become evident to the world, but no one could have imagined how precariously dovetailed was I in this battle between the Gandhi men.

In those trying moments of our life, Mohandas decided to write a letter to Harilal. It was a pained cry of a father to a son. He hoped to get across to him in his vulnerability; a message to tell him to hold a mirror to himself and stop his certain self-destruction. Harilal was even more infuriated by his Bapu's letter. On reading those unwarranted preachings from his father, he was once again struck by self pity, for never having been appreciated or understood by the man whom he had eulogized as a child and emulated in his early adulthood. Once again he was reminded that his father had used me, his beloved Ba, as an instrument to get at him through my open letter that had been published nationwide.

'Ba is just a shadow of Bapu,' he ruminated contemptuously.

'He has never allowed her to have her own identity.'

When the fury inside him mounted to a point of explosion, he sat down to write a befitting reply to his father.

Respected Bapu

I received your letter. Whenever you write to me you use just one approach. I don't think it is compassionate but you seem to like it that way, so what can I say?

In ancient times kings used elephants to break the gates of strong forts, and to shield their elephants, they used camels allowing them to die in the process.

You are using Ba in the same manner, as a cover. The letter published in the newspapers has your style. I know Ba did not write it.

You say that my misdeeds trouble Ba. But the pertinent question is who really troubles Ba? Is it you or I?

Ba only sees what you show her. In my opinion you have never allowed her to have an identity of her own.

In all these days she has not written a single letter to me. I know she will only write if you allow her to.

Your obedient son Harilal

It was clear to me that my son had become a rootless, aimless, vagrant all over again.

Sixty Five

March 1936

By the end of the year I had moved to the ashram Sevagram, into my own single-room hut with crude mud-plastered walls and earthen tiles. Segaon, where the ashram was built was a tiny village a few miles away from Wardha that had become the hub of activity after Mohandas had set his eyes on it. An industrialist-philanthropist, Jamnalal Bajaj, who owned a large portion of that arid land had donated his holdings to Mohandas. From what began as a single, thatched-roof hut for him soon turned into a vibrant ashram, with all the trappings of the earlier ones. After three long years of leading a nomadic life that consisted of endless train journeys and thousands of public meetings, to me this was nothing short of heaven.

Soon other followers joined in and a new "Gandhian community" came to life. Sevagram transformed into a small self-sufficient village with its well-defined roads mapped out in the wilderness, its manicured green lawns, ground-water wells, a large community kitchen, and a school for the children of the ashram as well as those of adjoining villages. While the number of new converts to the cause of *satyagraha* kept growing, Mohandas' old friends Henry Polak and Hermann Kallenbach also arrived and although they filled the air with bonhomie, reliving their days in South Africa, Mohandas remained unusually withdrawn. His health had been troubling him. He had frequent bouts of fluctuating blood pressure. The hot dry weather and the small stuffy rooms made it impossible for him to sleep indoors, so he slept out in the open, which was also part of his self-devised nature cure regimen. Though winter was bitterly cold in Segaon, Mohandas continued sleeping out in the open, but his frail health showed no signs of improvement. Eventually a doctor was called in, who advised him to move back indoors immediately, at least during the bitter winter or else face grave health issues.

Mohandas, obdurate and difficult as he was, paid no heed to the doctor's advice till one of ashram inmates, a British-born woman, Madeleine Slade who had been given the name Mirabehn by Mohandas, vacated her cottage for him. Mirabehn had been a devoted follower of the Mahatma since 1931. She was so taken up by his life and message that she cut her hair short, donned white *khadi* and undertook the mandatory vow of celibacy to join his inner circle of followers.

Mohandas was unmoved by Mirabehn's offer to let him sleep in her quarters, but I was greatly piqued. It was time for me to step in. That evening after the prayer service ended, I loudly proclaimed before all assembled there, 'From now on, Bapu shall sleep in my cottage.'

A low murmur broke out in the crowd, but without waiting for anyone to speak I marched out and the matter was settled. Mohandas' bed was moved in to my cottage while mine was moved out to the verandah. With me moved Ramdas' little son Karsandas, who had been in my care for some time.

Mohandas had a restful night in my hut after many sleepless ones and the stream of visitors that arrived the next day found him in a sombre mood.

'Poor Ba!' He lamented. 'This little cottage was specially built for her. I had supervised its construction myself to give her comfort and privacy in her old age. But now I have occupied it,' he sighed. 'Wherever I go, it becomes a dormitory. It hurts me, but she never complains…'

I interrupted them with a loud peal of laughter. The surprised visitors joined in and the place resounded with cheer and joy that had eluded us for a long time.

For now, my life seemed near perfect. Despite his overzealousness, in the quest for the ultimate truth, Mohandas was content. All the children and grandchildren were either with us, or led their own lives. Except Harilal. He was the one tragic casualty in my otherwise perfect universe who would never forgive me for his betrayal. As a mother, that was my lot!

✄ ✄ ✄

In September of 1939 the Second World War broke out in which two superpowers were engaged in a full-fledged, disastrous battle that threatened to destroy humankind. A sinister atmosphere of a deep insecurity prevailed all over. On the one hand, while representatives of the British Crown were completely at sea, the authorities in London were stretched to their limits in the ongoing war.

Menacing war clouds hovered over the cities of Bombay and Calcutta that had been vacated for fear of aerial bombings. The British were well aware that in order to tide over the grave war effort, they required the support of their colonies and foremost of those being India. Therefore, they lost no time and approached Mohandas to ensure that he used his influence over the large population to strengthen their might in the war against the enemy. But much to the chagrin of the Crown, Mohandas refused and was resolute in his decision to keep away from what was not only a clever political decision, considering he had been deceived once earlier during the First World War, but also more importantly, he was now the Mahatma, a prophet of peace who was opposed to violence of any kind. Mohandas however added a sting to the tail and informed the British that he and his fellow countrymen were now focussed on a common goal—total and unconditional freedom.

By this time a large number of revolutionaries who over the years had become ardent supporters of the *satyagraha* and devotees of the Mahatma, were out on the streets as part of a non-cooperation movement to counter-attack the British. Most prominent among them was a young, Kashmiri Brahmin, Jawaharlal Nehru, a highly qualified England-returned barrister with an impressive lineage, who swiftly became Mohandas' most trusted lieutenant.

Bristling with demonic frenzy, the government reacted to the protests violently. What followed was a spate of arrests and imprisonments, mass *lathi*-charges and sporadic cases of arson. Jawaharlal was arrested after being tried for sedition, a charge that he did not care to refute. He was sentenced to a four-year term of rigorous imprisonment, which sparked off a chain of violent protests and more arrests that threatened the stability of the subcontinent.

A young barrister, Mohammed Ali Jinnah, who had also returned from England to spearhead the cause of his fellowmen, was leader of a political party, the Indian Muslim League. Jinnah found himself sharply pitted against Nehru, who enjoyed undue favour with Mohandas.

The man born to a prosperous merchant in Kathiawar seven years after Mohandas' birth, could have never imagined that he would cross swords with him in a sharp conflict of ideology on his return. Himself an unorthodox Muslim, Jinnah had managed to persuade his brethren to throw their weight behind him. The religious divide between the Hindus and Muslims had never been this starker. The clamour for a separate Islamic state by a group of people, virtually perched on the mouth of a volcano, was growing to a deafening pitch. Arson, looting and riots could spark off at the slightest provocation and fear had penetrated deep into every Indian's heart.

Meanwhile, a spontaneous uprising against the centuries-old Indian monarchy had erupted all over India. Many of the revolutionary leaders feared that there would be mass violence if the movement was not checked. Moreover, the unity and stability of a free India would be in peril if the princely states were awarded self-rule, since they were insistent on securing their fiefdoms, which was obviously against the very kernel of a democracy. Although the Congress supported the campaign for protecting the civil and political rights of the people of Mysore, Travancore, Jaipur and Hyderabad, the crises showed no signs of abating. It escalated beyond control in the princely state of Rajkot where the cruel, despotic ruler was in no mood to relent. To add to that were rumours of the Thakore's sexual exploits with young women whom he frequently abducted and imprisoned in his summer palace, for his whimsical pleasures.

Mohandas appointed his close associate Vallabhbhai Patel, a trusted *satyagrahi* and an able administrator to oversee the negotiations between the people of Rajkot and their tyrannical Thakore. Assuming that the Thakore was being manipulated by the resident British Political Agent, the people of Rajkot decided to step up the protest against the misery unleashed by the regent. A large number of women who had been sexually exploited in the past, enlisted themselves and joined in the non-violent protests, offering to court arrest. The first to be detained was Vallabhbhai Patel's daughter, Maniben.

The news of this disturbing development was received with the greatest fury at Sevagram. I was particularly indignant because Maniben was one of the younger women *satyagrahis* closest to my heart. This was no longer a matter of political and civil rights, it was a question of women's honour.

On 31 January 1939, I left for Rajkot along with another dedicated young woman activist, Mridula, Ambalal Sarabhai's daughter. Immediately after my arrival, I began addressing large groups of women, urging them to join the protest to demand their rights and seek protection from the evil Thakore's sexual atrocities. I was arrested by the local authorities three days later and transported to Tramba, the royal summer palace of ill-repute, the place where sexual crimes were perpetrated by the fiendish Thakore of Rajkot, and was locked up inside a dark room for over a week. The Thakore believed that he could terrorize me into giving up my mission. At seventy, in solitary confinement with my history of frequent fainting spells, he thought he could easily break me, both in body and spirit.

That the satrap had grossly miscalculated became evident when outside the prison compound, fresh clashes broke out in protest of my arrest. He was compelled to relieve me of my solitary confinement and I was allowed brief strolls in the grounds of the summer palace under the strict watch of security guards.

Meanwhile, Mridula Sarabhai and Maniben Patel, who had been lodged in separate jails in Rajkot, were also brought to the palace to keep me company. Among other concessions, I was given access to letters Mohandas had been writing to me. He had heard that I had suffered several fainting spells in confinement that had made him deeply concerned about the state of my health. His letters were filled with apprehension.

Stay free of care wherever you are placed, Kastur. God is with you wherever you go…

This rare display of tenderness tugged at the strings of my heart, but Mohandas was in a state of extreme anxiety and that made me unhappy. He wrote,

You are being put to a severe test. You must tell us the difficulties you face. We at the ashram all feel your absence. Be brave…

And then, in another note to Mridula and Maniben that created a knot in my stomach, he said,

It is God's grace that you both are with her in Tramba…

Mohandas arrived in Rajkot three weeks later. He had been reluctant to get drawn into the locals' revolt against a tyrannical ruler. But reports of indiscriminate arrests and the cruel treatment being meted out to prisoners compelled him into action.

After a brief, tearful union with me at Tramba, he visited the two jails of Rajkot to meet the other imprisoned activists. He was convinced that the only way to deal with the situation was to begin his most dreaded, "fast-unto-death". The Thakore was duly notified of Mohandas' plan. Unless he agreed to the release of all prisoners unconditionally and initiate reforms, there would be a strong protest! A similar message was sent to Lord Linlithgow, the Viceroy in Delhi.

What had begun as a minor regional unrest in a remote state of India, now threatened to become a full-blown political war.

On 3 March, after receiving no response from the Thakore, Mohandas commenced his fast. After listening to a rendition of his favourite hymn, *Raghupati Raghav Raja Ram… Patita pavana Sita Ram,* he dictated a statement to the press.

The news of his "fast-unto-death" deeply troubled me for I knew it would pose a serious risk to his life.

God has taken care of him during all his earlier trials. He shall see him safely through this one too…

I said aloud, but the nervous tremor in my voice belied my words.

Three days later, the Thakore's deputies, acting on the advice of the weak-kneed authorities in Delhi, released me from Tramba Palace and I was escorted to Rajkot jail where Mohandas was held captive.

A day later, Maniben and Mridula were also set free. By the time Mohandas had entered the fourth day of his fast, an agreement had been arrived at. The Thakore granted amnesty to all prisoners arrested during the protest rallies and agreed to appoint a political reform committee to look into the various grouses and amend the excesses unleashed on his people.

Mohandas' fast ended on a note of triumph. We returned to Sevagram a jubilant lot, having crossed one more milestone of success in the long battle for the restoration of civil liberties and human rights of our people.

An uncontainable thrill racked my being. I knew we were steadily inching towards our glorious dream of a free India. With that infallible weapon of peaceful resistance at his command, nothing could stop Mohandas now!

✠ ✠ ✠

7 December 1941

Before the sun rose on the eastern horizon of the tranquil islands of Japan, hundreds of their fighter planes had bombarded the American naval base at Hawaii's, Pearl Harbour. It had been more than two years into the Second World War and America finally declared an offensive against Japan. In India, over 20,000 political prisoners were locked up, many for over a year, for participating in the civil disobedience campaign initiated by Gandhi.

Japan's involvement in the war posed a severe threat to South East Asia and all the other colonies of the British Empire. This precipitated a tremendous degree of discontentment that led the Congress Working Committee to convene at Wardha where a "Quit India" resolution was to be passed. It was an opportune time to leverage the position. In order to become willing partners of the colonial masters, the resolution demanded that all Indians must feel the "glow of freedom". It warned the British government that unless their rule ended immediately, the Congress would be compelled to start a nationwide civil disobedience movement under the leadership of Mahatma Gandhi.

Earlier in Calcutta, Subhash Chandra Bose's clarion call to hand India to Indians had led to massive revolts and he had been put in jail. Subsequently, to the embarrassment of the government, Bose flew the coup and reached Germany via Afghanistan and Russia.

For the next three weeks, tensions began to mount. The Congress Working Committee convened a meeting in Bombay where Gandhi's clarion call 'Leave India to God…or to anarchy' became the booming battle cry on every Indian's lips.

❃ ❃ ❃

By daybreak on 9 August 1942, Mohandas, Mahadevbhai and I, along with thousands of other Indians, were rounded up and stuffed into different jails across the country. Both Mohandas and I were locked up at the Aga Khan Palace in Poona, leading millions to court arrest, on the call of Gandhi.

Moments before he was whisked away by the police, Mohandas dictated a note to his secretary, Pyarelal:

Let every non-violent soldier of freedom write out the slogan 'Do or Die' on a piece of paper and pin it on his clothes so that in case he died in the course of satyagraha, he might be distinguished by that sign from the others who do not subscribe to non-violence.

Deluged by the mass hysteria of a movement that had become a flaming inferno of patriotic fervour, the entire nation was in the paroxysm of just one cry aimed at the British, "Quit India!"

❃ ❃ ❃

On the morning of 15 August 1942, there was an unusual flurry of activity on the grounds of the Aga Khan Palace. Before daybreak, sweepers were called to spruce up the place in anticipation of a visit by the Inspector General of Prisons. Guards could be seen pacing up and down the area nervously and prison officials were inspecting every nook and cranny of the jail premises. Gardeners were hurriedly pruning hedges and flowers were being gathered to put into vases.

Sarojini Naidu, another prison inmate and a long time *satyagrahi*, and I, arranged bouquets of flowers in each room awaiting the arrival of the Colonel. Mohandas, unperturbed by the frenzy outside, lay in his room getting his morning massage. At seventy-three, with his frequent fasts and lengthy detentions, his health was always a matter of concern for the authorities, so these small allowances had been granted to him.

The Colonel arrived with the customary paraphernalia amidst much fanfare. Mahadev and I rushed out to the verandah to greet him, but no sooner had Mahadev stretched his hand to the Inspector General, he collapsed in a heap on the floor. He clutched wildly at his chest gasping for breath, his eyes rolled into their sockets and he fainted.

'Someone help! Someone, Sushila—come quickly!' I screamed. Sushila Nayyar, the younger sister of Pyarelal, and a physician came rushing out on hearing the commotion. She bent over Mahadev's lifeless body to check his pulse. His heartbeat had slowed down, his heaving breath was spasmodic, and even as she knelt beside him, his breathing had stopped. Mahadevbhai was dead.

The sudden death of the gentle and sincere Mahadev, who had been Mohandas' indispensible aide, hit everyone like a bolt of lightning. A deep pall of gloom settled over the palace. The grieving inmates, who had collected outside, placed wreaths of flowers on his corpse. Within a few hours, a disconsolate Mohandas lit the funeral pyre of Mahadev Desai on the grounds of that ominous palace and his body was consigned to flames.

I felt an icy chill run down my spine. I folded my arms tightly across my hurting chest trying not to let the tremor pervade the rest of my body. Death had cast its shadow inside the walls of the Aga Khan Palace. It wouldn't be long before it struck again.

Meanwhile, Subhash Chandra Bose had been broadcasting messages from Berlin that his outfit the Azad Hind Fauj would join hands with Germany and Japan to fight against the British. He had begun a march from Singapore to India, to further his plan.

Sixty Six

Mahadev's ominous death had taken a heavy toll on us. Life had changed for all the inmates of the Aga Khan Palace and Mohandas looked increasingly restless with each passing day. We had not been receiving any newspapers or letters during the first few months of our imprisonment, but Mohandas had written a letter to the authorities to protest against this, following which the ban was revoked.

It was only after reading the newspapers did we learn that Gandhi's arrest had sparked off massive and widespread riots across the nation. A frustrated and emotionally drained Mohandas began working out a time-schedule for the inmates of the palace jail to keep their morale from sagging further.

Imprisoned together in the 61st year of our married life, the long abandoned project of my education was reactivated and became a compulsory part of my timetable. Over the years I had picked up a working knowledge of English and was able to read simple Gujarati, but now Mohandas began proper tutorials in history and geography as well. And one hour a day was reserved for lessons in the Bhagavad Gita, much of which I had already memorized.

In the beginning, these lessons were a great source of enjoyment for me and I looked forward to them eagerly, but at seventy-three, with my failing memory and weakened faculties, it was an onerous task to memorize and recall so many facts and figures.

'Perhaps those frequent bouts of illness have damaged my brain,' I moaned to a despairing Mohandas after I had failed to recall a couple of dates from the history lesson.

But my Gujarati lessons were enjoyable. Mohandas had found a textbook of Gujarati poetry, the contents of which could be sung to a rhythm. He was aware of my love for music, and he devised an easy method to help me memorize them. Every evening before the prayer service, he would sit with me in the verandah that overlooked the lush green gardens of the palace and sing. It was as if the two of us, united by the thread of eternal love, had rediscovered a mystical plane that brought us closer. It made me feel complete once again. However, like all dreams, this one too would come to an abrupt end.

The tutorials rolled along each day, some enjoyable and others, deeply frustrating, but they never stopped. My lessons in reading progressed at a snail's pace and since my writing skills were not that developed, an extra hour was allocated to me for writing-practice. In keeping with Mohandas' belief of conservation and no wastage, I was given a chalk and slate for my practice.

One day, at what turned out to be an ill-timed moment, I said to Mohandas, 'Can you get me a notebook and pen, please? I don't want to practice my writing on this silly old slate.'

Mohandas grimaced. With political tensions mounting outside and the authorities paying no heed to his demands, he was at his wits' end. What was worse was that even the *satyagrahis* seemed to be disregarding his word. There had been reports of protestors turning violent in some places. Although the entire nation was electrified by the battle cry for freedom, he was losing control over the activists. Mohandas' patience snapped.

'I'll get you a notebook only after you learn to write properly,' he lashed out. 'Until then you shall use the slate.' His mouth curved downwards into a scowl.

Those stinging words hit me hard. I flung the piece of chalk and slammed the slate on the table and stood up.

'I am done with my lessons for life, thank you,' I shouted as I bowed my head and hurried out of the room holding back my tears.

A few days later, I saw Pyarelal enter my room carrying a pen and a new notebook.

'This is for your writing practice, Ba,' he said cheerily.

I knew it was an effort on the part of Mohandas to make amends. I took the book from Pyarelal, marched into Mohandas' room and flung it on his desk.

'Why would an illiterate like me need a notebook?' I fumed and stomped out. That was the end of my husband's zealous literacy scheme.

Mohandas apologized to me several times that day, but my vanity had been piqued once too often and I was not in a mood to relent this time.

That ominous notebook stayed with him like a dark reminder of an irreparable blow he had delivered to me in the twilight of my life. But with time, my resentment dulled and finally, faded away.

⚜ ⚜ ⚜

1943

The day began with a walk to the spot where Mahadev had been cremated. Mohandas and I placed a garland of fresh marigolds on his *samadhi* with a prayer on our lips. Mohandas was in a sombre mood. There was malicious propaganda being spread in the country against his call for the British to "Quit India". Taking advantage of his confinement in the Aga Khan Palace and a complete black out of communication from their leader, the people were being fed with all kinds of mischievous lies. Vile rumours were floating around that the "Quit India" movement was going to be a violent attempt by the Indians to overthrow the British. Mohandas had even written a letter of clarification to the Viceroy, but on receiving no satisfactory reply he had decided to undertake a fast-unto-death.

Once again, the news of his fast spread like wildfire across the country. Gripped by anxiety, thousands of people gathered outside the palace gates to keep vigil. The authorities were well aware that Gandhi was in poor health and if he died in custody, then the country would surely combust. In order to pre-empt any such calamity, the British administration had deputed a government physician at the palace to take care of him.

Meanwhile, three members of the Viceroy's Council who were known for their strong anti-Congress views resigned, demanding the immediate release of the Mahatma.

The government was caught in a bind. Hundreds of requests for the release of Mohandas flooded the offices at London and Delhi. But despite the mounting pressure, the authorities not only ignored all the pleas, but further hardened their stance. The Viceroy believed that there was no moral justification to bow down to this mischievous political blackmail. British Prime Minister Winston Churchill was even harsher in his retort that was broadcast to the world.

'Let him starve to death, if he insists.' It was clear that the government was in no mood to relent.

Inside the Aga Khan Palace, Mohandas was sinking by the hour and outside, national hysteria had peaked to a point of no return.

✖ ✖ ✖

After a gruelling twenty days, Mohandas finally broke his fast. The government eventually succumbed to pressure and opened the gates for the public to prove that their beloved and revered messiah was alive and was no longer in the grips of a deathly starvation. Throughout the three-week period of his perilous fast I had been fired by a demonic energy that kept me going, but once it ended I felt completely drained of my strength.

Barely a fortnight later, it was my turn to fall ill. I suffered severe breathlessness and a violent bout of coughing that lasted for two hours. A week later I had another attack that subsided after four agonizing hours of continuous coughing. All day long I felt a constant ache in my chest that made me weak and anxious.

Meanwhile, a strong rumour began circulating outside the palace walls that Kasturba Gandhi was dead. Fearing a massive outbreak of riots, the government was out of its depth trying to scotch the rumour and on Mohandas' constant urging, the authorities agreed to allow my sons to visit me in jail.

In response to my pleas, my fifteen-year-old grand-niece Manu was transferred to the Aga Khan Palace where she had been imprisoned during the mass arrests following the call to

Quit India. Manu, a namesake of my beloved Harilal's daughter was the great-granddaughter of Mohandas' uncle Tulsidas. She had lived with us for a long time in Sevagram, after the death of her mother. I had virtually adopted her and she cared for me as a daughter, nurse and a companion. I felt a sense of comfort with her nursing me in prison.

Each day, I eagerly looked forward to the visits of my sons Ramdas and Devdas that made me forget that I was seriously ill. At times my beloved granddaughter Manu accompanied them, and I was overjoyed to see her cheerful and happy in their company. The sight of Manu tugged at my aching heart that went out to the missing Harilal. I had not heard from him in months. I had last seen him at the Katni station, some time ago, after which he had written a brief postcard to greet me on new year.

Ba,

Now when I am rendered a bit disabled what can I pray for? I only ask God to give you and Bapu another 10 years for I do not have many years to live.

Sadly, God had other plans.

❊ ❊ ❊

Harilal's piteous face came alive before my misting eyes. I felt that excruciating pain sear up my chest again. I clutched at my ribs and shouted out to Manu. It did not take very long for the prison doctor to diagnose that I had a dangerous heart condition and needed complete rest.

How could I tell the doctor that I could give my body all the rest it required, but who would help me calm my strung-out mind?

I had propped myself up on my pillows when I met Ramdas the next day. Every word I spoke sent a stabbing pain into my chest.

'Find Harilal for me, son,' I said between laboured breaths. 'And tell him his Ba waits constantly for his letters…' I sank back on the bed racked by sobs that couldn't slow down my racing heart.

All the other jail inmates had been informed of my deteriorating condition. No medicines were of any help. Even the doctors had failed.

In January 1944 I suffered two successive heart attacks after which, seriously debilitated in body and spirit I contracted the dreaded pneumonia. I was dying and the only hope to save me was the administering of penicillin, a drug manufactured exclusively in America. The jail authorities sent an urgent message to Delhi to procure the drug without any further delay.

Meanwhile Ramdas' frantic attempts to locate Harilal bore fruit. He found him wandering aimlessly after he had been reconverted from Abdullah to Heeralal, but in an even more deplorable state than before. In the grip of extreme poverty, his addictions and depravity, he was barely managing to survive on some meagre financial help that he received from friends.

On hearing of my critical condition, Harilal first rushed to Poona and then arrived at the Aga Khan Palace. Frail and emaciated, I lay listless on my bed when he entered. He bent down and touched his forehead to my feet. My eyes brimmed over. My throat was locked in a painful spasm. I ruffled his dry, unkempt hair and pulled him close. 'Come here, son,' I rasped. 'You don't look well.'

Mohandas was seated cross-legged beside me on the floor. He watched the emotional union between mother and son silently. A painful expression flickered across his eyes.

'Stay here, close to me, Hari.' I whispered. 'Don't go away. I worry for you. You can come and see me anytime. Come like Ramdas and Devdas do…'

Harilal clasped my hands and wrapped his arms tightly around me.

'Don't worry, Ba,' he said. 'I shall come as often as you want me to… I shall be with you for as long as you say, Ba; I shall never leave you, never.'

I wept. Harilal wept and Mohandas…he bowed his head without speaking a word.

✂ ✂ ✂

The next day I woke up feeling slightly stronger. The meeting with Harilal and the hope that I would henceforth be seeing him regularly had brought a glow to my face. Or perhaps my face had brightened to reflect the quiet arrival of my impending death, waiting to strike.

Later that day all the inmates gathered around me to chant and pray.

I could see Devdas, but there was no sign of Harilal. The day crawled at a painfully slow pace. The evening shadows lengthened and merged in the cover of darkness, but there was still no sign of Harilal. I could not get myself to shut my eyes that waited to catch a glimpse of my beloved son. I waited all night, drifting in and out of consciousness, calling out his name.

When the sun rose the next morning, I could see a faint glimmer of light in the room that had filled with people. My eyes flitted in the dimly-lit room from face to face, person to person, searching desperately for Harilal.

'Can someone telephone Harilal?' I managed a barely audible whisper. My chest heaved violently and slowed down.

'Call him someone. Please!' I whispered again. 'I don't have much time.'

My eyelids, heavy with the effect of the disease had closed. My mind was bursting with crazy thoughts. Did Harilal fall asleep in a drunken stupor? Did he not care that his mother was on her deathbed? I felt a rush of tears fill my eyes, after which I lost all consciousness. But rest eluded me. How could I leave without bidding my Harilal a final farewell?

Harilal staggered into my room late that afternoon. He was in the same unwashed and tattered clothes that he had worn the day before. There was a soiled cloth bag slung on his drooping shoulders. His eyes were bloodshot, his face unshaved and haggard and his legs were trembling. He could barely stand. He steadied himself against the door and took slow faltering steps towards me. A hushed silence engulfed the people collected there. He stretched his arms forward to touch my feet.

'Ba, how are you feeling now?' he mumbled.

The quivering sound of my son's voice fell on my numbed ears and my eyes fluttered open. I focussed on his face and a deep sigh escaped my lips. I tried to raise my hands to touch him, but did not have the strength to lift them. I saw him sway to one side as he moved closer to my face. A strong smell of alcohol hit my nostrils and permeated the air. My face contorted with the foul stench. Another laboured sigh escaped from my slack mouth.

'You are drunk, Hari? At this time? When your Ba is dying? I don't know which of my sins are revisiting me that I have to see you drunk like this, standing by your mother's deathbed.'

My chest heaved violently again. Broken, piteous sobs rent the air. They did not stop till my breath turned into a painful rasp and someone propped me up to help me sip some water.

Harilal stood beside me. He held my face in his rough palms and put his head on my frail chest.

'No! I am not drunk, Ba…I am not drunk.' His words slurred and his rotting teeth were visible through his parched lips. It was hard for him to speak a single coherent word. I mustered up all my strength to prevent myself from weeping loudly, but a long guttural wail gushed out from my heaving chest.

'Why do you lie to me, son? Why? Oh God! What sins have I committed that I am being tortured thus?' I let out a loud moan. 'Hey Govinda! Hey Govinda! Why am I being punished like this in the last hours of my life?'

My clenched fists were striking my forehead with a fiendish force as I kept on chanting 'Govinda! Govinda!' till I fell silent. The tears kept flowing out of my closed eyes.

Harilal collapsed on the floor in a heap. He was scooped up by two men who dragged him out of the room. Mohandas and Devdas jumped up and clasped my hands. Everyone present in the room began to cry. I lay still on the bed, exhausted and numb. I had not noticed Mohandas stare at my face helplessly. By then, darkness had engulfed me.

I was still in a semi-conscious state when the penicillin arrived. The doctor had checked my heartbeat and pulse. I heard someone say, 'It won't be of much help. She is too feeble to withstand this.' I heard Mohandas say, 'Don't give it to her.'

Then I heard Devdas' pleading voice. It came in receding echoes from a distance. 'Please Bapu, please, let them give her that penicillin injection. It's her only chance.'

The rising crescendo of continuous chants of verses from the Ramayana drowned out all else. The rendition continued through the night. I drifted in and out of darkness and light. Mohandas' voice was the loudest of all. I forced my eyes open and saw him sitting beside me, at dawn.

'You go and sleep…I shall call you before I die. I won't leave until you are near me…' I barely managed to say.

My eyes had shut. My breathing was hard and rapid. My most adored granddaughter Manu was sitting beside me. My hand dropped lifelessly on her lap and I drifted away. I felt Harilal by my side a little later. He took the holy *Ganga-jal* from an urn that had been placed near my bed. With trembling hands he held the spoon to my mouth.

'Are you still drunk, Hari?' I asked, but no sound came from my mouth. I felt the sweet nectar of the gods trickle down my constricted throat drop by drop.

I forced my eyes open and focussed on the people standing around me. Mohandas, Harilal, Devdas, Manu, all blurred faces stricken with fear looking intently at me. I stretched my clammy hand to Mohandas. He held it tenderly in his palms.

'God, my refuge… Thy mercy I crave!'

The last words that escaped from my dying lips rose up in the air and mingled with the ether. My mouth froze in a crooked smile as my body contorted and then went limp. I felt myself merge into a shaft of blinding blue light that cocooned me. I did not see Harilal double over on the floor, overcome with grief.

Nor did I hear the loud and piteous wail of my loved ones, rent the air.

❊   ❊   ❊

Afterword

Sixty Seven

August 1946

A warm, humid night hangs over the marshes of Noakhali. It has rained incessantly and the muffling downpour has clogged the lungs of the people living there. The house reeks of mildew and damp clothes. Mosquitoes are out in droves, humming about, seeking blood with the persistence that no 'neem' leaves can diminish. Gossamer-thin white nets lie draped like ghosts over the cot and mattress where Mohandas lies. The air is thick with the putrid smell of death. Thousands of Hindus and Muslims have been raped, looted and butchered in the frenzied riots that erupted on Id and continued unabated for days after.

Hark! I hear the cry of a distraught man. He is overcome with anguish and tears flow out of his rheumy eyes. He beckons me. I hear him again. He is calling out my name. His voice trembles amidst sobs and recedes into a deep chasm of nothingness. I hear that piteous cry again and again. I feel myself floating down into his vista. He turns his face upwards to the yellowed ceiling covered with cracked and peeling paint.

'Kastur, my beloved, don't turn your back on me,' he mumbles. 'In the eyes of the world, I am a selfish pursuant of my experiments with truth, a sinner. The vile compulsion to preserve the vital fluid of life drives me to desperation. My motherland, the country that I have loved with every fibre of my soul is being sawn mercilessly into two. I am wading through rivers of fire and blood, bare-bodied, bare feet, to carry my message of peace, but no one heeds my word. I am flailing desperately to stay afloat. This

is my sad plight? But Kastur, my soul! The life long torchbearer of my vision, I know you see me differently. Who can know better than you how my heart bleeds when my failures stare me in my face? I have only my sexual lapses and mortal imperfections to blame for the crises and calamities in the world. Only you can help me discover what is blocking my single minded pursuit of celibacy and ahimsa.

Yet, in the eyes of the world I am a sinner, an egocentric self-obsessed freak. They think my propensity for intense self-absorption has clouded my vision. All of them do. Jawahar, Patel and all the rest. Even those whom I nurtured in my lap like a mother.

Tell me, my beloved Kastur. Tell me that you do not believe that the onset of old age has impaired my thought and distorted my perceptions.

I make my last effort to acquire absolute control over my libido. It has to be both in my thoughts and my actions. This is my last hope of injecting spiritual energy into the cosmos that can stem the ongoing bloody massacre that fast envelops my motherland.

I sleep naked. And on either side of me in my bed, lie Manu and Abha, also disrobed. Our souls intertwined, their breath resonates with mine. Our bodies touch, but they are flung far apart, separated by a vast universe of carnal desires. I make no pretense about this. What is not secret, is no sin. I have endeavoured to practice complete restraint, and master my carnality.

Is this a sin, to drift along in pursuit of that ever-elusive mirage? Help me, Kastur. Don't dismiss it as a diversion of my vitality. My grief and my failures cannot be shared. They cannot be transferred, but please don't call this a barren pursuit of a selfish dream.

Not you Kastur, not you! You must understand.

His body racks with uncontrollable sobs. His glazed eyes fix on a crack in the ceiling. I peer into his deep sockets ridden with bloodied veins that throb with pain. I feel his searing torment, far greater than a burning fresh wound. His tears dry up on the gaunt and sallow cheeks sucked into the oral cavity of his age-lined face and his stark body lies crumpled in a heap on the metal charpoy that has become his regular sexual laboratory.

I can see him drenched in sweat. Beads of perspiration line the folds of his brow. The two naked women that lie on either side must experience deeply conflicting emotions, but appear to be asleep. For them the experiment has eradicated the fine line that exists between the spiritual and the sensual, for they have surrendered their personal dilemmas, body and soul at the feet of their lord. They are totally oblivious of the violently conflicting demons warring inside the mind and body of the magnificent mahatma who has chosen them to be his bedmates that day in this union of bizarre uncoupling. To be the chosen one is a great elevation in their status. The squabble for that proud privilege erupts each night before his bedtime at the ashram. All the female inmates clamour to be his partners in this experiment, but no trace of the tussle shows on the quiet countenance of the two sleeping girls.

How could this be a successful test of their celibacy? In this a two-way street, how can he not think of their feelings, their arousal? To test the limits of sexual desires of these craving nubile women, who revere and love Mohandas as a superior divine being, to whom they have wedded their souls is cruel, as it is unholy. Shouldn't someone be monitoring their levels of arousal? Do their stirrings go unnoticed or are they ignored and suppressed because they don't matter? They sleep in his bed because they have succumbed to their irresistible attraction for a man whom the world venerates and adores as a saint; but who they pine for.

Bathed in sweat, he turns over and falls asleep. The telltale pool of that felonious, wasted life-force mocks at him, portending failure of gargantuan proportions and sure damnation to hell. Indeed truth is a good slogan, but confronted in the corridors of reality, it doesn't enlighten, it emasculates. And if stretched to an absurd level of madness, destroys all peace within.

I cannot deny that I am deeply moved by his plight, but what can I do to alleviate his agony? He is doomed to wallow in the failure of his pledge and his mission. And I? I am a helpless spectre, devoid of power. I quietly recede into the ether, back to my quintessential haven of death's solitude.

'Kastur my beloved, set me free!' The agonizing rasps of the anguished and failed emperor of peace, have robbed me of mine!

❈ ❈ ❈

SIXTY EIGHT

14 August 1947

It is the midnight hour when the dream of a nation has come to fruition. A jubilant crowd of men and women has filled the benches of a vast assembly hall in Delhi.

A tall handsome man wearing a *khadi* cap, a white *achkan* with a red rose affixed in its lapel, strides up to the podium and takes hold of the microphone. Upon his shoulders shall rest the onus of a "Free India". Jawaharlal Nehru, the favourite protégé of my husband Mohandas Karamchand Gandhi, wears the mantle of Prime Minister-to-be with ease. He has trounced all his competitors for the post, effortlessly.

Two years earlier, Subhash Chandra Bose perished in a plane crash flying over Taipei. And the towering son of Gujarat, Vallabhbhai Patel has been marginalized, as he does not enjoy the mandate of the Mahatma.

As the microphone crackles to life, Nehru's impassioned voice reverberates over the length and breadth of a nation celebrating its much-awaited day of independence. His words are impassioned and sincere. The people of India, stirred by a feeling of patriotic fervour, hang on to each word he speaks.

Long years ago we made a tryst with destiny, and now the time comes when we shall redeem our pledge, not wholly or in full measure, but very substantially. At the stroke of the midnight hour, when the world sleeps, India will awake to life and freedom…

Outside the hall a loud crack of thunder rips the midnight sky and a torrential monsoon downpour drenches the triumphant crowds waiting to unfurl the glorious tricolour and herald the dawn of a free nation.

But freedom has come at a heavy price.

Nehru's greatest political adversary, the intractable Mohammed Ali Jinnah, has had his way. The nation has been cleaved into two entities, India and Pakistan. Earlier that day, Jinnah flew to Karachi, a proud and triumphant man, poised to take over the mantle of Prime Minister, Quaid-e-Azam Mohammed Ali Jinnah, in the newly-formed Islamic state of Pakistan.

The ominous Partition has magnified the existing religious tensions between Hindus and Muslims who are baying for each other's blood. Raging fires of communal violence have consumed the entire nation. Blood curdling cries of *"Har har Mahadev"* and *"Allahu Akbar"* from hordes of maddened lumpens roaming the streets to loot and massacre their brethren have rent the air. Trains filled with slain and mangled bodies of panic-stricken Hindus fleeing from Pakistan, roar into railway stations, sending terror into every Indian's heart. Thousands of people have been slaughtered and their bodies are piled up on the streets reeking with the stench of rotting human flesh. The peace and brotherhood of the subcontinent has been wrecked forever.

Mohandas Gandhi is overcome with grief. This is not the free India of his dreams. He blames his own lapses, his own flawed *brahmacharya* for this unprecedented genocide. Unable to arrest the frenzied bloodshed and communal riots that have spiralled out of control, he stares at defeat, a sad and broken man.

In the twilight of his life at seventy-nine years, it is not in spiritual serenity or self-realization, but in a state of piteous ruin that he shall reach his tragic end.

The miserable epitome of a fallen God who failed.

❄ ❄ ❄

Sixty Nine

In the heart of Delhi, the capital city of free India, no different from any other day, a chilly winter morning begins with a pre-dawn prayer.

'The path to God is for the brave, not for cowards,' he says in a low voice that wafts out in the darkness.

After his last frugal meal of two rotis, a glass of goat's milk and half a grapefruit, leaning his frail body on the shoulders of Manu and Abha, he ambles on to the lawns of the sprawling mansion in New Delhi that belongs to a devotee and industrialist, Ghanshyam Das Birla. In sharp contrast to his decree of simple living, this grand manor has become his home for a while now.

The straw pallet on which Manu sleeps is still spread out on the floor of his room near his frayed mat. Outside, they wait for him to commence his fast. He shall lie on a weather-beaten rope *charpoy* all day. Both Abha and Manu, his human walking-sticks and the chosen partners of his experiments, stand beside him. His grim-faced secretary Pyarelal and physician Sushila Nayyar are in attendance. I see Jawaharlal, his spiritual and political heir sitting close to him on the floor, with his head bowed. A sombre look clouds his face.

After a weary start to a momentous day, Mohandas stretches out on his creaking cot to take a nap. Soaking in the soft rays of a winter sun, he rests. For the world, this newly-imposed ordeal is perplexing. There have been no fresh outbursts of violence, the kind that had preceded his last bout of penance by starvation. The bloody communal massacres across the subcontinent have come to a total halt.

Then what is it? Could he have sensed another impending violent eruption? Is this fast a pre-emption of something sinister that only he can see or is he watching his own death hover around him like a dark shadow, waiting to strike?

The news of his fast of penance is greeted with mixed feelings of hostility, anger and concern. To most, the conditions laid down by this feeble octogenarian, emaciated in body and seemingly unfit in spirit, are preposterous. It has infuriated a large section of the people and there are murmurs of discontent even in the corridors of power, in Delhi. He has demanded an immediate payment of five hundred and fifty million rupees to Pakistan. Those hordes of refugees who trudge past the borders with the blood of revenge in their eyes and insurmountable grief in their hearts are never going to forgive him.

To many, Mohandas Gandhi has become a forgotten messiah; his voice and message a discarded ethic. It is as if he has turned upon his own fellowmen, shaking them up once more, to dwell on who he is, what he symbolizes and for one last time, ponder upon the meaning of his life and message.

❈ ❈ ❈

Poona
13 January 1948

Seven hundred miles away from the hub of feverish activity in the capital, the news of Gandhi's fast-unto-death has particularly enraged two self-appointed upholders of the Hindu *dharma*. As their emotions catalyze into virulent fanaticism, they are being propelled on a perilous path of crime so macabre and brutal in its ambit that it threatens to send ripples of shock across the world and beyond.

These two crazed Hindu zealots, Nathuram Godse and Narayan Apte, have bloody revenge on their minds. Incensed by Gandhi's political blackmailing that they believe largely favours the Muslims, they clamour for justice. These fanatics, appalled by his tilt towards the newly created state of Pakistan, want to avenge the death, destruction and uprooting of their brethren without any delay. They will not allow him to dole out package after package for the appeasement of an enemy-neighbour who has unleashed terror on an ever-forgiving, peace-loving and highly tolerant Hindu populace.

Nathuram Godse particularly loathes him. The pusillanimous conduct of the government in meekly surrendering to the demands of Muslim rapists, plunderers and murderers has made him contemptuous. He draws upon his inner power to help him execute this heroic and altruistic deed. He must eradicate Gandhi from the face of the "Hindu" republic, even if it's the last thing he does. Consumed by a blinding rage, a passion rooted in what he believes to be an act of courage and sacrifice, the perceived martyr-to-be has only one thought on his mind—Gandhi must die!

Someone, anyone, stop them; stop them now, please…! Oh God! They are going to kill him!

I shout myself hoarse, but no one heeds my cries. My phantom voice bounces off the impenetrable wall that separates me from his temporal world.

✄　✄　✄

The last rays of the winter sun reflect on the stooping shoulders of Mohandas as he shuffles unsteadily across the manicured lawns of Birla House. One hand resting lightly on Manu and the other gently brushing the neck of a stone-faced Abha, he approaches a raised platform that has become a favoured spot for his evening discourse and prayers. He lowers himself onto the straw mat on a six-inch high platform. A copy of the Bhagavad Gita, a notebook with the text of his speech for the day, and his brass spittoon are placed in front of him.

As on most days, the front lawns of Birla House is bursting at its seams; over six hundred people have assembled there to listen to their Mahatma. A halo hovers over the head of that frail figure, so earnest in his conviction and so impassioned in his oratory that I feel a sharp tug inside my heart. As the deepening shadows of twilight fall over the vast garden space, his faint quivering voice pierces every pore and cell of the audience. The hymn that has echoed timelessly through the marshes of that mosquito-ridden, muddy, Noakhali delta comes alive in Delhi's Birla House as the microphone crackles to life and the crowds join in to sing a song written by Rabindranath Tagore:

Jodi tor dak shune keu na ashey tobey ekla cholo re
Ekla cholo, ekla
cholo, ekla cholo re…

(If they answer not your call, walk alone

Walk alone, walk alone, walk alone…)

A hush descends on the crowd as he begins to speak.

My fast is an appeal to God to purify the souls of mankind and make them equal. Hindus, Sikhs and Muslims must live in amity here as brothers. Delhi is on trial now. We should not deflect from our call of duty. The senseless killings of our brothers should not derail us from our paths of deliverance. No matter if every single Hindu loses his life in this unholy war, it is upon us to protect the life of every Muslim who lives in our sacred motherland. Bestiality should be replaced with kindness…with humaneness… and if I cannot do what I say, I am unworthy of my existence in this world. My life is futile.

An uneasy calm settles on the tranquil beauty of the rolling green lawns of Birla House. Manu rises first. She gathers the spittoon and the sacred Gita in one hand and helps Gandhi up with the other, leaning her full body against his, to support his shaky legs.

I watch the forlorn figure of my Mohandas, his arms resting weakly on those two young women, recede into the dense ivy-covered sandstone arches in the distance. He doesn't know he is being closely trailed by a shadowy figure, shrouded in a black-hooded cloak and I have no way of warning him.

✁ ✁ ✁

Day 2
Wednesday, 14 January
3:30 am

He is up long before sunrise, reciting verses from the Gita, massaging his gums gently with a freshly shredded *neem* twig. Manu stands beside him, alert in attendance. There are no signs of the long sleepless hours she suffered the night before, standing vigil, checking on him, covering him with his coarse blanket to keep out the bitter cold. She hands him his first meal of the day, a glass of warm water with soda bicarbonate. He gulps it down with a grimace and turns to read an earnest appeal sent to him from Devdas. My adored Devdas…it is he…!

I feel a lump in my throat choking me, my eyes brimming with tears, as I focus on my son's handwritten note.

What you can achieve by staying alive Bapu, you cannot achieve by dying….

I see Mohandas sit still for a long while after that. He caresses that piece of paper, those tender words, with his moist eyes. He raises it to his gaunt cheeks with his hands and calls out to Manu.

'Write what I dictate to you. My son awaits my reply. Come sit beside me and write what I say...'

Only God who has ordained this fast, can make me give it up. You and all others should bear in mind that it is not for me to live or die. My single prayer to God is to keep me firm in my resolve, lest I get overpowered by the temptation to live.

Ah! Those words he utters in the spirit of a stubborn crusader! They sear through me as they shall sear through the chest of my son. I feel distraught. Mohandas has decided to end his life. Death shall strike him with brutal swiftness.

✖ ✖ ✖

At midday members of the newly-formed Indian Cabinet gather around the *charpoy* of the feeble Mahatma, his life ebbing out with each laboured breath. Summoned by Nehru and Patel, who have both failed in prevailing upon Bapu to give up the fast-unto-death, the motley crowd of Congress workers congregate beside him to hold a crucial meeting. No different from the sinister assassin who waits stealthily for the right moment to mow him down, these people are also incensed at the obduracy of their leader. Their pleas hang in the air, unheeded. Weak and dizzy with his vital organs shutting down, Mohandas lies there silent, eyes glazed, staring at the ceiling. After a while, he heaves himself onto his elbows, his eyes brimming with tears.

'You are not the Sardar I knew,' he rasps at Vallabhbhai Patel.

His barely audible words are punctured with heavy breathing as he falls back onto the thin, frayed mattress and goes silent again. My throat chokes up once more. I cannot see the faces of the two men through the veil of tears that blind me. What a sorry plight, Mohandas! What a sorry plight!

Unending streams of people are filing past his bed, beseeching him to abandon his suicidal fast that has stirred up an unprecedented wave of nationwide resentment. Thronging the street outside Birla House, a group of irate demonstrators are shouting slogans that penetrate the walls of the dying man's abode. Mohandas stirs. He beckons Pyarelal.

'What are they saying?' he whispers into his ear.

Pyarelal is silent, head bowed. He is mortified as he listens to that chorus of blasphemy. He gulps hard as the brutal sounds escape his dry lips.

'Bapu, they are saying, "Let Gandhi die!"'

That icy chill grips my heart again.

❊ ❊ ❊

Bombay
14 January 1948

In a northern suburb of Bombay, inside a double-storied building of crumbling concrete covered in slimy green moss, three men are stirred by a passion of a different kind. At that moment, there couldn't have been anyone else in the entire subcontinent who loathed the dying Gandhi more than those who had converged there. Sharply contrasting with the mission of the prophet of peace, these self-appointed upholders of religion also had a mission albeit diabolical that would send shivers down the spine of the entire human race.

The murderous trio, Nathuram Godse, Narayan Apte and Digambar Bagde, split up after meticulous discussions to execute their plan. They headed off in three different directions and vanished into darkness. They were united by just a single thought that night—'Death to Gandhi!'

✵ ✵ ✵

New Delhi
15 January 1948

Mohandas was sinking rapidly. A fatal metabolic breakdown had overcome his frail body. Sushila Nayyar was in panic. She had tried explaining to him about the seriousness of his condition, but Gandhi was unmoved. Manu despaired. She mechanically administered his ritualistic, colonic irrigation to purify his body. The reticent, grandniece of Gandhi had withstood several outbursts of temper and regularly acquiesced to his unyielding demands. This was not the man the world viewed as a peaceful, serene prophet, detached from material and carnal desires. This was a different man. One more such angry outburst that day, on a delay in bringing the enema apparatus, had failed to perturb her. She saw him exhausted and weak, pale as a ghost, crumpled on the rope *charpoy*. Fear gripped her as she stood silently, eyes brimming over watching his image de-focus through the veil of her tears. His obdurate demands were nowhere near resolution and his life was fast ebbing out.

Outside the compounds of Birla House, the city was racked with tremors of a different kind. While a large part of the populace was forming processions, calling for communal harmony and earnestly praying for the Mahatma's life, there was a radical shift in the mood of the people of Calcutta. A scary disquiet crept into the mind of Manu. It was a nagging fear that her fellowmen may actually, 'Let Gandhi die!'

Late that afternoon a message was flashed by news agencies across the subcontinent. It was a shot in the arm for the dying leader. The government of India had announced an immediate payout of fifty-five million rupees to the bankrupt state of the newly-created Pakistan. Gandhi had been accorded his last victory. Peace was restored to the troubled nation. Gandhi would live!

❃ ❃ ❃

30 January 1948
New Delhi

It is a chilly, foggy morning. The day begins with a prayer before the rays of the rising sun have reached down to play with the city's skyline. I see him sitting cross-legged, frail and wasted after his death-defying fast, chanting a familiar verse from the Gita. His high-pitched, weak voice wafts across the dimly-lit room rising upwards to the sky. This does not augur well. A morbid fear grips me again. I could see a faint dark shadow descend furtively on the city that misty day. And not too far away from Birla House, I see the silhouette of three men moving stealthily and swiftly, all finely synchronized in words and action. They are on a mission of deliverance, wired together in unison, with a singular thought on their minds—'Kill him!'

Providence has granted them yet another chance. The slack investigation on the part of the local police and CID, in a perceived threat to the Mahatma, last time is enough reason to finally firm up their bloody agenda. They must not fail. After an arduous search for a suitable weapon, Nathuram Godse and his two accomplices, Narayan Apte and Vishnu Karkare, have managed to lay their hands on an automatic Beretta and twenty rounds of ammunition. The lean Godse is the chosen one—only he has the requisite skill to operate the weapon and most importantly, also a murderous determination to get to his target before the police can get to him. There is no room for error. There better be not!

❃ ❃ ❃

It is going to be his last walk through the lush gardens of Birla House. Manu and Abha are close by his side. The canny, murderous trio, smoothly saunter into the lawns where a motley crowd has congregated for the evening prayers.

Barely twenty-four hours earlier, as the emaciated figure of Mohandas had shuffled down the granite steps to address his prayer meet, an enraged man had jumped up at him. He belonged to a group of Hindus and Sikhs, victims of a brutal massacre that had erupted after a train from Pakistan, filled with mangled bodies had chugged into the Old Delhi railway station.

'Why don't you go back and retire in the Himalayas?' he screamed.

'You have done us enough harm. You have brought us to ruination. Leave us alone. You infidel. Retreat to the Himalayas where you belong! Get out now!' He was frothing at the mouth. Sparks flashed from his eyes.

The crushed and bewildered Mohandas had shrunk into himself. He clutched the shoulders of Abha and Manu and stumbled ahead. Tears spilled down those hollowed cheeks and his swollen eyes sank deeper into their dark sockets.

'I do what god commands, my brother. I seek peace amidst chaos. My Himalayas are here.' His feeble voice trailed off and drowned in the melee, as the policemen on duty roughed up the slogan-shouting man and pushed him out of sight.

The meeting had ended peacefully.

But this is another day, when the three assassins are roaming free in the lawns, wired up to seize the moment. Mohandas' short-lived triumph at having been able to get Patel and Jawaharlal to resolve their differences a little while ago has delayed him by a precious ten minutes and he is agitated. The gentle despot, a stickler for punctuality has already ticked off Manu and Abha. The irritation is visible on his face as he peers into his pocket watch. Ten vital minutes lost. He rebukes them again as he shuffles across the garden hurriedly, alighting the four sandstone steps that lead to the prayer ground. He folds his hands together to greet the restive crowd. A soft ripple engulfs them.

The endearing cheer of 'Bapuji! Bapuji!' overcomes all else. But on the enraged minds of the three rabid killers, just two words resonate, 'Kill him!'

Wait! I see the crowd part. I see Godse in a grey shirt and loose trousers with one hand inside his pocket. I hear the click of the safety catch of his Beretta being released. He is just two steps away from the edge of the human wall. In a couple of seconds he closes in. Manu looks at a stocky, inconspicuous man in a grey shirt. She takes him to be a keen devotee from the thronging crowd. She has not seen him tighten his fingers around the trigger of the hidden Beretta. She watches him like I do, step effortlessly into the human corridor. He bows down slowly from the waist as if to touch the Mahatma's feet.

'Not now, brother,' Manu whispers. 'He's already late.'

I see Manu being violently pushed to one side by the man in grey. She stumbles and then regains her balance. The spittoon and notebook fall from her hands on to the grassy path. Three loud shots rip through the air. I hear the blood-curdling sounds break the mortal barrier and travel far, far above into thinning ether. No one has seen the blood freeze in the flaming eyes of the cold assassin. They were all reeling from shock at the sight of Mohandas' blood spilling on the white khadi shawl draped around his shoulders, the last raiment of the slain prophet of peace.

The lifeless bundle falls heavily to the ground uttering the name of the Lord before he drops dead. As if to summon the holy deity to deliver him from his temporal hell, he cries out—'Hey Ram!'

My eyes are flooded with tears. Echoing the tenets of my slain husband, I speak aloud to the assassin, 'I neither hate you nor the sin you have committed, Nathuram Godse. You are a mere conduit in the execution of a divine karmic plan. I forgive you Godse! I forgive you, for you have allowed him his passage out of this world when his utility to his beloved motherland is over.'

I embrace the departing soul that fuses into my ever-expanding chest.

'Come home to me, Mohandas! Come home to me, my lord. Free India has no place for you!' I say, as I take him into my arms.

Inside the blood-stained shawl of the dead Mahatma, his pocket watch lies splattered with a few drops of blood. It is 5.17 pm. The heartrending wail of Manu and Abha fall upon his insensate ears.

❉   ❉   ❉

SEVENTY

30 January 1948

The lifeless, blood-soaked body of Mohandas is carried back into Birla House and placed on the straw pallet where he sat for the last time an hour ago. His spinning wheel stands beside him, a mute witness to the gory tragedy. Abha wraps a woollen shawl around his body. She looks at him intently and then covers her face and breaks into sobs. His wooden clogs, the three clay monkeys that symbolize his life's message, his copy of the holy Bhagavad Gita, his pocket watch, his shining spittoon and his brass bowl are all set out near his body. The room slowly fills up with mourners.

I lower myself near his head and gently caress his pallid brow. It is still warm.

I see Jawaharlal squatting on the floor. His face ashen, he leans on a wall and weeps. Patel is sitting a few feet away. His eyes have turned to stone. He stares in shock at the dead martyr with whom he had had an intense dialogue just a few hours ago.

A group of women clad in white *khadi* assembles near the makeshift bier and begins chanting *shlokas* from the Gita. A few earthen oil lamps are placed at the foot of the corpse. They emit an eerie yellow light that mingles with the aroma of the dense smoke of incense sticks that have been lit in the four corners of the room. I see Manu huddled near the body, weeping. She has cradled her beloved Bapu's head in her lap and is stroking his face continuously.

A twinge of jealousy stabs at my heart.

'That's my place, Manu. Move over now and let me hold his head.' I shout loudly but my words carry no sound. They flow unheeded into the myriad tones of the continuous chanting and blend with

the heady aroma of smoke rising from the incense sticks. I flow stealthily into the length of Manu's long fingers that are caressing the cold skull of my slain husband, a dejected martyr who can feel no pain and is free at last.

✄   ✄   ✄

For hours the body of the assassinated Mahatma lies under a mountain of roses and jasmines on a raised platform at Birla House. Mourners from all parts of the country are filing past for a last glimpse of their beloved messiah. They mourn the noble soldier of non-violence, who succumbed to the bullet of a crazed assassin.

Just after midnight, the body is brought in from the verandah for the rituals preceding the cremation. He lies still, surrounded by those who shared his intimate last moments and life of austerity. Manu, Abha, Pyarelal, Devdas and Ramdas sit around him, exhausted from the night-long vigil and emotional collapse.

All wear that sullen look that comes after being brushed by the hand of death. They are bound by the cruel finality and the deathly silence of knowing that he is gone forever.

But wait. Where is Harilal?

I float up to the ceiling and spread myself. He is nowhere. Call him someone! Someone tell him his Bapu is no more. I am certain no one has bothered to inform him and that poor, wretched firstborn son of Mohandas is lying somewhere in a drunken stupor with no idea that his rights are being usurped by his younger brothers, nephews and nieces and being handed over to a three hundred million-strong nation of mourners. They grieve for their universal father while his own precious firstborn lies drunk and dead to the world.

There is a layer of freshly spread cow dung on the marble floor. All the Gandhi men have bathed the body with *Ganga-jal* and wrapped it in a new sheet of white *khadi*. A priest has anointed his bare chest with a freshly ground paste of saffron and sandalwood.

I float along with Manu's hand and together we dot his forehead with a red tilak. We touch the lines of his crumpled brow with our outstretched fingers. Manu and I make a rangoli of mango leaves and rose petals that trace "Hey Ram" on the floor near his head and a similar one spelling "Om" by his feet.

The wall clock strikes the half-hour. It is 3.30 am.

Wake up, Mohandas, I whisper in his ear. It is time for you to rise for your morning prayers. I hear the sounds of weeping and then the melodious notes of a farewell hymn punctuated with sobs emanate in an eerie rhythm from within me –

Cover yourself with dust
Because dust you are
And dust you shall be
Bathe and change your clothes
For there is no come back
From where
you shall go with me….with me…

My loud cries must surely shatter the soulful solemnity of the moment, but no one is disturbed. The agony of being near, yet so far, the desperation of the dead welcoming one of their own from amongst a room full of mourning devotees hits me hard. I shrink into myself and nestle around the red tilak on Mohandas' forehead. I shall accompany him undisturbed, to his cremation.

Manu and Abha look on with grief. Devdas pulls out thick strands of knotted handspun yarn and wreaths them around his father's neck. His trembling hands linger just a wee bit longer on the raw thread garland as he pats it down. It is the last and only accessory that shall accompany his father to his pyre.

My head hurts and my heart beats wildly. I look around desperately, searching for that one face that could afford me succor.

Where are you, Harilal? I swiftly scan the crowd that waits to receive the body of Mohandas. A deafening cry drowns my thoughts while I am immersed in the morbid silence of my mind.

Frozen into the serenity of the ultimate usurper of life, Mohandas is once again offered to millions of his fellowmen for a last *darshan* at the break of dawn. Drowned in a fresh pile of rose petals and jasmines, he lies for one last time on the open patio of Birla House, where wave upon wave of mourners are streaming past. They cry and wail, beat their chests as some walk in stony silence overcome by a torrent of grief.

> *I breeze into the constricted chest of my deceased husband, reliving my own painful, dying moments as I spread myself from the top of his head down to his toes. The icy rigor mortis that has overcome him vibrates with each expanding pore of my fluid form and I lie still, holding my breath for fear of rousing the silent one who lies in his final deep sleep.*

The wooden bier is lowered down from the balcony. It is set upon the open gun-carriage bedecked with flowers that will lead him to his funeral pyre by the banks of the River Jamuna. The stately Dodge weapon-carrier that will transport him to his cremation shall pay its final tribute to the prophet of non-violence with its engine switched off. It shall be drawn by a human chain comprising two hundred and fifty countrymen and sailors of the Royal Navy with the help of four thick ropes fastened on its bumper. Jawaharlal and Patel, their faces sullied with dried tears, their eyes swollen, along with Manu and Abha have placed two long sheets of red and white cotton on either side of his body that is shrouded in the tricolour, the glorious symbol of independent India befitting the grand Messiah of Peace.

> *I settle deep down into the decaying viscera of my husband, beneath the wide flag that had shrouded the two of us in death. Under the tightly secured tricolour, I feel it is our second union that now binds us together for eternity, inseparable and conjoined forever.*

The procession slow-marches into the ocean of humanity waiting outside Birla House led by four armoured cars and a squadron of the Governor-General's bodyguard. Honouring an Indian the first time ever, it is a gesture of reverence by Lord Mountbatten to his most intractable adversary. Bound together in sorrow, all barriers of caste, creed, religion and status have dissolved into the melting pot of human grief on that five-mile-long trek that is strewn with roses and marigolds all the way. For five agonizing hours, a sea of humanity trails the cortege to Rajghat, where the funeral pyre had been meticulously erected on a raised platform. It is stacked with thick round logs of sandalwood.

> *The wooden bier bearing Mohandas' body, with me embedded deep inside finally reaches the enclosure.*

The body is placed on top, with its head pointing north in accordance with the dictates of the Hindu religion. It is 4 pm. The mild rays of the winter sun illuminate the exposed face of Mohandas that has turned a darker brown.

> *I stretch out of the cramped visceral space to scan the crowd again. My heart lurches as I see Ramdas climb steadily on the pyramid where his father lies. Devdas is soaking the logs with a mixture of ghee, coconut, camphor and incense.*

> *Harilal, come forward, son! You must perform your duty as our firstborn to light the pyre of your father. It is a privilege bestowed on you at birth that compels you to release his soul from the clutches of this mortal world, into the cosmic umbra of nothingness. The Parabrahma awaits him, son. Come forward now or we shall be doomed forever. Where are you, Harilal? I see no sign of him.*

Ramdas has completed the five mandatory circumambulations around the pyre. A dozen saffron-robed priests begin chanting Vedic *mantras* in unison. Their rich sounds ricochet off his body and rebound high into the ether, resonating with the celestial music of the spheres. Ramdas holds an ignited *mashaal* over Mohandas' head and touches it to the sandalwood logs.

> *Oh God! Ramdas stop! Stop! That was your brother's right. Harilal has to light the pyre, not you!*

My deafening screams get lost in the crescendo of Vedic chants that rise with the thick orange flames of fire that consumes us. I feel a violent release of heat and light.

> *Come into my bosom, my beloved Mohandas. I shall embrace this fire to become a "sati". With you I shall depart to attain the*

highest "punya" demanded from a woman that shall grant her freedom from the endless cycles of birth and death.

As the flames and smoke engulf the sandalwood logs, the crowds surge forward and a loud chant fills the sky.

'Mahatma Gandhi *amar rahe*! Mahatma Gandhi *amar rahe*!'

The crackling flames lick up and greedily devour the tiny brown figure that disappears forever from the face of the earth. A twin spark of light races up towards the sky and explodes into a million particles leaving behind a crying, heaving and orphaned crowd below.

I take one last look at the ground below hoping to see Harilal and then dissolve into the thinning layers of the ether far above. Gone forever!

A stooped man with a grey stubble, wearing a cap and a soiled jacket stands at a distance watching the funeral proceedings. The sleeves of his jacket are torn at the elbows and collar tattered at the neck. He wears strapped *chappals* and carries a coarse, yellow jute bag. His eyes are bloodshot and there is a stench of stale alcohol on his breath.

As the flames rise higher and the chants get louder, he is shoved aside roughly by the hysterical mourners. He picks himself up and staggers towards the burning pyre. He stops when he is just ten feet away. Coughing violently as the dense oily column of acrid smoke hits his lungs, the lone, unkempt, inebriated man, mutters under his breath.

I'm here, Bapu... Look! Harilal, your son is here to bid you farewell. Peace has eluded me all my life, but may eternal peace be yours. May you rest in peace, my beloved Bapu. May you rest in peace. And forgive me Ba, for I could not be the son you wanted.

Harilal lifts his trembling hand to his forehead in a weary salutation, a sad farewell. He feels himself being roughed up again and pushed aside by the surging crowd. The loud, continuous chorus of 'Mahatma Gandhi *amar rahe*,' drowns out all else. The ocean of wailing mourners closes in above his head as he cowers on the soggy ground, watching the mortal remains of his father going up in smoke while he weeps.

May the heinous assassin of my father burn in hell! he mumbles.

✳ ✳ ✳

Select Bibliography

- *Ba And Bapu*
  By
  Mukulbhai Kalarthi

- *Freedom At Midnight*
  By
  Larry Collins and Dominique Lapierre

- *Gandhi: A Sublime Failure*
  By
  S.S. Gill

- *Gandhi: An illustrated Biography*
  By
  Pramod Kapoor

- *Gandhi: His Life And Message For The World*
  By
  Louis Fischer

- *Gandhi: Naked Ambition*
  By
  Jad Adams

- *Harilal Gandhi: A Life*
  By
  Chandulal Bhagubhai Dalal

- *Mahatma Gandhi and his Apostles*
  By
  Ved Mehta

- *Mahatma Gandhi's Letters on Brahmacharya, Sexuality And Love*
By
Girija Kumar

- *Mahatma vs Gandhi*
By
Dinkar Joshi

- *My Days with Gandhi*
By
Nirmal Kumar Bose

- *My Experiments With Truth*
By
Mohandas Karamchand Gandhi

- *Nine Hours To Rama*
By
Stanley Wolpert

- *The Forgotten Woman*
By
Arun and Sunanda Gandhi

- *The Men who killed Gandhi*
By
Manohar Malgonkar

- *Thus Spoke Gandhi*
Compiled By
Dr Ramesh Bharadwaj